EXTRANETS

EXTRANETS
The Complete Sourcebook

Richard H. Baker

McGraw-Hill
New York San Francisco Washington, D.C. Auckland Bogotá
Caracas Lisbon London Madrid Mexico City Milan
Montreal New Delhi San Juan Singapore
Sydney Tokyo Toronto

Library of Congress catalog card number: 97-70565

McGraw-Hill

A Division of The *McGraw-Hill* Companies

1 2 3 4 5 6 7 8 9 0   DOC/DOC   9 0 2 1 0 9 8 7

ISBN 0-07-006302-8

The sponsoring editor for this book was Scott L. Grillo, the editing supervisor was Paul R. Sobel, and the production supervisor was Claire B. Stanley. It was set in Vendome by Terry Leaden of McGraw-Hill's Professional Book Group composition unit.

Printed and bound by R. R. Donnelley & Sons Company.

McGraw-Hill books are available at special quantity discounts to use as premiums and sales promotions, or for use in corporate training programs. For more information, please write to the Director of Special Sales, McGraw-Hill, 11 West 19th Street, New York, NY 10011. Or contact your local bookstore.

CONTENTS

Contents

Contents

INTRODUCTION

Not long ago, Federal Express—FedEx for short—opened its shipment tracking system to the public. FedEx customers can go to the company's web site and schedule shipments, fill out the necessary forms, and even track their own shipments.

The FedEx web site is one of the earliest and best-known examples of an *extranet*—an intranet that is opened to external use. Most likely, the FedEx folks weren't particularly interested in adding a new term to computing lexicon. More likely, they were looking to gain a competitive edge through better customer service. Whatever their motivation, though, they created something that did not fit neatly into any existing categories.

It is not, strictly speaking, an Internet application. Although anyone can open the FedEx web site, it is mainly of interest only to customers or prospective customers. Neither does it meet the strict definition of an intranet, hunkered behind a corporate firewall and available only to insiders. Thus it is neither and both at the same time. It is an *extranet*.

A new term demands a definition. In the absence of standards committees and the like, we can offer this:

An *extranet* is an intranet that is open to selective access by outside parties.

Unlike the Internet, an extranet is not wide open. Unlike an intranet, it is not restricted to internal use.

This is a simple definition—so simple that Netscape no doubt will soon offer beta downloads of its own extensions. And Microsoft, being Microsoft, will insist on doing things its own way. Expect ActiveExtranet real soon now.

However, it would be a mistake to overcomplicate things by insisting on a rigid definition that covers too many points too precisely. For the purposes of this book, there are only a few points worth remembering when trying to define an extranet:

■ An extranet is not confined to the sponsoring organization. It can reach outside the organization, particularly to the suppliers and customers with whom the organization wants to take an active role.

■ An extranet is not purely external either. As many intranet users have found, there is no rule that keeps them from setting up a mixture of internal and external information. The only necessity is to provide enough access control to keep the external users away from the internal stuff.

■ An extranet is a state of mind, not a technology. For the most part, it uses standard Web technology. What makes it different from its close relatives is the attitude with which extranet applications are created. An extranet simply requires an acknowledgment that there is a clear line, and no necessary distinction, between internal and external information.

■ The primary substance of an extranet is applications. It is these, not the system design, that amplify the usefulness of the technology.

By these standards, many people who thought they were running intranets are really operating extranets. Although there will always be value to standard intranet applications like putting a policy manual on line, companies have found that there is equal and greater value in using Internet technology to maintain partnership relationships with both their suppliers and their customers.

This book will show what many of these outward-looking companies have done, both internally and externally, to make full use of Internet technology. I invite both technicians and managers—and for that matter, technical managers—to learn more about this new way of looking at the networked world and about the types of applications that can bring it to practical reality.

—RICHARD H. BAKER

1

From Intranet to Extranet

An extranet has a lot in common with an intranet. Although intranets have been defined as existing behind firewalls and serving purely internal purposes, this has never really been the case. From the beginning, when intranet builders began to apply World Wide Web technology to specific organizational communication needs, their applications have always included both internal and external communication.

Take note: That's communication, with no *s*. I am not talking about the technical concept of communications here, but the singular form of *communication* that takes place between real people. And just as communication is important between members of an organization, it is just as important between organizations. Successful businesses no longer exist as isolated enterprises. They have come to see the value of active communication with their suppliers on one hand and their customers on the other. These customers and suppliers, in turn, are linked to other customers and suppliers. The result is an inter-

Figure 1-1
Most Intranet owners
either allow external
access or plan to
soon (Forrester
Research).

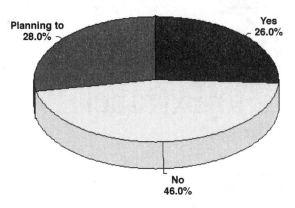

External access allowed

Do you allow external access?

Planning to
28.0%

Yes
26.0%

No
46.0%

locked chain that is something like a box of fishhooks, interlinked in multiple, unpredictable ways. Anything you do to one fishhook affects countless others.

This is why intranets have never been confined to strictly internal communication needs. That's also why an extranet cannot be confined completely to external communication. The line between internal and external communication was never observed strictly, and it is starting to disappear entirely. As businesses form partnerships with their suppliers and customers, there remains only the finest of distinctions between the inside and the outside. An extranet simply grants formal recognition to this long-established fact. Most intranet owners either allow external access already or plan to soon. (Figs. 1-1 and 1-2).

The reverse is also true. Although an extranet extends itself to outside communication, it should not be limited strictly to that. The test of a true extranet is that it is equally capable of handling internal *and* external information (Fig. 1-3).

How the Extranet Has Evolved

It all goes back to the Internet, a phenomenon that has transformed the computer industry and the way people use computers in many ways. As

Figure 1-2
Customers and other
business partners are
the main external
users.

Types of external access

External access is granted:

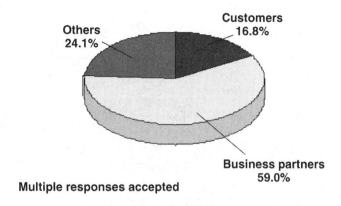

Multiple responses accepted

Figure 1-3
The differences are in
the details.

Networks compared

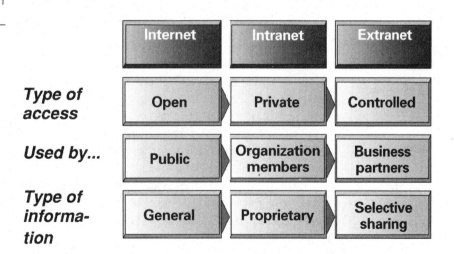

the Internet and the World Wide Web became established, organizations
have learned to use Web technology to distribute information to their
employees. By establishing intranets, these organizations have been able
to distribute information to their employees much more cost-effectively
than older means such as newsletters and memos.

Intranet priorities

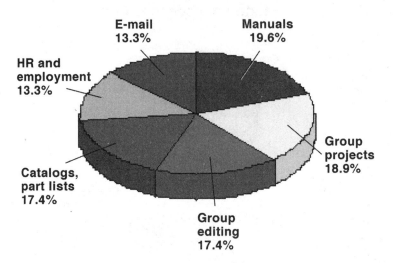

Multiple responses allowed

This is why the earliest uses of intranets were to distribute corporate information: newsletters, policies, employee handbooks, and internal telephone directories. According to a report published on the Netscape Web page, General Electric is no longer printing a standard directory of company information. By putting the directory on an intranet, the company is saving $240,000 a year in printing costs. Figure 1-4 shows that in 1996, planners were looking at familiar applications such as these, though several, like product planning and e-mail, had external uses as well.

Results like this can provide a quick payback for the costs of implementation, particularly when the implementation costs themselves are low. Eli Lilly linked about 3000 employees for a total cost of only $80,000.

The Intranet as Groupware

Although the intranet is still a technological toddler, applications like these already qualify for legacy status. In one of the shortest reproductive cycles on record, the intranet has spawned second- and third-generation applications that extend both ways from the original corporate base. One branch of the family extends downward from corporate-wide communication to allow exchange of information at departmental and workgroup levels.

Some developers asked this sensible question: If the Web provides an easy, facile way to communicate general company information, why not extend it to other types of information and applications? One of the first examples of this mode of thinking was to link an intranet to information stored in conventional databases. It was only one more logical step to extend their thinking to information sharing within departments and workgroups. One evolutionary path of the intranet, then, has been in the direction of groupware.

Publishing company-wide information remains a good way to get started with an extranet, but do not plan on stopping there. No doubt you have much information that is unique to departments and workgroups: information on different projects pursued by different teams. It has been predicted that the benefits of sharing this kind of information can be much greater than the savings you can get from intranetting internal communication alone.

Looking Outward

The same can easily be true when you look outward instead of downward. You and your business partners also have information to share. Product information, price lists, and delivery schedules are only part of the picture. This need has been recognized already in such areas as electronic document interchange (EDI), which allows business partners to place orders, deliver goods, and process payments electronically. The Federal Express do-it-yourself shipment tracking system (Fig. 1-5) represents yet another level of sophistication. Customers track their own shipments without requiring intervention by someone else. In addition, FedEx need not pay the cost of having someone there to intervene.

There is much to be gained by sharing information both internally and externally. The extranet gets rid of this distinction and lets you concentrate on sharing information whenever and wherever good communication is important. And good communication is important just about everywhere.

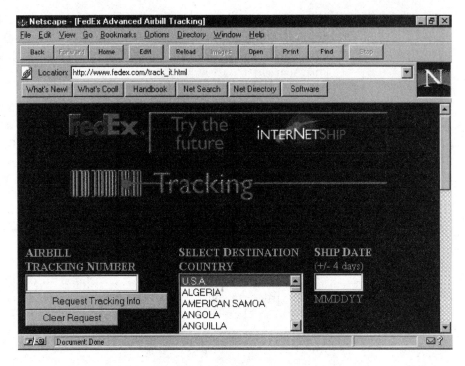

New Tools for Better Sharing

That was the first generation of Intranet evolution, extending its outlook downward toward departments and workgroups. The departmental
intranet still did little, at least deliberately, to look beyond the firewall
toward essential business partners outside the organization.

The downward-looking generation did produce some things of value.
First, it established the point that intranet technology need not be limited to obvious, enterprise-level applications. Second, it brought valuable
new tools into common use. These tools vastly enhance the process of
sharing information with fellow team members, both inside and outside
the organization.

Not Designed for Sharing

Consider the typical corporate computer today. It contains a suite of
desktop applications including, most likely, a word processor and a
spreadsheet. It is networked to a file server, often more than one. It is
also likely to be served by electronic mail.

None of these tools is truly designed to share information. The word processor, spreadsheet, and other applications that make up a desktop suite are designed for use by individuals working alone. The suites have gained some communication functions in recent years, but these have been grafted onto what are still essentially single-use applications.

The file server? It is a great place to store files but a horrible place to find them. Furthermore, it has no inherent facilities for sharing work and resources. File servers let you share disk space but little else. It is a static sort of storage, with little to foster group dynamics.

E-mail is closer to becoming a workgroup product—in fact, the newest versions of e-mail are evolving into sophisticated work-sharing applications. Nevertheless, simply trading e-mail messages is not enough by itself to foster group dynamics. E-mail is also plagued by problems of compatibility between systems, challenges of directory management, and other uncured ailments. Not the least of the problems is the prevalence of junk e-mail that diverts attention from more important forms of communication.

There are, of course, dedicated workgroup tools like Notes and Exchange, and they cannot be written out of the picture easily. Nevertheless, the advent of Web technology for internal communication heralds the use of the same technology for communication throughout a much-extended workgroup. In particular, Notes is being revamped to work with the Web rather than as a self-contained system.

Better Things from the Web

First-generation intranet developers have demonstrated how you can use Web technology and Web page development methods to improve group communication, both inside and outside your organization. Web techniques have made it easier to find your way through the massive amounts of information on the Internet. Surely they can help people find their way through the less massive amounts of information you want to exchange with employees and external trading partners.

In its more visionary statements, Netscape envisions a model in which virtually all corporate information is stored on a Web server. Creating a Web page is much like creating a word processing document, and it certainly is no more difficult. Nearly anyone can learn how to do it.

But—and here's a key element—not just anyone can read or edit your information. A Web administrator can use modern access control features to determine who can read and who can edit a Web document.

The advantage to this approach is that anyone with information to share can readily share it—with someone in the next cubicle or someone in the next country. Furthermore, the information can be made easier to find and use.

Benefits of this approach include the ability to

- *Share information with less effort.* A document can be posted on a Web server and updated instantly when necessary. You need not send e-mail to a list of intended recipients. The recipients can come to the message.

- *Find information with less effort.* Search tools are now readily available that can help find information no matter where it is posted. Unlike older forms of data storage, you need not even know that the resource exists. The search tools can find it anyway.

- *Reduce printing and mailing costs.* Electronic documents may not save as much paper and postage as the optimists like to think, but savings still are possible.

Of course, there are potential drawbacks as well. Security and access control are vital if you are to open information to parties outside the organization. However, these are also important in a strictly internal intranet, so the challenges are not that much greater.

Applications Emphasize the Workgroup

As intranet developers concentrated their attentions on the department and the workgroup, they created several new types of applications. Although originally intended for internal workgroups, these applications also have external potential:

- *Sharing information with cross-functional teams.* It has become a common business situation for project teams to be formed from members of different departments. Team members can be at different locations and may operate different kinds of computers. A team Web page on an intranet or extranet can be an ideal way to share information.

- *Extranet potential:* Project teams can be built that extend beyond single organizations to customer and vendor locations. In these different firms, the differences in equipment and location will be even greater. An extranet can help these cross-corporate teams share schedules, product information, development plans, reference material, and to-do lists.

- *Sharing information throughout departments.* This kind of sharing can be critical. People need to know what others in their departments are doing and how they can best get the job done. They can share resources like document templates, standard procedures, best practices, status reports, and technical support.

- *Extranet potential:* Technical support is an obvious and fruitful way to share information with business partners via an extranet. And when working together to produce a better quality product, multi-corporate workgroups can benefit from shared information just as well as internal workgroups.

- *Sharing information between organizational levels.* Good communication with sales representatives and other mobile workers is a major challenge. These dispersed workers often lack regular contact with the home office. Yet it is they who must often answer customers' questions and shoot the customers' troubles. For them, an extranet is a way to get accurate, timely information. The same link can work the other way, too. Customer contact employees get some of the first and best feedback from the field. The extranet can help them relay this valuable information to the decision makers back at headquarters.

- *Extranet potential:* This kind of application already extends well beyond the firewall at headquarters. It would be only one more small step to give customers direct access to important information and to let them send their feedback directly to the executive suite.

Why Internal Communication Is Not Enough

The expansion of the intranet for internal communication has been spectacular. It has been so much so, in fact, that intranet development will soon overtake and far surpass public Internet applications. Nevertheless, David Moschella, senior vice president for research at *Computerworld*, recently wrote that, "Despite this apparent stampede, the industry's emphasis on intranets can be described only as disappointing."

"Since the beginning of enterprise computing, information technology suppliers have sold their wares based on promises of internal productivity," Moschella explained. "Accounting, human resources, payroll, manufacturing, and word processing systems were designed to improve internal company efficiency. They have often succeeded."

But, he continued, "the relationship between internal efficiency and business productivity has never been a one-to-one correlation, and it's ultimately subject to diminishing returns. Unless information technology can be used to directly provide customers with superior products and services, its potential long-term potential will remain elusive."

Moschella cites EDI, digital cash, on-line banking, and of course, the FedEx shipment tracking system as examples of technology applications that can transform major business activities. He acknowledges that many of these applications need time to mature and that many purely intranet applications are valuable. Nevertheless, he believes it is wrong to focus strictly on conventional intranet applications. "Every dollar invested in internal automation is a dollar that could have gone to a more compelling and useful [external] presence," he said. These external applications could include "a useful presence on the World Wide Web, a supply-chain EDI application, or an on-line customer service capability. The sooner the industry makes these external, customer-centric applications its top priority, the sooner the great potential of the Internet will be realized."

More of the Same to Come

Expect more of this kind of commentary in the future. The same issue of *Computerworld* that carried Moschella's column also described how Countrywide Home Loans (Pasadena, CA) built a hybrid extranet—half Internet, half intranet—that could serve as a prototype for the kind. In fact, Countrywide was one of the first organizations to describe its installation as an extranet.

Through this application, Countrywide can share information with the banks and mortgage brokers who are its business partners. At the same time, strictly internal information such as financial databases are screened from outside disclosure.

Called Platinum Lender Access, the system lets a banker who is processing a mortgage application call up the Platinum site to check such information as the loan's status, the account history, and current interest rates.

A bank of firewalls restricts access to banks that can supply the proper name, password, ID number, and other proprietary information. An access control system is designed to reveal only information to which the specific bank is entitled.

Countrywide reports substantial savings, just in a limited initial trial, over traditional methods that involved telephone messages, faxes, and mailed documents.

Controlling Access

The biggest risk, of course, is that someone will use the system to obtain information they should not have. Countrywide not only worries about competitors and hackers, but it also fears individual home buyers might gain access to data that are intended for the banks and brokers alone. Business partners share these concerns.

To meet the security need, the firm has established several layers of access control, the full details of which it keeps to itself. One element is the Secure Sockets Layer encryption scheme used in Netscape products. There are also several firewalls in place, including some custom-built installations.

How Internal Applications Can Become External

The range of possible extranet applications is almost infinite. In particular, nearly anything you can devise for an intranet can have external implications. Nevertheless, the early applications generally have fit into one of these categories:

- *One-to-many communication between teams, departments, or entire corporations.* You can post information on a Web page, reducing paper documents and making the information available almost immediately. The cost savings in printing can be significant, but even more important is the savings that come from better communication.

- *Applications that require two-way interaction.* If there is such a thing as a classic extranet application, it is technical help and support. Many computer-oriented companies have found it easy and cost saving to post specifications and problem-solving information on the Web and to use Web e-mail as a vehicle for receiving and answering inquiries. In other instances, an employee needs information to prepare a report, analyze data, or learn about suppliers and customers. Here, a Web site linked to corporate database resources can be easier and quicker than relying on printed reports.

■ *Collaboration that requires many-to-many interactions.* In this category are news groups whose members exchange information. Their posted messages can form a valuable knowledge base for others. At times, of course, you will want exchanges of confidential information to remain within a controlled group. Even in this case, though, it is not always necessary to confine that group to internal members. Trusted suppliers and customers can, and often should, be in the communication chain.

Types of Applications

Within these general classifications, application development to date has focused on several particular types:

■ Sales and marketing
■ Product development
■ Customer service
■ Human resources
■ Financial

Sales and Marketing

The departments that sell products face a continuing challenge delivering up-to-date reference information to customers who often are dispersed over a large area: the nation or even the world.

Sales representatives know that having the right information available at a critical moment can be the difference between winning and losing a sale. An extranet can give them information like this:

■ Product specifications and prices
■ Sales leads
■ Competitive information gleaned from competitors' Web sites
■ Calendars of sales activities

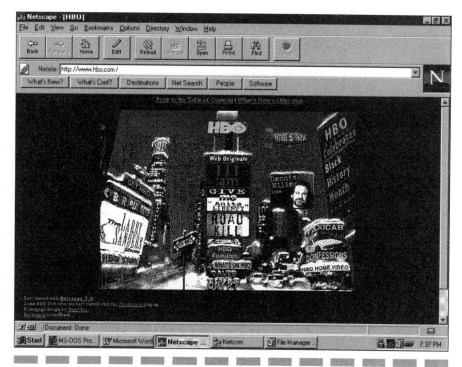

Figure 1-6
HBO offers a host of features for its home page viewers, but it also has internal/external features that support its sales representatives (http://www.hbo.com).

- Just-in-time training
- Instant sales presentations

Marketing people, meanwhile, need access to database-type information on current and potential customers. For example, Home Box Office (Fig. 1-6) has converted its marketing campaign materials from printed and videocasette forms to a Web site that gives the sales force instant access from just about anywhere.

Cadence Design Systems built a dynamic Web database of sales and marketing information. This system maps out each step of the sales cycle with links to sales support resources. It also

- Uses Web-page forms for communication with headquarters.
- Lets global account teams share information in a secure environment.

Figure 1-7
Cadence Design also uses the Web to support its sales representatives
(http://www.cadence.com).

- Provides a storehouse of sales and reference materials.
- Offers links to key Internet sites.
- Provides a daily news report on industry developments (Fig. 1-7).

Product Development

The external elements of sales and marketing applications are indirect, but this does not mean they do not exist. Even when an application does not offer customers direct access to your system, it supports the people who are making customer contact, and this is an essential element of an extranet. It is important that good customer relations be encouraged; whether you do it through direct electronic contact is secondary.

You can say much the same about product development. Even when extranet information does not reach outside parties directly, it enhances the ability of those who do maintain the contact.

Also like sales and marketing departments, product development groups need quick, current information. Product development activities often center on project management. Team members need good communication to update project schedules, report and coordinate their progress, and—here's the external part—receive and assess customer feedback.

Not all product development information should be shared directly in any event. This is a sensitive area, and information on future product plans is often highly confidential. You need strict access controls on this type of information. Still, you can use the extranet to supply your own people with the information they need to respond to customer needs.

The types of information available through an extranet can include

- Product specifications, designs, schedules, and changes
- Team rosters and individual areas of responsibility
- Customer comments and desires
- Features of key competing products

National Semiconductor Corporation has taken the extranet route in this area. It has developed a network whose main purpose is to help its customers get their own products to market faster. Not only does this aid the customers, but National Semiconductor uses it as an educational experience. By getting the products to market more rapidly, the firm is able to get timely feedback about its products' features and shortcomings (Fig. 1-8). With this knowledge, the firm can get a jump on its competition in designing the next generation of products.

Electronic Arts, the multimedia entertainment company, uses news groups to assemble virtual workgroups. Even widely separated employees can use the network to exchange information and participate in on-line discussions. Team members also have access to a database of product test reports.

Customer Service and Support

Here, the external contact is more direct. And even while calling their installations intranets or something else, organizations often use what are really extranets to exchange information with their customers.

For example, Mobil Corporation uses the Web to serve its customers and communicate more effectively with them. Customers have always made calls or sent letters to tell the company what they thought of its

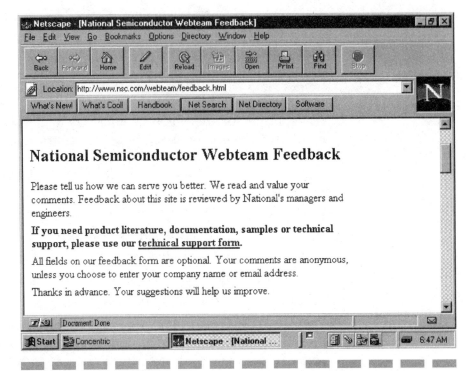

Figure 1-8
National Semiconductor uses this page to solicit feedback from business partners (http://www.nsc.com/webteam/feedback.html).

products and services and to discuss other subjects such as environmental issues. It takes a fair amount of motivation to write or call, so Mobil is using the Web to make it easier. The company can hear from more people and get more immediate responses to its statements and activities (Fig. 1-9).

Customer service extranets can foster communication in other ways, too:

- Community applications let the service and support staff dig more deeply into particular issues.

- News groups with threaded discussions provide forums for detailed discussions of frequent customer problems and their causes.

- Employees can trade their knowledge of which solutions have succeeded or failed in the past.

- News groups can alert individual team members to changes or other important information.

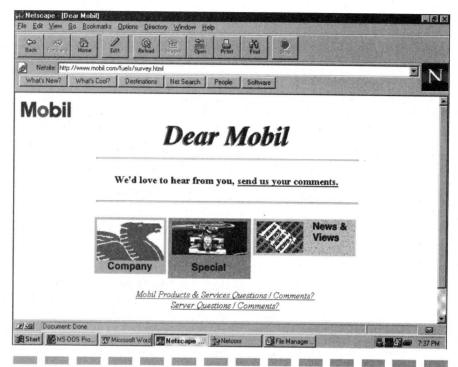

Figure 1-9
Mobil wanted more and better feedback from its customers
(http://www.mobil.com/fuels/survey.html).

Human Resources Applications

Here you find the classic intranet applications, but human resources applications also can reach outside the organization. Personnel recruiting is the major case in point. You can post job openings on the net and use Internet e-mail to receive applications and resumés. One small step further is the use of hypertext markup language (HTML) application forms.

Other human resource applications have less external impact:

- Benefits information
- On-line enrollment in 401k plans and optional benefit packages
- Policy statements and manuals
- Mission and goal statements
- Job postings for possible internal transfers

- Searchable internal telephone directories
- Annual reports
- Personal and departmental home pages
- Employee surveys
- Personal classified ads for employees
- A lookup service where employees can check their available leave time

Financial Applications

Here, purchasing is the main external component. Purchasing departments can maintain on-line catalogs of approved supplies and equipment, and client departments can call up the Web and order what they need. At the same time, the network can simplify the billing and purchasing from external vendors. In this role, the Web application is a form of electronic data interchange (EDI).

In another area of finance, investment firms are starting to use extranets to provide information to their customers and, if security concerns can be overcome, to handle customer transactions over the Web.

A pioneer in this area has been the Vanguard Group (Fig. 1-10), a major mutual funds company. Vanguard's Participant Online (POL) was developed for a business client whose employees now can look up details of their 401k accounts, use a retirement planning tool, download prospectuses of Vanguard funds, and educate themselves on mutual funds in general. Initially, POL was limited to business clients, but Vanguard has been making plans to extend its extranet services to the public. Eventually, the firm plans to use the POL structure and a secure commercial Web server to give individual customers access to their accounts.

Of course, the essence of an extranet is that it need not artificially observe distinctions between external and internal applications. Aside from the reporting requirements for public corporations, a business organization's finances are primarily an internal matter.

Careful monitoring of financial indicators helps a company's management set clear objectives. The continuing challenge has been to keep this information secure while also making it available, ideally in an easy-to-use form. With extranet applications, a finance department can more easily spread this information to key managers by posting data in a

Figure 1-10
The Vanguard Group's Web site offers many kinds of information but is only a preview of the group's extranet plans (http://www.vanguard.com/).

secure fashion or by providing query forms to help managers frame their requests for information.

The Web lends itself to innovation as well. At Allen-Bradley, employees can take advantage of a database swap shop to find buyers for older computer equipment.

Looking Outward for Profits

Many extranet applications are simply intranet applications that have implications outside the organization. As intranets take hold, however, a few organizations are discovering that looking externally can boost income and cut costs at the same time.

Brian R. Blackmarr, host of the on-line Phantom of the Internet (http://www.brba.com/news/apr96/news.htm) has identified these extranet sales opportunities:

- *Retail businesses and financial institutions with multiple sites.* These firms are strong extranet candidates because they need regular communication. The data include sales reports, inventories and restocking, and labor. Many retailers also need low-cost ways to handle large numbers of low-dollar credit card transactions.

- *Catalog sales.* Here, you find businesses that cater both to retail customers and to other businesses. An extranet approach can be much less expensive than printing and mailing catalogs. In addition, an extranet can make inventory replenishment quicker and more accurate. When you can readily restock, you can maintain lower inventories with a lower investment and less risk. An extranet-based customer link also can ensure that you quote current prices.

- *Fast-paced markets.* Stock and commodity markets are the models for this type of transaction. Traders can already make use of the Intranet to make investment and trading decisions. You could extend this concept to all types of financial transactions such as home banking. They key here is the time value of money; even small amounts of time and interest saved can add up to major sums.

- *High-technology businesses.* Here, an extranet can help a customer obtain the latest technical specifications, stock levels, and other information. The customer can check the price and availability of each component of a custom design. Meanwhile, the vendor can use the extranet to make sure customers always have the latest prices and specifications.

Why Web Technology Is So Attractive

Richard Villars, an Internet analyst at International Data Corporation (IDC), says that in order for an intranet offering to succeed, it "must meet one or more specific needs better than an alternative."

He could have been speaking about extranets as well. Compared with the Web technology used in an intranet, many current means of external communication are limited. For example, Vanguard adopted an extranet policy after considering and rejecting a graphic front end for a traditional client/server configuration. The company's planners decided a browser would be accessible to more people. This choice also would eliminate the cost and trouble of delivering software to clients and could be readily adapted to Web use.

Extranet benefits can include

- Ready access to information
- Freedom of choice
- Security
- Ease of use
- Moderate setup cost
- Lower printing and processing costs
- Simplified work flow
- Lower training costs
- Better group interaction

Ready Access to Information

An extranet's easy access to many types of media can make it an ideal vehicle for both internal and external communication. As presented in a Netscape corporate statement, an extranet can provide information in a way that is

- Immediate
- Cost-effective
- Easy to use
- Rich in format
- Versatile

Freedom of Choice

Web technology does not lock you into a single vendor's system, not even Netscape's or Microsoft's. Web technology is available for nearly all leading operating systems and hardware platforms and can enhance the value of existing database systems.

Security

The Web is neither as insecure as it is sometimes reputed to be nor as secure as its most ardent advocates would like to think. This is a particularly important issue where extranets are concerned, because you will want to control both who has access to the system and what kinds of access they have. There are ways to make an extranet more secure, Chapter 15 is devoted to the subject.

Ease of Use

Hypertext is a big factor in making it easy to use a Web-based extranet. Customers and suppliers can learn how to follow Web links readily; many of them already know. Furthermore, Web technology uses a single

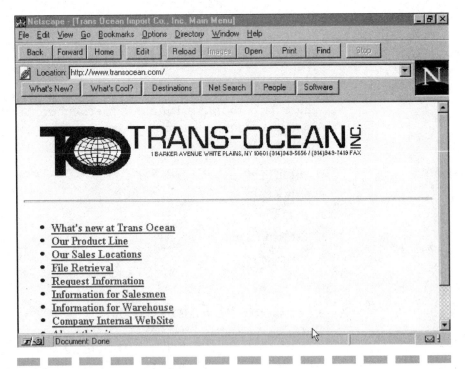

Figure 1-11
Trans Ocean, Ltd., piggybacks an intranet/extranet on its Web home page. Here, customers can use the system to retrieve product and service specifications (http://www.tolcontainers.com/).

Web browser front end. Once someone has learned to use that tool, he or she can use it for all Web activities. He or she does not need to learn new applications to retrieve new information. Trans Ocean Ltd. (Fig. 1-11) has reduced the number of screens needed to use its inventory and order entry systems from ten screens to one.

Moderate Setup Cost

An extranet is not as low-cost an option as it might seem initially. An extranet can be surprisingly inexpensive—or surprisingly expensive. Netscape says the typical cost of an enterprise or large department system is $40 or less per user. This is much less than any other kind of communication or workgroup system.

Lower Printing and Processing Costs

Early intranet users cited this advantage, particularly when they put printed manuals on-line. The on-line employee manual is almost an intranet cliché. Other fertile ground for cost savings include telephone directories—which need not be limited to internal listings—material safety data sheets, and employee and customer surveys.

Simplified Work-flow

An extranet can simplify work-flow in such areas as ordering supplies, filing reports, and managing customer service requests. Looking externally, Diamond Shamrock lets approved employees order office supplies directly from company purchasing agents. Other companies extend similar links to outside vendors.

Lower Training Costs

The Web lends itself to just-in-time training, delivered directly to the people who need it, when and where they need it. Even internal training programs can have indirect external impact. AT&T used this method to cut the training time for customer service representatives in half.

Better Group Dynamics

Discussion groups, bulletin boards, mailing lists, and on-line knowledge bases make it easier for people to learn from each other. These links can be extended easily to outside information, providing a foundation for easy exchange of information with your business partners.

The Flip Side of Web Technology

There must be some kind of rule—perhaps an offshoot of Murphy's law—that for every advantage, there is an equal and opposite disadvantage. Extranets are no exception, except maybe for the equal and opposite part. Certainly you cannot gain the benefits of an extranet without risking some of the pitfalls that inevitably exist.

If you do not spot all the possible problems yourself, management almost certainly will do it for you. One of the biggest potential problems is measuring the costs and benefits and computing the return on an extranet investment. Early intranet and extranet projects have been more or less experimental, and their proponents have gotten by with citing the relatively low costs of implementing these applications.

This will not last forever. Management will soon be demanding that you provide hard numbers to justify an extranet investment. And both the costs and returns of an extranet are frustratingly soft.

Startup Costs Are Just the Beginning

Netscape's $40 per user directly plops into the squishy category. This number may reflect the initial investment accurately, but the startup cost is only the first of many bills to be presented.

The Meta Group (Westport, CT) has published figures that multiply the cost by more than 100. By the time you figure in the costs of hardware and support, you can count on about $4100 per user, this source estimates. And that is just for basic hypertext markup language (HTML) service. If you want added functions like the ability to collaborate on plans and projects, expect to spend even more.

You certainly should not be lulled by installation costs alone. Measure and allow for other costs such as these:

- Staff time
- Training
- Support
- Application development

Finding Hidden Costs

Then there are the costs that often do not reveal themselves until too late to avoid or control them. Consider these:

- Support for multiple browsers
- Necessary hardware upgrades
- Business process redesign
- Firewalls
- System management
- Integration of existing databases and other applications
- Complexity of all kinds

These can quadruple your initial budget estimates, warns John Gantz of International Data Corporation (IDC). If the original $40 has already become $4100, the Gantz estimate now puts us in the $16,400 ballpark.

There are yet other possible drains on your budget:

- Developing and maintaining the content
- Browser version control
- Installing and maintaining high-speed telephone lines
- Managing libraries of Internet applets
- Rising product costs

These costs will be greatest, the Meta Group says, if you do not yet have a solid network infrastructure in place. A robust enterprise-wide network is a major asset; the lack of one, as in mainframe shops that have yet to seriously adopt client/server, is a major liability.

The list of potential costs is not yet exhausted. If your extranet succeeds, there is one way in which that success will become a liability. If more people use the network more often, the costs of supporting them naturally will rise. More significantly, the more experience people gain with the network, the more good ideas they will have for adding and improving applications. Many of these ideas will have merit. All of them will cost something to implement.

Soft Benefits to Hard Numbers

The greatest benefits of an extranet are things like improved communication and better access to information. These are valuable benefits, but it is hard to put firm dollar figures on their value. Even if you learn how to assess the current costs for communication and access, then you often must still find a way to measure the costs of these same activities without the extranet. This makes it hard to show the benefits.

This indeed can be a serious problem. Consultants point to the earlier example of videotext which, they say, failed largely because its proponents were not able to show specific benefits.

Extranets, like the Internet and intranets that came before, require that you find new ways to measure value. Several approaches have been tried. None is perfect, but any or all might help make the case when management starts asking hard questions:

- *Do not look for profits.* Do not try to justify an extranet on the basis of the profits it can generate. Instead, evaluate the extranet as a cost item like sales and administrative costs. Diamond Shamrock used a proof-of-concept approach in which a few selected employees were given dial-up access. After the company identified the potential benefits, the service was extended to senior executives and board members—decision makers who could thus see the benefits themselves.

- *Get cost information from client departments.* There are certain departments and activities that are likely to become the most active internal customers of an extranet. Find out how much they spend now on communication and information gathering. This will give you valuable "before" data to compare with your "after" expenses.

- *Emphasize opportunity cost.* Ask, "What is the value of better communication and improved customer service? What would be the cost of failing to provide it?" Focus your presentation on new opportunities that will make the organization more competitive. Then compare the cost of an extranet with the cost of not having one.

Other Considerations

Corporate warfare like the Internet supremacy battle between Netscape and Microsoft makes plenty of fodder for the trade press. It may have only limited significance to you and your operations. Nevertheless, when giants fight, even microscopic organisms must exist in the ground they tear up. So it is with those of you who plan and use extranets.

When you pick a vendor, you will always have to wonder whether the chosen company and its technology will still be around in its present form.

More to the point, an extranet faces many potential compatibility problems. Web technology can cross platform and operating system barriers at a single bound, but the leap is not always effortless. Already, the major Web browsers have gone their own way in supporting frames, tables, Java, and other features.

You can avoid this kind of compatibility problem by selecting a standard browser in your own organization, but you cannot do this as easily with a customer or a trading partner. The unsatisfactory alternative is to try to maintain a generic extranet that supports only those features all the major browsers will recognize. When you limit features, you also risk limiting the things your extranet can do.

2

Where Do Extranets Come From?

Back in geologic time—1996 to be exact—Forrester Research published a report that introduced the idea of a full-service intranet. Netscape has since adopted the idea as a way to promote its own version of intranet technology. Netscape describes the full-service model as a way to use standard Internet technology to deploy a versatile environment for communicating, sharing information, and running applications.

It takes only a little imagination to extend the idea even further and envision a full-service extranet—taking the same ideas outside the organization that Forrester and Netscape have been using inside. In this role, the full-service concept can serve as the very model of a modern extranet.

A full-service extranet could be defined as a network that combines the Transmission Control and Internet protocols into the more familiar TCP/CCP. This network links an organization's employees, customers, suppliers, and other business partners. It does so in a way that

■ Makes all these parties more productive

■ Makes information more accessible

■ Makes it easier to navigate through all the resources and applications the organization has available.

An extranet takes advantage of the open standards and protocols that originated with the Internet, although—and here we depart from the Forrester/Netscape definition—it also can include proprietary systems such as Notes, particularly as that product has become more Internet aware.

The Extranet at Your Service

The heart of an extranet is not in technical definitions that happen to fit some vendor's products. The best way to think about an extranet is in terms of the services it provides. Thanks to these services, people can look up information, send and receive e-mail, and search for information. They also provide for custom and third-party applications that take advantage of the extranet's features. These services make it easy for information services (IS) managers to manage the network and provide for further essential services such as directories and security.

There are two basic kinds of services. Network services provide the fabric that keeps things running. User services provide the resources people use to communicate and share information.

The network services include

■ Directories

■ Replication

■ Security

■ Management

They support user services like these:

■ Information sharing and management

■ Communication and collaboration

■ Navigation

■ Access to applications

How People Can Use an Extranet

Sharing Information.   You can use an extranet to publish your latest product information, possibly including an on-line demonstration or training video. You then can make this material instantly available, worldwide, to any audience with access rights.

This is an example of how an extranet can provide painless, transparent publishing across the entire network, to internal and external patrons alike. This information is easy to update, making sure everyone who has access rights to the information also sees the latest available intelligence.

The key here is hyptertext markup language (HTML). Even existing word processing documents can be converted to HTML. With HTML, you can create hypertext links, present multimedia, and use embedded objects to create interactive on-line publications, customized, perhaps, for each reader.

You also can index and organize documents as they are published and manage the publication program from a single location, no matter how widespread the audience.

Navigational Aids.   A customer looking for information about your company or products can enter a single query. It will return all the available internal and external information about that subject. The only requirement is that the researcher be authorized to see the information.

An extranet makes it easy to find any kind of information or any other resource that is available on the network. You can type a single query that produces an organized list of all matching information on any server throughout the organization or even throughout the Internet. You can create indexes and browsing abilities, just like the search engines that cruise Internet sites.

Another possibility is to create an agent that alerts a customer whenever new information of possible interest is added to the network.

Of necessity, an extranet also provides for access control. A sophisticated security system—which at the same time is the least you can get by with—gives different people different levels of access. With a well-planned security system, it is possible to maintain control over access yet let customers and other authorized users have access to important information.

Working Together. Workgroups and project teams are important parts of modern business. Whether these groups are permanent or ad hoc, communication is their lifeblood. This is the type of service that lets a sales representative look up a customer record, find the customer's e-mail address, and send the customer an e-mail message.

Current Internet standards provide for open e-mail and groupware available across the network. Again, access control is important. You need it to make sure e-mail and discussion groups can be limited to those who properly should participate.

You can conduct e-mail and discussion groups across the network or take them off-line for disconnected use. Some e-mail packages let you send formatted messages that include audio and video. An on-line address book can help you find the e-mail addresses of customers, suppliers, and coworkers around the world.

Access To Applications. A customer given access to the extranet could run an application that displays an on-line catalog, checks prices, and places an order, all without intervention from the seller's staff. If you do not want to go this far, you can have an employee place the order for the customer.

Web-centered programming languages like Java let you build an application and quickly deploy it to all kinds of client and server operating systems and hardware platforms. The extranet is a true client/server system, in which client-side application logic can be downloaded whenever the application is opened. Updates are noted automatically.

Network Services Provide Support

Directory Services. The network services that are part of an extranet exist primarily to support the user services and the users themselves. For example, directory services track and manage

- Information about the people who use the network
- Access control
- Server operation and configuration
- Resources needed by particular applications

Ideally, when a new employee joins the organization, a network administrator can record the addition with a single entry, noting the employee's personal information and assigning the proper access privileges. This information then can be instantly available to anyone connected to any server anywhere on the network.

The Lightweight Directory Access Protocol (LDAP) provides directory services across all operating environments and applications with which the network connects. It is designed so that individuals can find information readily about the people with whom they want to correspond, including e-mail addresses and security keys. At the same time, network managers can manage directory services and access control from a single location.

Applications can take advantage of these directory services to enhance their communication functions. These could include acquiring information from legacy e-mail systems or replicating information to allow universal single login.

Maintaining Security.   Security is important, even when an intranet is maintained within the corporate walls. It is even more vital when you extend your reach beyond the drawbridge via an extranet. Security should be both universal and easy to manage, no matter how contradictory these goals might be. At the same time, it must not place such a burden on legitimate users that they circumvent the security system and in the process leave you vulnerable to unauthorized access.

In a secure extranet environment, you and a business partner should be able to maintain secure communication, perhaps the electronic billing and payment that characterizes electronic data interchange (EDI). The foundation of EDI is that such exchanges must be quick and simple. At the same time, they must be protected from outside intrusion.

The Web has been justly criticized for lacking security, but it is not totally lacking. An extranet can provide ways to

- Protect resources against unauthorized access
- Encrypt communication
- Authenticate communication to verify the sender's identity
- Verify that the information you received is the same information that was sent.

A secure extranet can protect services of all kinds, including applications, Web pages, directories, discussion groups, and databases. Central management can link user privileges to the appropriate resources and include access controls in the directory service. Meanwhile, e-mail correspondents can encrypt and decrypt their messages, with assurance that the senders and recipients have been identified properly and the messages' contents verified.

In addition, you should be able to manage the distribution and use of security keys so that employees and trusted business partners can conduct business easily and in a secure atmosphere. In addition, you should be able to use the extranet to extend applications across the network.

Replication Services. A company with several branch offices could produce catalogs and price lists, drawing on the resources of its inventory database. It then could send replicas of this information to the branches. Local customers would have ready access to this information at higher speed and reduced network traffic than if the information was concentrated at headquarters.

This is one of the ways replication services can support an extranet. Replication maximizes the network's efficiency by distributing information to multiple locations along the network. This information could include Web content, discussion group messages, directories, and database tables.

Replication also makes it easy to take discussion groups and directories off-line, so that they are not taking place on the network. This can improve security while reducing network traffic. At intervals that could range from a few minutes to a few weeks, any updates and other changes made at the local level could be recorded on the server.

Central Administration. A well-configured extranet can let a single person administer all servers on the network. If necessary, this individual could update information and install software at branch offices on several continents. The Internet lends itself to instant updates, if necessary.

The technical background of this service is in an HTML-based management interface that allows all servers and other resources to be managed from anywhere on the Internet. The Simple Network Management Protocol (SNMP) can be integrated with most other network management systems. Directory services provide for simple, centralized management of user information, access-control standards, and information on server configurations.

Multiple Generations of Applications

Intranet/extranet applications have moved quickly through a reproductive cycle that already extends to the third generation. The first-generation intranet applications were usually like these:

- *Publishing corporate documents.* The human resource guides are the staples of this category. Other documents include company newsletters, annual reports, and maps of company facilities.

- *Directory service.* This group includes corporate telephone books, perhaps with the information mirrored at a Web site.

- *Departmental Web pages.* Intranets often have started as grass roots developments in the form of personal Web pages posted by individuals or small groups. Departmental pages came next, and in a few companies the intranet actually includes the corporate Web site, with pointers to departmental and personal pages.

- *Simple groupware applications.* With forms support, the site can provide sign-up sheets for benefits or activities, conduct employee surveys, and do simple scheduling.

- *Software distribution.* Network administrators often have considered, and sometimes have used, Web pages as a way to deliver applications and updates on demand to users throughout the network.

The Second Generation

The first-generation products showed the potential of the intranet. Developing and using them also gave the pioneering organizations some useful experience. They set the stage for second-generation products that looked downward, toward lower levels of the organization.

If an Internet client provides a simple interface for using the Internet to obtain general company information, the logic went, why not extend this feature to other types of company information and applications, such

Figure 2-1
Second-generation
intranet development
proceeded down-
ward from the corpo-
rate level.

Typical development pattern

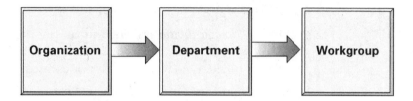

as those stored on databases? In fact, you can take another step and extend down to department- and workgroup-level information sharing.

While there are good reasons for companies to start their intranet deployments by publishing company-wide information, this is only the beginning. Most of an organization's information is specific to a department or workgroup, where people work in teams to complete projects and achieve objectives. Web publishing at the department or workgroup level can yield even greater benefits by boosting information sharing, collaboration, and ultimately workgroup productivity (Fig. 2-1).

Unshared Information

The sharing of information was an important development, because until recently, the typical personal computer (PC) was an individual-use tool with a suite of desktop applications intended for individual use. Some application suites are now developing workgroup capabilities, but at the heart, these are still single-user applications.

Fundamentally, none of these tools was designed to share information easily across an enterprise. Word processors were designed to create printed documents; sharing them with others was an afterthought. Even in the typical network installation, file servers were designed to provide shared access to files and applications, but not for easy searching or retrieval.

"Does Not Play Well with Others"

Even some ostensible workgroup applications fall short of their apparent potential. E-mail, for example, is a popular tool for sharing information and keeping people informed. E-mail certainly has an important, long-term future as a business communication tool, and it is rightfully a part of most Internet-based installations. Still, it cannot do everything, and it has some significant drawbacks:

- *Directory difficulties.* Maintaining an e-mail directory system in a large organization is a major challenge for administrators. E-mail patrons do not have it much better. They do not always know who to send documents to. Even if the directory is comprehensive and up to date, it is hard to know all the people in an organization who might benefit from your information. When in doubt, the easy way out is to send copies to everybody. In effect, these copies are sent to nobody. When e-mail runs to excess, as it often does, inboxes become so flooded with unimportant messages that recipients are hard-pressed to identify the truly important material.

- *Compatibility problems.* Different e-mail systems are notoriously incompatible with each other. They assume that everyone else is using the same system, when the reverse is usually the case. Even in the best-case scenario, messages may be garbled when transferred from one mail system to another. Attachments are not always handled properly, either.

- *Transient status.* When you send a document via e-mail, you can be assured only that it is stored on your own hard drive. Others may or may not store the document, and even if they do, they will likely delete it when cleaning out their inbox or e-mail folders. The information is not stored permanently in a generally accessible way.

- *Bandwidth.* E-mail places heavy demands on a company's networks and disk drives. Attachments that are sent to many people are potentially duplicated numerous times and then also often stored by default on the user's desktop machine. These numerous copies of documents take up unnecessary network bandwidth and computer storage. Not all e-mail systems are guilty of this, but a fair number of them are.

The Line at the Copier

Neither have traditional systems cut down on the need to print, duplicate, and distribute information on paper. They still require that people often

- Stand at the printer waiting for a document
- Stand at the copier to make copies
- Walk around and drop off copies at people's desks
- Go through this process again when the information is updated

Dreams of a paperless office have been largely unfulfilled, and the intranet is no exception. Even though Internet technology promises to reduce the volume of printed documents, there will always be paper to be shuffled. In a television commercial that ran a few years ago, an executive complained about having to use e-mail instead of the paper memos he was used to. "You could always print your e-mail," his assistant suggested. Many people do just that.

Confession: Much of the research for this book consists of documents downloaded from the Web, stored on disk—and printed for easier reading.

The real advantage of Internet technology over traditional paper distribution comes when the extranet extends the network outside corporate boundaries. There, it will reach people who have no access to your printers or copiers. Of course, they probably have access to their own.

Intranets as a Better Way

This is not to say that other types of products are seriously faulty. Modern PC software does many things well. Nevertheless, intranet developers found that Web technology could overcome some of their limitations in information-sharing service. Web technology has made it easier for users to navigate through massive amounts of information. It was natural to extend this information-access capability to include departmental- and workgroup-level information, where the most pertinent data exist.

Using personal Web page authoring tools, users can share information like a new product proposal, a schedule for a project, a cost-reduction plan, quarterly objectives, and information on a competitor.

Information like this can be stored on Web servers. Each document or directory of documents can have strict access control. An administrator can decide who can read and who can edit the documents.

Sharing all information on Web servers gives authorized users access to all information. For content creators, it greatly simplifies the task of distributing information. An author can post information on one server and then have users find out about it through a variety of mechanisms, including

- Links from other Web pages
- Links in e-mail messages
- Web search engines
- Full-text searching

Unlike e-mail, you do not have to identify the proper recipients of a message. You can let them find you.

Counting the Benefits

This approach has several benefits:

- *The ability to unlock information that is not currently available.* In every organization there are hundreds or even thousands of important documents that many users do not know about or cannot find. The opportunity cost of this lost potential is tremendous.

- *Reduced effort to share information.* Instead of repeatedly sending a document via e-mail, the latest version can be posted and updated dynamically, while users find out about it automatically.

- *Less time and energy spent trying to find and read information.* People often struggle to find the information they need. Web technology is far from ideal in this respect, but posting documents on Web servers lets people take advantage of such tools as full-text searching, cataloging, and links from other documents. Because documents are in HTML format, there is no need to launch a specific application to read documents.

- *Reduced load on the network and server infrastructure.* Documents are often e-mailed, copied, or replicated, so you end up with multiple copies, some at unknown locations. All these copies consume network bandwidth to distribute and disk space to store. Having a single current copy of a document in one place is much more efficient.

■ *Saved printing and distribution costs.* It is less likely that people will print and manually distribute documents.

The Second Generation

The second generation of intranet development has produced applications like these:

■ Sharing information among members of project teams
■ Sharing information within departments
■ Sharing information with other departments

Project Teamwork.   Modern project teams are often cross-functional, made up of people who can contribute to the effort, whatever their place in the organizational structure. Team members often work at different locations and sometimes use different computing platforms. With Web communication, they can share documents easily such as

■ Schedules
■ Product specifications
■ Product plans
■ Reference materials
■ Meeting agendas, minutes, and action items

Within Departments.   In a way, the department is an enlarged project team. Members need to know what others in the department are doing. They often can exchange information profitably on the best ways to get things done. To meet these needs, members can use Web technology to share

■ Templates or previous examples of standard documents
■ Procedures
■ Best practices
■ The status of ongoing projects

Sharing Between Departments.   A challenge many companies face is the need to maintain good communication between headquarters and a widespread sales force. Salespeople must respond constantly to customers' questions and requests for more information or assistance. They also receive daily feedback on why the company's products do or do not meet customers' expectations. Traditionally, it has been hard to exchange timely and accurate information between sales representatives and people at headquarters. With Web technology, several types of information can be exchanged easily:

- Proposals
- Product information
- Product and company presentations
- Frequently asked questions
- Sales reports
- Enhancement requests
- Competitive information

Ready for the Third Generation

Instead of looking downward toward lower levels of the organization, a third generation of intranet development looks outward, toward supporting partnerships with suppliers and customers. The extranet uses many of the techniques of earlier intranet development, but with the additions necessary to provide access to outsiders.

This is not just any kind of access. Unlike a Web site, which is open to almost anyone, an extranet maintains controlled access. And unlike an intranet, which encourages personal and departmental Web page authoring, an extranet requires some control over the information that is made available even to authorized outsiders.

With these exceptions, though, an extranet and an intranet are close relatives; an extranet is simply a new-generation development of an intranet, extended beyond the limits of the organization (Fig. 2-2). You can adapt intranet applications readily to extranet service. In fact, many existing intranets have external features and applications.

Improving the Breed

An extranet lends itself to many of the same kinds of applications as an intranet. The main difference is that the communication is external as well as internal.

Figure 2-2
En extranet can communicate internally
or externally—or
both.

An extranet goes both ways

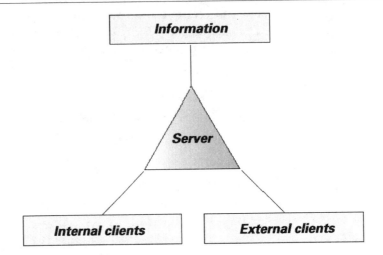

- *Project team sharing.* Not only can these groups cross departmental lines, but often they can cross organizational boundaries as well. A major example is the automobile industry, where manufacturers work closely with their suppliers in the design and manufacture of parts. They sometimes work so closely, in fact, that it seems the members are all part of the same company. This was a response to the industry's quality problems relative to imports, and it has been a response that has worked. Moreover, if information sharing works well for internal project teams, it can work even better when extended to business partners.

- *Sharing product information.* These applications serve the customer side of the chain. Sometimes the sharing is indirect. A salesperson responding to a customer's query often can make a better response when he or she has access to product information and pricing via an intranet. You could go a big step further and let the customer have direct network access to prices and specifications. Even information filtered through a human intermediary is valuable, though. In addition, this approach reduces security risks, and it maintains the valuable asset of direct people-to-people contact.

At the proverbial bottom line, the extranet represents one more step in a continuing process of improving communication using Web technology. It is an extension of the thinking that formed the Internet and intranets in the first place. The extranet is another move forward, and do not expect it to be the last.

Where Extranets Began

The extranet, of course, has its roots in the intranet movement. Forrester Research says that one in four Fortune 1000 companies now uses an internal Web server. Even small companies have been building them (Fig. 2-3). As one authority put it, intranets offer "the ability to connect product information, employees, customers, and vendors. Intranets are considered by many to be the building blocks of electronic commerce."

This is hardly a behind-the-firewall view of an intranet. The customers and vendors both exist out beyond corporate walls, and if you are going to build electronic commerce, you must stack at least some of your blocks outside.

Even when used for external communication, intranets offer two advantages the Internet does not:

- *Security.* Because intranets are parts of secure organizational networks, they can routinely offer valuable information that the company does not want to make available to the general public.

Figure 2-3
Corporate interest in intranets has been growing fast, even when the intranets are used externally. (*Courtesy of Business Research Group.*)

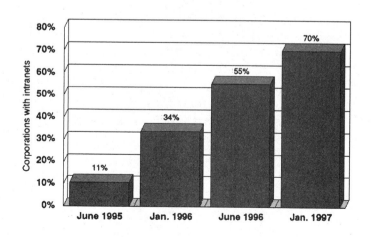

Intranet growth

■ *Bandwidth.* Although this is a problem with Internet fixtures like the World Wide Web, the opposite is true at the corporate level. Intranets run on corporate networks that are several times faster than Internet communication.

Early Adopters Get Surprised

Intranets had a fairly inauspicious start. The typical growth pattern was for one or two people to start a modest bulletin board—which immediately would be swamped by thousands of users with expanded ideas about how they could use the technology. Earlier intranets were not really planned. They just happened. Often they grew in unexpected ways, unto the third generation.

This was the experience at Genentech (South San Francisco, CA), a biotechnology pioneer that discovers, develops, manufactures, and markets pharmaceuticals such as a human growth hormone and a blood clot–dissolving drug for heart attack patients. Based in South San Francisco, the company's business focuses on research and development, filing of applications for new drugs, clinical trials, data analysis, manufacturing, and shipping (Fig. 2.-4).

When its intranet was installed in 1994, the idea was to set up a common bulletin board to replace a home-grown system. It soon grew into a multipurpose network serving more than 3000 people. The network now helps employees improve their efficiency by providing a common interface to applications and facilitating new ways to share information. An application, once developed, becomes available to the entire company, saving both development time and money.

Typical of many intranets, the system serves as Genentech's on-line employee handbook. The company's human resources, engineering, environmental safety, legal, corporate communications, library, medical affairs, quality assurance, and security departments, among others, all have home pages. It puts more information in the hands of employees to help them get their work done more effectively. Employees are also using Web-based news groups and bulletin boards to increase communications and provide links between organizations.

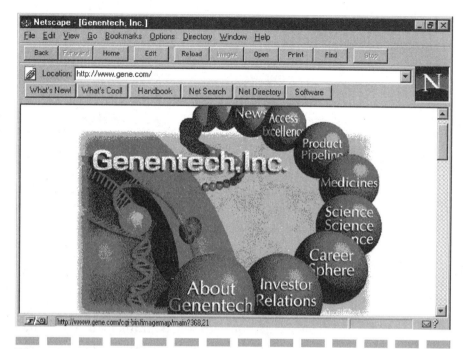

Figure 2-4
Genentech started with a small internal network, but it has expanded in size and outlook (http://www.gene.com/).

Looking Outward

Even here, the outlook is not entirely internal. Genentech is using the Web for other external purposes. Access Excellence (AE), available through the Genentech Web site, is a national educational program designed to enhance high school biology education by

- Linking teachers and scientists through an interactive computer network that provides peer support and access to critical sources of new information about research and developments in biologic science.

- Supporting teachers and scientists in developing strategies and resources to communicate this knowledge. The audience for this communication is not limited to students. It also includes educators, policymakers, and the public.

■ Creating partnerships between teachers and scientists in implementing national science education reform agendas.

Each year, about 100 outstanding biology and life science teachers are selected by the National Science Teachers Association to become AE fellows. The first group of fellows was selected in the spring of 1994. The AE fellows are selected based on their demonstrated capacities and interest in advancing the state of the art of secondary school biology education. Once selected, AE fellows attend an annual Access Excellence Summit. There they receive a laptop computer and special training on how to use the laptop and the interactive network.

AE fellows use America Online, the Internet, professional meetings and complementary print and multimedia resources to assist the science, education, and policy communities in developing an advanced understanding of the biologic sciences and information technologies. Through this greater understanding of science and what it takes to teach it, Genentech hopes to aid in implementing national science education reform agendas, both locally and regionally.

It Takes a Global Village

U.S. West (Denver) is another early user that has seen its network, known internally as the Global Village Project, expand in ways the originators could not have expected. One popular development has been the Virtual Secretary, a collection of useful tips on how to get things done, from ordering catered lunches to sending paperwork to the proper destination.

At Sun Microsystems, which should be about as network conscious as any company on the planet, a network that connected about 200 people in 1994 had grown to more than 3000 people a year and a half later. Employees now can open SunWIN, a Web site that connects to a Sybase database of sales and marketing information. This information was once available only to sales and support employees.

Extranet Applications

Such an extranet can run a variety of applications, both packaged and custom made. Some are suggested by the range of services available over an extranet. Others are custom developed, and still others are purchased over the counter. These applications can address many business needs, including

- *Order processing.* Customers need up-to-date information about your products and services. An extranet can let them place orders, receive invoices, track shipments, and process payments, no matter where they are.

- *Joint projects.* Members of a team developing a new product can coordinate with suppliers on product specifications and production methods. An extranet lets them share information so that they can work together as a single team, even though they represent different companies. Customers can be added to the team to make sure their requirements are met.

- *Ungarbled communication.* People in different organizations need a common way to share information. Because it is based on familiar Web technology and is basically ignorant of various platforms, an extranet can provide a common ground for clear communication.

- *Customer service and support.* An extranet can provide a way for customers to obtain self-help information and solutions to their problems. At the same time, a technical support staff can use the problem reports to track customers' problems, making sure that all are resolved properly.

- *Electronic mail.* A large organization easily can have half a dozen e-mail systems, and proprietary e-mail is notorious for its lack of compatibility between systems. When you add suppliers and customers to the mix, the compatibility problems can become even worse. Consider what can happen when a customer support employee has no way of knowing what the sales force has promised a key customer.

■ *Full access.* An organization may maintain all manner of databases filled with customer information and market research data. An extranet gives any authorized person a way to tap all this information.

You probably have many other application needs, many of which have not been addressed because there has been no way for people to gain access to a full range of applications and information resources. An extranet provides access to these applications, be they inherent Web applications, custom-built applications, or commercial over-the-counter applications.

Native Applications

The Web technology used in an extranet includes several built-in applications that are inherent in the technology. These include

■ Electronic mail
■ Group collaboration
■ Real-time audio and video communication
■ Information publishing and sharing
■ Network navigation
■ Full-text indexing and searching
■ Directories

Custom Work

In addition to these built-in applications, Web technology lends itself to easy development of custom applications. These can be made available to anyone you choose, anywhere, on any platform. Development and deployment are both much faster than with traditional programming methods. There are yet other savings to be had, too: Since all applications can use the same browser interface, training costs and time can be reduced sharply.

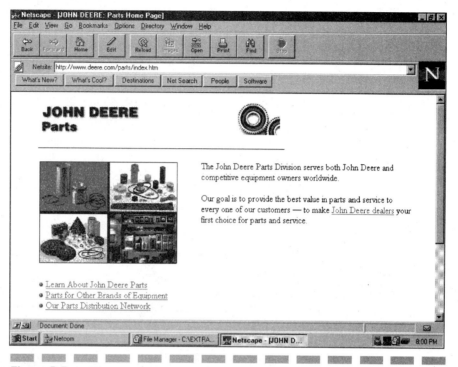

Figure 2-5
John Deere provides parts information and dealer locations at its Web site. Employees can go further and retrieve information from a parts database
(http://www.deere.com/parts/index.htm).

Database Access

An extranet can use its uniform interface to link people to databases and applications on traditional platforms. For example, John Deere has implemented a parts database that is available via the network (Fig. 2-5).

Employees can look up a picture and description of a part, including its size, materials, assembly instructions, and a list of the operations used to put the part together. Purchasing department members can solicit quotes by sending a picture and description of a part to potential vendors. In a true extranet, key vendors would have direct access to this information so that they could prepare the quotes and plan the manufacturing process with the help of immediate, direct information.

Multiple Purposes

John Deere's Waterloo Works Division also uses a Netscape-based extranet to

- Allow company-wide access to results from remote test sites
- Provide technical documentation to employees
- Offer a visual front end to the parts database
- Find new uses for otherwise obsolete equipment
- Integrate corporate information with agricultural data on the World Wide Web.

Building an Information Structure

John Deere's traditions may be rooted in agriculture, but it views information as critical to its long-term success. Several years ago the company started planning a systems architecture for information. Its purpose is to let various divisions rapidly build custom applications that work alongside traditional desktop programs. The firm chose an intranet, later expanded to external service.

At its most basic, the Netscape-based network lets people examine design, product, marketing, and manufacturing data on all platforms. But the company needed more: the ability not just to "view" data but to work with them. For this purpose, John Deere is using Java applets that can be downloaded from the network and run on any client.

For example, John Deere is putting a catalog of its tractors and equipment on-line. Instead of just looking at pictures of the tractors, employees can send queries to various databases and bring a variety of product information to their screens.

Remote Access

John Deere is using its intranet to distribute information from remote test sites, where new models of tractors and heavy equipment are put through their paces. Test results are more than just numbers. They also can include pictures and sound. For example, you might want to listen to what an engine sounds like. This is no small part of John Deere's history. In years past, farmers either swore by or swore at John Deere's two-cylinder engines. Regardless of these strongly-held opinions, a John Deere's exhaust note was distinctive.

More fundamentally, distributing information on the Web means it is available instantly to all authorized Deere employees. Because of its sensitive nature, the information must also be delivered securely. For this purpose, Deere chose a Netscape Commerce Server, with its Secure Sockets Layer (SSL) that lets sensitive data be encrypted.

Distributing Documentation

John Deere is finding a better way to distribute and use technical documentation by making it available over its net. The company describes this as "moving from a static, paper-based environment to a dynamic, on-line environment." It has begun to store computer systems documentation on a Web server and deliver it to people throughout the company. New documentation can be added hourly. The parts database fits into the system as an extension to on-line documentation.

The Web-based parts database will have many applications throughout John Deere. For example, a purchasing agent could send a picture of a part to a vendor. In addition, the people on the shop floor could call up information on how a part is put together. Engineers could automatically develop bills of materials for their designs.

John Deere's information architecture enables it to combine corporate knowledge with resources available on the World Wide Web. There is a wealth of agricultural information on the Web, such as crop reports, weather reports, and U.S. Department of Agriculture (USDA) information. This information can be integrated with John Deere's rich store of internal information.

Recycling Old Computers

The Web even lends itself to recycling older computers. John Deere has found a way to get more mileage out of them by turning them into dedicated Web clients. Recently, the Waterloo plant decided to convert several hundred 6-year-old Macintosh IIcx computers to dedicated Web browsers running Netscape Navigator.

Olivetti Builds a "Virtual Laboratory"

Olivetti, the Italian technology firm, has used Internet technology to create what it calls a "virtual laboratory." *Olivetti Ricerca in Rete* (Olivetti research by network) is a network of research laboratories designed to provide advanced tools and services for communication and cooperative work (Fig. 2-6).

The network supports Olivetti Ricerca, a research and development organization established in 1987, which is at the core of the organization's research and development activities. Its stated mission is "to become the Olivetti group's center of excellence for the development of innovation and applications." The network serves research and develop-

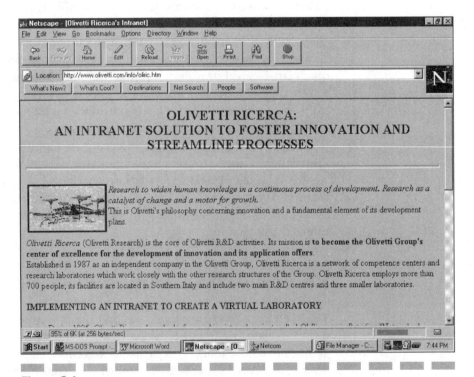

Figure 2-6
Olivetti Ricerca uses Internet-style communication at the core of its research and development programs (http://www.olivetti.com/info/oliric.htm).

ment employees at corporate headquarters, two main research and development centers, and three smaller laboratories.

Researchers use the network to retrieve a wealth of product development information, to conduct debates in network discussion groups, and to share experiences and information with their colleagues. This network provides Olivetti researchers with information on advanced topics such as asynchronous transfer mode (ATM), intelligent agents, new Web development, and multimedia applications. There are also many links to external sources of information.

The network is also used to speed up internal processes, thus contributing to an overall gain in efficiency and effectiveness. Project leaders now have instant access to administrative information such as costs incurred, resources spent on each product, and the status of procurement requests. Naturally, access to sensitive information is restricted to authorized people.

Sales and Marketing

Distributing information to a widely scattered sales force is a natural extranet application. Sales representatives can use an intranet to enjoy instant access to the latest product, pricing, and competitive information. Make this information available to selected customers, and you have a natural extranet application.

Gilding the Lilly Sales Force

Eli Lilly has taken the first of these two steps, setting up a network to distribute sales information to the field (Fig. 2-7). In the past, documents and presentations were sent by overnight mail—a major cost when these materials must go to as many as 300 salespeople worldwide.

As a pilot application, the Indianapolis-based company began distributing information to sales offices in seven European countries via an internal web. Expansion plans called for reaching all sales representatives worldwide.

Lilly also has been working on a forms-based system for its salespeople to use when calling on health care providers. When a representative visits a physician, the doctor may ask for a written notice of the charac-

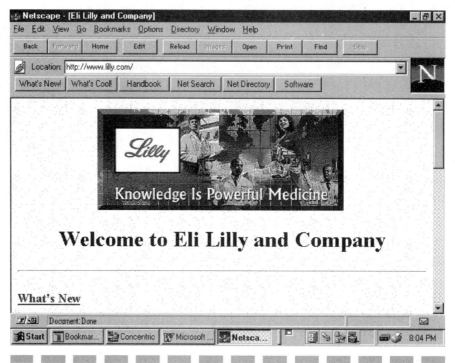

Figure 2-7
Eli Lilly uses a network to distribute sales information to representatives around the globe (http://home.netscape.com/comprod/at_work/customer_profiles/lilly.HTML).

teristics of a particular drug. The salesperson can call up a form, enter the doctor's name, address, and the requested information, and the request goes to headquarters immediately.

Extranets do not necessarily cut out the proverbial "middleman." Although a Lilly representative actually files the information request, it is a direct, specific, and immediate response to a customer's need. And this is the main point.

Charting the Sales Cycle

Cadence Design Systems has built a dynamic sales and marketing intranet that provides a different kind of information. It maps out each step of the sales cycle and links each step with the necessary sales support resources. Account teams can share information—sent in encrypted form—and take advantage of a repository of sales tools and reference materials.

Extending the Intranet

Of course, most extranet applications do not even know they are extranet applications. They are intranet applications that reach outside the sponsoring organization because it makes sense to do so. Their sponsors were less interested in forming a new kind of network than in finding new opportunities to take advantage of Internet technology.

For example, AT&T has developed a system that lets employees order office supplies directly from the stockroom. Typically, it is an intranet program with an extranet component: It is also possible to place an order outside the organization through an office supply catalog.

Direct to the Customers

Other networks are directed more strongly toward the outside. McDonnell Douglas uses an extranet to provide its customers with fast, complete transmissions of technical bulletins (Fig. 2-8).

McDonnell Douglas's commercial aircraft manufacturing division, Douglas Aircraft, is using Netscape and the World Wide Web to build a system to distribute aircraft service bulletins to their customers around the world.

This new document distribution system provides several benefits. It is

- *Less expensive.* Electronic distribution costs less than half as much as mailing paper.
- *Faster.* Customers receive service bulletins immediately compared with 2 to 3 weeks in the case of international customers.
- *More flexible.* Customers can integrate the standard generalized markup language (SGML) files into their own documents.

Based in Long Beach, California, the 11,000-person Douglas Aircraft builds airplanes for more than 200 airlines around the world. In addition to delivering airplanes, it delivers a staggering volume of aircraft service bulletins. These provide crucial information on how to modify and service the company's airplanes.

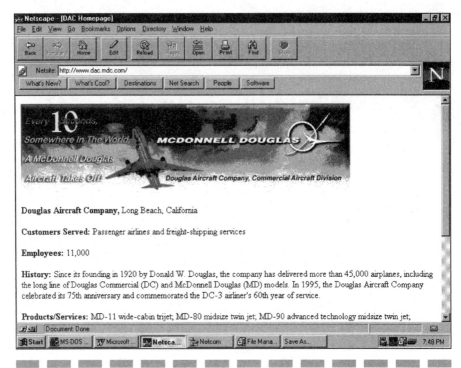

Figure 2-8
McDonnell Douglas has extended its Web page into an extranet that feeds information directly to customers (http://www.dac.mdc.com/).

The average bulletin is 25 pages long, and the firm sends four or five each day to customers around the world. This accounts for over 4 million pages of documentation every year. Now the firm can distribute service bulletins electronically.

Since the firm has customers and suppliers all over the world, it began a search for the best platform for communicating with such a widespread audience. The answer was the World Wide Web. It was there now, people understood it, and you could use it from anywhere in the world.

Providing Security

McDonnell Douglas had already set up a Web page to provide general information about the company and its products to all visitors. This was

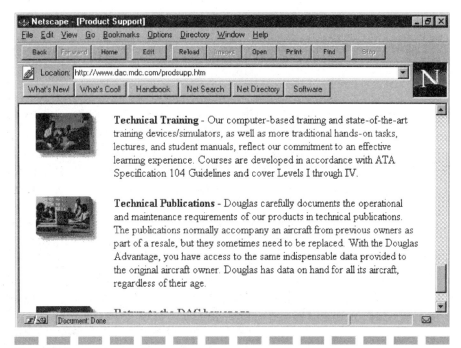

Figure 2-9
Customers can download service bulletins and other information via a protected entry point from the World Wide Web (http://www.dac.mdc.com/prodsupp.htm).

an ideal place to provide customers with access to service bulletins. However, service bulletins often contain proprietary information. Thus the issue of security came up immediately. If you just put information on the Internet, anyone can gain access to it unless you do something to secure it. The Netscape Commerce Server was used because it provides a way to encrypt the data using RSA encryption, which is a standard the organization wanted to follow.

To read or download service bulletins, customers call up McDonnell Douglas's home page and choose a button labeled *Access Service Bulletins* (Fig. 2-9). They then are required to enter passwords. Security precautions are designed to make the service bulletins' area private.

Douglas Aircraft runs Netscape's Commerce Server on a Hewlett-Packard HP9000 Model 800E Unix server. The service bulletins are stored as SGML files in an Oracle 7.1 database, with access from the Web page.

Benefits of Electronic Distribution

Douglas Aircraft saw three problems with their existing paper-based system for distributing service bulletins:

- Paper takes time, often too much time, to travel from the copy room to the customer's desk. The technical information in the bulletin is crucial, so every missed week counts.

- Once the paper actually gets to the customer, it is no longer live information that customers can incorporate into their own systems. Now, since the information is on-line, it is available almost as soon as it is created. This improves the quality of the data. Customers receive service bulletins in SGML (a superset of the HTML standard), and they can cut and paste the information into their own documents.

- Paper is hard to store and retrieve. After 20 years, you can end up with a building full of documents. Now customers can store all the bulletins digitally and retrieve them via the Web. Both McDonnell Douglas's customers and employees can access service bulletins right from their desktops.

Yet More Paper to Be Converted

There is yet another class of documents, maintenance manuals, that awaits conversion to the Web. A set of manuals for an aircraft runs 45,000 to 50,000 pages. Most of the airlines still store these on paper or magnetic tape. Experiments are also under way to use Pentium-based computers on jets so that crew members can connect to the Web directly.

The Web can be used in other ways, too. There are several ways the Web could be used to streamline other internal operations. Eventually, the company probably will share manufacturing, financial, and engineering data on the Internet across different parts of the company. Thinking even longer range, the firm wants to use the Internet for all information transfers, even from one building to another.

Already, the document service for customers has a matching Web-based service for suppliers. McDonnell Douglas also uses the Web for EDI, exchanging purchase orders, shipping documents, and payments electronically (Fig. 2-10).

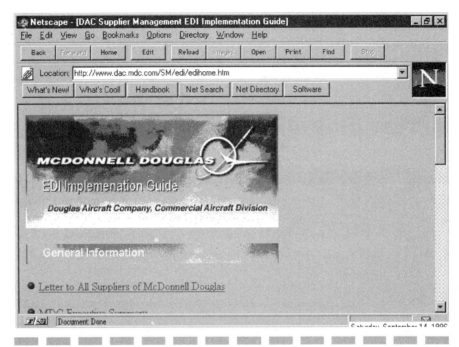

Figure 2-10
McDonnell Douglas also offers EDI through its Web site
(http://www.dac.mdc.com/SM/edi/edihome.htm).

Mobil Looks Outside

Mobil Corporation is also using the World Wide Web to forge new links
with employees, customers, and business partners. Its network has both
intranet and extranet components.

Mobil's extranet enhances employee communication by

- Sharing internal company information
- Publishing Internet guidelines and procedures
- Enabling divisions to collaborate on projects more efficiently

The external Web site provides customers, shareholders, and other
audiences with

- Company information, financial results, and news announcements
- Mobil's well-known editorial ads on economic and political issues

- An on-line application for Mobil's credit cards
- An electronic catalog of Mobil merchandise such as hats, jackets, and mugs
- Coverage of Mobil-supported sporting events, including the Indy and Nascar racing circuits

Building Relationships

Mobil is using the Web to build closer relationships with employees, customers, business partners, and the general public. In addition to its internal and external Web sites, Mobil is using the Web to develop new channels of communication and commerce with its business partners.

Mobil's external Web site uses Netscape's Commerce Server software running on an IBM AIX system. It is paired with internal Web sites that use Netscape Communications Servers. Mobil is rolling out Netscape Navigator to its employees as part of a standardized "common computing environment" for the desktop. Mobil's network includes a wide variety of Intel-based PCs running Windows as well as Unix workstations.

Boosting Employee Communication

Mobil's internal Web provides employees with three general types of information:

- *Employee information,* such as announcements, reference materials, and news posted by individual departments, divisions, and organizations
- *Internet guidelines and procedures,* such as style guides, security guidelines, answers to frequently asked questions, how to get software, how to access the Internet, and how to identify business opportunities to port to a Web server
- *Application platform.* The site gives divisions and affiliates a way to put up their own Web applications, maintain bulletin boards, and collaborate on projects. For example, oil exploration is a very collaborative environment. The Exploration Group in New Orleans puts its daily operations status report on-line for the team to read. Mobil's geophysicists, geologists, and reservoir engineers use the

Internet to share knowledge on research and software or to point to where information can be found.

Talking Back

Mobil has long been known for its editorial advertisements that state the company's opinion on public affairs. Among other things, the external site gives customers a way to talk back.

The company says it invites public comments on its editorials. It provides a way to monitor public reactions to the positions the company expresses. If they want, customers also can send their views directly to Congress from the Mobil home page (Fig. 2-11).

People have always called or written to Mobil with comments or questions about products, services, or environmental issues. However, the company only got feedback from people who were motivated to write or to find the right person within Mobil. With the Internet, the firm gets a broader, more immediate response. It helps make quick changes, if necessary, in the way the company serves its customers.

News & Views

Recent announcements about Mobil businesses and other activities. Plus a forum of ideas. Let us hear from you, too.

Where Are We Heading?
Remarks by Mobil Chairman and CEO Lucio A. Noto to the
1996 Offshore Northern Seas Conference, Stavanger, Norway,
August 27, 1996.

Gasoline Price Information
Answers to your questions

News Releases
Updated Frequently

Figure 2-11
Mobil uses this Web page to express—and listen to—public opinion (http://www.mobil.com/news.HTML).

For shareholders and customers, the company publishes business information, such as financial results, environmental information, and news releases.

Customers can use Mobil's Web site to apply for a Mobil credit card, the Go gas card, and business fleet credit cards on-line through the secure capabilities of the Netscape Commerce Server. Future additions to the external Web site include the Mobil Travel Guide and interactive services for consumers and distributors of Mobil lubricants and fuels.

Mobil also posts information about company activities beyond its main businesses. For example, Mobil supports the Indy and Nascar racing circuits and hosts racer fan clubs. The Web page publishes hourly updates on the races. And Mobil hats, jackets, and mugs are available for credit card purchase from the on-line catalog.

Serving Business Partners

An extranet can be extremely important in building relationships with external business partners. Mobil has been phasing in this part of its extranet. The first phase has involved some rudimentary forms of electronic commerce. This gradually will evolve into full business-to-business communication.

Mobil is moving into the last phase with a Web application that provides timely data to its North American distributors for heavy product lubricants. Mobil distributors will be able to obtain information via Netscape's Commerce Server, which is fed by Mobil's mainframe applications. This application saves the company money by reducing or eliminating reports and phone calls. It also permits an opportunity to provide a valuable service to business partners, and it is relatively inexpensive.

CHAPTER 3

The Extranet in Your Communication Strategy

The Internet is fun. An intranet helps your employees do better jobs. An extranet helps your company do a better job.

It does this by creating better relationships with suppliers and customers. This makes an extranet an important part of business and communication strategy.

An intranet should be a home-grown, self-guiding installation, and it will probably never come under the kind of central control information services (IS) specialists visualize. An extranet, on the other hand, opens possibly sensitive information to people outside the organization. You must be very careful to determine exactly what information will be made available to whom and on what terms. In short, an extranet must be planned.

While there are uncounted numbers of Web sites on the Internet, there are equally uncounted numbers of intranet sites in America's corporations. Digital Equipment Corporation (DEC) is said to have more than 400 internal Web sites. This is still far short of Sun Microsystems, which has more than 1000. The Meta Group estimates that about 75 percent of the Web servers now going into service are for internal use.

Someone has to create them and then take care of them. Many intranet projects consist of individual departmental Web sites. While they do require IS to support the effort and maintain the network and communication infrastructure, the best role for IS is to provide the structure and then leave well enough alone. An extranet requires a greater degree of technical attention, particularly in the critical area of access control. An extranet is usually a top-down project, specifically planned and executed to meet a stated objective.

Even with this added responsibility, maintaining an extranet is simpler—probably much simpler—than maintaining a standard client/server system. An intranet has been described as client/server done right. It also can be described as client/server done more easily.

Developing a Strategy for Success

No local-area network (LAN) is an island, and neither is any piece of today's corporate communication strategy. An extranet can, and should, be only one element in a wider-ranging communication strategy that extends both within and beyond the organization.

Alliances are a major business trend. Growing numbers of organizations are establishing partnerships with suppliers and customers and distributing more information to employees. Sound, timely business decisions depend on communication among all these parties. Transmitting essential information from wherever it is stored to wherever it is needed is critical to timely decisions and streamlined business processes.

The key to success today is to give the right people access to the right information without exposing the corporate network to security risks. The three access technologies that companies are using to facilitate communication and extend the reach of information include remote, Internet, and intranet access.

One way to accomplish this is to provide remote access to mobile employees and to business partners outside the organization. Remote

Figure 3-1
You can try the rest,
or you can try an
extranet.

Ways to boost communication

- Provide outside access
- Use dial-up service
- Use the extranet for selective external service

access gives these key people the ability to contact the corporate LAN from remote locations.

Another approach is to provide Internet access via a dial-up service with a modem redirect on a remote access server or over a dedicated leased line attached to a local Internet point of presence.

The extranet represents a third approach. It involves the implementation of Internet technologies such as Web servers and browsers within an organization rather than in the form of an external connection to the global Internet. This approach uses access controls to provide information to employees and business partners, but to keep out the public at large. (Fig. 3-1).

These options are not mutually exclusive. You can use any of them, alone or in combination, to meet your strategic objectives. The best choices depend on your level of ambition, how quickly you adopt new technology, and what types of changes your corporate culture will accommodate.

A Remote-Access Strategy

If you have traveling workers or telecommuters or these might be part of your future, consider implementing remote access. A remote node is the best way to give employees remote corporate local-area-network (LAN) access. Another method, remote control, requires that a dedicated PC be linked to the corporate LAN and is subject to access and control by another PC at a remote location.

The basic equipment requirements for remote node access are a dedicated remote access server and the software that runs on the client PC. The remote access server should support the different protocols on the corporate LAN including Internet Protocol (IP) and IPX. Client software should be available for different operating systems, including Windows NT and 95, Macintosh, and OS/2.

An Internet Strategy

A corporate Internet strategy has two components:

■ *Providing Internet access for employees.* There are many reasons to provide Internet access for your employees. These include obtaining market and competitive research, receiving updated industry news and information, and assembling large networks of diverse people from the business community. For example, the e-mail component of the Internet provides an alternative to voice communication with customers, suppliers, and partners. The key criteria for determining the nature of your firm's Internet commitment include the size of the company, the number of people who use the Internet, and the types of applications they want to use

■ *Using the Web or an extranet to make information about your company available to the public.* A Web site home page lets you promote your products and services on-line to a huge audience of prospective customers. This service easily could include providing information on demand. Maintaining a Web site is less costly than mailing bulky product catalogs, and customers waste less time manually sifting through volumes of directories. An extranet is a better choice when you want to confine access to authorized business partners and other acceptable outsiders and when the information you provide is solely for their eyes.

An Intranet/Extranet Strategy

While the Internet provides the technologies available for communicating via the Web, the intranet applies these technologies within the organization by way of the corporate LAN. Here, all the Internet's benefits can be applied to the corporate LAN by using Internet tools. Since the Internet is based on standards, the infrastructure setup is simple. The classic one-to-many IS problem is solved with the help of Internet technologies on the LAN. Intranet deployment involves developing a private, secure network based on a Web server available for use by employees. The extranet extends this network to business partners and other parties.

Web servers send and receive e-mail, compile data and feedback, and can encrypt messages, depending on the level of security the Web server provides. Companies install them on their LANs so that employees can find and use corporate newsletters, updates on company events, corporate phone books, and benefit policies.

Most companies introduce the intranet as a pilot before implementing a full blown Internet solution. For example, a dedicated Web server could be established on one part of the LAN or at a single site to address a certain issue such as storing and reviewing resumés. User feedback could be compiled and used to design the strategy for implementing an intranet company-wide.

Assessing Your Assets

If you are going to institute a managed extranet, the first step is to take inventory of your assets and liabilities. Three factors will do much to determine whether you will have a smooth transition from legacy systems to extranet technology:

- A pool of expertise in Internet technology
- A sound implementation plan
- How strong a management role IS can be expected to play (Fig. 3-2).

Is the Know-how Available?

This is a no-brainer. If you have experts in Web technology on board, you will be better off than if you do not. It stands to reason that the greater your organization's experience with open systems and Internet-related technologies, the easier will be the transition to the extranet. Corporate development groups that have gotten their hands into Unix,

Figure 3-2
Things to check be-
fore you get started.

Questions to ask

- Is the knowledge available?
- Do you have a sound implementation plan?
- Can IS take the lead?

TCP/IP, HTML, and Perl will stand a better chance than those which have yet to use these technologies.

Have a Plan

A typical enterprise network is a jumble of protocols. TCP/IP can provide a single, nearly universal replacement for these multiple protocols; as a practical matter, though, it will not replace all of them, or even many of them. This means that TCP/IP must run alongside and in concert with existing PC, host-based, and client/server networks. Consequently, when you add TCP/IP to the mix, you must make many decisions depending on multiple factors. Among the points to consider are

- Which protocols are required to support which legacy applications
- What staff and equipment resources are required to support each protocol
- The cost of purchasing new hardware to handle routing or gateway functions.

There are three ways to achieve this kind of technical cooperation:

- *The direct approach.* Load an IP stack on every machine in the organization. Since this is often the most effective approach, it also is naturally often the most expensive. This is particularly true if you must upgrade or replace a great number of PCs.

- *Gateway servers.* These let PC networks continue to run Novell and related protocols, and IP remains on the server.
- *Mixed response.* This approach runs multiple protocols on both desktop systems and servers. Newer operating systems, including Windows 95 and NT and the Macintosh operating system, are designed to handle multiprotocol operations.

Can IS Take the Lead?

For the transition to be effective, IS professionals must take the lead and manage the Web services for their enterprises. This could be difficult, particularly since the skill level required to set up a Web server continues to drop.

However, just setting up a Web server is not enough. Maintaining its content and keeping up with the changes in corporate information are the real challenges. You need the ability to deploy corporate publishing and conferencing services over the extranet as a core technology for distributing information.

This is where IS may need some help. IS departments have people who know how to maintain information, and these folks can readily serve as mentors to department heads who want to produce their own net pages. In truth, though, establishing and maintaining Web site content is best done by editorial professionals—technical writers, graphic artists, and the like. Content authorship requires a completely different skill set than network management, and if you want professional results, you should use professionals in each field. Notably, some employment advertisements are beginning to appear, placed by organizations that want to assemble editorial staffs for their Web sites.

What IS does have are people who are qualified to manage information in a variety of forms. One way to demonstrate competence is in the area of applications that use data from legacy databases.

Of course, where IS and central management are concerned, the issues are as likely to be political as technical. As a group, Web enthusiasts are the spiritual successors to those who originally saw PCs as instruments of freedom and individuality. They tend to be suspicious of central control. Such intramural warfare is as unnecessary as it is unproductive. The best way to avoid it is for IS to demonstrate that it can bring value as well as control to the project.

A New Look at Net Management

An extranet cannot afford the ad hoc, free-form nature of the Internet or the home-grown atmosphere of many intranets. When you extend critical information outside the company, it must be done with a strong sense of organization and control. You cannot have just anyone putting material in an extranet for outside consumption. While most employees would exercise good judgment in what they post, there is always the grave danger that a thoughtless employee—or one bent on retribution—will post something that outsiders should not have.

This poses the political problem of employees who are suspicious of IS intentions. Sometimes this stems from unreasonable paranoia. Sometimes it stems from painful experience with high-handed administration.

IS Must Change Some Habits

If IS has gotten into the habit of being high-handed, this is the one thing that should change. However, there is another habit to be broken, and it is both more subtle and more important. This is the habit of seeing a network in terms of its physical components.

Most networks are made up of easy-to-identify devices: routers, servers, cabling, and the like. The cabling and topology are only slightly less tangible. The people who manage networks are accustomed to managing *things*.

Internet technology usually does not involve many new physical components. A manager accustomed to dealing with devices is left with little of the kind to manage. Yet this same manager carries the responsibility for management of the network, a particularly great responsibility in the case of an extranet. An extranet manager must learn to deal with a concept that is a lot less tangible than the networks that have come before.

A Service, Not a Product

In the familiar distinction between products and services, a traditional network is primarily a product. An extranet is primarily a service.

Certainly, an extranet user does not think primarily in terms of using a physical product. He or she takes advantage of the service the extranet provides. The service comes in the form of information. This individual probably does not think much about the routers, servers, and connections through which that information passes. There is a much greater interest in the quality of the service, measured in easy access to useful information. Extranet managers, then, must think of themselves as managing a service, and the measure of their success should be that its customers, both internal and external, feel well served.

Few Service Management Tools

Many of the people who install intranets and extranets are focused primarily on the service aspects of what they do. However, even when they adopt this attitude, they face another obstacle. Most of the network management tools available are products of the product orientation. They concentrate on managing physical devices.

Thomas Nolle, *Network World* columnist and president of CIMI Corporation (Voorhees, NJ), sees some hope in recent trends. "The description of the connections and quality of service associated with the service view . . .[could] be converted into a set of virtual network objects that would be linked to the real devices. Service managers and users could see and possibly control these virtual network objects. Any changes they are permitted to make would be reflected downward to the real network based on rules that control just the part of real network resources this particular service is allowed to consume."

Some Web-based management tools appear to be on this path, Nolle continues, but "We're still likely to be managing devices down in the core of the management center. With all the interest in Web-based management, we're missing the boat here. Instead of trying to figure out how to deliver intranet management through a multikilobuck software product on a Unix workstation of similar price, why not just do the job using the same Web tools that made up the intranets in the first place?"

Not Part of the Web

If intranets and extranets are not defined by their physical networks, neither are they really part of the Web. Instead of spreading information Web-style, the object of an intranet is to make workers more powerful and productive by giving them access to better information and tools. In the process, an intranet empowers the organization to be more efficient and competitive.

An extranet extends this idea. If an organization can become more powerful and efficient sharing information among its own people, it could become even more so by sharing information with its business partners. Of course, it is important to be selective in choosing both the information and the partners. This works against the intranet tradition—if something so new could yet have any traditions—of do-it-yourself authorship by individuals and department heads.

Another columnist, *InfoWorld's* Dave Taylor, recently asked, "If you were a medium-size company and were feeling the crunch of competitive market pressures, would you want your salespeople, your marketing whiz, and your engineers dedicating their precious working hours playing with company Web pages? Definitely not."

Trans Ocean Gets Organized

Trans Ocean Ltd. (San Bruno, CA), a maritime container leasing company, is a major international business with 200 offices and depots around the world. Employees need direct access to the firm's order entry and inventory applications 24 hours a day, from anywhere in the world. The solution might be called an *indirect extranet.* It is an intranet directed to agents and customer service employees around the globe.

This last requirement was the toughest to meet. Previously, employees had used a system of leased lines that lead to a proprietary wide-area network (WAN). There were holes in this scheme, particularly in places like South America and China, where agents might be unable to make connections for days at a time.

Today, agents still can use the WAN, but now it leads to the company's intranet. And they have a new service: local point of presence (POP) access providers who can be reached by telephone line from anywhere in the world. In its 15 main locations, Trans Ocean has leased lines; outside these areas, the company relies on the Internet for connections to its intranet. Sometimes there are problems finding good connections, and the major problem sites are still in South America and China. For the most part, though, the new network meets the goal of full-time, worldwide access.

The intranet also has boosted productivity. The former terminal-based application was slow and hard to use. Customer service representatives, who are on-line all day, say they appreciate the new system's ease of use. Where once they had to plow through ten screens to find information they wanted, now they can get it on one.

For example, a customer service representative might receive a call from a shipping line. This customer wants to pick up 100 refrigerated containers to ship bananas from Chile to San Francisco. The representative can use the network to determine that the company has 80 containers in Chile and another 20 in Brazil. The representative can book the order and at the same time move the 20 containers from Brazil to Chile. At the same time, the representative can look at the contract, quote prices, and send a confirmation to the depot authorizing release of the units.

The Trans Ocean extranet is an extension of the corporate Web site. When either internal employees or external visitors sign on, they see much the same screen. The employees, however, have access to additional resources (Fig. 3-3). Trans Ocean says this approach cut development cost

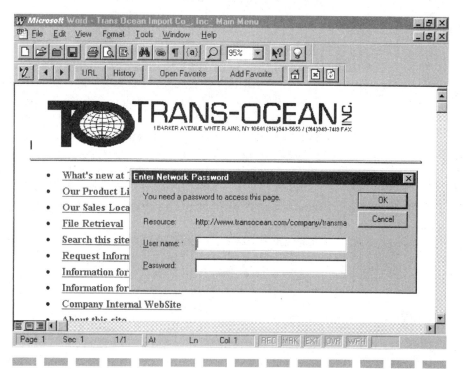

Figure 3-3
The Trans Ocean intranet appears on the Web site menu, but you need a password to get in. (http://www.transglobal.com)

and time in half; it needed to create only one master system. Development took a little more than 3 months and cost about $100,000.

Emphasis on Security

The system reflects a lot of effort to provide security. Security is important even though the company did not place actual financial data in the system initially. What is more, its containers are hard to steal. They weigh several tons and are 40 ft long. Each container is worth several thousand dollars, though, and the industry in general is very concerned about security. Building a highly secure system was important to make management comfortable with the whole project. Table 3-1 provides a Trans Ocean technical summary.

The People Who Make It Work

Trans Ocean did find itself with a shortage of net expertise. Its IS people had strong backgrounds in mainframe and client/server development, but none of them had done much with the Internet. Thus, other than the project manager, it was necessary to staff the project with outsiders. This in itself was a problem. The company found many people who had done Web pages and some who had database experience. Few had the full set of qualifications, and competition for them was intense. To add injury to the insult, the project generated a lot of publicity for the project manager, who was hired away by another company.

With this loss, the project team included part-time consultants for database administration, project management, and documentation and full-time consultants handling graphic design, HTML, and Common Gateway Interface (CGI)/Oracle programming.

TABLE 3-1 Trans Ocean technical summary.		
	Firewall	Three Digital Alpha systems
	Server	Digital AlphaServer 1000
	Server software	Netscape
	Database	Oracle running on Alpha 8200
	Public Web site	http:/www.transglobal.com

Emphasis on Training

There also was a heavy training investment in existing IS employees. This was a very visible project, using forefront technology, so naturally the internal IS people were concerned when the company went outside to staff it. To show support and get these employees involved, the company sent everyone in IS to intranet classes at a local university. The cost was reasonable, and the program eventually eliminated the need to use outside consultants.

In addition, nearly everyone in the company was given an Internet tutorial. The developers also built good on-line help into the system and published good documentation, including a glossy job aid sent out to every user.

Future Plans

The next project for this intranet is a full human resources system. It is to give employees the means to review health benefits, manage their 401k investments, and check their available vacation and sick days. Plans after that call for an EDI billing and collection application that will extend its functions to Web site customers as well as internal patrons.

How Extranets Are Built

With one significant exception, the technology of an intranet and an extranet are the same. Both have several distinguishing features:

- They use TCP/IP for both local-area and wide area networking.
- They use HTML, the Simple Mail Transport Protocol (SMTP), and other open, widely used standards to move information between clients and servers.
- They can be managed by many of the same methods as are used currently to manage existing host or client/server networks.

The big exception:used is that an intranet is completely owned by the organization and is not generally accessible to the public at large. As most owners have found, though, keeping an intranet purely internal is neither practical nor a particularly good idea. Regardless of whether it has been so labeled, an intranet is often really an extranet. It is not available for general access, but it is available for controlled access. Almost by definition, then, an extranet depends heavily on access control.

Using TCP/IP

When Lewis and Clark negotiated with Native American leaders, they often had to use a tortuous method of translation. A chief would speak in his native language, which an interpreter with the expedition would translate into the Shoshone tongue. Sacagawea, a Shoshone, then would translate the message into the language understood by yet another interpreter, who finally could relay the communication in English. It was even more difficult when one or more of the translation steps had to be done in sign language. Understandably, even routine discussions could take all day.

In the same way, modern enterprise networks often use a mixture of protocols. These networks must speak multiple languages to communicate with different platforms and network installations. Many organizations have decided to replace their multiple protocols with one, and the natural choice is Internet Protocol (IP).

In many ways, IP is an obvious choice. It can handle both LAN and WAN traffic, and nearly all the major computing platforms support it. It has a strong set of management tools, and there is an active development community whose members know how to use the protocol to best effect. IP is also the native tongue of the Internet.

In addition, some old shortcomings are being cured. In the DOS era, IP was widely reputed as a memory hog. But particularly under Windows 95 and NT, IP is better integrated with the operating system, and memory use is becoming less of a problem.

Using Familiar Standards

If sign language was the standard tongue of the Great Plains, Hypertext Markup Language (HTML) is equally at home on the World Wide Web. Alhough competing vendors have rushed out their own major modifications to HTML, it did begin life as an open standard, and much of the openness remains intact. This means a Web browser running on any client, Unix, Intel, or Macintosh included, can enjoy similar access to the

Web. This makes even a proprietary enhancement of HTML an attractive choice to many organizations that have mixtures of such systems.

The availability of HTML is one reason that Web technology has become so popular for intranets and extranets. There are other reasons as well:

- Unlike older Internet services, the Web can present graphics, sound, video clips, and other nontext items. The most advanced Web sites have become multimedia extravaganzas.

- Web sites can range from the personal to corporate, depending on who is posting what kind of content and how much effort is going into the process. Highly visible companies such as Disney, ESPN, and Hershey's Chocolate have begun using the Web both to provide corporate information and to extend the value of their identities and services.

- Each Web server contains information that can be linked to other sites and documents, whether they are in some other country or on the same server. This ability to link—if designed correctly— gives the Web its power. Linking also makes the Web attractive as a distributed corporate information resource.

The Web has adopted or popularized other standards as well. Along with HTML it supports other standards such as file transfer protocol (ftp) servers, Simple Mail Transport Protocol (SMTP), and others. These were developed originally for Unix computers, but they have spread throughout the corporate world as IS has embraced them.

E-mail is a major example. Ten years ago, PROFS and DISSOS were the de facto standards running on proprietary hosts. Now these products seem like dinosaurs, and many corporations are looking to Internet-based e-mail for better service. Nearly every e-mail product now in use has Internet or SMTP gateways, making it easier to reach anyone via e-mail. Internet e-mail systems also avoid the problems of multiple e-mail systems that do not talk or share directories with other e-mail systems. Most corporations are moving toward such a common backbone to tie their own disparate e-mail systems together. In fact, many have already done so.

Using Familiar Methods

Alhough an extranet is truly a client/server system, its administration and management can easily emulate the familiar, legacy corporate System Network Architecture (SNA) backbone in terms of purpose and procedures. You simply must do the same job with different tools. Many of these tools originate in the Unix community that spawned the Internet. Many others are being created to provide greater control and higher levels of service.

Just because the extranet uses the protocols and languages of the Internet does not mean that it has to adopt the wide-open, unmanaged environment that is one of the Internet hallmarks. In fact, the Internet has spawned some important design principles for building reliable extranets.

One example is the ability to assign maintenance chores for particular pieces of content to different corporate departments who develop and maintain the information. Other management issues include

- Providing a local cache of popular or useful Web sites for better performance or to ease network congestion. These shadowed sites are often available on internal proxy servers without going outside the organization's network.
- Providing fine-grained, user-based access control and usage statistics reporting. These help corporate Intranet developers fine-tune their applications.

Not for Our Eyes Only

The distinctions between the Internet, an intranet, and an extranet are mainly fine points of terminology. The Internet is open to all comers; an intranet is a closed corporate system. The extranet allows public access, but with controls over who has access to what material.

All use the same tools, techniques, protocols and products, drawing heavily on TCP/IP standards. Often, Intranet projects began as pilot projects of departmental Web sites. They since have been been opened to the public on the Internet or in controlled fashion through an extranet.

There are some differences between the Internet and its corporate offspring:

- Much corporate data are not for public consumption. Payroll, sales projections, internal discounts, and client memos illustrate the types of information an organization needs to protect carefully. This is no great change from the past, when host-based or client/server databases were protected by security programs. An extranet should be available only to trusted individuals, whether from inside or outside the organization.

■ Many intranets began with pilot projects to test out the technologies and understand the skills required. They quickly have grown into full-time, production-quality information systems that have taken on a particular corporation's culture and methods.

■ Many corporations want their own networks to have the same level of service as their existing networks, and this is only possible when the networks are under corporate control from end to end.

Key Extranet Components

Regardless of the access technology you use, an extranet will require a substantial list of key components. Consider these in your implementation plans. Not all may be necessary, but any might be useful:

■ *Universal TCP/IP deployment.* Since Internet communication is primarily built on TCP/IP, the corporate LAN protocol must include an IP application that is installed on every desktop and remote computer.

■ *Web browser.* The Web browser is the desktop viewer that makes Web-based content readily available to all authorized users. The browser runs on top of the IP stack and communicates with the server using the industry standard point-to-point protocol (PPP). This valuable software should be installed on every desktop and remote computer.

■ *Web server.* A Web server usually runs on Unix or Windows NT, although other platforms including the Macintosh can accommodate server applications. Server software ranges in function from simply displaying information to providing secure, encryption-based transactions.

■ *Remote access server.* A multiprotocol remote access server links remote users to corporate resources, extranet applications, and Internet access via phone lines. Plan on plenty of communication ports. Most companies use one port for every eight to ten dial-in users. The remote access server should support all the multiple protocols that appear on the typical corporate LAN.

■ *Client dial-in software.* Remote dial-in client software should be installed on remote users' PCs. Since remote service often involves multiple computing environments, the remote access client should be available for different operating systems. The client software initiates the call, negotiates the connection, and terminates the connection when the remote session is over.

■ *Internet connection device.* A router connects the corporate site to an Internet Service Provider (ISP). The Internet connection device typically provides IP and IPX protocol support and IP packet level filtering.

■ *Leased-line connection.* There are several ways to connect to the Internet, including modems and ordinary telephone lines. A high-volume operation may want to use one or more dedicated leased lines. Any ISP that serves the corporate market probably can provide a leased line connection through the local telephone company. Leased line connections are available in a variety of speeds and configurations. The choice depends on how much activity you expect between the corporation and the ISP's point of presence.

■ *Firewall security.* Extranet access creates new security needs. It is particularly essential in extending controlled access to outsiders. A typical firewall is a Unix- or Windows NT-based application that identifies IP addresses, source applications, and other indicators that it uses to screen out unwanted users.

Security

Regardless of whether you want to allow only internal access or control external access, security is vital. A highly recommended approach is to place a series on the network, beginning with the Internet connection device that connects the corporate site with the ISP. The device, a router, forms the connection and screens out unwanted users from the network. Screening routers use packet filtering to verify the source and destination of every packet sent to the network. A screening router allows the network manager to set a series of criteria that every packet must filter through. The criteria are based on the source address, destination address, source port, destination port, and type of packet. Each criterion is set to permit or deny packets from the network.

Packet filtering was the basic technology of early firewalls, and it still exists in many hybrid types. And a firewall represents the second layer of security. This protection can be applied to the application and presentation layers of the OSI model. Firewalls allow the organization to protect corporate IP addresses from the outside world and prevent unwanted users from gaining access. You can build in business rules such as a list of individual, address, and application filtering criteria to examine incoming connection requests

Other security features to consider include passwords, user authentication, dialback, and compatibility with third-party security devices. Since the remote user needs a specific authorized user name and password to log into the network, this type of access is considered less risky than that posed by Internet traffic.

Some ISPs are promoting the use of dedicated Internet access at the corporate site as a way to also do remote access. This is a viable solution for corporations that may want to reduce their investment in hardware or maintenance costs. This solution does introduce a security risk unless the solution uses Virtual Private Networking (VPN). VPN provides an encrypted tunnel from the client to the corporate site. At the corporate site, a firewall is still recommended.

It Takes All Kinds—of Clients

A communication strategy must be prepared to manage at least five types of access from internal and external sources:

- LAN-based employee access to the Internet
- Remote employee multiprotocol access to corporate LAN, internal Web server, and the Internet
- Remote partner multiprotocol access to a dedicated Web server or Intranet
- Public Web services to the outside world
- Multiprotocol remote access to public LAN

A LAN-based Employee Connects to the Internet

Suppose you have a small business, fewer than 100 employees, including a few telecommuters. These employees want access to Internet

TABLE 3-2

The right kind of
Internet access
depends on how
many people need
what kind of
access.

Number of users	Access type	Options
1-10	Dial-up access over analog	Any browser that has a dialer application
1-20	Dial-up access over basic rate ISDN	Browser with a dialer that supports ISDN or a dedicated router that supports 1 or 2 BRI channels
10-50	Dial-out from a corporate network over analog or ISDN	Remote access server that supports dial-out connections
50 and up	Dedicated service, always available from the network	Full time router and connection to the Internet via no-dialing ISDN, leased line (56K, fractional T1 or T1/E1

SOURCE: Shiva Technologies.

information, including industry news, market data, and competitive information.

Depending on the number of users and the size of the company, there are several ways to provide Internet access. Shiva Technology offers the guidance in Table 3-2.

According to this analysis, a dedicated leased line is the best solution for basic access by a smaller group. This requires an Internet connection device. Most dedicated services come in bandwidths of 56, 128, 256, 384, and 512 kb/s or a full T1 at 1.544 Mb/s (or E1). Your ISP can help you secure the leased-line connection. The collision-avoidance system (CSU/DSU) you choose will determine the connection speed and type that you need.

Providing Remote Access

On the other hand, you may be part of a global organization that wants to provide remote and Internet access to traveling workers and a significant telecommuting population. All the core business information and processes are on the multiprotocol corporate LAN, and employees need access to them from anywhere at any time. In addition to files and databases, the organization would like employees to have access to other types of private information such as medical insurance benefits, 401 updates, stock quotes, and the employee handbook. The organization wants to ensure that the information meant only for employees is secure, while giving access to the important information on an extranet connection.

You can meet this need by providing all types of access—remote, intranet/extranet, and Internet—through a security firewall.

With remote access software, a distant employee will be able to dial in to the server site and connect to the network using a dial-in client. Once connected, the remote employee becomes a node on the network and can use all its resources, including the private Web server and the Internet. Plan to prevent unwanted users from gaining access to the corporate network through the use of user names, passwords, and other security options.

To set up such a system, configure a Web server on your corporate LAN to house private information for employees. Install a Web browser on each remote PC. Employees can use the browser to find important corporate information, and the organization does not have to worry about mailing catalogs and binders each time the information is updated. The firewall makes sure the employee is the only person who has access to the segment of the LAN where the private Web server resides.

Granting Access to Business Partners

A typical corporation has an extensive network of resellers, suppliers, and customers. The printing, mailing, and human resource costs of communicating with these partners can become overwhelming. You might want to provide current information to these important partners and at the same time receive information from them. As you exchange information with your expanded and expanding network of partners, you will extend the reach of your products, services, and corporate message.

You can provide your partners with both remote and extranet access. Install a dedicated remote access server and Web server at the corporate site, and provide partners with dial-in software for use on their remote PCs along with a Web browser. The dedicated servers ensure that information intended for partners will only be available to partners. Configuring the firewall behind the partner remote-access server restricts partners from access to the sensitive information on the corporate network.

Providing Web Services to the World

A company can find itself at a competitive disadvantage if it does not have a Web site to display information for the general public. Other companies use this avenue to announce and advertise products, provide end-user product support, post bulletins, and generally enhance their image. To stay even, much less gain an advantage, you need your own Web site.

Configure a Web server on the corporate LAN in front of the firewall. People all over the world will be able to see information about your company at any time. Visitors to the site can be prompted to provide information, download software, and even provide feedback and comments via e-mail. The public Web site provides an avenue to communicate with current and potential customers and to gather important information about them.

Making the Business Case

The low cost and easy production of a Web site can make an extranet sound like a no-lose proposition (Fig. 3-4). After all, who could object to something that costs so little and brings so much value?

A 1000 Percent Return?

Certainly, an extranet can be easy and inexpensive to install. Ian Campbell of Internet Data Corporation (IDC) reports on an IDC survey of Netscape intranets. It found the return on investment to be well over 1000 percent. Payback periods ranged from 6 weeks to 3 months. These

Figure 3-4
The selling of an extranet.

Selling the extranet

- Prove the concept; don't try to justify costs
- Put people before technology
- Have a goal and a strategy to get there
- Have a prototype ready early
- Use the prototype to make your case
- Know what the competition is doing
- Be honest about how much it costs
- Don't get mad -- get better

results led Campbell to make this unvarnished recommendation: Install an intranet, immediately if not sooner.

Although there have been few cost studies yet of extranets, there is little doubt that you could achieve similar results. Extending the extranet to a selected audience of business partners does add to the cost, but the extra cost is not so high as to put more than a fender-bender dent in the IDC 1000 percent return.

Do Not Make Assumptions

Nevertheless, it can be dangerous to make assumptions about the cost. There are many not very well hidden expenses involved in setting up an extranet, particularly when you consider the security measures necessary to keep unwanted outsiders outside. Furthermore, although the technical challenges of building a Web site are relatively modest, creating and maintaining good content are a major professional challenges and something not within the skill set of an ordinary IS professional. Figure 3-5 shows the experience of one firm where content management involves the proverbial lion's share of the costs. This is an extreme case, but it is not *that* extreme.

This is just one of the "soft issues" with which you will have to deal. You also will have to take on such squishy chores as selling the idea to management.

Figure 3-5
Much of the cost is ongoing, well beyond the startup.

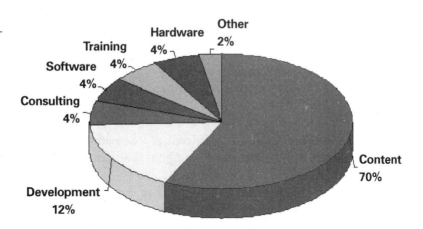

Content really is king

- Other 2%
- Hardware 4%
- Training 4%
- Software 4%
- Consulting 4%
- Development 12%
- Content 70%

This is one area where an extranet differs sharply from an intranet. An intranet tends to be a home-grown product that grows by its own momentum. As the system demonstrates its value, departments and even individuals add their contributions. IS can manage the process, but it should not even think about controlling it. The intranet is a bottom-up phenomenon. It is not at all uncommon to hear IS professionals vow that they will not lose control as they did when PCs first entered the organization. Where intranets are concerned, they are locking the proverbial barn door.

An extranet is not home grown. Although it usually stems from an intranet, the process of exposing information to outside view needs professional supervision. Both the technology and the content can be crucial and should not be left to internal freelancers.

This means that an extranet should be a top-down process, with all the meetings, memos, budgeting, and approval-getting this term implies. It means that you must sell the extranet to management. Although the process is not difficult, it will be ongoing. You must first master not just the technology but the human side of the organization.

Don't Try to Justify Costs

It would seem natural for an extranet sponsor to conduct a formal cost-benefit analysis of the proposal. After all, the costs will be low and the benefits great. In practice, though, this has not turned out to be a good idea. Not only can it be a drawn-out process, taking centuries in computer years, but so many of the costs also are uncertain and intangible.

Instead, use the proof of concept approach. Use a prototype and examples of other successful extranets to demonstrate the potential of the process. Take key decision makers to trade shows and seminars so that they can see how the technology would fit into the business world. Put Web browsers on their PCs.

For example, Diamond Shamrock, Inc., a petroleum refiner and marketer based in San Antonio, Texas, put Netscape browsers on its 2000-node Novell Netware 4.1 network using Windows NT servers. The sponsors had no doubts that the benefits would far exceed costs, particularly since one goal was to reduce value-added network costs. However, they saw little value in a traditional cost-benefit analysis.

Instead, the sponsors decided to prove the concept. They started with dial-up service in the hands of a few specific users. This demonstrated where the benefits could be found. When rolling out the system, it went first to strategic people, including directors and senior executives. Instead of taking the bottom-up approach that has characterized many intranets, Diamond Shamrock worked top-down.

As the decision makers become familiar with the network, they can gain confidence in it. They will be less inclined to look at Web technology as a technological toy, and they can begin to see where it will fit into the business. As a Diamond Shamrock executive put it, "My job is to take the hurdles away from the folks, get them to the tools, and give them the empowerment and the education."

Put People First

The preceding has opened the touchy subject of people. It has been conventional wisdom for years that IS professionals must learn to function in a human organization as well as a technical one. Unfortunately, there still are some who view fellow members of the human race as beings to be avoided—or worse, "end users."

In fact, the first network to build is not electronic but human. Before you even start an extranet project, get the support of the internal customers who will use your creation. This requires two-way communication. The IS professional should learn as much as possible about the organization's business process, methods, and objectives. At the same time, IS should educate department heads and other potential clients about the benefits an extranet could offer.

The two kinds of education are complementary. If you understand the business process, you can do a better job of showing how an extranet could benefit an individual or department. And if you can show the benefits, the people who would enjoy them will become your natural supporters.

Create a Strategy

The benefits of an extranet must be more than just good ideas. It is just as important to develop a sound, overall strategy for including an extranet in your overall communication program.

Although it is nice to say that an extranet will provide better communication with business partners, it is even nicer to present it in terms that evoke a higher vision, a larger objective, or an overarching principle. Set a theme for the project. For example, if you have business partners scattered around the world, use the theme of drawing everyone into a community. Use this theme to help build enthusiasm and support.

Another important part of the human element is to make sure you understand the corporate culture. Awful though this term might be, it is important to understand the way your organization traditionally thinks and goes about its business. Just as Microsoft is vastly different from Nordstrom's, any well-established organization is also a well-established little society.

For example, I worked for many years for a corporation that was much like a Victorian era family: strong on tradition and highly paternalistic but showing undying loyalty to its employees/relatives, even though there were a few episodes of bad behavior. (Regrettably, a corporate merger has since assimilated this unique social structure.) An organization like this is not likely to be found on the leading edge of anything. If you are planning an extranet for such an organization, it would be a mistake to trot out all the flashy screens and animated pictures you can put on a Web page.

On the other hand, a fast-rising technology company probably thrives on visual stimulation and would find a simple text-based page impossibly stodgy.

Build and Display a Prototype

There may be nothing like the real thing, but a good imitation can come close. This is particularly important when it comes to demonstrating the benefits of an extranet. What you can show people is much more effective than what you can simply tell them.

Assemble a prototype extranet, stocking it with the kind of information a full implementation might contain. This should not be live data of sensitive information; use outdated or fictional material for the sake of the demonstration. You need not put a lot of information in the prototype. Just include enough to support a "dog and pony show" you can use to demonstrate how the extranet would work. For example, you could simulate the kind of data an external supplier might see when plugging into the network. Or find an interesting Web site that provides information and services similar to those you plan to provide.

Humor columnist Dave Barry has described the Web as the multimedia version of the Internet. Keep that in mind as you build the prototype and later as you put the real thing together. It is the substantive content of an extranet that will win or lose favor, but it is the graphics that get the attention in the first place. Do not limit yourself to dry facts. Use the power of Web technology to put on a good show. The old phrase, "seeing is believing," has some truth to it.

In fact, if your prototype stirs interest, it would be a good next step to demonstrate a real, working demonstration of an active site. Find one that interests you, and arrange a brief visit.

Make Your Case

When demonstrating the prototype, it is important to understand the audience—that people thing again. Some executives understand technology and want to understand exactly how your proposed extranet would work. Others want to skip the mechanics and go right to the main point: How will this project achieve a business goal? Adapt your sales pitch accordingly.

In either case, you should demonstrate that you understand exactly how the extranet will fit into the relationships between your organization and the target outsiders. You should display a comprehensive understanding of how the organization communicates, internally and with others. Show how the extranet would enhance this process. Be honest about its drawbacks, too.

Your object is not to make an unvarnished sales pitch but to help management make a rational decision. If the proposal is really as good as you think it is, a decision based on all the facts, pro and con, is much stronger and more lasting than one made before important information comes to light.

Know the Competition

Know and explain exactly what the competition is doing in this area. Find out and evaluate the ways in which competitors handle internal and external information exchange, collaboration, and other operations that might be involved in an extranet.

You probably will find that you have two options: build an extranet because it gives you an advantage over competitors who do not have one, or build an extranet because others already are working on it and you do not want to fall behind.

Be Honest About the Costs

An extranet can be inexpensive to develop initially, particularly when compared with a larger mainframe or client/server project. Make sure management understands that you can extend Web technology to the organization and key outsiders without investing the kinds of sums that require special funds and accounting.

Here too, honesty pays, and it is important to be up front about all the costs. Training and equipment upgrades are two areas where you can expect the unexpected expense. It is better to present this information at the outset than to have to explain later why things are not as rosy as you had pictured. Be assured that even a worst-case financial scenario probably will compare very favorably with the costs of other types of projects with similar impact and value.

For example, when Hewlett-Packard (HP) replaced an older communication system with what HP calls an ESP intranet for sales representatives, it found that training was a major need. Even a well-designed interface needed some explaining, the company found. More important, having installed the new system, HP wanted to motivate its employees to make use of it.

Be a Good Loser

Even the best-prepared presentations sometimes fail. Be prepared to accept the defeat, and resist the temptation to fight. This is particularly important in the frequent case when management approves some elements of your proposal but rejects others. Accept your victories, and work to succeed within the terms of the management decision. There is no better way to get a rehearing of your case than a show of proven success.

Making Dollars and Sense of an Extranet

Many companies have been attracted to an intranet because of the apparent low cost. Pilot projects tend to be the simple, familiar applications, such as internal telephone directories, that are easy and inexpensive to install.

Almost inevitably, though, the intranet becomes an extranet. Once this happens, the cost picture begins to change radically. The data you carry become more critical to the mission. You need to establish and maintain a 7×24 server. Web-site technology and authorship become major challenges. Security and access control become critical needs. You need more specialized people working with more specialized equipment. And the costs become as hard to figure as the benefits.

It Starts Out Easy and Cheap

Acquisition costs are the easiest to figure. Start by identifying the tools you need. The shopping list can include

- Web-specific hardware such as servers and peripherals
- Communication hardware such as routers
- Leased lines, Internet access, and other access options
- Software, including operating systems, servers, add-ons, database management, utilities, and graphics packages

Figure out what you need, and get a few price quotes. It probably will come in a little higher than you expected, but not seriously out of line.

Hard to Find, Hard to Figure

What does get seriously out of line is all the rest of the costs. Other expenses can be both hard to recognize and hard to compute. Consider the cost of

- Creating content and keeping it current
- Designing Web presentations
- Building hyperlinks and making sure they remain current and active

These are the types of activities that eat up the time and effort on the part of a large paid staff. Early intranets often are built by volunteers who work on the project for the fun of it. When things get serious enough to become an extranet, this spirit can fade rapidly. As Web work eats up more and more of their time, people develop the desire for formal recognition as Web experts and increased pay to boot.

One of the Biggest Costs Is for People

At Access Health (Rancho Cordova, CA), the staff costs alone to develop and administer an intranet became prohibitive. The type of centrally managed intranet Access Health wanted would require that the firm dedicate several people full time to creating and maintaining it. But the most knowledgeable people already were committed to other projects, and the company was not yet prepared to devote the necessary resources for a central administrative body.

Instead, management agreed to let departments set up job-related sites as needed. If a department needed a site and had the means to build and support one, it was free to do so. IS, however, did not have the resources to help.

Not only can the costs be much higher than the initial simple projections, but they cannot be quantified readily. And most of them are for people, not technology.

Often, no one actually knows how much time people spend on the continuing details of running an extranet. Expect to spend more than you expected managing and administering the site, creating applications and plug-ins, developing applications, integrating those applications with legacy systems and databases, and learning new technology. Continuing training and self-education are major projects, since Web products have rapid turnover cycles. Do not underestimate either the cost of creating or maintaining the content.

Access Health estimated it would have to spend about $20,000 for browser licenses, Web server software, and hardware needed to support an intranet for 400 to 500 people. If your organization is larger, as many are, be prepared to spend even more. Major corporations should think millions—perhaps $10 million. And again, these are just the opening hardware and software costs. The people costs still must be added in.

Finding the People Costs

To start identifying the human costs of an extranet, start by talking to management and other leaders who have goals and expectations for the project. Try to gain an understanding of their applications needs and find out what they have in mind for the project. This process identifies the type of network you will need and the volume and nature of its content. Then you can apply human and other resources and calculate their costs.

Carefully examine your business processes, internal and external, before you launch an extranet program. Take each process and determine the most efficient way to quickly and effectively communicate vital information out to the target audience.

If you plan to invest in a full-scale extranet, make sure you include an organizational structure that will support the ongoing commitment an extranet requires. If you lack commitment, eventually so will the assigned employees. The content will become stale and lose its value, and people will revert to less efficient systems. You will then have spent a whole lot of money on nothing.

Costs Come Out of Hiding

As the process moves forward, expect to confront all kinds of hidden costs. You may need additional personnel, even above those you have already anticipated. As the scope of the project progresses beyond directories and policy manuals, so does the need for people and other sources.

Of course, there are also many substantial costs that can be subtracted out. Although direct profits from Web commerce have been slow to materialize, many companies have been able to use the Web's superior information flow to reduce costs and improve their competitive positions.

It also can be hard, though, to compute the benefits, but when you find them, they can be significant. For example, try to figure in the significant costs of staff filing, updating, and referring to paper-based material.

Business Will Demand an Accounting

Despite these obstacles, as companies move toward larger and more comprehensive extranets, there will have to be an accounting. The only way to do this is by closely examining the requirements for content publishing, transaction-processing, and access to legacy systems and groupware.

Think in terms of fitting the intranet into the overall infrastructure. Few people have considered this yet, but they must. Start immediately if not sooner. Until then, many extranet managers will remain convinced that their creations save money, but they still will not be able to figure out how or how much.

Slow Down, You Go Too Fast

The relative ease with which you can implement an extranet project can have one drawback: You may find yourself moving too fast. Your progress may outstrip your planning.

One company that found itself ahead of its best schedule was Financial Service Corporation (FSC), an Atlanta-based distributor of financial products and services. It took all of about 6 weeks to get the site up and running. Then its managers stood back to take a longer look at what they were or were not accomplishing.

FSC wanted to use the intranet to reduce the amount of paper it ships to its 1500 affiliated brokers and financial advisers. Eventually, the extranet is intended to replace a customer transaction network that now connects brokers to FSC's mainframes through a private node provided by CompuServe. However, after its quick start, FSC is taking a more deliberate approach.

For example, the company has slowed down the process of converting its brokers from paper to electronic documents. Reducing the amount of paperwork is now a goal for the ensuing year, not an immediate objective.

The company is also moving slowly toward allowing broker transactions over the extranet. One reason for the slowdown is that regulatory agencies have only recently begun to publish guidelines for electronic customer transactions.

In the meantime, the FSC intranet is giving brokers the benefit of other types of applications such as real-time Java-based chat, bulletin boards, and databases where brokers can search for counterparts according to geography or specialties. The entire broker network, as well as FSC's headquarters staff of 130, can now use Internet e-mail.

The company also has been setting up a database that will let brokers and financial planners search for information about particular types of financial products by category. Enhancements in the work include a financial news feed and research on specific companies and industries. Also in the works are links to FSC business partners so that field associates can cross-sell a variety of products.

Despite the delays in some areas, FSC seems satisfied with the progress. One advantage of Web technology is that a site can be enhanced as time goes on.

4

How to *Really* Profit from the Internet

If you are a customer of CSX Transportation, you can open the company's Web page, call up a map of the system, click on a destination point, and find out when your shipment is due to arrive. This external service is a major function of the CSX intranet which, like so many others, has really become an extranet.

In the process, this is providing a significant object lesson for those who seek profits in Internet commerce. Not only can you use an extranet to serve your customers better, you also can serve them less expensively.

Many folks have been searching for success in Web commerce—success that always seems to be right on the next home page. A few have found it. Some companies have managed to earn income from direct sales over the Web. Others have profited by accepting advertising, although little profit has yet been demonstrated from *placing* the ads. Others wait for the elusive killer Web commerce application to show up.

The Stealth Killer App

Well, the killer application has arrived, and we barely noticed. Direct Web commerce may yet bear substantial fruit; it might even do so real soon now. But the companies that are profiting from Web commerce are looking in an entirely different direction. Economic success on the Web comes not from selling things in Web commerce but from using better communication to serve customers better.

Good customer service is a basic business necessity. Just about everyone has learned how to do this. Even government agencies and quasi-government agencies like the Postal Service have shown greater tendencies to serve their customers and are less anxious to impose arcane rules to their own advantage. Nearly everyone serves customers well. If you are to gain a competitive edge, you must achieve *outstanding* customer service.

It Costs Money to Make Money

Good customer service can be expensive. In most business situations it requires good information communicated quickly. A sales representative needs current details about product specifications and other key sales information. Sometimes, this need arises suddenly, in the customer's office in the middle of a sales presentation. Even in less demanding circumstances, the customer expects a quick answer if not an immediate one. Customers are not inclined to wait while sales representatives play voice mail tag with the folks at the home office or try to make a timely exchange of faxes. Ironically, as the customer waits impatiently, the sales representative is running up major-league telephone bills trying to get the needed information.

Likewise, a help desk hand or service technician often needs detailed, timely technical information to help a customer get up and running or to repair a malfunctioning device. Again, there is often the impatient customer waiting to be served quickly but forced to wait out a slow, procedure-bound exchange of information between the central office and the field. And again, this process is expensive.

Serving customers in situations like these requires good communication and immediate access to detailed, timely information. At the same time, there is a serious need to reduce the costs of customer service. This is where the Web comes in.

The Intranet Goes Public

In the last year or so, the intranet has become a business buzzword. But a funny thing happened on the way to the intranet. It became an extranet. Companies loaded their policy manuals onto their intranets. They put together on-line internal telephone directories. They let employees look up information on benefits or on the status of their 401k plans. Individuals and departments put up their own pages and formed discussion groups. Then folks looked around and asked the question popularized long ago by singer Peggy Lee: Is that all there is?

No, That's Not All There Is

Emphatically no. But this answer also does not lie either in the wide-open spaces of the Web or within the confines of the corporate firewall. A purely internal intranet has many uses, but in the end it is a limited option. There is much more to be accomplished by looking outside the organization. Thus without really intending to do so, companies have turned their intranets into extranets, offering controlled access to the outside world.

An extranet is neither a Web site nor a closely held intranet. What an extranet uniquely offers is the ability to exchange information with selected people outside the organization. These people, by and large, are business partners: suppliers on one side and customers on the other. Your customers may have customers of their own, and your suppliers may have suppliers of their own. Your suppliers certainly have at least one customer of their own: you.

No business organization exists in isolation. It is one link in a chain that extends from one business to another in an extended network of supplier/customer relations. This is the principle behind electronic document interchange (EDI), the electronic transmission of documents such as purchase orders, shipping documents, and payment vouchers. Your best chance to become a strong, vital link in such a chain is to serve your customers better than anyone else. This often means working back down the chain to your suppliers and helping them produce quality components that not only meet your customers' needs but also exceed their expectations.

It also means getting information quickly to your customers. The simple way is to give key customers direct, immediate access to your catalogs and sales information. A less direct method, but a popular choice, is to do so indirectly: making sure your people in the field have quick, effective access to the things their customers need to know. This is a form of internal customer service: serving the person who's serving the customer.

Works Better, Costs Less

An extranet is an ideal way to meet these needs. It offers controlled access to selected business partners, managing both who shall have access and what they can do or see once they acquire it. Or sales and service representatives can gain immediate access to the information the need in their customer-contact jobs. Organizations that have taken the extranet approach feel that it has vastly improved their ability to serve customers and to gain competitive advantage over those who offer lesser degrees of service.

Furthermore, although some of these extranet projects have hardly been inexpensive, nearly all report that their customer service costs have been reduced sharply. Just imagine the aging athletes of beer commercial fame, one group chanting "works better" and the other responding "costs less."

Given this fortunate confrontation, these companies have found the real killer application of the Internet. It is customer service.

Goal: Reduced Cost

CSX is a 39,000-employee global transportation company based in Jacksonville, Florida. Not long ago the firm set out to develop a Web-based strategy that involved both internal and external services (Fig. 4-1). The goals were to reduce operating costs while taking advantage of its network infrastructure.

With a six-member development team and a budget of less than $1 million, the company was quickly able to make a combined Internet/intranet system available to about 500 people in its technology group. Ultimately, the goal is to place the service in the hands of customers and employees worldwide. Table 4-1 presents CSX's tecnical summary.

Figure 4-1

CSX links its internal and external networks.

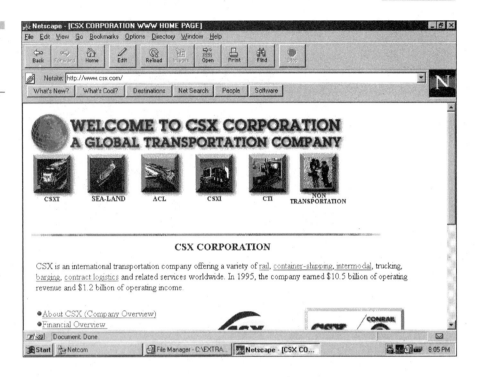

TABLE 4-1	Browsers	Netscape Navigator on Windows 95 and NT
CSX's technical summary	Servers	Netscape Enterprise and News servers running on Solaris; Oracle database; GIS mapping tools developed in-house. Sun Ultra SPARCservers
	Development tools	Java software development kit; Microsoft Exchange and Internet Assistants for Word and Excel
	Public Web site	http://www.csx.com/

Java Applets Energize the Map

Of main interest to customers is a Java-built system that provides graphic links to critical shipment tracking information. Business partners with Web browsers can display a map of the United States, click on rail hubs, and drill down further to the specific trains and cars that carry their shipments. They then can check lists of contents and find out when the shipment is scheduled to arrive (Fig. 4-2).

This application, called *Transportation Workstation Net* (TWSnet), was

Figure 4-2
A system map is the
key to advanced EDI.

CSX Transportation Route Map

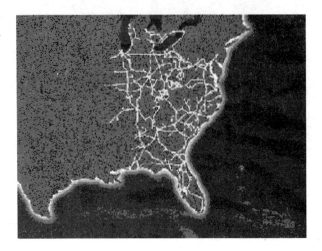

developed in about 3 months. It is considered a step beyond EDI, which processes orders and payments electronically. TWSnet goes further and, in the view of at lease one consultant, gives the shipping firm a big competitive advantage.

Web the Choice for External Information

The graphic application that serves external customers originated in a prototype that was presented to display some of the emerging possibilities of EDI. The prototype was created in Notes, but the final version was developed using Web technology and Java. The main reason for the switch was that many customers would have had to implement Notes in their organizations in order to use the system. The Web technology makes the information universally available and lets the customers avoid major installation and training costs.

Another internal/external service that has been under development is to replace a mainframe-based imaging system that maintains regulatory documents. This system will make the information available to anyone with a Web browser and the proper access privileges.

Reversed Priorities

In a reversal of normal priorities, the development of this external service preceded work on developing internal communication. The key internal piece is Integrated Measures, a management system that tracks 35 key measurements of business performance. These include statistics on how frequently rail cars arrive on time and the costs of handling cars at each terminal.

Integrated Measures implemented an idea that had been on the table for some time, waiting for the technology that could implement it. The intranet proved to be the right solution. Managers can tap the intranet and see to-the-moment reports on how well they are doing. Response has made this the most popular intranet site, and the greatest problem is that internal customers want more. Initially, the system provided information only for the transportation group, but it is being expanded to the entire organization. Data for the measurements come from systems throughout the company, and expanded development involves the creation of a data warehouse to store and distribute the large volume of data that will be involved.

Intranets Become Extranets

CSX worked in the reverse of the normal pattern, starting with an external function and developing an internal one later. In most other ways, though, its experience is typical of a well-established pattern. An intranet does not often remain confined to strictly internal information. It soon offers controlled access to the outside as well.

This has been particularly true in customer service. It often becomes obvious that you can use an extranet to serve external customers as well as your own employees. In many quarters, in fact, there is little distinction between the two. The employee is simply an internal customer, one link in a seamless chain that extends from suppliers, through the organization, and on to the customers. A frequently stated motto says, "If you aren't serving a customer, you'd better be serving someone who is."

In this spirit, the typical customer service application has both internal and external components. Often, as at CSX, customers are given access to important information. A company that does this offers a new dimension in customer service that can provide a competitive edge.

Meanwhile, the same extranet can serve employees such as sales representatives and support technicians—the internal customers who serve the external customers. One of the most common intranet functions is to provide an information resource to these representatives so that they can provide better, quicker service to the customers. Although this is an indirect form of customer service, it is really an external function because customers are the primary beneficiaries. There are times when it is better to filter information through your own employees than to feed it directly to the customers. But this is a business decision, not a technical one.

Two Sites with One Network

Trans Ocean, Ltd., is another shipping company that has combined internal and external forms of customer service in its extranet. Both groups enjoy controlled access to the same information database (Fig. 4-3).

From the outside, customers interested in container shipping can visit a corporate Web site to place lease orders for containers, inquire about available containers, get specifications, and send messages to Trans Ocean management. There is even a game they can play.

Meanwhile, employees can use the same Web site to take and execute orders, including any necessary follow-up. There are also the usual employee services, including corporate documents, discussion databases, links to other sites in the company, and a help desk.

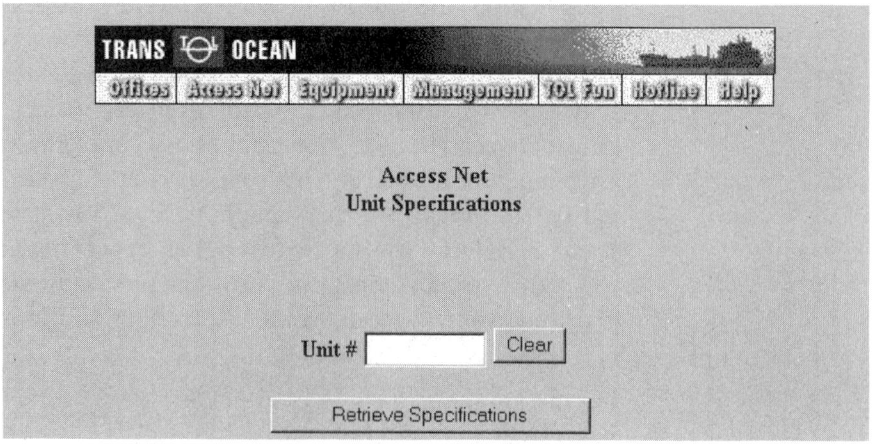

Figure 4-3
Trans Ocean looks both inward and outward.

Not Making Money, Saving Costs

These sites provide examples for those who are concerned about making money on the Web, if their success is any example. The real value of Web-based customer services is not direct sales; it is the reduced cost of customer service, coupled with improved service, that keeps these customers coming back. In the end, these may well prove much more profitable than direct income-producing activities on the Web. For example, Trans Ocean reports that its $250,000 in development costs repaid $700,000 in the costs of making sales and serving the customers—and this was just in the first 6 months.

Federal Express has saved about $10 million in the cost of serving customers. A FedEx customer can do nearly anything, from making a shipment to tracking its progress, through this firm's pioneering extranet. And furthermore, the company has been aggressively looking for more ways to use its extranet to expand customer service.

Sales and Delivery Service

In fact, FedEx has been busy building on this customer service foundation. Originally, customers were able to track their packages on the Web. Now the company will help them sell the products they ship. FedEx has introduced a business-to-business service that displays Web catalogs, takes orders, and delivers the merchandise, via FedEx of course. The company's stated strategy is to serve companies that need someone to handle the daily details of conducting business on the Web. It is seen as one of many things the firm can do to expand the range of its services from mere delivery to the full logistics of order processing and delivery.

BusinessLink customers have their own Web pages on the FedEx server. Each appears to be the customer's own site, with catalog and pricing information displayed as the customer wants it. Orders are transmitted initially to the selling customer's server, but shipping is handled at FedEx.

Marketing Gets Involved

The marketing department has had a large, early role in development of an extranet at Columbia Healthcare Corporation. The site has become

TABLE 4-2

Columbia Health-care's technical summary

Browsers	Customized versions of Netscape Navigator. It includes an animated corporate symbol, and the toolbar buttons lead to company-selected sites.
Servers	Two Silicon Graphics, Inc. Challenge S servers, running Netscape products including Commerce, News, and Proxy servers. The intranet ties into other database servers running SQL Server and Oracle7. The sites use a Checkpoint Software firewall.
Development tools	Microsoft Visual Basic ActiveX objects
Public Web site	http://www.columbia.net

notable for both the quality and scope of its content, including professional networking services for doctors and nurses.

Columbia, based in Nashville, Tennessee, is a $20 billion company with 280,000 employees. It has enjoyed the fast track up the Fortune 500 list to its recent ranking of fifty-first. Early in the planning stages, marketing and other involved departments decided that they would rather do the job well than quickly. The marketing department also had the luxury of operating under neither a fixed deadline nor an expected return on investment. Notably, too, a director of interactive marketing is responsible for both internal and external Web services. Table 4-2 presents Columbia's technical summary.

The network service, called *Koala*, provides applications for materials management, job placement, employee training, and most recently, the professional networking service.

All Deliberate Speed

Columbia has 347 hospitals and 280,000 employees. It will be a while before all of them are connected to the extranet. Plans are to have about 20,000 people on the net by the end of 1997. One reason for the deliberate speed is that many health professionals are not regular computer users. It will take time to train them and, more important, to convince them of the value of the network service. In fact, many do not even have PCs available. It is not unusual for 15 to 20 people to share a single workstation. Columbia has found it necessary to give people reasons to use

Figure 4-4
Even extranets can carry internal information.

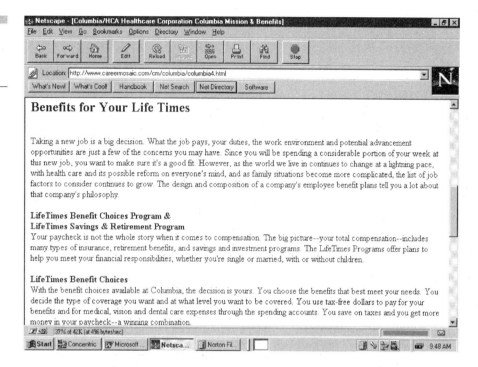

the Internet and other on-line services. Accordingly, the planners have incorporated interactive training programs offering subjects such as health care economics and patient satisfaction (Fig. 4-4).

Sharing Knowledge Worldwide

As part of the Koala project, the company's technology group has been creating the conferencing system on its Web site. The idea is to set up doctors and nurses in separate discussion areas where security and privacy are ensured. The object is to promote the free exchange of ideas, suggestions, and even complaints.

The sponsors want this application to provide secure areas for interactions so that physicians can talk to physicians and nurses can talk to nurses without involvement from the lay public. The company had placed a message board for its physicians on America Online, but the general public seized on it to ask questions about personal health. Their involvement cut heavily into the use of the system for communication among professionals.

Managing Supplies

Another application at Columbia serves materials managers at far-flung company facilities. Called *CEQUIP,* the application allows managers to create internal markets for used or overstocked products. After 30 days, any equipment not selected internally is listed on the corporate Web site, where outsiders can bid on it.

Another business process that has both internal and external components is physician recruitment. Jobs are posted on the external Web site. When resumés are received, they are moved to Koala. Recruiters at various hospitals can retrieve these resumés from a searchable, Web-compatible, database in HTML format.

Patients Go On-Line

A Dutch health care firm, de Heel General Hospital, is going a step further in extending itself outside the organization. With support from the government, the hospital has been building an extranet that ultimately will give patients access to both medical information and their own health records.

The hospital is one of many health care organizations worldwide that have found extranets valuable for two key elements of patient relations:

- Health care information and education
- Administrative chores such as admissions, discharges, and billing

For example, a patient facing surgery might not fully understand or absorb a doctor's explanation of the procedure. Using established techniques of teaching and communication, a Web site can give the patient a more graphic presentation that could be easier to understand. Some of these tutorials are so graphic they include QuickTime movies of the procedures.

Paperwork On-Line

When the Dutch project is completed, each patient's complete records will be available to physicians and nurses. Other administrative records also can be put on-line.

Like their American counterparts, the Dutch sponsors are finding one limitation: Health care professionals are not, by and large, experienced computer users. This means that the system must be easy to learn and understand. It also requires that the content be useful enough to induce the professionals to learn and take advantage of the system.

At de Heel General, the first application developed allowed physicians and patients to look up information about illnesses, treatments, and surgical procedures. This information is available through both desktop computers and stand-alone kiosks with touch screens. Patients who visit the kiosks can read articles, see pictures, and watch videos that help explain their medical situations.

The kiosks are meant to supplement the traditional fliers. Electronic distribution has several advantages over the traditional paper. You can post changes readily, without having to reprint the entire document. Also, patients have the option of reading the information on the spot or taking home a print-out.

Positive Reviews

Studies of both patient and professional reactions to the system have shown an enthusiastic response. Another positive factor has demonstrated itself, too: The system has become a form of self-paced personal health education. A patient who looks up information about a current condition often continues and finds information about other health care topics as well.

American doctors have praised the program, too, but they would like to see one improvement: Take on-line health care education beyond the waiting room and into the home. With home access to the on-line education material, patients can learn and practice preventative techniques, before their complaints become so serious they must visit a hospital.

Buying Hardware by Computer

Bell Fasteners (Pawtucket, RI) sells hardware by computer, but it does not sell computer hardware. Its industrial customers can now search the firm's 35,000-plus inventory of nuts, bolts, and screws and execute orders via a Web browser.

Although Bell still accepts and processes most of its orders by tele-

TABLE 4-3	Server	Nine DEC VAX minicomputers on a wide-area network
Bell Fasteners' technical summary	Database software	Quanta/D based on an Apache Group server, implementing Secure Sockets Layer security

phone, it has always been looking for ways to computerize the ordering process. Each week for a few years it would send inventory data to customers on diskettes. This was becoming hard to manage as the customer base grew to about 2500. It was not fully satisfactory to major customers, either. They were asking for direct access to the inventory database.

The new Web-based system makes use of an interactive inventory management and order entry system developed for Bell to run on Web servers. The system, Quanta/D from Sprintout Internet Services (Providence, RI), has since been released as a commercial product. Table 4-3 presents Bell Fasteners' technical summary

Access to the Bell inventory system will be limited to top customers. This is not just a security measure. It is intended as an incentive for all customers to do more business with Bell.

In Bell's configuration, the inventory system responds to structured query language (SQL) queries built from a series of Web forms that ask for the item, material, and style of part. After the inventory is checked, the part can be ordered. One improvement Sprintout made to this user interface was a shopping cart function, which lets customers see a running total of their purchases.

Bell wants to use the technology at Sharon Philstone Fasteners, a sister company that sells to hardware chains and home improvement stores.

Paper Company Cuts Paper Use

Wisconsin Tissue (Menesha, WI) supplies napkins and other paper products to all the major food groups (translation: fast food chains). When it established an intranet, the objective—more or less natural—was to reduce paperwork.

Specifically, the vendor of recycled paper products wanted to reduce the waste and delay of written reports and frequent games of voice mail tag with its sales force. In its place, the company sought an electronic, interactive system based on the Internet. A second objective was to

TABLE 4-4	Sales automation software	Aurum Software, Inc., IntraIntelligence
Wisconsin Tissue's technical summary	Marketing catalog	MediaShare Corporation
	Agent technology	First Floor

boost the century-old company's sales and visibility. The result has been a 2-year project to get its sales representatives selling more paper and preparing less.

Although the 2-year time span is long for an Internet-based project, this one is more complex and comprehensive than most. And Wisconsin Tissue is hardly a startup. It is a century old and still growing, with more than $300 million in annual sales.

The network will be a combination of Aurum Software Inc.'s sales automation software, MediaShare Corporation's multimedia marketing catalog, and First Floor's agent technologies. This combination will give sales representatives access to dynamic, interactive marketing materials and up-to-the-minute information located on the company's intranet server, something they have not had before and in an area where the company threatened to lag badly behind its competition. With tools for tracking, measuring, and managing the entire sales cycle and Web browser access to the interactive marketing system, the company believes it can put these shortcomings in the past.

The new approach uses Aurum's IntraIntelligence Center to connect dissimilar islands of information that clog communication between sales and marketing staffs. Instead of weeding through mounds of general information, sales representatives can use Web monitoring software and intelligent agents to fetch current, specific sales data directly from the Internet. Each employee can organize and personalize a view of the interactive marketing encyclopedia. Mobile sales representatives can hook up to the Intranet server and get instant access to changes that have occurred since they last entered the system. Table 4-4 presents Wisonsin Tissues's technical summary.

Salespeople Are Different

One basic premise behind the project is that sales representatives are a different audience than other kinds of employees. They need information immediately and in an easy-to-use form. Time spent in training or dealing with a cumbersome application is time spent away from commission-generating activities. A sales data information program must provide simple, accurate information and impose strong security.

The goal is not really to provide more information. It is to make existing information more useful and to get it to the right people quickly. Wisconsin Tissue wants to be able to

- Determine potential markets open to sales opportunity
- Conduct presale company analysis
- Perform profit analysis
- Determine sales call progress

The presale analysis is particularly important. It gives the sales force tips to tailor its pitch to the individual company, such as lowering inventory costs, consolidating products to lower cost, and training in recycling programs.

Even as they make on-site presentations, the sales representatives can open a multimedia encyclopedia for CD-ROM, PowerPoint presentations, and testimonial videos by other buyers. Having information readily available increases effectiveness and efficiency. Where it used to take five sales calls to make a typical sale, it now often can be done in one.

It helps both parties that the Web can make the process interactive and enjoyable. It also enables the company to demonstrate the benefits of its recycling programs, of reducing inventory costs, and of the products themselves. Still to come is a process of making the catalog interactive so that more sales can be concluded on the spot.

"Virtual Distribution" with an Extranet

A guiding principle at Marshall Industries (El Monte, CA) is that "the heart and soul of the business is service." An extranet link that starts with suppliers and extends through the company to its customers is adding electronic support to this principle (Fig. 4-5).

The El Monte, California, company sells electronics components to more than 100,000 customers worldwide. Although its suppliers include such well-recognized manufacturers as IBM, Texas Instruments, Inc., Toshiba America, Inc., and NEC, all these products are also available

Figure 4-5
On-line ordering.

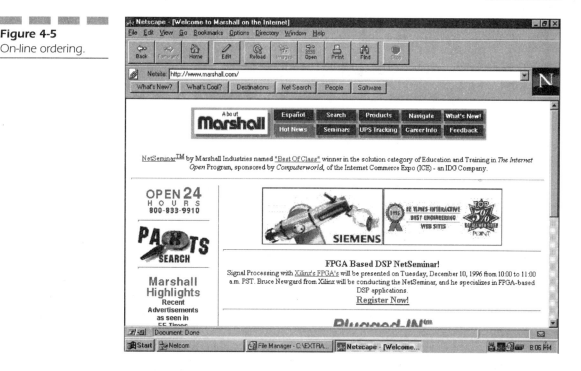

from someone else. Accordingly, Marshall decided that the best way to beat the competition was to offer outstanding customer service.

Maintaining such a level of service requires efficient, accurate communication. To meet this need, Marshall has established its intranet as a central communication channel for employees, customers, and suppliers alike. The intranet—again really an extranet—is at the heart of a service concept called *virtual distribution.*

Three groups of people—suppliers, employees, and customers—make use of this network and its information. Each group has a distinct need.

Electronics suppliers tap the extranet to find out about such things as sales volume, design registration activity, pending sales opportunities, and answers to quotations. Customers need access to information on backlogs, credit limits, work in process, purchases to date, pricing, and inventory. Marshall's employees can find routine information about their 401k plans, medical insurance options, and employee directories. They also can look up digital pictures of fellow employees and locations from around the world. For each of these constituencies, having behind-the-firewall access to their own distinct Marshall intranet saves time and money and increases flexibility over the traditional methods of data

TABLE 4-5	Hardware	Multiple client/server platforms
Marshall Industries' technical summary	Database software	Oracle, DB2
	Mobile connections	Lotus Notes
	Video conferencing	Intel ProShare
	Public Web site	http://www.marshall.com

access. The available information is updated constantly to support sound business decisions. Customers and suppliers are guaranteed accurate information about their Marshall accounts without making multiple phone calls and wasting time. Table 4-5 presents Marshall's technical summary.

Total Restructuring

The extranet is part of a major corporate restructuring begun about 4 years ago. Marshall's IT platforms were completely redesigned, and more recently, the intranet was added to the revamped structure. The restructuring, in turn, was part of a larger effort to improve customer service using the principles of total quality management (TQM).

The result is that everyone in the chain from suppliers to customers can work seamlessly from locations anywhere in the world. Not only has global communication been restructured, but so has corporate management. An old system of management by objectives has been replaced with management by method. The goal is not to make the employer happy. It is to make the customer happy.

Delivering Information

A key element in this program is the ability of the extranet to deliver information to the key people who need it, inside and outside the organization. In particular, it has helped keep track of a widely diverse product line. Marshall distributes about 170,000 different products from 150 suppliers. In the process, it records about 700,000 transactions per day. Internal and external customers alike can use the system to penetrate this product diversity and find the right item that answers their needs.

Another advantage of the extranet is its ability to deliver on-line training and presentations. Marshall employees can hold live video "cyberseminars" that provide training on a variety of subjects. Training topics range from how to sell a particular product to how to make informed choices about company benefits.

Many of these on-line training sessions extend outside the organization. For example, suppliers can take advantage of seminars on product design; and customers can receive training on how to use the product. Both ends of the communication chain can share information about how best to design a product that increases the customers' satisfaction. If they like, they can share this information through live remote conferencing.

Reducing Sales Costs

In a development that must have some kind of irony, an international telecommunications firm has cut the cost of supporting its salespeople drastically by getting them off the telephone and onto an extranet.

MTC Management Corporation (Petaluma, CA) sells cellular phones and switching services, primarily in overseas markets. Through subsidiaries, it works with more than 15,000 sales representatives in 90 countries.

In the past, this large, widespread sales force was linked to the company by telephone: long-distance lines, faxes, and voice mail. The cost and slow response of this system had become a major problem.

Even an Advanced System Has Problems

Even an effective dial-up order entry system implemented just a few years earlier was unacceptably expensive. The order entry system allowed sales representatives with portable computers to meet their customers, take orders, and activate the service almost instantly by dialing into a network of California-based PCs.

It worked well and was infinitely faster than competitors' methods, which usually were based on faxes and headquarters-centered order entries. However, as MTC enjoyed a healthy boost in sales, the dial-in system became increasingly expensive to maintain. The company was spending as much as $30,000 a month in long-distance charges. To relieve the growing cost, the company developed an extranet.

Maintaining Database Access

An objective of the project was to give sales representatives access to financial and administrative information held in a variety of database systems. Furthermore, sales representatives had to gain this access without compromising security. The company established two other conditions as well: It should not add to the expense of restructuring the databases, and everything should be accessible with a Web browser.

The resulting extranet lets authorized users send queries to the company databases across a firewall. The firewall, run on a dedicated Windows NT server, isolates the internal and external functions of the network. It will accept only a controlled number of remote procedure calls (RPCs). For example, a sales representative who has the right authorization and provides an account number can retrieve the credit card number of the customer who holds that account. But there is no comparable way for someone to request credit card information for other customers.

Authorized users are assigned IDs and passwords. An individual's identification is matched against user profiles in the corporate database and matched with the provided password. The profiles also contain information on the specific types of access to which the individual is entitled. This is how the system screens requests for credit card information.

This is only one of two levels of security through which an information request must pass. Requests for information are entered on Web-page forms that support Secure Sockets Layer technology. They are passed via RPCs to the NT server that runs the firewall. All MTC databases support open database connectivity (ODBC). Using this feature, an accepted request is processed in the database server, which formats and delivers it in a way the requesting party can see on a Web browser.

Because the databases use ODBC, changes at the server end will not require any matching changes in the front-end system. This is an important feature, since MTC has plans to convert all its databases to SQL. Table 4-6 presents MTC's technical summary.

Substantial Payback

MTC has not disclosed the cost of its system, but it does acknowledge that planning and development cost well into six figures. Nevertheless,

TABLE 4-6	Firewall	Dedicated Windows NT server. Separate network cards communicate with intranet and Web servers.
MTC Telemanagement Corporation's technical summary	Web browsers	Netscape Navigator 2.0 or Microsoft Explorer 2.0
	Server software	Netscape Commerce Server
	Databases	Access, dBASE, SQL (converting to all SQL). ODBC access
	Communication	T1 like, with ISDN line as backup. Local access for most field representatives
	Public Web site	http://www.mtc.com

the project has already paid for itself in cost savings, and it will probably pay for itself several times more in the future. The company believes that its extranet will support as many as 100,000 sales representatives worldwide without having to expand the support staff in California.

In addition to eliminating some of the expense of dial-up access, the system has boosted sales and service effectiveness. For example, should a customer halfway around the world experience a garbled data transmission or a disrupted telephone call, the customer can enter a trouble ticket into the system. MTC's computers are programmed to search the files for data on the particular transmission and can notify the responsible carrier automatically about the trouble.

Training sales representatives is another area in which the extranet has reduced expenses sharply. In the past, MTC flew its representatives from their overseas posts to California for 2-day training sessions that often cost $50,000 to $100,000. Today, all of MTC's training manuals are available on-line at a fraction of the cost.

Representatives also can see PowerPoint presentations and other multimedia materials in the MTC electronic library, which can be used on-line or downloaded for use at a later time or at a customer's office.

Previously, slide shows given to the representatives would be out of date within several weeks. Whenever this happened, the company would have to send out new sets of slides. Now a representative can play an up-to-date slide presentation live off the net. Changes in the presentation can be entered in about 5 minutes after they are ordered.

Meanwhile, because all the information remains in company databases and is not housed on Web-accessible servers, information does not have to be carried between the two systems and is immediately available to anyone with access to the system.

Getting into EDI

The company has been moving into EDI, with a new system that bills some customers directly via the extranet. Some bills are hundreds of pages long and can cost $5 to $10 to send through the mail. As the new system is developed and extended, customers will be able to see detailed information about their accounts and upload graphic and statistical information into their own PC software.

AT&T Prepares for the Future

For now, at least, AT&T is limiting itself to an intranet—if any network that serves more than 300,000 scattered employees could be called purely internal. But the telecommunications giant is using its internal network to lay the groundwork for future external projects, particularly in the area of electronic commerce.

Already, AT&T has built services like these:

- A system that integrates the varied billing systems of various business units
- Connections to library services, internal research sources, and external news feeds
- A system for ordering office supplies
- An employee-contacts database with more than 300,000 names

One major objective of this program has been to expand employees'information resources. People are able to find the information they want rather than waiting for the information to come to them—and hoping it is what they need. The intranet also has helped employees collaborate more effectively, particularly in research and development.

Getting Integrated

For a company that was once the symbol of corporate giantism, AT&T in its modern form is highly decentralized. Although it has formed several separate business units, these organizations still need to collaborate on sometimes complex projects. Managing the budgets and expense transfers between these billing units can be a major project in itself, because there are several different billing systems.

Instead of trying to translate data between different types of systems, the company is using its intranet to let the separate units exchange payments in the form of digital cash. A universal transaction system lets the units exchange this electronic currency. One official compares the system to the economic community in Europe.

If you are looking for a model, you need not look much further than this one. If AT&T can exchange digital cash with its internal business units, a similar system could process payments to external business partners. In fact, an EDI system is one of AT&T's major goals when it expands this intranet into an extranet.

Electronic Shopping Trips

Electronic commerce is already available in miniature. Employees now can order office supplies via the intranet, connecting to the company's global procurement organization. The intranet adds a Web interface to the internal ordering systems so that employees can place orders on-line. In some cases, an employee can pick up supplies from a drag-and-drop, Java-based interface to an office supply catalog. Table 4-7 presents AT&T's technical summary.

Steps Toward the Outside

Although the intranet is now primarily an internal resource, AT&T has already taken a few steps outside. One is an external service, secured by passwords transmitted via a Secure Sockets Layer protocol. It is considered secure enough to process credit card transactions (Figs. 4-6 through 4-8).

Another venture with external implications is a knowledge management system for customer service representatives. It gives 10,000 frontline employees direct access to a library of business procedures and policies. The system replaces collections of binders, substitutes for hours of classroom training, and provides access to 20 legacy systems.

With the help of this system, AT&T has consolidated 27 call centers

TABLE 4-7	Servers	Netscape Commerce Servers for internal applications, Netscape Proxy Servers
AT&T's technical summary	Browsers	Netscape Navigator
	Security	Secure Sockets Layer with a basic password authentication scheme

Figure 4-6
The AT&T credit card application opens a secured transaction.

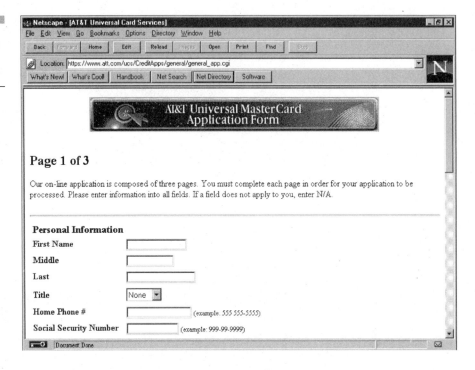

Figure 4-7
Encrypted transmissions help protect credit card information.

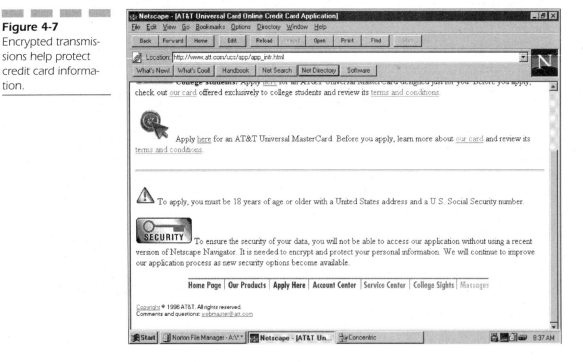

Figure 4-8
Netscape Navigator posts this notice of a secure transaction.

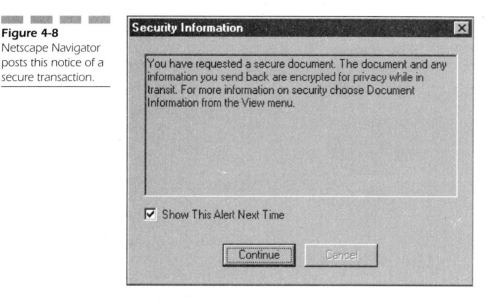

into one and cut 50 days of annual training time to 25. More important where customer service is concerned, the system creates a single contact point for customers and has cut the average call length in half. It is seen as a key resource as AT&T enters the local service market.

Where Customer Service Counts

Customer service can sometimes go more than one layer deep. When Vanguard Financial Services established its Participant Online (POL) Program, it was interested in serving a customer by serving the customer's employees (Fig. 4-9).

The program originated when Vanguard was negotiating to obtain the 401k retirement plan of a large computer manufacturer. The potential client wanted Vanguard to supply a secure, interactive way for employees to get information about their individual accounts.

At the time, Vanguard did not yet even have a Web site, although it was working on ways to capitalize on developing technology. The customer was not thinking about the Web either. It had in mind, perhaps, a CD-ROM or a kiosk.

The Web Via Kiosk

In fact, the Web-based POL does use kiosks, which ensure that the information is available to everyone in the client company, not just those who have regular access to PCs. The kiosks are connected to Vanguard's Web server via a dedicated T1 line, with links to databases that hold the account information. An employee who uses the system enters a personal identification number (PIN) to gain access to personal account information.

There is another security feature, too: If an employee walks away and forgets to log off, the system does it automatically.

Design Questions

The technical problems were fairly easy to conquer. Good design was the greater challenge. Unlike many Web-page proprietors, Vanguard did not want to leave its contents to the same technicians who built the system. It brought in communications professionals and design experts to make sure the site would reach its intended audience effectively.

That audience specifically included customer employees who were new to 401k plans and to investments in general. The site was designed to help unsophisticated users easily find the information they need. For customers on all levels, Vanguard wanted the site to be inviting and to encourage exploration.

Therefore, designers at Logical Designs Solutions (Murray Hill, NJ) coupled attractive artwork with large, simple buttons that lead employees to information on investing in general, on the available Vanguard funds, and on their personal accounts. The designers also used hypertext links sparingly to guide users and to keep them from getting lost in the system.

The site offers several features to help customers make investment decisions. For example, you can download the prospectus of the funds in which you are invested or are considering. Then you can run various scenarios based on different allocations between the funds.

Although designed initially for a single large customer, the Vanguard site serves others as well, including other employers and individual investors using their home PCs. Table 4-8 presents Vanguard's technical summary.

TABLE 4-8

Vanguard Financial Services' technical summary

Server	Sun SPARC workstation running Solaris operating system
Database	Sybase, running on Unix servers; MVS on IBM mainframe
Browsers	Customized kiosk browsers based on Spyglass
Added feature	Document assembly tool to integrate database information
Public Web site	http://www/vanguard.com

The Extranet in Electronic Commerce

Marketing people have taken strongly to the Internet. More recently, they have discovered that an intranet offers equal possibilities, particularly if it is expanded to the scope of an extranet.

Marketing executives now know that they can use an extranet as a major element in their strategy of getting the word out, attracting prospective customers, and keeping up with fast-changing markets. Just like everyone else who needs to exchange information, people in marketing have a two-way need for communication: to inform and to be informed.

Many Ways to Boost Marketing

The extranet offers many ways to support a marketing campaign. Start with the campaign itself. There is a need to coordinate a long list of activities such as publishing price sheets, press releases, brochures, and other documents, getting the necessary approval, and getting everything finished on time. This is a workflow project, a natural extranet application.

The extranet can meet other marketing needs as well:

- Obtaining quick competitive information on new products by competitors
- Conducting online discussions about product plans
- Providing interactive calendars for smooth scheduling
- And most of all, seeking and serving customers

Reaching Out to Customers

The external features of an extranet can be invaluable in reaching out to current and potential customers. In the business world, automatic customer loyalty unfortunately has gone the way of many other kinds of loyalty. If even a long-term customer finds a better deal or quicker service somewhere else, you can bet that that customer will soon be doing business somewhere else.

Like Alice in Wonderland, you must keep running just to stay in the same place. Customers are becoming more sophisticated and are getting used to better, quicker service. They want better access to product information. And if you cannot provide it, the modern marketplace offers overnight service from just about anywhere in the world. An international order might take 2 days, tops.

Quick delivery, however, is only the first level of customer service. Customers also have problems that need solutions. And contrary to so much computer lore, a product is not usually the "solution." More often you must solve problems with information and trouble shooting.

However, there is yet a third level of customer interest: Your customers really want to become your business partners. They even want to be involved in your decision making.

Expand on What You Have

If you are an active Web-using company, you probably have product information available on your Web site. You also may have a knowledge base of solutions to common problems. It is the third level—the customer as business partner—where an extranet can be a key marketing tool.

Often, you have the necessary information already. An intranet usually has plenty of information designated for internal use that could just as easily be opened to external customers. For example, you and your colleagues might have created a problem-reporting database. It might have a few rough edges, but with a little work it can be made available to the customers.

One company that has done this is Intersolv, Inc., which markets software development tools. Anyone who is interested can review the questions posted by other customers and the answers they received. The database now has more than 100,000 documents (Fig. 5-1).

Figure 5-1
The Intersolv information base provides access to more than 100,000 documents.

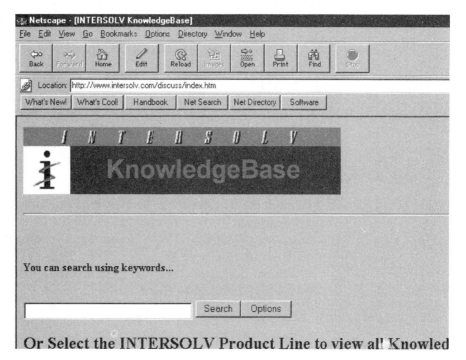

Figure 5-2
Intersolv is even open
about errors.

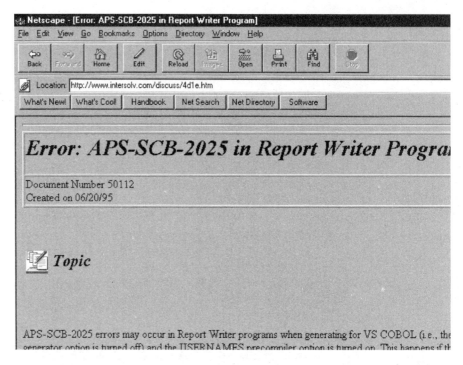

There is some risk in doing this. Competitors who learn about the service will be quick to exploit it. Still, Intersolv has found it is better to address customer problems openly and directly than to try to hide them in a corner. If customers can resolve their problems more quickly and inexpensively, the venture is worth the risk (Fig. 5-2).

Tracking Orders

As customers become more savvy, they know that order-tracking information exists. You keep information about them and their orders in computerized databases. Why should they not have access to information about themselves?

With an extranet, you can provide that information, including answers to questions like these:

- What was the last order I placed?
- When will it be shipped?
- When can I expect delivery?

- If on back-order status, how long must I wait?
- If a shipment will be delayed, are there alternative products that would meet my needs?
- How much have I ordered this year?
- What is my current discount status? When will I reach the next level?

An extranet should answer questions like these. Otherwise, the customers are likely to look to your competitors for answers—and are increasingly likely to find them.

Finding the Target Market

Through nearly all its short life, the Internet has been a marketing mechanism. In fact, this probably has been its most productive corporate use. However, an extranet can be a marketing tool, too. Its controlled access can be particularly important when your target audience is not the public at large but a discrete customer group.

This is the case at Turner Broadcasting Sales, Inc. (TBSI), where there is one clear, specialized target audience: advertising agencies. In fact, Turner's extranet was created specifically for this role. It did not follow the typical pattern of an intranet that developed an external role.

Called *Turner Mania*, the extranet does have the usual internal functions. As the advertising sales arm of Turner Broadcasting, however, TBSI's main object is to communicate directly and personally with the agents who represent the advertisers.

Helping Customers Find the Proverbial Needle

The Turner extranet solves a long-standing problem in advertising: how to give potential advertisers the information they need without overwhelming them with reams of data they do not need. In the past, advertising agencies evaluating media placements had to force their way through a mountainous overkill of documents dealing with programming, demographics, ratings, and promotional opportunities. Now they

TABLE 5-1

TBSI's technical summary

Site development	Sausage Software Hot Dog HTML editor
Database software	Microsoft SQL Server 6.5; NuTech Software Solutions Web2SQ
Web server	Netscape Commerce Server
Browser	Netscape Navigator

can search the TBSI data on their own, writing customized searches that focus on their specific needs.

The extranet was developed in response to a search for better ways to communicate with potential customers. Since Turner Broadcasting maintains a separate identity for each of its many networks, just keeping track of the different accounts and account representatives was a major challenge. TBSI executives decided to set up a clearinghouse mechanism that would give ad agencies access to information they need, not just what their internal contacts thought they might need. It also would give the agencies a fast way to identify and communicate with their representatives.

TBSI was fortunate to have a good model. Turner Broadcasting, the parent corporation, had installed its own successful intranet. Much of the early planning process involved tapping this project for ideas. An outside consultant, i3 Information and Imagination, Inc., helped select and organize the information and present it in an attractive way. For the most part, the extranet displays the same information TBSI already distributes in printed form.

The plans did bring one bonus: Since management saw the project as enhancing customer service, it did not require a formal return on investment analysis. Table 5-1 presents TBSI's technical summary.

Inform and Inspire

The home page is designed to accomplish two things:

- Help customers get the specific information they need
- Inspire them to think of other ways they could be advertising their clients' products

A client interested in a specific network such as TNT can click on that icon and get a report on the historic or current ratings for a particular show, and the demographic makeup of an audience. Clients also can download logos and photographs for a presentation. This approach allows them to work independently to see what is available. They need not contact sales representatives until they are ready to take the next step.

A menu on each network's page offers drill-down information such as analysis of how the cable and television networks are faring, research on who is watching, and even a party section where ad representatives needing a break can play a game and win a prize.

While offering its business partners the freedom to obtain timely information, the extranet gives TBSI a vehicle for better communication. A simple click on a red phone icon, part of each page except the home page, provides a list of the client's Turner representatives and their phone numbers. With another click on a name, an e-mail template appears, and a message can be sent to the representative.

This is seen as an advantage for smaller ad agencies that work with Turner. Since every client has the same access to the page, large and small companies will have the same timely information and opportunity to best serve their clients.

Security Lite

Security is mainly a matter of matching user names and passwords. Otherwise, TBSI has decided not to implement a more rigorous security system. To make that decision easier, there is no direct access from Turner Mania to any of the organization's other systems.

As a basis for the access-control system, the TBSI sales staff prepared a database of more than 12,000 advertising agency employees. When one of these employees logs on for the first time, the individual's name and agency are checked against this list. If there is no match, the individual can go no further. Otherwise, the individual then can create a password for use in future contacts.

Larger Plans

Few extranet projects stand still; their sponsors keep finding new things to accomplish. TBSI officials envision a future application in which the system will exchange information with agency representatives instead of just providing it to them. TBSI could collect information that would allow it to track which pages are being read most often and by whom.

Another goal is to build a cross-selling tool. An advertiser who wants to buy a spot during a Braves baseball game, for example, also could be informed of the opportunities on a Turner Sports Network basketball broadcast.

Levi's Strikes Gold Again

Levi Strauss & Company sells its jeans around the world, but it had been having trouble sharing information on the same scope. Levi's, whose origins are in the California Gold Rush days, now has 37,500 employees in 60 countries. When it comes to sharing good marketing ideas, however, information sometimes seemed to travel no faster than the horseback speed of the firm's early days.

Levi's needed a way to quickly and effectively capture and share corporate knowledge across the globe. When Levi's communications executives hit on the idea of using an internal Web site to share best-practices information, they said, "Eureka!" which is Greek for "you found it." It is also now the name of the new intranet.

The object is to empower the organization by cutting down barriers to communication. One of the major barriers was created by different time zones. Instead of trying to synchronize time zones, employees can post their experiences and insights on Eureka to be tapped by someone who could use that information literally halfway around the globe.

The worldwide network was built on a Web server that was already available. The first content placed on the site was standard intranet fare such as product fact sheets, executive biographies, press releases, and copies of speeches. Each document featured links to other useful documents. For example, a press release could contain links to a fact sheet linked to a picture of the product. The Report Card, a twice-monthly report on financial results, is available on-line with links to other financial information and a video clip of the chairman's speech about financial results, with a further link to the chairman's biography.

Levi's North American and European organizations had recently completed a long reengineering process aimed at improving customer service to retailers. The Asia-Pacific region had become the next target for the same process and will benefit from the experiences of the other two regions. One of the biggest benefits of publishing this type of information is that employees get ideas they might not otherwise have thought of. Eureka is expected to be the cornerstone of continuous improvement.

Learning about the Business

In addition to publishing this best-practices information, Eureka has been designed to help employees learn more about the business they are in. The global marketing project will collect and publish brand information, including the results of customer research, information collected on an external World Wide Web site, and data from a company sales kiosk. When the technology is available, the subject matter might include video clips from Levi's television commercials around the world. The site also will offer a tour of the products, displaying all the information presented to customers.

This will be useful to someone working on an ad campaign or a merchandiser coordinating major accounts. However, it also will be a training resource used to expand basic business literacy. Any employee who wants to can take a "Capitalism 101" tutorial explaining such concepts as cash-flow analysis, return on investment, sales and earnings growth, and competitive information. Employees who previously might have been reluctant to acknowledge ignorance can find the information quickly and discretely when it is posted on the intranet. Furthermore, the training project will use the company's own data. After reading a brief explanation of cash flow, for example, a user could click to see the financial data underlying company cash-flow information and see exactly where the numbers came from.

Of course, this kind of information will not be of much interest or benefit to many employees. Nevertheless, it can be useful if all employees gain some perspective on what is important to the company. All employees will benefit from learning about emerging markets, which will benefit the company because it will help employees expand their thinking from local to global.

Procedural Matters

Content is largely in the hands of the net's creators. Levi's has been careful not to create unnecessary procedural barriers to placing good ideas before its colleagues. The company recommends that the communications department of each region act as a content gatekeeper, but the regions are free to disperse their publishing capability. An Editor's Guild, a group of early Web developers, has drafted guidelines on standards for consistent look and feel, appropriate formatting, proper use of logos, and other issues. Beyond these appearance issues, though, neither the communications department nor the IS department will manage or maintain other divisions' content.

Hewlett-Packard Saves Trees

Sales department managers at Hewlett-Packard (HP) noticed that their sales representatives were throwing away too much paper. Reports, brochures, and other sales-related information tended to pile up on desks. More than half, the company found, either never reached the intended recipients or were thrown away unread. Now, an electronic sales partner (ESP) has put more than 13,000 of these documents on-line, with better communication and less waste.

ESP is a typical intranet with an external marketing and customer service function. It gives HP service representatives worldwide direct access to information on products, services, and new marketing programs. The contents include sales presentation materials, white papers, and interviews with HP executives. This material shares one of the world's largest intranets with personal information for thousands of employees.

The network is also a showcase for HP's own intranet products and services. More than 7000 desktop browsers have access to the firewalled system from any location. The system has links to databases both inside and outside the company; more than five terabytes of data are available through hundreds of routers and tens of thousands of links.

More Knowledge, Less Waste

ESP has changed the way sales representatives receive information. Instead of the often-wasted paper materials, the system offers easy access to current, graphically enhanced materials. The ability to obtain information has improved the recipients' desire to receive and use it.

For example, a business partner wanted a set of slides for a presentation and called an HP representative. The representative downloaded the slides from ESP and e-mailed them to the partner.

There is also a feedback form that lets sales representatives send feedback, anonymously if they prefer, to the people who create presentations and other documents. There are several of these messages every day, so the contents are updated regularly.

Not Plug and Play

This is not an example of a system that was installed overnight and immediately put to use. Downloads can be slow, so sales representatives receive monthly updates on CD-ROM, to give them faster access to the material.

It also was necessary to train the employees in how to use the system. Although ESP uses a straightforward point-and-click interface, the change in systems still required some classroom instruction. One-hour training workshops were held to build awareness and motivate employees to use the system. Six trainers made the rounds of the major sales offices; staff members at smaller offices were invited to attend the workshops at other locations or received videotaped versions of the training.

Documented Savings

Surveys have documented the network's effectiveness. Early returns indicate that the typical sales representative has saved a substantial 5 hours a week. Printing and mailing costs were down by $10,000 per mailing.

Long-term plans call for extending ESP to business partners, providing content oriented to their needs. The network also may transport multimedia and videotaped messages and provide for internal news groups.

Helping the Sales Force Keep Up

Telegroup (Fairfield, IA) has been ranked as one of the nation's fastest-growing companies. The long-distance service provider has enjoyed the success, but it is not without problems. One of those problems is to keep abreast of an expanding customer base and with a worldwide network of independent resellers. The solution has been an extranet.

As suits a growing telecommunications company, Telegroup has been able to establish itself as an international organization while operating from a base in the rural Midwest. Nevertheless, the problems of growth and communication have challenged the fast-growing company in its own field: communication.

Trying to manage a global network of independent sales representatives is neither easy nor inexpensive. It is a necessity, though, since the

Figure 5-3
Telegroup supports
its sales force.

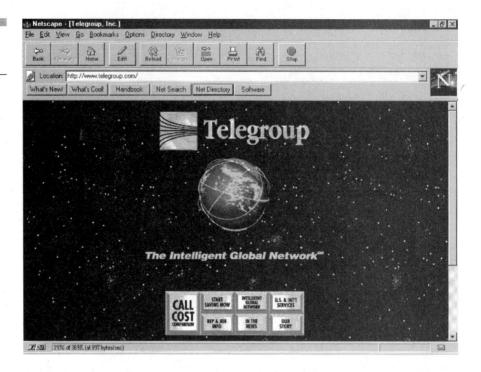

company is in a highly competitive market where it is important to maintain low prices. Accordingly, the company has looked to Web technology as a vehicle for streamlining the way it handles incoming orders from resellers (Fig. 5-3).

This has been a major change for the company's sales force, which historically has used fax to activate service for new customers. Often, sales representatives would follow up with expensive international phone calls to check on the status of their new customers.

Now all this information is available to representatives equipped with a computer, Internet access, and a Netscape browser. Telegroup has established a Web server, devoted specifically to serve its sales force, that allows users to place orders and check to ensure that new customers have been connected properly to Telegroup's long-distance service. A network of three Power Macintosh computers equipped with a relational database called *Fourth Dimension* serves as Telegroup's gateway between its sales force on the Web and its established in-house computer system.

The Power Macintoshes provide a menu-driven Web site that lets salespeople choose from a variety of options, including placing orders. The system speeds the process of establishing new service from a week to less than 2 days.

Figure 5-4
Telegroup maps its
network.

An important asset of the net applications is that they can deliver digitized information. The data arrive in a form that can be processed immediately by the company's in-house system. There is no need to wait for order-entry clerks to key the information into the system.

The database in the company's Web server screens order applications immediately to determine whether the forms have been filled out properly by the salespeople. Applications with missing information are returned immediately, eliminating what could otherwise be a serious delay.

The information also must pass through fewer steps. Previously, orders arriving by fax would pass through as many as five sets of hands before Telegroup had collected all the information it needed to activate a customer's account. Now the process often can be completed by an automated process (Fig. 5-4).

Encryption for Security

The system does expose part of the company's database resources to the Internet, with its attendant security issue. Telegroup feels that the limit-

TABLE 5-2	Web servers	Network of Power Macintosh servers
Telegroup's technical summary	Browser	Netscape Navigator
	Server database	Fourth Dimension
	Main corporate database	SQL Server running on Windows NT
	Database interface software	NetLink (Foresight Technology, Fort Worth, TX)

ed information available over the Web has minimal value to illegitimate users. At the same time, the company has taken several measures to safeguard its data. Sales representatives must use Netscape browsers, for instance, so that they can use Netscape's encryption feature to protect transmissions of sensitive transactions.

The company also has set up firewalls designed to protect its in-house system, and it requires password entry into its Web server. The company also tries to use standard off-the-shelf software that will allow it to upgrade its systems as new security services become available.

The server network is also set up to handle higher traffic volumes if necessary; the company can simply add more computers to the Web server network. Table 5-2 presents Telegroup's technical summary.

Serving a Mobile Sales Force

You need not be a large company to set up an extranet to serve remote and mobile sales employees. You need not be a high-tech company either, although CogniTech (Atlanta, GA) does have this advantage.

The 4-year-old company with about 30 employees is in the business of selling sales force automation products. The primary text bed for the firm's own Sharkware sales management products is its mobile sales force.

There is little doubt that an extranet serving mobile employees can boost productivity. There still are many issues to be solved, though, such as what kinds of information should be exchanged and under what forms of security. Other issues include the ability of the sales force's existing laptops to handle the job and to what degree the process should be automated.

Well Equipped

By most standards, particularly those of smaller companies, the sales force and the network are well equipped. Pentium notebooks running the company's own sales management software can use the extranet to contact a client/server database maintained at headquarters. The database contains records of about 75,000 sales contacts and divides them into groups according to the company's activities with them. Both remote and local users can upgrade the information as it changes. The sales representatives get replicated versions of the database every time they pick up their e-mail.

Looking for More

If this extranet has one major challenge, it is to provide even more information. Management would like to make a variety of information available, particularly to keep remote employees well informed about what is happening at the home office. The extranet is seen as a means of technical support and a way to distribute product information. And since the extranet both sells and uses Sharkware, there is the need to keep the network up to date with the product's features.

So far the extranet carries no proprietary information, so it is maintained as an open Web site. There is no firewall and few security measures beyond the basic combination of user ID and password.

Serving the Sales Force

Since the network serves the sales force and, by extension, the customers, planners started by asking what kind of information the sales representatives wanted the network to carry. In addition to the sales management functions, an often-requested feature was a calendar application that could help both the sales representatives and their home-office coworkers keep track of their schedules. Other requests include technical support and a product pricing template. As the company develops these for its own sales force, they also become potential additions to the Sharkware product. Table 5-3 presents CogniTech's technical summary.

TABLE 5-3 CogniTech's tech- nical summary	Sales management software	Sharkware
	Sales representative notebooks	Pentium processor running Windows 95
	Client/server database	Sybase/Powersoft
	Database interface	Sybase Net Impact Dynamo
	Web home page	http://www.sharkware.com

Not Just One Company

Business partnerships can cover many interlinked organizations, and there is no rule that says an extranet always has to be run by a single company. To demonstrate, a group of 15 businesses, in varied roles as customers and vendors, has been developing a prototype extranet that will let manufacturers, their suppliers, and customers work together on-line.

This extranet amounts to a virtual private network running on the Internet. Participating companies can collaborate easily and in confidence on such subjects as customer requests for product improvements. Should a manufacturing firm's customers request certain improvements in a product, the manufacturer can easily maintain dialogues with both the customer and the supplier to make sure that the product and all its components respond to the customer's needs.

A leading organization in the project is InfoTest International (Denver, CO), a private combine that develops practical applications for testing on the Internet. The manufacturing extranet is such a trial. It will combine Web technology with other fields such as computer-aided design and manufacturing, product data management, electronic data interchange, videoconferencing, and other more traditional technology (Fig. 5-5).

Manufacturers already use most of these applications, but usually through proprietary systems that make it hard to establish links along the full product chain from suppliers to ultimate customers.

The 18-month project, called *Enhanced Product Realization* (EPR), will set up a system for product design and supply-chain management and will study the costs and benefits of such a system. Participating organizations will assume the roles of manufacturers, suppliers, customers, and others in the product delivery chain. The sponsors hope to demonstrate that the extranet can improve customer response times and can get products to market more rapidly. The anticipated cost savings are about 30 percent over present methods.

Figure 5-5
InfoTest is a continuing test of network applications.

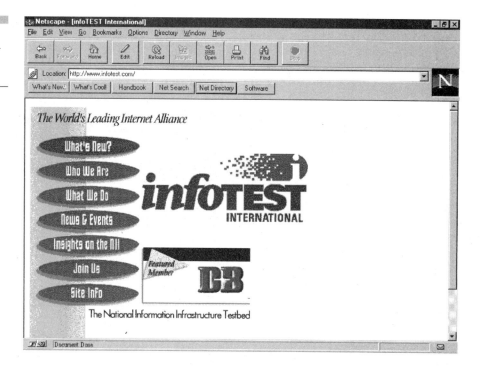

The test will address an actual business problem. One participant, Caterpillar, Inc. (Peoria, IL), wants to improve its response to custom requests for product modifications. The goal is to take a process that now often consumes several days and complete it within 5 days.

Bank Lets Customers Check on Checks

Need a copy of that canceled check? You soon might be able to get a look at it on-line.

This is the promise of an extranet-based check-verification system pioneered by Bank One (Columbus, OH). Its OneImage service lets customers review their incoming and outgoing checks using a standard Web browser. The system is currently designed for high-volume customers like insurance companies who need better management controls to prevent fraud and errors, but it has possibilities for smaller customers as well (Fig. 5-6).

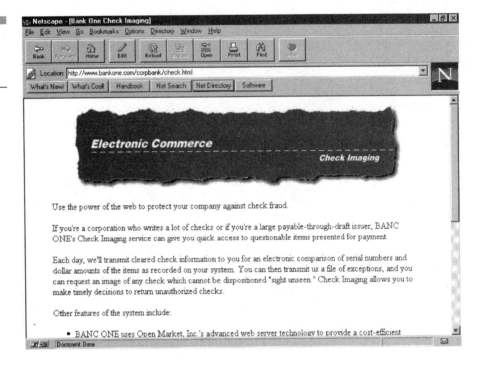

Most bank transactions take place automatically. When a deposit is received, it is credited to the customer's account. A check is deducted automatically. But sometimes major customers want to examine specific items—perhaps checks or deposits of more than a certain amount—before the transaction is completed. The large customers have been entitled to fax or courier service, but this can be awkward and time consuming.

The new system lets a customer log on to the bank's service and review images of exceptional checks. Once the image is displayed, the customer can decide whether to complete the transaction.

Maintaining Security

Security is important to nearly any banking endeavor, and this is no exception. Any data that move over the Internet are encrypted using standard Secure Sockets Layer technology. Bank One also uses access-control software to verify customers' identities and control the terms of their access. If the customer is properly identified, the software issues a "ticket" in the form of an encrypted data string. The customers then can

TABLE 5-4	Access-control software	Open Market OM-Access
Bank One's technical summary	Key devices and software	Digital Pathways SecureNet Key

use the ticket to gain access to the Web services they have requested. Table 5-4 presents Bank One's technical summary.

This is only the beginning of a security gauntlet. Each customer is issued a security key device that generates passwords for one-time use. When a customer enters the system, the Web server generates a "challenge" character string. The customer enters the challenge into the key, which generates the correct response. The customer then must type that response to gain full access.

Pictures via the Extranet

If a picture is worth a thousand words, 30,000 pictures must be worth... well, you get the picture. This is the number of pictures John Deere & Company (Moline, IL) takes every year of the company's tractors and other equipment. Now, John Deere is able to use its extranet to keep track of every image (Fig. 5-7).

Figure 5-7
At John Deere, a word can be worth 1000 pictures.

John Deere products are photographed from every possible angle in all kinds of settings to create a library of pictures. These can be used in advertising and publicity, customer presentations, and internal newsletters. The company has been digitizing its corporate photo album and storing the pictures on a Web server. The new technology makes the photographs available to every employee, whether at headquarters or at an overseas sales office.

Camera Ready

The object was to find a better way to distribute images throughout the company. The extranet provides pictures in a format that lets them take their publications directly to press. Previously, when someone needed a photograph, it had to be selected from sheets full of thumbnail-sized proofs. When—or if—the right picture was found, selecting, ordering, and processing a specific picture could sometimes take a week or longer.

The company has been considering some form of electronic image distribution for some time and had considered a system that used proprietary software and traveled a wide area network (WAN). However, the company was reluctant to commit itself to a stand-alone application. The people responsible for the photograph collection did not want to get involved in software support as well.

Under the new system, the image digitization process is outsourced. The contractor scans the images and stores them on a CD-ROM. John Deere then takes the images from the compact disc and transfers them to a 10-GB hard drive. Table 5-5 presents John Deere's technical summary.

Some clients want high image quality; others are more concerned with file sizes and transmission speeds. Accordingly, John Deere stores different versions of each photograph—a high-resolution version occupying 4 million bits of storage, a less detailed version occupying 1 mil-

TABLE 5-5		
	Digitizing software	Developed by SRI International
John Deere's technical summary	Web browsers	Netscape Navigator
	Digitizing contractor	Wace, Inc.
	CD storage	Kodak Photo CD
	Server	Sun workstation

lion bits, and a basic version at 250,000 bits. Each version can be selected and retrieved, depending on the resolution quality needed in the photograph. For example, people who are developing newsletters for our dealers or incorporating photographs into PowerPoint presentations usually opt for the higher-quality versions.

Improving the Breed

The intranet image application is also intended as a prelude to more sophisticated technologies, such as digital photography, in which specialized cameras can store images electronically instead of on film. Eventually, photographs may be able to go directly from the camera to the company's image database.

Most employees have ready access to the available photographs. With most workers equipped with connections that can handle 56,000 bits of data per second, most pictures can be downloaded in less than 2 minutes. A tagline accompanying each photograph describes the product, model, photograph dimensions, and setting. The tagline also lets the company protect photographs of yet-to-be-released products by requiring password access.

The tagline is designed primarily to let employees look through the photograph database using a search engine. The searches can be based on business unit, product category, or how equipment is being used in the photograph. An employee can time stamp a query; should the employee run the same query again, it would return all the photographs that have been added to the database since the previous search request. The product of search results also can be stored in an individual file, from which the searcher can recall pictures retrieved in earlier searches. Also, when the pictures have been published, the system can catalog the use.

HBO Distributes Information

Some chains of business relationships have multiple links. For example, Home Box Office (HBO) distributes marketing information through an extranet, not for its own sales staff but for use by the cable operators who sell HBO services to consumers.

HBO does not sell directly to retail customers, but it does provide marketing materials to help cable operators promote HBO. The marketing assistance ranges from previews of coming attractions to free installation and introductory service for new customers for use at the cable operators' option. HBO also produces customized direct-mail pieces personalized with the operator's logo and other local information.

The object, of course, is to generate business. What the programs also do is generate huge amounts of data for account executives to manage. It includes subscription numbers, data on marketing participation and campaigns used, and the types of marketing support given to cable operators. The information is stored in a data warehouse. The need was a query tool that would allow salespeople to get into all these data.

It would have to be easy to use. Most sales people fall well short of power-user status. It was not reasonable to expect them to understand how to find databases or build effective queries. With 250 sales employees spread over eight regional offices, HBO also needed a tool that would make it easier to distribute the information.

One response was to implement improved query tools the IS staff could use to present in table and graphic form material the sales staff could readily read and absorb. A second response was to implement an HBO InfoNet, an in-house intranet, to deliver information company-wide. Table 5-6 presents HBO's technical summary.

HBO InfoNet provides general company information, such as company policies and job postings, and also delivers specific information for departments. For example, the sales force page displays all the available marketing materials, which sales employees can dial up to read and, if they want, download as clips.

Another goal is to integrate the improved query tools with the Web browser so that queries can be launched from a customized HTML-based intranet page.

TABLE 5-6

HBO's technical summary

Web software	Netscape
Query tool	BrioQuery Enterprise 3.0
Database	Oracle

Controlling Access

The database includes a profile of each person. On one level, the profiles serve as a means of access control, allowing even authorized employees to enter only certain queries. The profiles also serve another personalized purpose. For example, a sales representative can see a presentation of his or her own accounts but can pass up queries of other accounts.

6

Browsers and Servers

Mosaic was the first of the popular Web browsers. It is a few years old now. Ergo, it is obsolete. Web browsers have advanced rapidly since then, and the pace of new releases has become legendary. When this was written, the two leading browser products both were at version 3. By the time you read this, who knows?

Despite the rapid development pace, the choice of Web browsers is now down to two: Netscape Navigator and the Microsoft Internet Explorer. It is hard to make a wrong choice between the two. There may be some circumstances in which one or the other works better for you.

For example, Texas Instruments (TI) had intranets long before the term had been invented. A few engineer types installed some early versions of Mosaic and some freeware servers and used these products to swap information.

Later, TI recognized the value of these early intranets and decided to formalize the process. The goal was to keep the grass roots nature of the original intranets but to boost their value for exchanging information between a greater variety of employee groups. As a browser, TI has standardized, more or less, on Netscape, taking out an enterprise license for that product.

Typically, TI had a reason unique to itself: It felt that Netscape's Unix implementation was ahead of Microsoft's, and this was important in TI's scheme of things. At the same time, however, IS officials at TI recognize that they may end up supporting both leading browsers, each for the things it does best and because individuals will tend to try both before settling on personal favorites.

Basis of a Selection

Browser choice is an area where an extranet differs significantly from other forms of Web technology. When you install an intranet, your organization's browser choice becomes very important in your plans. When you install an extranet, the emphasis shifts to your partners' browser choices.

Like it or not, browsers often come into an organization more by chance than by plan. You can download either of the leading products from the Web. They come bundled with some operating systems or software packages. They are free or inexpensive, and the cost of experimenting to find a personal favorite is low.

Nevertheless, the choice of a browser can be important. It can have an important impact on how useful your extranet will be in years to come. Some analysts even describe a browser as a strategic product. It certainly is important to remember that although a browser may be a giveaway, it is not a throwaway. It is the window to your extranet, and everything passes this way.

Equal Opportunity Browsing

In an extranet, you also must grapple with this nonvirtual reality: You must be prepared to accommodate a multitude of browser types. Although there are only two leading market contenders at the moment, the rapid release of new versions has left a multitude of browser types out there. Even some copies of Mosaic are still in use. This means that you cannot design your extranet around the features of a particular browser. You must have a page that is accessible to the least well equipped of your business partners.

It is hard enough to standardize internally on a particular browser. It is next to impossible to standardize externally. As the promoters of EDI learned some time ago, suppliers and customers resist when you try to set standards for *their* networks. This kind of resistance has been one big factor in limiting the spread of electronic commerce.

The Multimedia Challenge

The big factor in browser selection is multimedia. At any given time, Netscape or Explorer might have an edge in multimedia technology, but this advantage probably will not last long. Basically, you can expect that if people start using a particular form of multimedia technology, both browsers will soon support it if they do not do so already.

Nevertheless, multimedia decisions still are not simple. For example, you might want to liven up a Web page by using animated graphics generated by Java. This means that your business partners should have Java-enabled browsers. Although both version 3 browsers support Java, not all your business partners may yet have the most advanced products.

If an organization already uses Microsoft Office products and relies on Object Linking and Embedding (OLE) custom controls, it might be more comfortable with Microsoft's ActiveX, which is an extension of OLE to the network. Explorer also has close links to all of its parent company's desktop applications.

For example, one firm initially adopted Netscape, which was on the market earlier than Explorer. Later, though, it began to take a serious look at Explorer. This firm was already using Visual Basic for internal applications. Since ActiveX is based on Visual Basic, it makes sense for this firm.

However, this preference is not universal. Believe it or not, there are organizations that do not use Microsoft Office. Some of these are Unix shops that feel more comfortable with Netscape's background in that area.

Internal Factors

Internal factors—your own and those of your partners'—will guide most browser decisions. Though Netscape has been the early market leader, the TI experience is typical: So many individuals are making their own evaluations and decisions; most likely you will find both products present and supported.

You may find some business partners who have heavily customized their browsers. AT&T is an example. It uses a modified version of Netscape for its intranet. Each new version of the product means the company must update its installations and get the new versions to about 75,000 people.

There Are Other Browsers

Despite the dominant positions of two products, including the trade press, there really are other browsers on the market, and some of your partners might use them.

There are several vendors who sell entire desktop application suites that include schedulers and database access tools along with Web browsers. Examples include Emissary Host Publishing from Attachment Corporation, Chameleon from NetManage, Inc., and the Columbus Desktop from Hummingbird Communications.

Many of these have special functions that appeal to particular customers. For example, a consultant who specializes in law office automation says his clients like the Hummingbird product because it includes a document management system that can convert text documents to HTML.

Some analysts predict that the leading products took hold largely on the basis of their low or nonexistent prices. They also were designed to handle basic tasks such as delivering standard Web pages. Future browsers may include more specialized features that appeal to particular markets. Whatever appeals to your business partners' markets, your extranet should be designed to accommodate it.

Services from the Servers

If the browsers have been essentially giveaways, the motive has been simple: to attract people to the rest of the product line, including Web servers. Here, there is a great deal more variety. And just as with the browsers, market conditions change faster than you can display a Web page.

Although a browser is the window to your extranet, the server determines what you can see. Others may pick their browsers, but you pick your own Web server. What you need is a server that is muscular enough to accommodate the material and the use you expect and to allow for future expansion.

Decisions, Decisions

The Web server you choose actually involves several related decisions. The first is to decide what kind of server product you want. Should it be software, hardware, or both?

Vendors, including Digital Equipment Corporation, IBM, Silicon Graphics, Inc., and Sun Microsystems, Inc., offer powerful bundles of Unix-based hardware preloaded with Web server software, more often than not obtained from Netscape Communications Corporation. Or you can pick a software-only Web server from any number of sources, including Netscape, which sells users a different, more functional version of the package it provides to other vendors.

A second decision, tied to the first, is to determine what kind of hardware and operating system platform you want to use. Vendors such as Process Software Corporation and TGV Software, Inc. have packages that run on everything from NetWare to Digital's Open VMS. Others have single-platform offerings. These include American Internet Corporation's NetWare-based product, Incognito Software's entry for Banyan Systems' VINES, and Quarterdeck Corporation's line of servers for MacOS, Windows 95, Windows NT, and Windows 3.1.

Microsoft has been giving away its Internet Information Server (IIS) 1.0 to licensed Windows NT users. This product lacks some of the features and functions other vendors offer, but product testers say it makes up for its minimal functions with ease of installation.

Ease of use certainly should be a consideration in selecting a server. The easier a product is to install and configure, the less likely you are to make errors that could bring down your extranet at a critical time or could leave serious security gaps.

How difficult it is to install and use a particular package depends on how familiar you are with the server's operating system. You need to know about a whole range of server attributes, including memory, data storage structure, file organization and security.

Other selection factors include which version of HTML the Web server supports, whether it provides such features as use and activity reports or remote administration, and the type of security it provides.

HTML Delivery

A Web server has one primary function: to deliver HTML files in response to requests from HTML-compatible Web browsers. This is an essential function, but most servers now provide more. The availability of the extra services you need could make the difference in picking one server over another.

Basic added services include e-mail, File Transfer Protocol (ftp) support, and a Domain Name Server (DNS). These features can save you from having to operate separate servers to support these functions. For instance, some Web servers can double as Simple Mail Transfer Protocol-based e-mail, DNS, and ftp servers.

Running one or more of these other server applications concurrently with the Web server can decrease overall performance. If you want the Web server platform to support more concurrent browsers or to shorten response times, then move all other applications off it.

Proxy Service

A proxy server means different things to different people. Basically, it is a server that increases a server's responsiveness and security by maintaining a separate storehouse of data that are used frequently or, in the case of an extranet, offered outside the organization.

This form of proxy server usually works with the operating system to forward browser requests or distribute the processing workload. Browser requests could be received initially by a primary Web server, but the Web-page file actually may come from a nearby system. Likewise, a Web server asked to execute a Common Gateway Interface (CGI) script can instruct another machine to kick off that process.

Some vendors say that this architecture can, if properly tuned, yield a very high-performance multiprocessor Web server cluster. This proxy architecture also could be applied to a cluster of Web-server nodes, working collaboratively as a single logical Web site.

Another, less common use of proxy servers is to host multiple Web sites by concurrently supporting multiple IP address identities. The IP address mapped to a domain name distinguishes one Web site from another. While some vendors use proxy servers to describe this multiple IP address/domain-name support, others apply different terms for the same thing. Microsoft, for example, calls them *virtual Web servers.*

Yet another use of proxies is in firewalls, where they form part of an application filtering scheme.

Extra Service

Many Web servers have added software functions as well. These include utilities for creating and authoring Web pages, importing and exporting non-HTML files and data, and a graphic user interface (GUI) for managing files.

Also a consideration is the fact that some products have been optimized to deliver maximum performance on a specific hardware platform. This is particularly true of the bundled hardware/software combinations.

Authoring Help

Another added feature is the ability to design and create Web pages. In an extranet, this is a function best left to professional writers and graphic designers, but even they can benefit from a little built-in help.

Nearly all servers now come with sample Web pages already installed. You can place your content in these designs and have almost an instant Web page.

Security Factors

All Web servers use some form of encryption feature for security, but there are two competing standards:

- Secure HTTP (SHTTP)
- Secure Sockets Layer (SSL), which has wider support, including its use by Netscape

Which is more effective is still open to debate. Use of either security feature depends on the server and browser speaking the same language. Even though most browsers can still connect and talk to most servers, they cannot always make use of optional security measures if the server supports a different security protocol.

Other Selection Factors

The features offered by Web servers vary as much as their ease of use. For servers that will host multiple sites—the pages of multiple organizations or departments, for example—a multilayered system of administrative access can be useful. The person given the highest level of access can tap into all portions of the server and files. Subordinate levels can be set up to limit access to specific files so that different users can access and update their own Web pages but nobody else's.

A Selection Checklist

As you consider your server selection, consultant Edwin E. Mier, writing in *Network World*, suggests you consider these factors:

- *HTML version support.* Nearly all vendors claim to support HTML versions 1.X, 2.X, and 3.0, which is the latest version. Picking a Web server supporting all three versions means you will be able to support the widest range of browsers.

- *Activity tracking.* Whether for intranet or Internet use, knowing how your Web server is being accessed is a real plus. In an intranet environment, activity tracking helps with departmental charge-backs as well as general traffic management.

- *Use reports.* Some Web servers can track activity but do not offer integral facilities for reporting these data. One set of servers may only export usage statistics and log into certain third-party spreadsheets or databases. Others can report usage data in various ways, including via automated e-mail messages.

- *Simple Network Management Protocol agent.* If you want to manage a Web server at the enterprise level, make sure it can respond to polls from an SNMP-based console. Otherwise, you will have to rely on the administrator interface provided with all Web servers. Increasingly, a standard Web browser is being used for local and remote administration.

- *Remote administration.* Some products rely on the underlying hardware platform and operating system to enable administrators to access and control the Web server. Depending on the platform, a local console may be the only option. For maximum flexibility, though, users should look for products that support management access via different paths. Common access methods include in-band management over the server's main LAN interface and out-of-band via a serial port. It is best if both are supported concurrently so that you have a backup path should one fail.

■ *Authoring/editing tools.* It makes sense for a server to have utilities for creating and editing Web pages. At a minimum, the package should provide an editing viewer—a browser emulator that enables administrators to view new or edited Web pages without having to go on-line.

■ *GUI-based file management.* This is a must for multisite Web servers, where the administrator is constantly adding or moving new or revised Web page files. In some cases, the file management GUI may use the server operating system's integral facilities. But this is usually not oriented to Web page files. Instead, look at the integral interface that some Web server packages offer for manipulating and moving Web pages. Some use intuitive object-oriented displays that clearly show—in flowchart fashion—the relationship between the pages of a Web site and even display hypertext links and jumps between pages and sites.

■ *Non-HTML file import and export.* Along with tools for authoring/editing Web pages, other useful features of some Web servers are utilities for converting data to and from HTML. In some cases, a Web server can convert certain non-HTML formats, such as data from spreadsheets or word processors, into HTML format without administrator intervention.

Looking at the Market

You can buy a server as a hardware/software package, or you can buy the software and install it on your own system. The first course requires more money; the second, more time and effort. Notably, many of the hardware vendors who sell bundled packages use Netscape software. Also notably, the Netscape software you get directly from Netscape sometimes has more features than the bundled OEM versions.

The Web server market is much more crowded than the browser market; you cannot limit your discussion to a couple of market leaders. Some servers are simple shareware products; others are major commercial productions. And one comes from a book publisher. Nevertheless, the field has become more stratified lately into a few market leaders and a bunch of market followers.

O'Reilly's WebSite Professional

Instruction manuals have gotten increasingly skinny; some are now no wider than a CD-ROM. But there is at least one Web server that has been praised for having a well-written manual. It is WebSite Professional, from the technical book publisher O'Reilly & Associates.

After Microsoft hit the market with its giveaway server software, O'Reilly matched the price—but with an expanded version of its previous product. Reviewers have described WebSite Professional as a solid performer with a good range of tools and utilities. Mark Gibbs of *Network World* recommends it for midsized Web sites that see 300,000 to 500,000 hits per day.

One of the added features is a document management system called *WebView*. This product presents a tree-structured view of the contents of any HTTP server. If that server is WebSite Pro, not only can you look at the document titles, but you can use it to keep the documents up to date and to avoid or repair broken links.

WebView also provides an automated page generating service, with templates for a home page, a What's New page, a search page, and a page that is under construction.

Security features include access control broken down to users, groups, and combinations of these, plus controls based on IP address and host domain names. It supports both SSL and Secure HTTP for encrypted communication.

This is also one of the only major Web servers that will run on Windows 95.

Reviewers have given WebSite Pro high marks for easy setup and management. Criticisms have been few and have centered around limited remote management ability, particularly under Windows 95.

Microsoft's IIS

A product that (perhaps surprisingly) has not gotten high marks for ease of use is the Microsoft Internet Information Server (IIS). Easy installation is supposed to be a strong point of this product, but *Computer-*

*world*s Ted Vegvari feels that this is true only if you have a properly configured system in the first place. If not, the installation becomes much more difficult, and Microsoft offers little guidance. Vegvari is not the only reviewer to point out that Microsoft, which invented the Wizard, provides few of them in this product.

However, the price is right—it is free to NT customers—and when the setup procedure works right, it appears to work very well. Vegvari recommends IIS for large NT shops with remote locations and heavy administration requirements. In this service, NT's extensive access control functions are available to IIS.

IIS uses SSL security and includes a key-generating application that can be installed with the product. Like the basic installation, though, it is easy only if you have the right information available in advance.

Netscape Enterprise Server

Enterprise Server does have a wizard that guides you through the initial installation. Once installed, you can use the Navigator browser to manage the server using conventional Web pages.

This is, after all, the defending champion in its league, and reviewers have pronounced it rugged and reliable. The biggest gripes seem to come from Windows users: Like all Netscape products, its Unix heritage is visible. This means that it does not operate exactly like you would expect a Windows program to do. The HTML management interface also was deemed less flexible than the management application programs used with other products.

Commerce Server also has been judged strong in logging and reporting errors and storing a wealth of information for every server connection. With a built-in analyzer, you can identify the server's busiest times of day, the volume being processed, and the most popular addresses.

For security, Netscape is strong on Secure Sockets Layer (SSL) technology for the encryption and authentication that maintain secure transactions. Generating and sending SSL keys to a certification authority is an involved process demanding multiple layers of electronic bureaucracy.

Enterprise Server is part of the Suite Spot product group that also includes:

- *Live Wire Pro,* which provides a visual development environment for creating live content and applications that can connect to databases legacy systems

■ *Mail Server,* which provides open systems e-mail across an intranet and the Internet

■ *News Server,* which facilitates secure groupware-style discussion groups that enable team collaboration and easy information sharing

■ *Catalog Server,* which provides indexing, searching, and browsing of all the content and services on an intranet

■ *Directory Server,* which provides a universal directory service for enterprise-wide management of user, access control, and server configuration information

■ *Certificate Server,* which issues and manages public-key certificates and security keys for users and servers

■ *Proxy Server,* which replicates and filters content, improving performance, control of content, and network security

On the Hardware Side

Many servers that combine hardware and software are from hardware manufacturers who sell OEM versions of Netscape or other makers' server software.

Among them is Sun Microsystems, whose three Netra Internet server models are based on Sun UltraSPARC platforms. The products range from an entry-level server to an enterprise-ready rack-mountable Web site configuration that can work with up to 350 GB of data. This super-server model also comes with not-pluggable components and an uninterruptible power supply. All run Sun's Solaris 2.5 operating system, tuned for use in intranet or public Web environments.

Standard offerings on the Netra servers include:

■ Checkpoint's FireWall-First, which allows organizations to set up and secure individual departments or workgroups and comes pre-installed on the Netra systems

■ Netscape Web server software, including the LiveWire site management system, Netscape Enterprise Server, and Netscape Navigator Gold, which combines browsing and authoring software

■ A recently enhanced version of the Netra servers HTML-based administration software

- Bundled IPX gateway, e-mail, and DNS service with multihost and multidomain support, and one-button backup and restore
- The ability to expand the server's functions by adding a variety of Sun and third-party software, such as database integration products and commerce applications

Netscape for the Extranet

Netscape not only holds grandfather status in this competition but also has some special features that apply themselves directly to extranet use. These are

- *Publishing System.* A suite of applications and tools for a comprehensive, transaction-oriented system for publishing information.
- *Community System.* A suite of applications and tools to let users communicate and collaborate in a transaction-oriented on-line service environment.
- *Merchant System.* A suite of merchandise management and transaction-processing tools and applications.
- *Live-Payment.* The basic tools and applications to extend SuiteSpot into electronic commerce.
- *Wallet.* A system that organizes a customer's on-line payment activities.

These extensions to the base browser and server products are designed in particular to extend an intranet to business partners.

Transaction-oriented Publishing

The Publishing System extends the usual content creation and publishing capabilities of the browser and server into the transaction-processing realm. The system includes

- Transaction services you can use to register and bill customers. You also can use these services to publish information for their use.
- Billing services take on the all-important role of helping you collect your money. You can create a customized invoice form, auto-

matically generate billing statements, and use Secure Sockets Layer SSL encryption for credit card processing.

■ Registration services let you use custom registration templates to help you keep track of your customers and their transactions. You can set up different kinds of counts for individuals, corporations, or families, and you can generate preset membership reports from a structured query language (SQL) database.

You can link access control to the registration and billing process, granting access to individual documents, articles, issues, or entire publications. Your partners also can take advantage of such features as a search engine for content and attribute searching. You can create personalized contents based on information about your users.

The Publishing System also provides advanced content creation features, beyond those in the standard Netscape products. Content staging helps you update information, synchronize content, and provide automatic archiving, indexing, and backup. You also can import material from other systems such as news and satellite fields. The system formats, tags, and loads the documents into the system. This feature works with all major text, desktop publishing, graphic, and newswire services; the formats are converted into HTML.

From Chatting to Finished Products

Business partners often work together on product design and development. Communication across business boundaries lets you create products that are both feasible to produce and satisfactory to the customer. Netscape's Community System lets you conduct these discussions through newsgroups, on-line bulletin boards, and e-mail. You also have the means to exercise substantial control over the look and feel of the environment where these discussions are held.

These messages are not limited to text—you can add graphics, audio, and video. You can even go on-line with traditional auditorium and conference room meetings. Meanwhile, the bulletin board service provides for threaded discussions that link discussions on various topics.

The Community System also incorporates many of the same registration and transaction elements of the Publishing System. This includes several payment options, including credit cards, you can use to create billable products.

Commercial Services

In addition, features aimed at Internet commerce also might be used to bolster relations with business partners. For example, LivePayment provides the functions needed to maintain an Internet storefront, including access to banking services.

The Merchant System provides back office support for on-line mall operations with merchandise-management and transaction processing tools. A front-end server component handles customer requests. If you use it to display an on-line catalog, you can specify rules for the display. For example, you might offer some merchandise only to wholesale customers, or you might instruct the system not to display items that are not currently in stock.

The back-end component is a transaction server that processes completed purchases, calculates sales taxes and shipping charges, and delivers the orders to the warehouse for fulfillment.

CHAPTER **7**

Setting Up
a Server

As previous chapters probably made obvious, there is
more than one kind of Web server on the market. Any
and all could be candidates for extranet duty. This chapter will focus on two of these. One is the Netscape Commerce Server, chosen partly because it is the most popular product in the field and in larger part because it
boasts so many accessories that can be valuable in
extranet service. The other is the leading contender,
Microsoft's Internet Information Server (IIS).

Both are the flagships of larger fleets. Netscape offers
several types of servers that are close relatives of each
other, adapted to different purposes. Two of the most
popular, the Commerce Server and the Communications
Server, are identical except for one thing: The Commerce
Server has security features the Communications Server
lacks. Microsoft has been expanding its own product
line from an IIS base, offering both heavier- and lighter-
duty versions.

Whatever your server, it will be the working partner
of your browser client. It is not necessary but it might
occasionally be useful to have a browser and server from
the same source.

The Role of a Server

A Web server uses the Hypertext Transport Protocol (HTTP) to send documents and data to an HTTP-compatible browser. HTTP runs on any TCP/IP network, of which the Internet, of course, is probably the most important. A server also can offer security, as the Commerce Server does by way of the Secure Sockets Layer (SSL) protocol.

In a typical exchange of information, the browser, as the client, requests information from the server. The request is sent over the Internet. The server receives the request, processes it, and sends the information back over the Internet to the client.

Internet Design

Because no one is really in charge of the Internet, its real unifying force is that it employs well-understood standards for its use—at least they are well-understood once you have been around the Internet for a while. Like the scoring systems in tennis or bowling, newcomers can find the whole Internet arena intimidating.

The World Wide Web is part of the Internet. This particular part expands the Internet's basic abilities with multimedia features such as sound, animated graphics, and movies. Because the Web uses graphics instead of text, it requires that a browser also be able to handle graphics.

Web addresses are hypertext links to documents where each page has a Uniform Resource Location (URL) in this format:

$$protocol://computer/directory/file.$$

Each Web address begins with a protocol for the link. In the case of a Web site, this usually is http (for Hypertext Transport Protocol) or https (Secure HTTP). When used in the protocol position, *file* refers to a file on your hard disk or network, as opposed to one retrieved over the Internet. Other protocols include gopher, ftp (File Transfer Protocol), telnet, and news (Usenet news).

The second part of the URL, after the //, is the computer address, in the form *machine.subdomain.domain*.

Example: The machine *home.easttech.com* is the machine recognized as *home* in the easttech section of the *com* domain.

Domain names refer to various groups and subgroups in an organization, and they can have as many subdivisions as the biggest organization chart allows. Domains are generally grouped into these categories:

- .com: commercial organizations
- .edu: educational institutions
- .mil: military
- .net: network organizations
- .org: other types of organizations

Then come elements that might be more familiar: a directory and a file name. Text files usually have .html or .htm extensions, which mean the document is a Hypertext Markup Language document that might contain jumps to other pages.

Example: The Netscape home page is */home/welcome.html,* which means the page is a hypertext (.html) document in the home directory on the *home.netscape.com* computer.

Actually Making Things Simple

Complicated as they are, URLs are designed to simplify the job of identifying Web sites and pages. They substitute for Internet Protocol (IP) addresses that are even more obtuse.

All Internet hosts are identified by their IP addresses. An IP address is a series of numbers separated by periods, or dots. An IP address can range from 0.0.0.0 to 255.255.255.255. The first of the four numbers can be a clue to the type of organization that holds it. In general, the lower the first number, the larger is the organization. You may have to find and enter one or two IP addresses in the course of setting up a browser or server.

The rest of this chapter will explain the requirements for setting up the Netscape and Microsoft servers. The intent is not only to take you through the steps involved but also to help you understand how the various elements of Web communication go together. We will start with Netscape:

Netscape System Requirements

If you are going to install a server, count on needing some heavy-duty hardware. Netscape has one server, the Fast Track, that is designed to run on Windows 95; otherwise, count on a rugged Unix or Windows NT product with as much memory as you can afford.

For a Unix system, Netscape says the Commerce Server requires

- One of these operating systems:

  DEC (OSF/1 2.0)

  HP-UX 9.03, 9.04 and series 700, 800, and 9000 hardware

  IBM RS/6000 (AIX 3.2.5) SGI (IRIX 5.2)

  Sun (SunOS 4.1.3) Sun (Solaris 2.3, 2.4)

  386/486/Pentium (BSDI 1.1, 2.0)

- At least 32 MB of RAM. Count on 64 MB or more if you expect to handle a lot of traffic.
- 5 MB hard disk space for the server, plus 2 to 3 MB for log files
- A browser that will handle forms

  For a Windows NT system, Netscape has set these requirements:

- An 80486 processor or higher
- NT version 3.5 or higher
- At least 16 MB of RAM (More is strongly recommended.)
- A swap size at least as large as the RAM size (For high-load servers, this should be between 100 and 150 MB)
- 30 MB of free disk space for the installation
- 30 MB of free disk space for log files (for approximately 300,000 accesses per day)
- A forms-capable browser

People who are not accustomed to managing Unix systems probably will lean toward the NT version. Some reviewers have found the NT server less capable, though, than its Unix counterpart. In particular, NT does not readily handle Common Gateway Interface (CGI) scripts that exchange variables, as most do.

The choice may come down to your in-house expertise. If you have Unix programming and system administration talent on board, a Unix system is probably a better choice for an extranet. Otherwise, you can opt for the familiar face of NT.

The Right Hardware

Your hardware selections are linked, of course, to your choice of an operating system. The options include

- *Intel processors.* With this choice, you can run either Windows NT or the BSDI version of Unix. If you go this route, get the fastest processor and most amount of memory you can afford. If you do, you will have a server that will perform nearly as well as some options that are much more expensive.
- *Digital Alpha.* These systems can run either NT or Digital's OSF/1 version of Unix. If you must, you can get by with 16 MB of RAM here, but it is not recommended.
- *Silicon Graphics.* A line of Web servers can be had with the Netscape server of your choice at a discount price. This line uses the X-Windows, the Unix graphic interface, which is both much like and frustratingly unlike the more familiar Windows look. If you are comfortable with Netscape Navigator, even as a Windows or Mac product, you probably also will be comfortable with X-Windows.
- *Sun.* This firm's SPARCstations and Netra servers appeal more to experienced Unix hands than to Unix beginners. These are professional tools that should be assigned accordingly.

Making the Right Connections

In theory, you can link your server to any Internet connection that can give the server a distinctive IP address. In practice, it is not quite this simple.

Your site needs its own name and address. This means that your server should be attached to a system that will provide a unique, permanent IP address. You also should make sure there is enough bandwidth to carry the amount of information you expect to be moving around at any given time. This connection should be rock solid. People who cannot get through often do not come back to try again. This is why the major Web site operators have T1 lines or at least fractional T1 service.

An Internet Service Provider's (ISP's) pricing scheme can be a selection factor, too. This is not just a matter of picking the best base rates. Pricing is often based on the greatest amount of bandwidth you demand at some established measuring point on the network. Heavy traffic can drive up your bill in a hurry, and you might find that the price of popularity is more than you want to pay. It might be better to choose a plan that lets you select a maximum bandwidth. If you find yourself crowding the limit, you can always increase it. This extra capacity will have a price, of course, but you will have more control.

Installing a Unix Server

Installing the server is not a hard job, but some advance preparation can make it a lot easier and quicker. These advance steps include

- Make sure your domain naming service (DNS) is in operation.
- Create a home page for your Web site.
- Create an alias for the server.
- Create a user account.
- Choose a unique set of port numbers.

Starting DNS

At various times during the installation, you will be asked to supply a host name, an Internet Protocol (IP) address, or both.

To review: A host name is given a specific computer. It uses the form *machine.subdomain.domain*. The IP address, discussed earlier in this chapter, is a set of four numbers, separated by dots: *123.45.678.90*. It is the numeric address that corresponds to the computer name.

If the DNS is not up and running when you start the installation, the server cannot identify host names or connect to any remote hosts.

Every Site Needs a Home Page

The home page is usually the first thing someone will see when they visit your extranet. It should introduce both your Web site and your organization. It also should provide a table of contents for the information your site provides.

If you are fortunate enough to already have a home page ready, you can specify it during the installation process. If not, you can create one before you start the installation. There is even a third alternative: let the installation process create a home page. You can tailor it to your own uses later.

Create an Alias

In many installations, the server software will run on one machine in a network. If so, you can identify the actual server system with a CNAME record in the DNS. Or you can assign an alias that points to the server—*www* can be a good enough alias. This could become important should you have to change the actual host name or IP address of the system. You can do so without having to change all your URL references.

Example: You might call the server *server.writtech.com*. You then could give it an alias like *www.writtech.com*. The URLs that point to your machine could point to the alias, which can remain constant despite other changes.

Creating a User Account

In addition to its various names and addresses, a server needs a user account. This is a matter of security and access control. The account you create now will be the "owner" of any subsequent accounts you create.

Specify this account during the installation. When the server operates, it will run under this account. The user account should have permission to read the server configuration files and write permission for the directory that contains the log files.

There is a good reason even this superuser should not have write access to the configuration files. If someone breaks into the server, they are likely to gain the privileges of the user account. Limiting the privileges associated with this account also limits the damage an invader could do.

There also is a reason you might want to avoid using the popular name *Nobody* for this account. First, it is one of those default names shipped with many machines. Many people leave themselves open to invasion because they fail to change the names on these accounts.

There is another reason, too. Some Unix systems give the user called *Nobody* a user ID (UID) of -2. A negative UID will generate an error message during installation. Check the password file to see if this UID exists, and if so, make sure it has a positive number. Better yet, avoid this troublesome name.

Port Numbers

You will need two port numbers: one for the administration server and one for the commerce server itself. The administration server is a separate program that lets you manage your server or servers from a single forms-based interface.

The standard HTTP port number is 80, but again this is something you may not want to use without question. You can install the server to any port that is not already in use. When you first use the administration forms, you will use the administration server's port number. It is a good idea to set a different port number for the administration server, again to remove a familiar default that could cause a security risk.

There is another consideration in assigning a port number: If you choose a port number of 1024 or less, you must log in as root to start the server. After the server is bound to the port, it will change from root to the user account you specify. This is not necessary if you choose a number larger than 1024.

One final point: When you start the installation, make sure your have write privileges to the root directory where you want to install the server. This means that you should be logged in under the server user account.

Starting the Installation

These have been just the preliminaries—the things you should do to get ready for the installation. What you do next depends on whether you have obtained the server software on CD-ROM or have downloaded a trial version directly from Netscape.

CD Setup

To start the installation from CD-ROM:

1. Put the CD-ROM in the drive, and change to the directory that houses your operating system.

Example: Type *cd solaris* or *cd osf_1*

2. Copy the file *httpds.tar* from the CD-ROM directory to the directory where you want the installation program to run. This should be a temporary directory, not the directory where you plan to install the server.

3. Type *https.tar.* This unpacks the server files and creates a temporary directory structure for the installation process.

4. Type *cd https.* You change to the new directory where there is a readme file.

5. Change to the directory *httpd/install.*

6. Type *./ns-setup.* The installation begins. If you are not properly logged in, you will see error messages to this effect.

7. When asked, enter the name of your browser. The browser starts and displays the installation forms.

Using a Downloaded File

Netscape offers downloaded server software for a free trial period. You can use the software until the trial period expires.

To install the downloaded server file:

1. Type *gzip −d* and the name of the downloaded file. This decompresses the downloaded file. You will need the gzip utility, which is also available for downloading. The decompression process produces a .TAR archive file.

2. Type *tar −xvf* and the name of the .TAR file. The decompressed files and directory structures are set up on the hard disk.

3. Type *cd https.* You change to the new directory where there is a readme file.

4. Change to the directory *httpd/install.*

5. Type *./ns-setup.*

6. When asked, enter the name of your browser.
   The browser starts and displays the installation forms.

Now the installation process is mainly a matter of filling out forms. These are HTML forms that collect data which the installation process uses to generate configuration files.

This is one area where Netscape differs significantly from other servers. Netscape uses HTML forms to transfer information to the installer, which then places that information in configuration files. Other servers use GUI interfaces to collect similar information.

Fill out the forms and click on the link labeled *Go For It*. This is when the installation process actually begins; until then, no files or directories have been modified except to set up the installation files themselves.

The installation process places all the files in and under the server root directory you specified on one of the installation forms. You will have these directories and files:

- *Start-admin* and *stop-admin* are scripts that start and close the server manager. The server manager is a tool that lets you configure the server.
- *Admserv* is a directory that holds the server administration files. It also contains the user name and password for the administration account and the binary files for running the server manager.
- *Bin* contains the binary files for the server. It includes the main program plus administration forms and other accessories.

  There is a type and port number directory for each server installed on the machine. Subdirectories contain configuration files, encryption information, and error and access log files.

  There are also shell scripts to start, stop, and restart the server and a script to rotate log files:
- *Userdb* is a directory that contains all user databases. It is a central directory any number of servers can use.
- *Mc-icons* contains icons for File Transfer Protocol (FTP) listings and Gopher menus.
- *Extras* contains utilities such as a log file analyzer.
- *Nsapi* contains header files and example for creating your own functions under the Netscape API.

Installing on Windows NT

Installation on a Windows NT system requires the same preliminaries as a Unix installation: Get a DNS up and running, create a home page, give the server an alias, set up a user account for the server, and create unique port numbers for both the basic server and the administration server.

There are some differences in the details. For example, when you create a user account for the NT server, you can restrict access through this route by setting up this account under a nonprivileged system. During installation, the process runs under a local system account, which has only a limited set of privileges. You can change the account after the installation is finished. At that time you can configure the account to include permission to get files on another machine. This lets your server use files from other machines.

The NT Installation

The installation process has two major steps:

- Copy the files from the CD ROM to your hard disk, or download the files from the Web.
- Configure and start the server.

An Event Viewer will log and report any errors that occur during the installation.

To start the installation from a downloaded file:

1. Decompress the files into a working directory. When you downloaded the file, you specified the type of compression you wanted to use. If you chose .EXE, you can run the downloaded file as an executable file. If you chose .ZIP, you must use a ZIP utility to decompress the files.
   Note: Avoid the temptation to name the working directory *\NETSCAPE.* This is the directory where the completed server program will be installed. Server files will be mixed with the installation files.

2. From your working directory, run *SETUP.EXE.* When prompted, click on *Continue.* A dialog box asks you in what directory to install the program files.

3. Unless you have a compelling reason to do otherwise, accept the default *\NETSCAPE.*

4. Click on *Continue.* The server installation files are installed.

To start the installation from a CD-ROM:

1. Run the program *SETUP.EXE* in the root directory of the CD-ROM. You see an opening message (Fig. 7-1).

Figure 7-1
Installation starts with an opening screen like this. The screen shots in this section are based on Netscape's Fast Track server under Windows 95, but other servers and NT installations are similar.

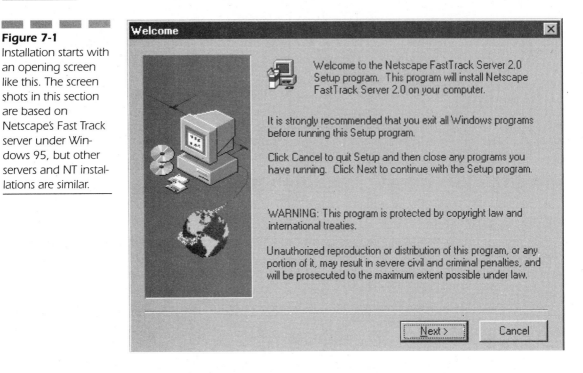

Figure 7-2
The default directory is the easiest choice to manage.

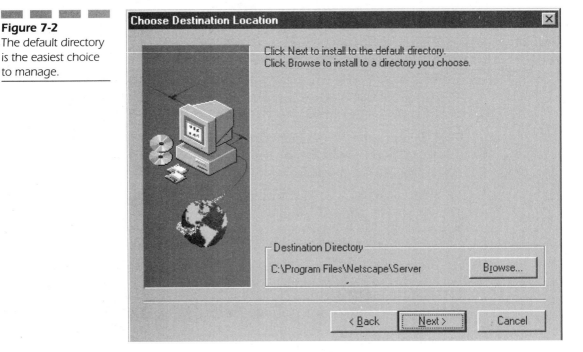

2. Click on *Continue*. A dialog box asks you in what directory to install the program files. Unless you have a compelling reason to do otherwise, accept the default **\NETSCAPE** (Fig. 7-2).

3. Click on *Continue* again. The server files are copied, and a configuration dialog box opens (Fig. 7-3).

To complete the installation: After the files are installed, a dialog box asks if your machine has a DNS entry in a DNS server.

1. If you know the DNS name of your server, select *DNS Configured*. Otherwise, select *No DNS Entry* to use IP addresses instead. A dialog box asks you to supply the DNS name or IP address. Normally, you can simply confirm the information retrieved from your computer's registry (Fig. 7-4).

2. You also may be asked to supply user names and other information (Figs. 7-5 and 7-6).

3. The installation program copies all the files to your hard disk and starts a service called *Netscape Install*. A message asks if you want to configure the server using Server Manager forms (Fig. 7-7).

4. Click on *OK*.

Figure 7-3
You are actually installing two servers.

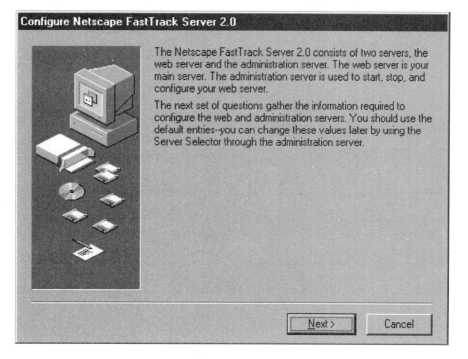

Figure 7-4
The installation program suggests a domain name.

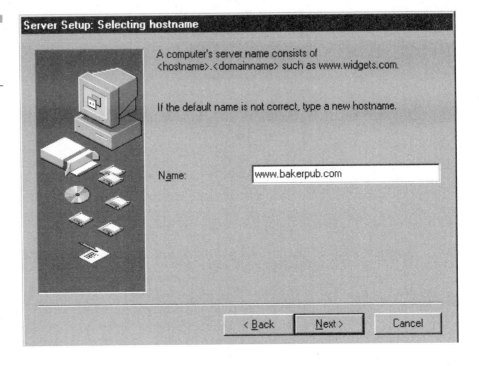

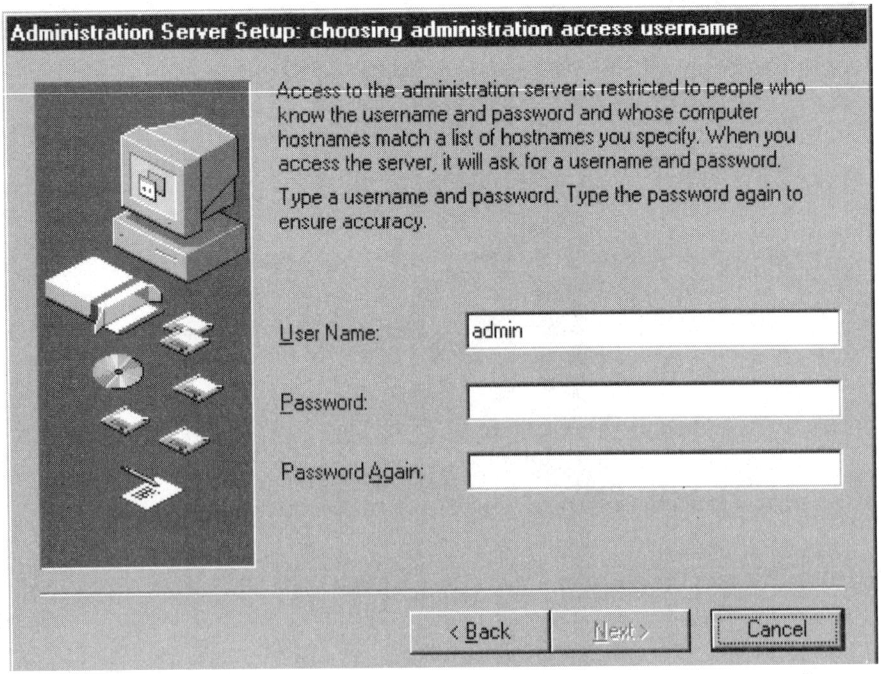

Server Setup: Selecting hostname

A computer's server name consists of
<hostname>.<domainname> such as www.widgets.com.

If the default name is not correct, type a new hostname.

Name: www.bakerpub.com

< Back   Next >   Cancel

Figure 7-5
Supply a user name and password for the administration server.

Administration Server Setup: choosing administration access username

Access to the administration server is restricted to people who
know the username and password and whose computer
hostnames match a list of hostnames you specify. When you
access the server, it will ask for a username and password.

Type a username and password. Type the password again to
ensure accuracy.

User Name: admin

Password:

Password Again:

< Back   Next >   Cancel

Figure 7-6
Choose a root directory for your documents.

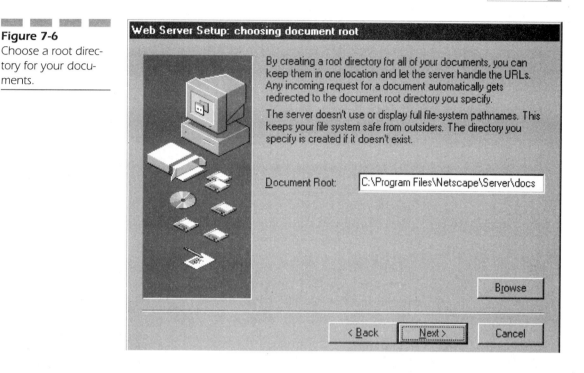

Figure 7-7
One more click finishes the job.

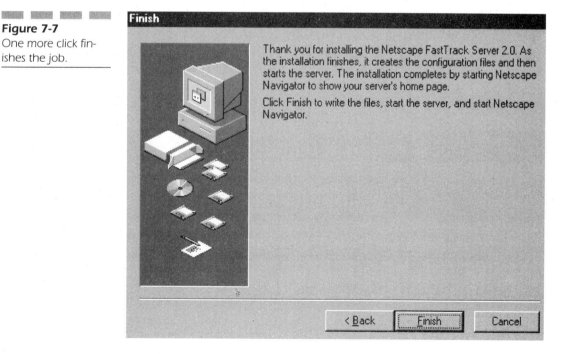

Installing IIS

Microsoft's Internet Information Server (IIS) is similar in concept; the main difference is that—no surprise—it is strictly a Windows NT product. In fact, the two are so closely linked that you can install IIS at the same time you install an NT Server.

The Internet Information Server requires

- A computer with the capacity to run Windows NT Server version 4.0.

- TCP/IP, which is included with Windows NT. Use the Network application in Control Panel to install and configure the TCP/IP protocol and related components.

- A CD-ROM drive to install from compact disk.

- Enough disk space for your Web-site information content. Microsoft recommends that all drives used with IIS be formatted with the Windows NT File System (NTFS).

If you want to publish information on an intranet, you also will need

- A network adapter card and local area network (LAN) connection.

- A Windows Internet Name Service (WINS) server or a Domain Name System (DNS) server installed on a computer in your intranet. This step is not strictly required, but as with the Netscape installation, it lets you use the relatively unintimidating language of URLs, rather than the all-number language of an IP address.

To publish on the Internet, you will need

- An Internet connection and Internet Protocol (IP) address from your Internet Service Provider (ISP).

- DNS registration for that IP address. Again, this is an optional step but one that promotes ease of use. Most ISPs can register your domain names for you.

- A network adapter card suitable for your connection to the Internet.

Getting NT Ready

You must configure the NT Server networking component so that your Web server can operate on the Internet. It also may be a good idea to check the current NT security settings and installed security measures and beef them up to control outside access.

You can use the Network application in the Control Panel to

- *Obtain an Internet Connection.* To publish on the Internet, you must have a connection to the Internet from an ISP.

- *Configure the TCP/IP Protocol.* Install the NT TCP/IP Protocol and Connectivity Utilities. Your ISP will provide your server's IP address, subnet mask, and the default gateway's IP address. The default gateway is the ISP computer through which your computer will route all Internet traffic.

- *Remove the FTP service provided with NT.* If it has already been removed, of course, this is not necessary. Also remove any other previously installed Internet services.

- *Configure the Site's Domain Name,* also called a *host name.*

- *Configure Name Resolution.* You need a name resolution system to map IP addresses to computer or domain names. On the Internet, Web sites usually use the Domain Name System. Once you have registered a domain name for your site, users can type your site's domain name in a browser to contact your site. On an intranet, you can use either DNS or the Windows Internet Name Service (WINS). Your network must have DNS or WINS servers to match IP addresses to host names, and client computers must know the IP address of the DNS or WINS server to contact.

- *WWW Virtual Servers.* If you have registered multiple domain names (such as www.easttech.com and www.easttech.com), you can host multiple domain names on the same computer running IIS. You can use Advanced TCP/IP Configuration settings to assign multiple IP addresses to the network adapter card connected to the Internet. Register a domain name for each IP address on your adapter.

Checking Security

There are several other things you can do at this stage to enhance extranet security. To boost the security of user accounts:

- Review the IUSR_computername account's rights to make sure that there are no unwanted openings.
- Make sure that all passwords conform to your policies and to standard security practices.
- Make sure that strict account management policies are in place and are used effectively.
- Limit the membership of the Administrators group to those whose responsibilities require it.
  Take these steps to make sure that NTFS file security is effective and in place:
- Use Access Control Lists (ACLs), available with NTFS.
- Enable auditing to track file access.
  Limit possible security breaches from running other network services as follows:
- Run only the services you need.
- Consider unbinding unnecessary services from your Internet adapter cards. This can enhance security, but there could be other undesirable effects.
- Check the permissions granted for network sharing.

Other Preliminaries

As with Netscape, most of the work of installing IIS is in the preliminaries. Like scraping and sanding before a paint job, this can be a chore. Also as in painting, though, the better your preparations, the better the finished job will be.

One important first step is to disable any other Internet services. If your server already has another version of File Transfer Protocol (ftp), gopher, or World Wide Web (WWW) services, disable these services before you install IIS. Each service has its own shutdown routine, which, you can hope, is well documented.

During the setup process, a screen will appear asking you whether you want to disable access by the Guest account to your ftp server.

In most cases, the right answer is *Yes*. This is the better choice to protect the contents of your system. If you choose *No* and enable guest access to your server, all existing files, plus any new files, will be available to the Guest account through ftp. You will need to disable access to each file or folder individually to prevent unauthorized access. Disabling ftp access for the Guest account will not affect an IUSR_computername account that is created during setup.

There is one set of privileges that you should make sure you do have. To install the services for IIS, you must be logged on to the server with administrator privileges. You also need administrator privileges to configure the services remotely through Internet Service Manager.

By default, IIS is installed from the compact disk to C:\Winnt\System32\Inetsrv. If you change the default, be sure to enter a full path name, including a drive letter. Relative paths and paths without drive letters can be misinterpreted.

Removing Old Files

When installing a new version of IIS to replace an older version, click on the *Remove All* button to delete the previous version.

The *Remove All* button in Setup removes all IIS program files but does not remove the directory structure or any content or sample files. This setting protects your content files from unintentional deletion. If you want to remove these folders and files after completing the Remove All process, you can delete them manually.

If there are data sources that refer to 16-bit Open Database Connectivity (ODBC) drivers on the system, Setup will detect them and ask you if you want to convert them to 32-bit. If you choose *Yes*, these data sources will be converted to refer to the 32-bit ODBC drivers.

Installing IIS

With all the preliminaries out of the way, the actual installation may seem relatively easy and quick. You can install IIS while installing a copy of NT Server, or you can do it separately.

When installing IIS during Windows_NT Server Setup, a dialog box during the process will give you the option of also installing IIS. At this point:

1. Make sure the *Install IIS* check box is selected and click the *Next* button. The IIS setup program begins.
2. Follow the instructions on the screen.

To install IIS separately, you must first be logged on with administrator privileges. Then follow these steps:

1. Insert the NT Server compact disc into the CD-ROM drive. An Install Internet Information Server icon appears on the NT Server desktop.
2. Double-click on the icon.

Completing the Process

Regardless of how you start the setup process, you soon arrive at a common point: a Welcome dialog box.

1. To continue the installation, click on *OK*. A second dialog box presents a list of options. You can click on *OK* to install them all, or you can remove the check marks from options you do not want to use. Table 7-1 describes the options.

   You can use the Setup program later to add or remove any of these components. The ODBC drivers are required for logging to ODBC files and for enabling ODBC access through the Internet Database Connector (IDC) from the WWW service. If you want to

TABLE 7-1

Server options

This service...	Does this...
Internet Service Manager	Installs the administration program for managing the services
World Wide Web Service	Creates a WWW publishing server
Gopher service	Creates a Gopher publishing server
ftp Service	Creates an ftp publishing server
ODBC drivers and administration	Installs Open Database Connectivity drivers
Sample files	Installs sample HTML files

provide access to databases though the IIS, you need to set up the ODBC drivers and data sources by using the ODBC application in Control Panel.

If you are running an application that uses ODBC, you may see an error message telling you that one or more components are in use. Before continuing, close all applications and services that use ODBC.

2. Select the options and click on *OK*. A new dialog box asks you to select an installation folder.

3. Accept the default folder, or click on *Change Directory* and enter a new folder.

4. Click on *OK*. When prompted, click on *Yes* to create the installation folder. The *Publishing Directories* dialog box opens.

5. Accept the default folders for the publishing services you have installed, or change the folders.

Note: If you already have files ready to publish, you can enter the full path to their current locations, or you can move them into the default folders later. If your files are on a network drive, you should accept the default folder. After setup is completed, use Internet Service Manager to change your default home directory to the path of the network folder that contains your files. Be sure to carefully check the permissions on the network drive. Make sure you will not be leaving any security gaps.

6. Click on *OK*. You are prompted to create several service folders.

7. Accept the default names, or enter new folders, and click on *OK*. The Setup program copies all remaining IIS files to their destinations. If you selected the ODBC Drivers and Administration option, the Install Drivers dialog box opens.

8. Select a driver, and click on *OK*. Setup completes copying files and presents a completion dialog box.

9. Click on *OK* to complete the setup.

Publishing Information

After IIS is installed and running, you are ready to publish information. If your files are in HTML format, publishing them is as easy as adding them to the appropriate home directory.

Example: To make the files available to a Web browser using WWW, place the files in the folder *Wwwroot*.

If you provide files with the gopher or FTP services, you can share these files immediately. Users can navigate through the files much as they do in Windows_NT Explorer or at the command prompt. With gopher, you can customize the way your folders and files appear to browsers; you also can include links to other servers in your files. Ftp can be used to accept files from or send files to Internet users.

Using Redirected Network Drives

The ftp, gopher, and WWW services cannot publish from redirected network drives, that is, from drive letters assigned to network shared folders. To use network drives, you must use the server and share name.

Example: \\Computername\Sharename\Wwwfiles. If you require a user name and password to connect to a network drive, all requests from remote users who want to use that drive must be made with the user name and password you specified, not the anonymous IUSR_computername account or any other account you may have specified.

This feature carries some security risk. Remote users possibly could make changes to a network drive by using the permissions of the user name specified to connect to the network drive.

Home Page

By default, IIS uses a file named *Default.htm>P>* as the home page for the various samples, tools, and demonstrations that come with the product. If the *Wwwroot* folder of your Web server already contains a file named *Default.htm* when you install IIS, your file will remain intact. The default IIS home page appears as */samples/default.htm* instead.

This is a tradeoff. If you retain your own home page, you will not have immediate access to the sample home page IIS provides and to the links it offers when you run IIS. In this case, to display the IIS version of *Default.htm* and its links it provides, use the URL

http://*computername*/samples/default.htm.

If you want to make the IIS version of *Default.htm* your home page, you can rename or move your version of Default.htm to a different folder and then copy Default.htm from the Samples folder.

Testing the Installation

You can test your installation by using a Web browser to display the files in your home directory. To test a Web server connected to the Internet

1. Ensure that your Web server has HTML files in the *Wwwroot* folder.

2. Start Internet Explorer on a computer that has an active connection to the Internet. This computer can be the computer you are testing, but Microsoft recommends that you use a different computer.

3. Type the URL of the home directory of your new Web server.

4. Press *Enter.* The home page will appear on the screen.

   To test a Web server on an intranet

1. Ensure that your computer has an active network connection and that the WINS service or other name-resolution method is functioning.

2. Start Internet Explorer.

3. Type the URL for the home directory of the server. The URL will be *http://,* followed by the Windows Networking name of your server, followed by the path of the file you want to view.

4. Press *enter.* The home page should appear on the screen.

CHAPTER 8

Managing the Server

Server configuration is an ongoing responsibility. Not only must you set up the server initially, but you also will have to make frequent adjustments as people come and go or, less frequently, when you need to change the server's name or port number.

The Netscape Administration Manager and the Microsoft Internet Service Manager are the central management points for configuring and administering their respective servers. In typical Netscape fashion, the Administration Manager uses hypertext markup language (HTML) pages as an administration tool; others use graphic dialog boxes. Not particularly typical of Microsoft, it gives you a choice between the two styles.

HTML documents use jumps, and this is one of the first things you will do in the Administration Manager. It lists the servers installed on your system—you can have more than one—according to the server type, such as Commerce or Communications, and their port numbers. Click on the link for the server you want to configure.

This takes you to the Server Manager for the particular server. A link at the bottom of the page can take you back to the Administration Manager when you are finished.

Once in the Server Manager, you can click on links to configure various parts of the server. Most links go to other forms that configure various aspects of the entire server. Still other forms let you concentrate on individual files and directories. Buttons at the top of the form let you specify the resource you want to configure.

- Server control
- URL configurations
- User databases
- Access control

Server Control

This resource lets you set up and control the technical options of the server itself. These include

- *The server location.* Perhaps you will never have to do this. On the other hand, there may be times when you need to move the server from one directory to another. To do this, you must change the server's location references so that the server can find its binary files. Once you have changed the location listing, you can shut down the server and copy its files and subdirectories to the new location.
- *The server's user account.* This is the account that the server itself uses. You can expand or restrict the server's types of access by assigning it to a different user account that allows the kinds of access you want.
- *Server threads.* When someone contacts the server, the server uses background threads to process the requests. You can specify the minimum number of threads that will be dedicated to the server. These threads become available when the server is started, and they remain idle until needed. The server itself imposes a maximum number of threads; you can set the minimum. The actual number of threads in use will fluctuate between the two figures.
- *Domain Name Service (DNS).* You can identify a server by DNS or by its Internet Protocol (IP) address. Although DNS can be easier to use, it also can exact a performance penalty. If you wish, you can configure the server never to use DNS lookups during normal

operation. At the risk of stating the obvious, you cannot use DNS if the server machine has no entry in a DNS server. The same is true if the machine is not configured to use the DNS lookups. (If you turn off DNS on your server, host names will not appear in your log files, and you cannot restrict host name use.)

- *Starting and stopping the server.* When you change a port number, enable security, or do some other tasks, you must stop and restart the server. You can do this from the Server Manager. When you stop the server, the system shuts down completely. If you want, you can configure the server to restart when the system fires up.

- *Rotating log files.* The server maintains several log files, including lists of access attempts and any errors that occur. Depending on the level of activity, these files can collect substantial amounts of information that soon becomes outdated. Plan to periodically archive the current log files and have the server create new ones. When you rotate the log files, the server renames the existing files and creates new log files with the original names. The archived files are renamed to reflect the date they were rotated.

Using the Server Selector

When you install a Netscape server, you actually install two servers: the Web server and an administration server. The administration server lets you manage one or more servers from a single interface called the *Server Selector.* The administration server must be running before you can use the Server Manager, which is a collection of forms you can use to change options and control the server.

Using the Server Selector, you can manage

- A single Web server
- Multiple Web servers installed on different ports on one machine
- Multiple servers from different domains.

The Server Selector can perform tasks like these:

- Choose a server to configure
- Install another Web server on the machine
- Remove a server from the list of servers you can configure

■ Configure your administration server

■ Start and stop a Web server

Opening the Server Selector

When you install a server under Windows NT, the installation program creates a program group or menu selection with several server management icons. Double-click the *Administer Netscape Servers* icon to start the administration server. If you are using Windows 95 or the NT version 4 interface:

1. Click the *Start* button in the Windows 95 taskbar.

2. Select *[Programs][Netscape Servers][Administer Netscape Servers].* The administration server starts.

3. Type the administration user name and password you specified during installation.

4. The Server Selector opens (Fig. 8-1).

To configure a server using the Server Manager, click on the name of the server you want to configure.

Managing Multiple Servers

If you are using Windows NT, the administration server runs as a service. You can use the Control Panel to start this service directly. Once the administration service is running, you can use any network navigator that has access to the administration server to configure your servers, as described in the following steps.

Remote Access

As long as you have access to client software such as Navigator, you can use the Server Selector from remote locations to configure your Web server. To open the Server Selector from a remote location:

1. Using a browser that supports frames and JavaScript, type the URL for the administration server:

Figure 8-1
The Netscape Server
Selector lets you do
just that: select a
server to administer.

http://[servername].[your_domain].[domain]:[port_number]/

Use the port number for the administration server; this is not the port number for the Web server. You are prompted for a user name and password.

2. Type the administration server user name and password you specified during the installation. The Server Selector opens and lists all the servers installed on this system.

3. Click on the name of the server you want to configure.

Shutting Down the Administration Server

To minimize chances of a break-in, shut down the administration server when you are not actively using it.

1. From the Server Selector, click on *Configure Administration,* and then on the *Shut down your admin server* link.

2. Click on *Shut down the admin server.*

If you are using Windows NT, use the Control Panel Services to shut down the administration server:

1. Open the Control Panel and double-click on the *Services* icon.

2. In list of services, select *Netscape Admin Server.*

3. Click on *Stop.*

4. Confirm that you want to stop the service.

Installing Multiple Web Servers

You can install another Web server on your current machine without going through the installation program. Your new Web server can share its configuration with an existing Web server on your system, or it can use its own separate configuration files.

Each Web server you have installed can run on any TCP/IP port on your system, but you cannot run two Web servers on the same port at the same time.

If your system is not set up to handle multiple IP addresses, you need not enter an IP address for each server. If your system is configured to use more than one IP address, two or more Web servers can share the same port as long as they use different IP addresses. A Netscape Web server software license allows you to have as many Web server instances as you want on one system.

Removing a Server

You can remove a server from your system using the Server Selector.
To remove a server from your machine:

1. Shut down the server by clicking on the *On/Off* icon to the left of the server name in the Server Selector.

2. Click on *Remove a server from this machine* from the Server Selector.

3. Select the server you want to remove.

4. Select whether you want to remove the administration binaries, which include the server's configuration files and the server's binaries.

   Caution: Do not remove the administration binaries if there is more than one server installed.

5. Verify that you want to remove the server and the administration binaries.

6. Click on *OK*.

Configuring the Administration Server

You can use the Server Selector to configure these administration server items:

▪ *Daemon configuration Admin server user* (Windows NT only). This is the user account that can run the administration server. Make sure that this user account has both administrative and log-on as service rights and has a password set. Change the rights using the NT User Manager program. Leaving the password field blank leaves the administration server user unchanged.

▪ *Authentication password* (Windows NT only). This is the password used to authenticate the administration server user. Retype the password in the *Password (again)* field for verification.

▪ *Admin server port.* This is the port number used for server administration; it should be different from the port you used for the HTTP server.

▪ *Activate Secure Sockets Layer (SSL) and specify a key pair and certificate file.* You can configure the administration server to run in secure mode by activating SSL. Before activating SSL for your administration server, you must already have a certificate file and a key pair file. If you already have an SSL-enabled server running, you can use its key pair file for your administration server. If you type a path incorrectly when activating SSL for your administration server, the administration server will not start. In the \admservn\-admin.conf file, change Security to *Off* or edit the key pair file or certificate lines.

■ *Access control authentication.* You can change the user name you enter to verify that you are the server administrator. (This is the name you entered during installation.) This user name is an HTTP user name and can only be used within the server. The server will create the user you specify in this field.

■ *Authentication password.* You also can change the authentication password for the user name you specified. Leaving this password field blank does not remove the authentication password; the password will remain unchanged. The password can be up to eight characters.

■ *Hosts to allow.* You can change which hosts are allowed to administer the server. You can restrict access by host name or IP address. Using host names is more flexible; if a system's IP address changes, you will not need to update the server. Using IP addresses is more reliable; if a DNS lookup fails for the connected client, host name restriction cannot be used.

■ *Options access logging.* The administration server can keep access logs using the common log file format, the format the HTTP server usually uses. You can enter a relative path from your administration server root or a full path to where you want to keep the access logs. Leaving this field blank deactivates access logging.

■ *Detailed logging.* The server can keep a log of all the configuration changes you make. Enter a relative path from your administration server root or a full path to where you want to keep the access logs. Leaving this field blank deactivates detailed logging.

■ *Configuration file backups.* The administration server can keep backups of the Web server's configuration files; backups are made every time the server configuration changes. You can use the Server Manager to view or restore a backup configuration file.

You can start and stop any of the servers listed in the Server Selector by clicking on the *On/Off* icon located to the left of the server's name. If the server is on, you will see a green light under the icon. Click on the icon to turn the server off. To turn the server back on, click on the icon again.

Using the Server Manager

Even the best installations will require periodic maintenance, such as changing the server's name and port number or adding, changing, or

Figure 8-2
The Server Manager
is a configuration
management tool.

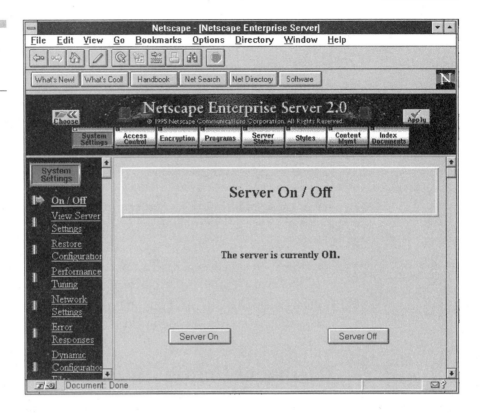

removing users in user database files. The Server Manager is a collection
of forms you can use to change options and control your server.

The Server Selector lists all the servers installed on your system
according to identifier. To use it, open the Server Manager by clicking
on the server name (Fig. 8-2).

You also can use the Server Manager from any remote machine as
long as the system you are working on is one of the hosts that can access
the administration server.

Note: You must save and apply your changes in order for your changes
to take effect. After you submit a form, you get a pointer to a script that
allows you to save and apply your changes.

You can return to the Server Selector by clicking *Choose* in the upper
left corner of the Server Manager.

Use the Server Manager forms to configure the Web server. The server
configuration buttons on the left side of the display let you select various configure settings. Click on one of these links, and a corresponding
form appears in the main window.

Configuring URLs

A URL refers to the server and to various directories and documents within it. If you change the server name and port number or the directories to your documents, you can map the URLs that referred to the old location to look in the new location instead.

Global Settings

There are several functions that can make global changes to all the URLs for your server. These include:

- *Server name.* This is the name clients use when they contact your server, such as *home.easttech.com* or *www.higher.edu.* The name can be a DNS alias if one has been created.

- *Server port number.* This is the TCP port where the server receives its messages from the outside world.

Document Configurations

Document configurations set the way the server deals with URLs:

- *Document root.* This is the root directory of the document storage system. All document paths specified in a URL are relative to the document root. For example, if your root directory is *\user\docs,* some of your documents might be in *\user\docs\policies.* A URL that reads *http://www.easttech.doc/policies/hiring* would actually look in the directory *\user\docs\policies\hiring.* If you decide to change the document root directory, you will need to change only this entry instead of every URL that refers to the old location.

  Caution: Be sure you designate a document root. Otherwise, the server will use your server's root directory, giving visitors direct access to the entire contents of the system.

- *Directory indexing.* When your documents are in several subdirectories it is useful to have an index to these locations. Dress them up and display them to the public. By default, the server looks for a document called *index.html.* You can write an index file and store it under this name, or you can designate another file as the index. If the system has no index file, the browser will create one.

■ *Server home page.* This is the first page visitors see when they call on your site. A URL such as *http://www.easttech.com/* retrieves the designated home page. If you do not specify a home page, the server will create and use an index file.

■ *Default MIME type.* Usually, when the server sends a document to a client, it includes information on the document's type, so the recipient can handle the document accordingly. If the server cannot determine the document type, which sometimes happens, it will report a default type.

URL Mappings

You can map URLs to other servers or directories. To do so, you can specify a prefix to map and the destination to which to map it. When a client uses a mapped URL, the server fills the requests from the mapped server or directory.

URL mappings are used to point to documents in directories outside the document root directory. You will usually keep all your documents in the document root and subordinate directories. At times, though, you may want to refer to a directory outside your document root. You can do this through directory mapping. To map a directory:

1. Choose the URL prefix to map. This is the URL users send to the server when they want documents in the mapped directory. For example, a mapped URL could be *http://www.easttech.com/products/index.html,* where *products/* is the prefix you specify. If you do not specify a drive letter, the server uses the drive it is installed on, so the path is relative to the root directory on that drive.

2. Specify the directory to which to map the URLs. For example, the directory could be called *\sales\tools\products.*

3. If you desire, select a template to specify how this directory should be configured. You can choose an existing template or choose *cgi* to specify that all files in this directory are CGI programs.

Mapping to Another Server

Misdirection is a type of football play. Redirection is more or less like looking for a secondary receiver. Redirection is a way for the server to tell a user that the document requested by a URL is now in a new location. For example, if you move a group of files to another directory or server, you can use redirection to reroute the contact from the original location to the new one. Your clients can still use their accustomed URLs and need not even know about, much less worry about, the change.

Setting up a redirection is very nearly as simple as entering the old location and then they new one. First, enter the prefix of the URL you want to redirect. You could say, for example, that you want to redirect the files that formerly were found under *▲sales/tools*. This could include the files in */sales/tools/products*. Then enter the new location. There are two ways to do this:

■ Name a specific new location, for example *http://www.west2.com/sales/tools/products/hammer.html*. If you take this approach, you must specify everything down to the file name.

■ Use a URL prefix. You can do this if the directory on the new server is the same as in the original site. You may need only enter something like *http://www.west2.com*.

Managing User Databases

User databases are lists of the people who have access to the server. Each individual has a unique user name and password. User databases are your main control on who can gain access to the server documents. The names and passwords appear in a file with the suffix *.pfw.*

The databases are stored in the directory *userdb*. You need not specify the directory when you open a user database; the filename is enough.

Creating a Database

To create a user database:

1. Click on the Server Manager link that creates a user database.

2. Type a name for the database.

3. Select the database type. You can encrypt the name and password listings, or leave the information unencrypted.

4. Enter a password for access to the database; enter it again for confirmation.

5. Click on *Make These Changes*. The server creates the new database and jumps to the page where you can add new names.

To remove a user database:

1. Click on the Server Manager link that removes a user database. A form displays a list of user databases.

2. Select the database you want to remove.

3. Enter the password for the database.

4. Click on *Make These Changes*. The database is removed.

Managing the Database Contents

Adding, editing, and removing user database entries is a continuing management task. In many installations, including extranets, you also can set up registration forms so that authorized clients can enter and change their own information. Either way, the process makes changes in the user database file.

To change a data in the user database using the Server Manager:

1. Click on the link to edit users.

2. Select the database that contains the entry you want to edit.

3. Type the password for the database file.

4. Type the user name of the person whose entry you want to edit.

5. Type the new user name and password.

6. Click on *Make These Changes*. The database accepts the revised information. You can make more changes or return to the Server Manager.

To remove an entry from the database:

1. Click on the link to remove users.

2. Choose the database that contains the name you want to remove.

3. Type the user name you want to delete.

4. Click on *Make These Changes.* You can remove more names or return to the Server Manager.

Controlling Access

You can use the server's access-control features to grant or deny access to all or part of the contents of your server. You can ask that would-be users to present proper authorization, or you can restrict access to those who come from particular hosts or IP addresses.

Authorizing Users

You can use this approach to admit specific individuals such as particular employees of your organization and business partners. You can apply these restrictions to the entire server or to selected directories and files.

A user database contains a list of authorized user names and passwords. When someone wants access to the server, the client application obtains the user name and password. This information is transmitted to the server, which checks it against the contents of the user database. The individual is admitted only if the name-password combination matches a user database entry.

To set up an authorization scheme, select the user database to be used. If you wish, enter a wildcard pattern that describes the database entries you want to accept. If you make no entry, all names in the user database are accepted.

You then must create a realm that describes the resources to which you are controlling access. For example, if you want to restrict access to records of mean times before failure (MTBF), you could name the realm *MTBF Records.*

Considering the Source

The kind of limited access used in an extranet often can be created using host name or IP address restrictions. For example, you could state that only contacts coming from a business partner's address have access to selected server resources. If your server has DNS and is configured to use DNS lookups, you can restrict access by either host name or IP address; otherwise, you can use only the IP addresses.

When a request for a document arrives, the server can identify its source. It then checks the host name with those in the user database. If it fails to find a match, it checks the IP address. If either identification matches, the document is released. Otherwise, the server rejects the attempt.

Managing the Contents

An extranet is nowhere without content. Server installation and configuration—and everything else connected with creating an extranet—exist solely for the purpose of making information available to Web clients. You can use the Server Manager to help manage the server's content. When clients connect with your server, they want access to the HTML pages, graphics, text, sound, video, and other content files you have created. The obvious first step is that they need access to these files.

Setting the Primary Directory

The first step in managing these documents is to set up a primary document directory. You can keep all your server's documents in this central location or its subdirectories. A benefit of maintaining a primary document directory is that you can move your documents to a new directory, perhaps on a different disk, without changing any of your URLs.

The paths specified in the URL are relative to the primary document directory. This means that you can designate the new location as the primary directory, and all the existing URLs that led to the original directory now go to the new location.

For example, if your document directory is *C:\Netscape\Server\docs*, a request such as *http://www.easttech.com/products/info.html* tells the server to look for the file in *C:\Netscape\Server\docs\products\info.html*. If you move all the files and subdirectories to a new directory, you need only change the primary document recorded in the server. There is no need to remap all URLs to the new directory or get the word out to clients that they should look in the new directory.

To set your server's primary document directory:

1. Select *[Content Mgmt][Primary Document Directory]*.

2. If you want to set the primary document directory, type the full path of the directory you want to be the primary document directory.

3. Click on *OK*.

4. Click on *Save and Apply* to confirm your changes.

Additional Document Directories

Sometimes you want to store documents in a directory outside your primary document directory. You can do this by setting additional document directories:

1. Choose the URL prefix to map. This is the URL clients send to the server when they want documents.

2. Specify the directory to which to map those URLs.

To add other document directories:

1. Select *[Content Mgmt][Additional Document Directories]*.

2. Type the URL prefix you want to map.
   Example: A mapped URL could be
   http://www.a.com/products/index.html, where *products/* is the prefix you specify.

3. Type the full path of the directory you want the URL prefix to map to.
   Example: C:\Netscape\Server\docs\sales\tools\products.

4. If you would like, select a configuration style to apply to this directory's configuration.

5. Click on *OK*.

Indexing Directories

Your document directory will no doubt have several subdirectories.
   Example: You might have separate subdirectories for product lists,

customer accounts, contacts, and other classes of information. Each of these might have subdirectories of its own.

In fact, you can have such a complex directory structure that it becomes confusing to your clients, even though this structure is supposed to be invisible. Thus they often can benefit from an index of these directories.

There are two ways the server can do this. It first searches the directory for an index file called *index.html* or *home.html,* which is a file you create and maintain as an overview of the directory's contents. You can specify any file as an index file for a directory. If no index file is found, the server generates an index file for you. This file lists all the files in the document root.

Server Home Page

When external visitors first contact your server, they usually use a URL such as *http://www.a.com/.* When the server receives a request for this document, it returns the designated home page. Usually this file has general information about your Web site and provides links to other documents. Either the server uses the index file you specified in the Index File-names field or you can specify a file to use as the home page.

Default MIME Type

When a document is sent to a client, the server includes a section that identifies the document's type so that the client knows what to do with the document. If the server cannot determine the proper type for the document, it sends a designated default response.

The default is usually text/plain, but it should reflect the most common type of file stored in your server. Some common types include

- Text/plain
- Text/html
- Text/richtext
- Image/tiff
- Image/jpeg
- Image/gif
- Application/x-tar

- Application/postscript
- Application/x-gzip
- Audio/basic

MIME types are stored in a file called *mime.types* in the *[server_root]* *[server_name] [config]* directory. A file in this directory might contain entries like these:

- type = application/x-excel
- exts = xls,xlc,xll,xlm,xlw
- type = application/mspowerpoint exts=ppt,ppz,pps,pot

To configure document preferences:

1. From the Server Manager, select *[Content Mgmt] [Document Prefer-ences]*.

2. Type a new index filename, or add a file to the Index Filenames field.

3. Select the kind of directory indexing you want.

4. Specify whether you want users to see a specified home page or an index file when they access your server.

5. Type the default MIME type you want the server to return if a client calls for a file with an extension that is not in the *mime.types* file.

6. Click on *OK*.

Configuring IIS

As they do in the setup procedures, Netscape and Microsoft present different interface options for configuring their servers.

Netscape uses HTML forms. Microsoft gives you a choice. IIS provides a graphic administration tool called Internet Service Manager that you can use to monitor, configure, and control Internet and extranet services. As an alternative, you can use an HTML-based Internet Service Manager you can run from any Web browser. You can perform the same administration tasks by using either version of Internet Service Manager.

Internet Service Manager is the central location from which you can control all the computers running IIS in your organization. You can run Internet Service Manager on any computer that is running Windows NT Workstation or Server and that is connected through the network to your Web server. With remote administration, you can administer your Web servers from the server computer itself, from a management workstation on the corporate local area network (LAN), or even over the Internet.

Internet Service Manager uses the Windows NT security model, so only validated administrators are allowed to administer services, and administrator passwords are transmitted in encrypted form over the network.

Connecting to a Web Server

You can administer any Internet Information Server on your network using either Internet Service Manager. You can specify a Web server by typing the computer's DNS host name, its IP address, its NetBIOS name, or its computer name.

You also can find all the computers on your network that are running Internet Information Server.

To connect to a Web server:

1. From the *Properties* menu in Internet Service Manager, select *Connect to Server*.

2. In the *Server Name* box, type the Web server's host name, IP address, or NetBIOS name.

To connect by selecting a Web server from a list:

1. From the *Properties* menu in Internet Service Manager, select *Find All Servers*.

2. From the list of servers displayed, double-click on the one you want to connect to.

Selecting a Vuiew

Internet Service Manager lets you select a graphic view of the services running on your servers. You can read a complete report, or you can sort information by the service type or by computer name. Views enable you to tell at a glance which services are running. You also can display or hide services and sort services by their state, such as running, paused, or stopped.

To select a view, from the *View* menu, choose *[Servers View] [Services View]*, or *[Report View]*.

To sort information in a view from the *View* menu, choose *[Sort by Server], [Sort by Service], [Sort by Comment]*, or *[Sort by State]*.

Example: If you sort by state, you can quickly see which services are currently running.

To display or hide services from the *View* menu, choose the service that you want to display or hide (ftp, gopher, or WWW).

Report View

The Report view is the default view. It alphabetically lists the selected computers, with each installed service shown on a separate line. You can click on the column headings to sort the entire list alphabetically. Report view is probably most useful for sites with only one or two computers running IIS.

If you are running other Internet services, such as Network News Transfer Protocol (NNTP) and Simple Mail Transfer Protocol (SMTP), they will be listed in the Report view along with the WWW, ftp, and gopher services.

Figure 8-3 lists the functions of the buttons and icons in Internet Service Manager; you also can use the *Properties* and *View* drop-down menus for the same functions.

Buttons, status bars, and other items in the Report view perform several types of roles. Table 8-1 describes the numbered features in Fig. 8-3.

Servers View

The Servers view displays the services running on network computers, arranged by the computer names. The plus and minus symbols expand or collapse the display. You can double-click on any service name to see its properties.

This view is most useful when you are running multiple Web servers and need to know the status of the services installed on a particular computer.

Figure 8-3
The Report view display.

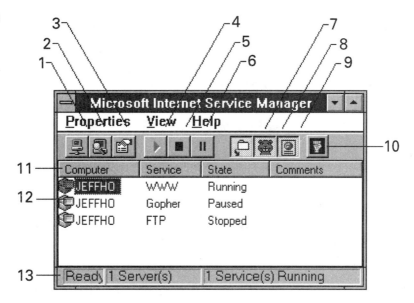

TABLE 8-1

Keys to Fig. 8-3

1. Connects to one specific Web server.

2. Finds all Web servers on the network.

3. Displays property sheets to configure the selected service.

4. Starts the selected service.

5. Stops the selected service.

6. Pauses the selected service.

7. Displays the ftp service in the Internet Service Manager main window.

8. Displays the gopher service in the Internet Service Manager main window.

9. Displays the WWW service in the Internet Service Manager main window.

10. Displays the Key Manager window.

11. Sorts the listings when you click a column heading.

12. Displays the property sheets for a service when you double-click it.

Displays server and service status.

Figure 8-4
The Services view display.

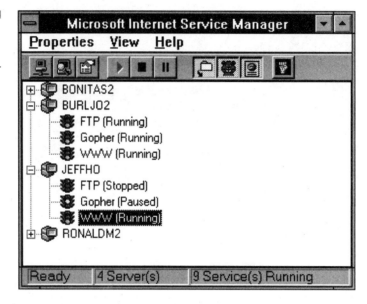

Figure 8-4
The Services view display.

Services View

The Services view (Fig. 8-4) also lists the services on each selected computer, but they are grouped by service name. You may find this view useful when you have widely separated Web services and you want to know which computers are running a particular service.

Configuring and Managing Services

You can use the Internet Service Manager to configure and manage WWW, ftp, and gopher services Internet Service Manager. In an extranet, WWW will undoubtedly be the most commonly used service.

In Internet Service Manager, you can double-click on a computer name or a service name to display its property sheets. Click on the tab at the top of each property sheet to display the properties for that category. After setting the properties for the service, click on *OK* to return to the main Internet Service Manager window.

The Service Property Sheet

Use the Service property sheet to control what kind of authentication is required to gain access to your Web site and to specify the account used for anonymous client requests to log on to the server. Most Internet sites allow anonymous logons.

The Directories Property Sheet

Use the Directories property sheet to specify which directories or folders are available to users and to create a Web site composed of folders on different computers. You also can designate a default document that appears if a remote user does not specify a particular file or you enable directory browsing. If you allow directory browsing, a visitor sees a hypertext listing of the directories and files with which to navigate through your directory structure.

The Logging Property Sheet

Use the Logging property sheet to log service activity. Logging provides valuable information about how a Web server is used. You can send log data to text files or to an Open Database Connectivity (ODBC)-supported database. If you have multiple Web servers or services on a network, you can log all their activity to a single database on any network computer.

By using the Logging property sheet, you also can select the format you want for logging, either Standard format or National Center for Supercomputing Applications (NCSA) Common Log File format.

The Advanced Property Sheet

The Advanced property sheet is a kind of minifirewall. You can use it to prevent certain individuals or groups from gaining access to your Web site. You control access by specifying the IP address of the computers to be granted or denied access.

You also can restrict the maximum amount of traffic on your site by setting a maximum network bandwidth for outbound traffic.

Limiting Network Use

You can keep your Internet traffic within limits by restricting the network bandwidth allowed for all Internet services. Limiting the bandwidth dedicated to IIS patrons is especially useful if your Internet line has multiple purposes. Limiting bandwidth allows other operations such as e-mail and remote logons to use the same line without being slowed down by too much activity on the Web server.

To change bandwidth:

1. In the Internet Service Manager, double-click on any service you want to change.

2. Click on the *Advanced* tab.

3. Select *Limit Network Use by all Internet Services on this computer.*

4. Select the number of kilobytes per second you want to allow for Internet services.

5. Click on *Apply* and then on *OK.*

If the bandwidth being used remains below the level you set, client requests for information are answered. If the bandwidth is close to the value you set, client requests are delayed until the network traffic decreases. Delaying responses enables the Web server to smooth out network traffic volumes without actually denying browser requests. If the bandwidth exceeds the level you set, client requests to read files are rejected and requests to transfer files are delayed until the bandwidth equals or falls below the set value.

Using a Browser

The HTML Internet Service Manager uses HTML forms to perform the same administrative functions as Internet Service Manager. You can use HTML Internet Service Manager with your Web browser to administer IIS over the Internet. To use HTML Internet Service Manager, use your Web browser to open *http://computername/iisadmin.*

To administer any of the services, you must be logged on to a user account that has administrator privileges on the computer being administered. You can use NT's Challenge/Response authentication if you have a browser that can handle it. Otherwise, you are can use only a more limited Basic authentication scheme.

When remotely administering a Web server through a browser, there are three actions you should guard against.

- If your browser supports only Basic authentication, do not turn off Basic authentication while you are administering Internet Information Server. The results would be just about what you might think.

- If you stop a service, you will be disconnected and will not be able to restart it using the HTML Internet Service Manager.

- If you delete the *Iisadmin* virtual directory on the server you are administering, you will be unable to use the HTML Internet Service Manager on that computer.

Using NT Tools

Since IIS is tailored to Windows NT, you can use NT tools to configure, control, and monitor many Internet services. Some of the NT tools duplicate those available in IIS; if you are already familiar with the NT versions, you may feel more comfortable using them.

Control Panel Options

You can use the Control Panel to set several NT systems and options. The Network application in the Control Panel configures your TCP/IP settings, including the IP address, subnet mask, and default gateway. In the *Installed Network Software* window, double-click on *TCP/IP Protocol* to display the TCP/IP Configuration dialog box (Fig. 8-5).

You can use the Services application to stop, start, and pause WWW, gopher, and ftp services. You also can use the Startup button to specify whether a service starts automatically when your server restarts. You also can override the account used by the WWW service, but do not do it without a good reason. Usually, this setting is better handled by the Service property sheet of the Internet Service Manager.

Figure 8-5
Set TCP/IP configurations here.

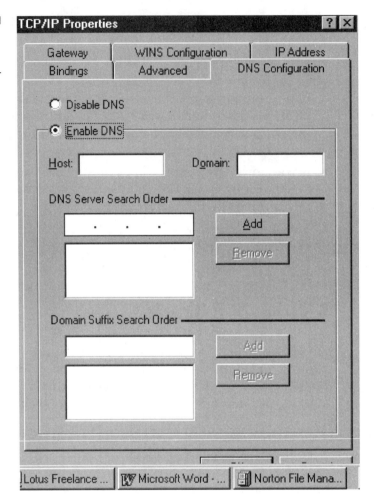

Using Windows Explorer

You can use Windows Explorer to set directory and file permissions on NT File System (NTFS) drives. Open the *Security* dialog box and select the *Permissions* options. This form of file access control is not available on file allocation table (FAT) systems.

Managing Accounts

User Manager for Domains, in the Administrative Tools submenu of the Start menu, is a tool that you can use to manage security for a Windows NT Server computer. With User Manager for Domains you can

- Create and manage user accounts
- Create and manage groups
- Manage the security policies
- Manage servers individually or as members of a domain

Tracking Problems

Event Viewer, in the Administrative Tools submenu of the Start menu, is a tool you can use to monitor events in your system. Event Viewer can notify administrators of critical events by displaying pop-up messages, or by adding event information to log files. The information helps you understand the sequence and types of events that led up to a particular situation.

Monitoring Performance

Another NT tool, the Performance Monitor utility, lets you measure the performance of NT objects such as process, memory allocation, and cache use. Each of these objects comes with a set of counters that provide information about the object. With Performance Monitor, you can create charts that provides snapshots of a service's activity. You also can

- Create logs of the service's performance
- Prepare reports of performance measurements
- Sound alerts when a service counter meets a predetermined threshold

IIS automatically installs Performance Monitor counters for WWW, ftp, and gopher services and for Internet Information Services Global. You can use these counters with the NT performance monitor for real-time measurement of your Internet service use. Table 8-2 lists the counters and their functions.

TABLE 8-2

Performance Monitor Counters

Counter	Description
Aborted Connections	Number of connections disconnected due to error or over-the-limit requests made to gopher service
Bytes Received/sec	Rate at which data bytes are received by service
Bytes Sent/sec	Rate at which data bytes are sent by service
Bytes Total/sec	Rate of total bytes transferred by service (sum of bytes sent and received)
CGI Requests	Total number of Common Gateway Interface (CGI) requests executed since WWW service startup; CGI requests invoke custom gateway executables, which the administrator can install to add forms processing or other dynamic data sources
Connection Attempts	Number of connection attempts made to service
Connections/sec	Rate at which HTTP requests are currently being handled
Connections in Error	Number of connections (since service startup) that resulted in errors when processed by gopher service
Current Anonymous Users	Number of anonymous users currently connected to service
Current CGI Requests	Current number of CGI requests simultaneously being processed by WWW service (includes WAIS index queries)
Current Connections	Current number of connections to the service (sum of anonymous and nonanonymous users)
Current ISAPI Extension Requests	Current ISAPI extension requests simultaneously being processed by WWW service
Current NonAnonymous Users	Number of nonanonymous users currently connected to a specific (WWW, ftp, or gopher) service
Files Received	Total files received by (uploaded to) service since service startup (WWW or ftp only)
Files Sent	Total files sent by (downloaded from) service since service startup
Files Total	Total files transferred by server since service startup (WWW or ftp only)
Get Requests	Total number of HTTP GET requests received by WWW service; GET requests are generally used for basic file retrievals or image maps, although they can be used with forms

TABLE 8-2 Performance Monitor Counters (*Continued*)	Gopher Plus Requests	Total number of Gopher Plus requests received by gopher service since service startup
	Head Requests	Total number of HTTP HEAD requests received by WWW service; HEAD requests typically indicate that a client is querying the state of a document they already have to see if it needs to be refreshed
	ISAPI Extension Requests	Total number of HTTP ISAPI extension requests received by WWW service; ISAPI Extension Requests are custom gateway dynamic-link libraries (DLLs), which the administrator can install to add forms processing or other dynamic data sources
	Logon Attempts	Number of logon attempts made by service since service startup
	Maximum Anonymous Users	Largest number of anonymous users simultaneously connected to service since service startup
	Maximum CGI Requests	Largest number of CGI requests simultaneously processed by the WWW service since service startup
	Maximum Connections	Largest number of users simultaneously connected to service since service startup
	Maximum ISAPI Extension Requests	Largest number of ISAPI extension requests simultaneously processed by WWW service since service startup
	Maximum NonAnonymous Users	Largest number of nonanonymous users simultaneously connected to service since service startup
	Not Found Errors	Number of requests that could not be satisfied by service because requested document could not be found; typically reported as HTTP 404 error code to client
	Other Request Methods	Number of HTTP requests that are not GET, POST, or HEAD methods; may include PUT, DELETE, LINK, or other methods supported by gateway applications
	Post Requests	Number of HTTP requests using POST method; generally used for forms or gateway requests
	Total Anonymous Users	Total number of anonymous users that have ever connected to service since service startup
	Total NonAnonymous Users	Total number of nonanonymous users that have connected to service since service startup

Logging Activity

You can configure each of the IIS services to log information about who has gained access to the server and what information they have obtained. This feature can help you in many ways:

- Improving Web site performance
- Providing a tool for volume and traffic planning
- Tracking content use
- Auditing the effectiveness of security measures

Configuring the Logging Service

When you set up IIS, you can activate and configure the logging service. Later, you can double-click on a service name to display its property sheets. Logging is one of these sheets; you can set the logging specifications for the selected service.

To configure a logging service:

- Determine in which folders the log files will be stored.
- Specify how often logs should be rotated
- Select the tools you want to use to analyze the logging data.
- Determine whether you want the logging data to be saved in a text file or in an ODBC or SQL database.

Logging to a File

To start logging, select the *Enable Logging* check box on the Logging property sheet. To stop logging, remove the check. To store logging activity in a text file, select *Log to File*. You can exercise the options described in Table 8-3.

To log to a file:

1. In Internet Service Manager, double-click on a service to display its property sheets and then click on the *Logging* tab.
2. Select the *Enable Logging* check box.
3. Select *Log to File*.
4. In the *Log Format* box, select the logging format you want.

TABLE 8-3

Log File Options

Use...	To...
Log Format	Selects the logging format you want. Click on the arrow and choose either Standard format or National Center for Supercomputing Applications (NCSA) format.
Automatically open new log	Generates new logs at the specified frequency. If not selected, the same log file will grow indefinitely.
Log file folder	Sets the folder that will contain the log file.
Filename	Shows the filename used for logging. If multiple services are configured to log to the same folder, they will use the same file.

5. To create a new log file when certain conditions are met, select *Automatically open new log.*

When the selected time span or file size is reached, the service will close the log file and create a new one with a different name in the same folder.

Logging to a Database

IIS will send its logging information to a text file unless you specify otherwise. If you install ODBC version 2.5 or later, you can elect to send the information to a database like SQL Server or any other database that uses ODBC.

To prepare for database logging:

1. Create a database table with the fields in Table 8-4.

2. Set up a database on your server and create a data source name (DSN) for the system. You will use this name when setting the logging instructions.

To log to a database:

1. In Internet Service Manager, double-click on the service for which you want to set up the database.

2. Click on the *Logging* tab.

3. Select the *Enable Logging* check box.

4. Select *Log to SQL/ODBC database.*

5. In the *ODBC Data Source Name (DSN)* box, type the system DSN.

6. In the *Table* field, type the name of the table (not the file name of the table).

7. In the *User Name* and *Password* fields, type a user name and password that is valid for the computer that houses the database.

8. Click on *Apply* and then on *OK*.

TABLE 8-4

Log Database
Fields

Field	Type
ClientHost	varchar(255)
user name	varchar(255)
LogTime	datetime
service	varchar(255)
machine	varchar(255)
serverip	varchar(50)
processingtime	int
bytesrecvd	int
bytessent	int
servicestatus	int
win32status	int
operation	varchar(255)

Assembling an Extranet

They say 1995 was the year of the Internet. Then 1996 became the year of the intranet. If logic follows, we may already be observing the year of the extranet.

Thousands of organizations have found that intranets can empower their employees by providing information that is both more timely and less expensive. This empowerment works to the company's competitive advantage. At the same time, it improves morale.

If a better information flow helps employees better serve their employers, it also can improve working relationships outside the organization. This is why, even as intranets were touted as the answer to internal communication problems, they also were becoming extranets: the answer to better communication with suppliers, customers, and other business partners.

When extended beyond the boundaries of a business, an extranet can provide benefits like these:

- Connected computers can share and transfer information between each other.

- These computers can communicate even if their hardware comes from multiple manufacturers and they run a variety of operating systems. This kind of variety is common enough within the typical organization. It is even more common when different companies link up.

- Common applications like e-mail and Web browsers are available for all these diverse platforms.

- Hypertext links make it easier to navigate and retrieve information.

The Browser as Gateway to Information

The Web browser is quickly becoming a widely used interface for retrieving information. Growing numbers of people are getting used to retrieving information in this way. This is not to say browsers are universal or as ubiquitous as some commentators like to say. There will always be people whose attitude toward computers ranges from hesitant to hostile. These are the folks to whom the URL is an intimidating string of gibberish. Come to think of it, a URL *is* an intimidating string of gibberish.

Nevertheless, growing numbers of people are using Web browsers as their primary windows to information. Like most Internet technology, the Web browser knows few boundaries of hardware platform or operating system. And people are becoming increasingly accustomed to using their browsers.

As Windows has become the dominant interface to PC applications, the Web browser has become the equally dominant interface to Internet resources. Although two browser products lead the market at this writing, the differences between them are a little more substantial than the artistry and labeling of their toolbar icons.

Web servers, the lesser known hearts of Web-style communication, have made their own contributions. They have been particularly effective as platforms for a host of supplemental applications like SQL database connections, audio and video services, video conferences, and multithreaded discussion groups. However, the server could do none of these things without the browsers to tap its facilities.

Finding Uses

The brief history of computing has seen plenty of products that turned out to be solutions to which there were no problems. It has proven all too easy to devise the technology and push it out the door, without thinking hard enough about what folks would use it for. Not so with the Web browser.

Management, information services (IS), and corporate departments quickly spotted the value of a new means of communication. They faced the opportunity—and sometimes the necessity—of making effective use of this new information resource. They found that they could set up a basic intranet in a few days and that an extranet takes only a little longer.

Content Really Is King

The first step in developing an extranet is to identify a pilot project, defined by the kind of content it will carry. Although your ultimate goal is an external network, it does not hurt to start with an inside job. Gain some experience and refine your design and methods before you inflict your work on outsiders.

Take a look at the paper flow within your organization. It is no accident that employee handbooks and sales brochures have been among the most popular intranet/extranet projects. They represent publications that can be produced and updated when the need arises, not when the calendar dictates another periodic edition.

What's the Source?

When you have identified a candidate application, take the next step and identify its content. Determine who is responsible for providing the information and getting it into print. Find out in what form the information currently exists. Possibilities include word processing documents, spreadsheets, or Notes or Oracle databases. While making this assessment, also make a judgment about who should turn this content into hypertext markup language (HTML) and where it should be stored in the new system.

One solution that frequently works well: Keep the files on the networked computer of the person responsible for maintaining them.

Your study usually will not stop with a single information source. You will probably find that one class of information has multiple authors, and there are other people out there preparing information that is much like the initial form.

This common situation suggests a team approach to content development. Let individual contributors save their documents in HTML, or have them forwarded in their original form to a desktop publishing technician for conversion. This individual can take care of turning the text into HTML, using a standard template for consistency with the organization's style.

As an alternative, you can have the material sent to an IS manager who can include it in an existing management scheme and can apply security and access control.

Who Gets to See It?

An important question, particularly with an extranet, is to determine exactly who will be authorized to see the material. Information that can be distributed generally can be made available on a Web server or even via e-mail. When people, internal or external, need this information, they can click on the right link and go directly to it. This simplicity and the lack of a need for control make such content an ideal candidate for a first project.

Picking a Pilot

A good candidate for the first project is something that is now delivered on paper, such as an employee handbook or product catalog. Turning these publications into Web pages is relatively easy and inexpensive. Furthermore, you have some benchmarks with which to compare the costs of the two methods.

For example, it is easy to calculate the cost of reproducing a document, whether measured in printers' bills or the cost of copier toner. When you move a publication onto the Web, you also can calculate what will probably be the sharply lower costs of electronic distribution.

The costs of other types of publications will not be quite as easy to compare. Although you can easily compare the costs for a particular report or memo, it can be harder to estimate the aggregate savings for documents that are not produced on a predictable schedule. In addition, the costs are not always as easy to identify. They tend to merge into general staff and supply costs, where they are harder to identify. If you cannot identify the costs, it is all but impossible to estimate the savings.

Measuring Information

However, there are other ways to measure success. Concentrate on quantifying the value of better communication and more access to information. A sales representative could say, "Having up-to-date information helped me gain three new sales last month." Or a customer service person could say, "I was able to double the number of problems I could resolve on the first call."

The object at this point is to establish the value of your pilot project. Once you have done this, it becomes increasingly easier to expand the extranet to other internal functions and, ultimately, to external business partners.

The Extranet Development Process

Setting up a Web-based network is easier than setting up most other kinds of networks. Nevertheless, a well-designed extranet represents a good-sized project for most organizations.

In fact, setting up an extranet is a classic work-flow management process. It has a sequence of operations that you must complete in order. Along the way, you must make many decisions, selecting components and services that include hardware, software, telephone service, and an independent service provider (ISP).

Know Your Applications

Application software is hard to use and harder to adapt to your situation. The applications you plan to use must be identified early in the process. You will have to adapt the network to its application. The network will not readily adapt to you.

For example, if you need access to some sort of legacy computer over a rare form of terminal emulation, there may be only one or two software products available for the purpose. If you have aggressive Java developments under way, remember that not every browser reads Java applets. All your software has compatibility and performance demands that will influence all the other components of your extranet design.

There is one factor in your favor: TCP/IP and its applications are better standardized than most other areas of computers and networks. Nevertheless, there are cases, mostly in DOS and Windows 3, in which applications will run successfully only on particular protocol stacks. Before the advent of the Winsock API, all these applications required custom interfaces with TCP/IP protocol stacks. In practice, it was nearly impossible for an application developer to support multiple IP stacks, so the vendor would stick with one. You were stuck with the same version.

Winsock provides a more standardized interface between network applications and TCP/IP. Furthermore, starting with Winsock 2.0, other protocols, can benefit from the standardized application interface.

Despite problems like these, some applications are easy to choose. Web access, e-mail, news readers, and file transfers are the most common Internet applications, and the best known of these applications work interchangeably with Winsock interfaces from multiple vendors.

Choose Compatibility

The next step may well be the easiest: Choose a compatible TCP/IP protocol stack. In Windows 95, Windows NT, OS/2, and the MacOS System 7, the choices have already been made. These operating systems come with TCP/IP implementations that support broad selections of applications.

If you are among the enduring throng of Windows 3.x users, you have more choices and a harder decision. Windows for Workgroups 3.11 does include TCP/IP. Commercial TCP/IP stacks are produced by a large number of vendors. However, these implementations for older products are 16-bit versions, half as wide as the 32-bit implementations available on more modern operating systems.

Despite this, it might be worthwhile to standardize on a 16-bit product even if you also have Windows 95 or NT, which include 32-bit versions. It is an option to consider if you expect the older Windows to stay around your organization for a while.

On the other hand, standardizing on the past means reducing everyone to least-common-denominator performance. This may not be the best strategy, and for more reasons than inhibited performance. As DOS and Windows 3 products disappear from the market, so does support for them. If your use of these older products is waning anyway, this might be the incentive you need to make a complete break.

Physical Access

The communication lines between yourself and your extranet partners will have a lot to do with both the cost and the performance of the system. Naturally, you can have low cost, high performance, or some combination, but you cannot have a full measure of both.

You have three possible means of access:

- A permanent, direct connection
- A switched circuit dial-up connection
- A shell account with an ISP or on-line service provider

The choice depends largely on the volume of extranet business you expect.

Of course, where an extranet is concerned, the business partner who makes contact with you will be able to select its own type of connection. However, you also have to communicate with the outside world, including your partners, so the choice of an access method affects your system's performance, too.

Direct Contact

A permanent direct connection makes sense for a large organization that expects to have dozens or hundreds of intranet/extranet connections going at the same time. In addition, any application that involves publishing information on the Web should be on a full-time link that does not depend on a dial-up connection.

This connection might be an over-leased line, a frame relay port, Switched Multimegabit Data Service (SMDS), or asynchronous transfer mode (ATM) service. It might even use a wireless or satellite link. When considering these options, look at

- Cost, including the costs of the link and of Internet access to that particular link

- Available capacity

- Quality factors such as the absence of congestion and noise and latency on the link (This last consideration is particularly important if you are considering multimedia applications.)

Frame relay and leased-line connections are the most common choices.

Telephone Connections

A dial-up connection can be as simple as plain old telephone service (POTS). In most parts of the United States, these lines offer free local calling to your ISP's local point of presence (POP). A big downside is the restricted upper limit on modem transmission speeds.

The Integrated Digital Services Network (ISDN) is a rapidly growing alternative for dial-up access. Single phone lines, little different from POTS lines, can transfer data at rates as high as 128 kB/s. The cost of ISDN hardware is dropping rapidly, and the service is widely available.

It still can be a challenge to get a network link working correctly over ISDN. A bad configuration can inadvertently reestablish a connection repeatedly in response to broadcasts or routing table updates. This activity can result in huge telephone bills that arrive without warning.

Switched access has a natural consistency in the small office/home office (SOHO) market. If ISDN service is priced right, a home worker or telecommuter may be able to use a single ISDN line in place of a dedicated fax line and business voice lines.

Modem transmission via POTS has its place, but that place is not in high-volume business service. If you have any significant need for business Web access, even the top speed of a modem connection will seem unusually slow.

Staying in Your Shell

The third access method, the shell account, could be implemented over a dedicated link, but it is more commonly used with dial-up links. Shell accounts do not actually link your computer to the Internet; instead, they allow you to use your computer as a terminal for Internet programs that execute on a host machine elsewhere—typically at the ISP's site.

For example, if you dial into America On-Line or CompuServe as an ordinary terminal, as opposed to logging on as a point-to-point protocol (PPP) client, you will not be able to run your own Web browser. You are just a remote terminal receiving the output of those programs running on the on-line services' systems. If you log on to the service as a PPP client, you can run your own Web browser.

Some ISPs have made shell services available at low prices. A shell client does not need a TCP/IP stack or any version of Windows; it is suitable for people with older computers and slower modems, but in a modern extranet it is not a valid commercial possibility.

Choosing an ISP

Internet service providers (ISPs) range in size from large telecommunications corporations to local PC user groups. The most common is a telecommunications company that offers Internet connectivity for a monthly fee. Small ISPs were the first in this field, but they now face high-powered competition from major telecommunications carriers. Some of the original ISPs have grown up and gone national. Many provide Web server hosting services, Web page design, or specialized technical support. Some also offer centralized multisite billing along with network management and reporting services.

The service, support, and prices you can expect from these companies have been in flux, but in recent months a standard of sorts has been reached at about $20 for no-time-limit service. Some discounts from this plan have become available.

The main thing you want to get from an ISP is clear access to an Internet backbone with a minimum number of hops along the way. *Clear access* means that when you make a connection, the link to the Internet has enough room for you. The communication line should have enough capacity to meet local demand at all but the most exceptional high-use periods.

The ISP is also your administrative contact with the Internet. ISP access can include an IP address for each dial-up account or one or more blocks of IP addresses with high-speed or dedicated accounts.

This is an important service, because IP addresses must be assigned and tracked carefully. It can be catastrophic to assign the same IP address to two devices. This problem can be particularly severe in an extranet, which will link multiple networks inside and outside the organization.

Whenever possible, it is a good idea to assign IP addresses dynamically through facilities like a Dynamic Host Configuration Protocol (DHCP). Even so, routers and servers must have fixed IP addresses.

In addition, you can register your domain name through the ISP. An ISP usually can provide mailbox services and a Usenet news feed. If you do not have a complete class C network or do not want to install your own Domain Name Service (DNS) server, the ISP can do it. Many ISPs provide IP stacks and a suite of Internet applications.

Many ISPs often sell or lease hardware. In any event, it is wise to use equipment that your ISP's support people understand. Often, the best way to ensure this is to use the same brand they use.

For dedicated links, you will need a router with a collision avoidance system (CSU/DSU) either built in or added on. Dial-up connections can take you to your local network over a router or bridge or over a remote access server, which is a bridge or router customized for dial-up connections.

Getting an IP Address

Because IP addressing is so tricky, many of the ISPs that offer dial-up accounts avoid problems by assigning IP addresses dynamically.

If you have a fixed IP address, you must connect to your own IP network; in particular, the network or subnet to which you connect must have a router interface with the same network and subnet as yours. With dynamic IP address assignments, the ISP can parcel out addresses on its subnet, no matter where you are dialing from. Dynamic addresses make it possible for traveling users to dial in to their ISPs in different cities and still connect.

Another major consideration in picking an ISP is the ISP's own business objectives. Some ISPs are clearly focused on the needs of business customers; others concentrate on the types of services SOHO customers might prefer.

If you have unique needs such as special routers, applications, or protocols, look for an ISP that can meet these. Better yet, reexamine your needs to determine whether they truly are needs.

Start Small

When you have found the right software and hardware, test it on a small scale. By now, your research and planning should have helped you narrow things down to a few leading candidates.

As you test applications, take note of the configuration details you will want to set up when you install the applications permanently. For example, you may want to point browser software to the organization's home page. Also use this period to try to head off problems that will otherwise arise when it is time to launch the full-scale network.

Your choice of hardware depends on the type of access you have decided to use and on the level of performance you hope to achieve. There are many midrange routers that can accommodate up to several hundred people using frame relay or leased lines. Prices are in the $2000 to $5000 range. Routers that cost even less than $2000 may be able to handle a few dozen users over 56-kB/s lines, ISDN lines, or even a few asynchronous dial-up lines set up with a modem pool.

The number of users any piece of hardware will support depends on how actively people use the network. People with demanding applications will consume more bandwidth than those who simply read a few e-mail messages.

Keep Track of IP Addresses

If you have decided to maintain a block of IP addresses for your extranet, it is important that you keep close track of them. As discussed earlier, there are many potential problems:

- Duplicate addresses are hard to correct.

- Remote users may not be able to use the same IP addresses they use at their desktops.

- Large-scale moves can present major reconfiguration problems.

In the current versions of NetWare, NT Server, and OS/2 Warp Server, most clients can share a pool of IP addresses that are assigned automatically when they connect to the network. If you have a fair number of mobile or light-duty users, you can "overbook" your IP addresses to use them more efficiently. Remote users and moves will no longer cause trouble because the address is assigned when the user connects.

NetWare users who have no IP stacks on desktop clients can use an IP gateway. Rather than installing a TCP/IP stack on every client, you install a slightly modified Winsock layer on each IPX client. A NetWare Loadable Module (NLM) converts IPX packets to IP packets. Because the applications still talk to Winsock, it makes no difference that IPX transports data between the client and the NetWare server.

Open for Business

If a project has been planned and tested carefully, the actual implementation will be almost an anticlimax. Nevertheless, any installation process that serves large numbers both inside and outside the organization is bound to have some significant problems. With good planning and testing, though, these should be fewer than usual, and they should be easier to solve.

At Your Service

Strictly speaking, an intranet does not need a server. Just put a set of linked HTML files on a shared network directory, and let folks roam through them.

This is not a great option, though, even for an intranet. It might work for a small site where management and access control are not major considerations. It will not work at all in a larger intranet, much less one that is open to selected outsiders. When you extend the intranet to an extranet, you need the combination of flexibility and muscle a good server can offer.

E-mail is one of those advantages. So are news groups, custom applications, and the ability to configure the server to meet your organization's needs. You also can use the important common gateway interface (CGI) programs that provide many benefits over a straight HTML installation:

- CGI applications are available for all the leading operating systems. They complement the Web browsers and other features that readily cross platform and operating system lines. Even if you are running a mix of Windows 95, NT, Unix, and Macintoshes plus some other operating systems, the only thing each individual on the network will need is a browser.

- CGI simplifies the job of managing workstation configurations. Since a CGI script operates on the server, there is only one place you must go to fix bugs or add features. The workstations run the scripts through HTML pages—which also come from the server.

- It is easy to provide security. Generally, the people who use a server-based extranet will not have direct access to applications or files. This reduces the potential for unauthorized access. In addition, the server can maintain a log of all access attempt, successful or unsuccessful.

Significantly, when you retrieve a file from a Web server, you really retrieve only a copy of the file. The server retains the original. Although someone might edit the copy they retrieve, unauthorized individuals can be blocked from access to the server where the root page is stored.

Added Services

Once you set up a server, the horizon of available services begins to expand. Internet e-mail is probably the first possibility to present itself. You can establish intranet and extranet mail using SMTP as the standard protocol for exchanging messages with the mail server. Most browsers have built-in support for SMTP mail service.

Newsgroups are a potentially fruitful extranet application. You, your customers, and your suppliers could conduct extended discussions of design, quality, and other issues. The extended chain that has your business at the center can put the best of these ideas to work, increasing quality and efficiency.

If a particular newsgroup attracts a lot of traffic, you might want to appoint a moderator to keep the discussion on track and divert extraneous material elsewhere. In this way you can avoid the experience of the hospital that set up an extranet for information exchange among medical professionals, only to have the general public take it over for discussions of personal health issues.

There is an important side benefit to supporting news groups: It reduces the amount of e-mail traffic. E-mail overload is a major problem in many organizations. A substantial part of that traffic is simple excess: mail on frivolous subjects, or excessive numbers of copies distributed. It is likely, though, that much of the e-mail traffic in a given organization is devoted to back-and-forth discussion of a particular subject. If you can divert these discussions to news groups, you can reduce the e-mail traffic, even though you may not be getting rid of the excess messaging that causes the real problem.

Also, unlike e-mail, a newsgroup can serve as a permanent information file. Someone who needs to understand traffic that was exchanged in the past simply can look up the old postings. This is a good way for a newcomer to a topic to get oriented.

Hardware Need Not Be Hard

The server hardware that can support an intranet may not be enough to handle an extranet. The choice of a server depends largely on the types of services you expect to run and the volume of traffic you expect. A smaller organization may be able to run an intranet on the same server that handles other file management duties. This probably is not true of an extranet.

It is not a problem of capacity but of security. If the extranet server is on the same machine as your internal database files, those files are at unnecessary risk. Any barrier you could erect between them would be unnecessarily thin. Do not even think about a firewall.

Physical separation is the first and best security. If outsiders break into your extranet, at least they will not have unimpeded direct access to your internal files.

Tuning for Top Performance

The Web is notorious for its sluggishness, and an extranet may not be far behind. There are many things that can delay an extranet transaction. Potential choke points include hardware components, network traffic and bandwidth, and the number and variety of images placed on Web pages.

In a typical installation, a Web service is indirectly connected to an intranet or extranet via a local-area network (LAN). The LAN, in turn, is linked to the outside world via a router and a transmission line. Even with a speedy transmission like T1, other links in this chain could slow things down.

In a corporate setting, a Web server can be placed on a geographically isolated LAN, which eliminates the need for a slower wide-area network (WAN) connection. In an extranet, though, or even in a larger organization's intranet, there probably are several of these separated LANs, connected by remote bridges or routers. Not only can the transmission facilities serve as bottlenecks, but a server's demands on its LAN also can be a factor in overall performance.

Faster May Not Be Speedier

The first response to performance problems might be to install a faster transmission line like a T1 circuit. You may well be disappointed with the results. Do not rush into a solution until you are sure you understand the problem. In the case of a Web server, the first step should be to understand exactly how people use your network. You may find that like a six-lane highway that suddenly narrows to two, the faster circuit may only cause traffic jams somewhere else.

For example, Ethernet and Token Ring are both shared-media LANs. Only one person at a time can use the network. As more users come on line and their level of activity grows, each person must make do with a smaller share of the available bandwidth.

Measuring the effect is a matter of simple arithmetic. If a 10-MB/s Ethernet network must support an average of 20 people at one time, each person gets 1/20th of the bandwidth. Thus, to any one of those 20 people, it is a 500-kB/s transmission.

Obstruction Inside

Another place to look for delays is inside the server. Processor speed, the amount and type of RAM, the type of network adapter, and the disk drive and controller all have an impact on a network's operating speed. Processor, disk, and RAM caches can boost speed; disk fragmentation can reduce it.

A processor's speed is important, of course, but tests show that the use of write-back caches speed performance by letting the processor write data to RAM more quickly. The amount of RAM is a major factor, too. Often, the best and least expensive way to boost performance is to add a few more RAM chips.

Optimizing RAM

The optimal amount of RAM depends heavily on the volume of Web traffic you expect to handle. Estimate the number of Web pages you will have. Examine their relationships, and estimate how many hits on a home page, for example, will lead to hits on other pages.

Try to maintain enough RAM to store the most frequently used pages in RAM. Some small intranets may get by with as little as 16 MB. In a larger network, this may be enough to store only a fraction of the needed pages. The more material you can keep in RAM, the fewer times the system will have to go to the disk. Having the pages in RAM saves some mechanical wear, too.

Keep Your Pages Composed

Web-page composition is another critical performance factor. Nearly everyone who has surfed the Web has had the experience of waiting, seemingly forever, while a graphics-laden page loads into their systems. It is not for nothing the Web has been called the "World Wide Wait."

Not only do the graphic elements require long transmission times, but each requires a separate transmission session. In an HTTP exchange, each graphic object has its own URL, and each must be retrieved and transmitted separately.

Curbing excess graphics may not suit your desire to have a flashy Web site, but it can satisfy your business partners by giving them quick, minimum-delay access to the information that lies behind the graphic display.

Another tip: Of the two types of graphic files transmitted by HTTP, the JPEG format moves more quickly than GIF.

Being Ready for the Future

Even by computer standards, the Internet has been a fast-moving form of technology. In fact, the idea of an extranet was barely thought of just a short time ago. It stands to reason that the extranet of next year, not to mention further down the proverbial road, will be even more different than what we expect.

While it is almost impossible to predict exactly what even the short-term future will bring, it certainly is safe to predict that Web technology will move rapidly into a central position in our computing lives.

One organization that has been making predictions of this kind is Forrester Research (Cambridge, MA). Forrester predicts that the intranet—including the extranet—will overtake even such familiar technology as the network operating system. A Forrester report predicts that by the turn of the century:

■ Intranet/extranet technology will offer five types of standards-based core services: directories, electronic mail, file, print, and network management.

■ Corporate computing gradually will switch from proprietary network operating systems to TCP/IP. As it does so, corporations will get the benefits of better communication, greater competition among suppliers, and lower costs.

■ Major current vendors such as Novell and Microsoft will have to overhaul their products drastically if they are to keep their leading positions.

The Extranet as an Operating System

If the Forrester folks are correct—and it is something to think about—the makers of computer and network operating systems face some future competition from a new quarter. One of the main purposes of an extranet is to build connections with business partners. Another of the expected benefits is to reduce cost. Both are areas where the extranet will have an advantage over operating systems as we currently think of them.

For example, EDI relies on a form of specialized software. An extranet, on the other hand, can handle this and many other functions using inexpensive, standards-based techniques. There is no need to lock yourself into a single product or a single vendor.

An extranet can be an antidote, too, for the complexity of much modern software. For example, many companies find themselves maintaining three or more sets of e-mail directories, each serving a different type of system. With extranet-based e-mail, you can do it all with one directory list.

Four Major Services

Over the remaining years of the century, Forrester predicts, forces like these will turn the extranet into something much more than it now is. It will support applications by providing four core, standards-based services: directories, e-mail, file and print services, and network management. In other words, the extranet will take over the key functions of computer and network operating systems. Should this come to pass as predicted, you will need to be prepared for some fast-paced evolution:

- A single, uniform directory will boost authentication and security. Not only will it replace the multiple directories that now make network administration much more difficult, but it also will make identification easier when deciding who will and will not be given entry to your information resources.

- Universal Internet-style e-mail will be both a cause and a beneficiary of the universal directory. The ability to get rid of multiple directories will inspire corporate managers to adopt a single e-mail system. With the help of the universal directory, the new e-mail system can provide such advanced services as message tracking, return receipts, and synchronized directories that show the same information no matter where you are when you look for information. In addition, the coming messaging systems will be based on HTML and linked messages, and will be able to receive messages from sources as diverse as pagers and databases.

- Today, the use of HTML is limited. In years to come, an enhanced HTTP standard will let authorized users, internal or external, check out, edit, and redeposit files in any format, including those used by the major desktop applications. The source will be a Web server.

- Workgroup printing was an original rationale of the local-area network (LAN). An open printing standard will move advanced printers onto the extranet. These advanced forms will include such services as sending output to paper, to fax or e-mail, or to a digital photograph processor.

- Network management may well represent the vanguard of change. The Simple Network Management Protocol (SNMP) already is an established uniform standard for network management. Coming developments could use Internet technology to administer network addressees and expand the list of supported resources and services.

Implementing the Future

The evolutionary process will not happen overnight, but there is not that much time either. There are some things that you can start doing right away:

- Add a Simple Mail Transfer Protocol (SMTP) gateway to your e-mail system—every e-mail system. A major benefit will be to open this means of communication to external business partners. Support this effort by establishing a consistent, easy-to-use name and address policy.

- Start publishing information on your extranet. Include both internal information such as employee handbooks and external material such as parts lists.

In the longer term, there are further things you can do:

- Upgrade your directories. This can be a gradual process. Start introducing open directories, particularly as you add or upgrade services.

- Convert to Internet-based e-mail in place of the proprietary systems.

- Issue standard digital IDs to all employees. As a certifying authority, you can distribute cryptographic keys that can be used for both access control and encryption. This is the start of establishing access control as your extranet extends both its reach and its abilities.

- Consolidate all directories. Put all personal and network configuration information in a common directory.

10

Building
Your Web Site

The first law of mass communication, including that done by Web, is to remember your audience. You can set up a Web site that has all the things you want to publish, or you can set up a Web site that contains the things your intended audience will want to see. The first approach fattens your ego. The second approach fattens your bank account.

In the case of an extranet, the audience is made up of your business partners and the employees who serve them. Particularly in the case of business partners, they have many other things to do, including visiting other Web sites that might be at least as interesting as yours. You have to design your site to attract these people, get their interest, and then keep it.

This means that both the design and the content should be appropriate to your target audience. A bank's Web site probably would have a much different audience than the site put up by a popular music promoter. The approach neither busines would be appropriate to the other. Compare the home pages of Vanguard mutual funds (Fig. 10-1) and entertainment-minded Home Box Office (HBO) (Fig. 10-2).

Figure 10-1
Vanguard's home
page is designed for
an audience of
investors.

Figure 10-1
Vanguard's home
page is designed for
an audience of
investors.

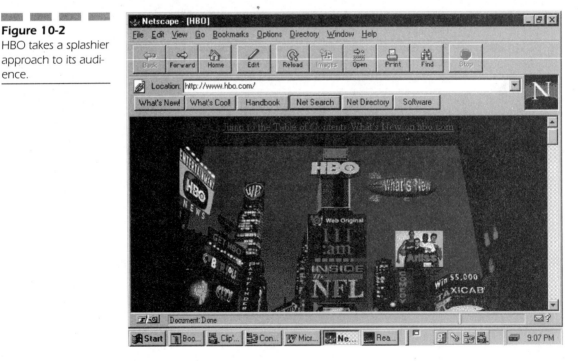

Figure 10-2
HBO takes a splashier
approach to its audi-
ence.

A second rule, just as important as the first, is that content counts. You hear a lot about sending multimedia extravaganzas over the Web or about Web sites that feature plenty of animated graphics. Used well, these can make a site more attractive and useful to its target audience. Used poorly, they will force people to wait while your bandwidth-hungry applications find their way to the browser screen. After all that delay, the audience is likely to decide that the wait was not worth it. The site is all style, with no substance worth waiting for. If this is the effect you have on people, they will leave and never come back. And in the well-known doctrine of customer service, few, if any, will pause to explain why.

Graphics and special effects can do much to enhance a site. They are no substitute for good information, of a kind and in a form that is useful to your audience.

HTML Is Elementary

A home page can have any of several elements, including text, links to other Web pages, images, and possibly sound and video.

Text Is the Easiest

A hypertext markup language (HTML) page is a text document—plain old ASCII text. The text includes codes that tell the browser how to present the material it receives. For example, <P> within a block of text is an instruction to start a new paragraph; </P> denotes the end of a paragraph. Bold type is bracketed by <B> and </B>. HTML has a million of 'em, particularly when you include the extensions added by browser makers to enhance the language and their products.

If you have a grasp of these commands, you can enter them along with the text, using any word process that will produce ASCII text. For all but the most advanced HTML practitioners, though, the easier course is probably to use one of the many HTML editors now on the market. They range from shareware to specialized Web publishing software. Many high-end word processing and desktop publishing programs now provide for HTML output. Whatever the product, the basic approach is this: You enter the text and other elements the way you want them to appear. The editor will provide the HTML codes to make it happen.

Figure 10-3
This is the typeface in
the Word Internet
Assistant...

Heading 1

Heading 2

Heading 3

Body type

Be aware, though, that Web page design is not quite like desktop publishing. Even using the most advanced HTML codes, you may find yourself with less control than you expected over the appearance of the final product. For example, you can specify that a line of text will be a second level headline, tagged with <H2> in HTML parlance. It is the browser, though, that will determine how it wants to display text with an <H2> designation. You can only assume that it will be somewhat smaller than <H1> and somewhat larger than H3. The typeface will be whatever the browser has been set to display. Compare the typefaces assigned to various heading levels used in Microsoft Word with its Internet Assistant in place (Fig. 10-3) and the same file opened in the Netscape Gold Editor (Fig. 10-4). In fact, successive attempts to switch between the two even produced variations in the way the two varied.

Figure 10-4
It could appear like
this in the Netscape
Gold HTML editor.

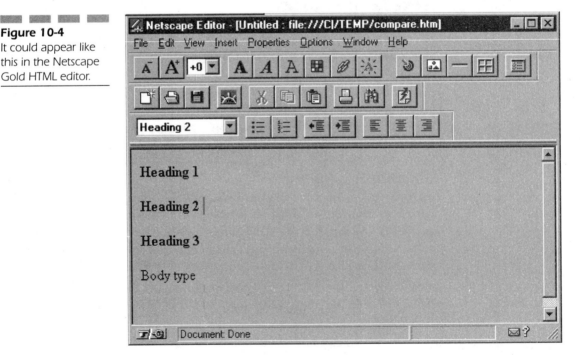

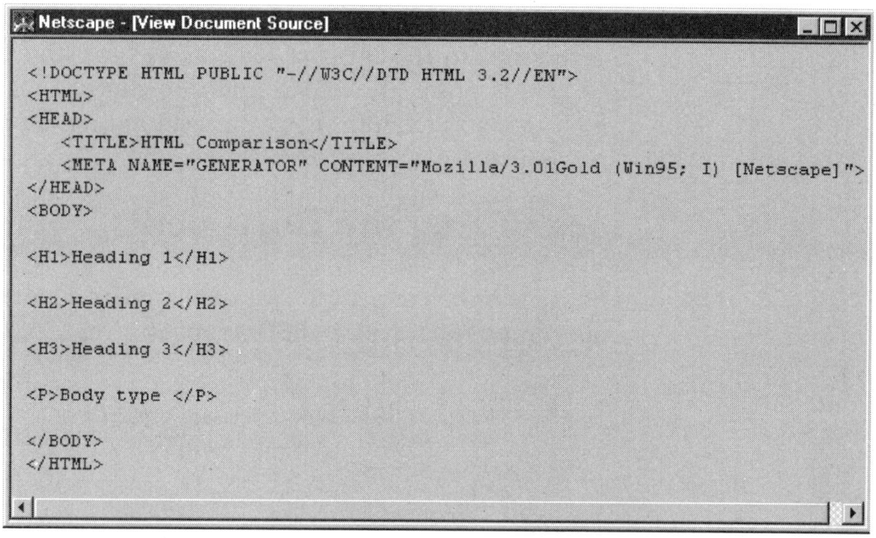

Figure 10-5
The same code works
in both browsers.

```
Netscape - [View Document Source]                                    _ □ ×
<!DOCTYPE HTML PUBLIC "-//W3C//DTD HTML 3.2//EN">
<HTML>
<HEAD>
    <TITLE>HTML Comparison</TITLE>
    <META NAME="GENERATOR" CONTENT="Mozilla/3.01Gold (Win95; I) [Netscape]">
</HEAD>
<BODY>

<H1>Heading 1</H1>

<H2>Heading 2</H2>

<H3>Heading 3</H3>

<P>Body type </P>

</BODY>
</HTML>
```

Both, however, used the same HTML code (Fig. 10-5) There is one difference: Each editor attributes the document to itself. But this is not part
of the displayed text.

Anatomy of a Simple Document

This is a simple document—the HTML equivalent of the program that
displays "Hello, world." Nevertheless, it does help demonstrate how
HTML works.

Elements of HTML

An HTML document is made up of various elements. An *element* is a
block of instructions that tells the browser what to display and how to
display it. These elements are identified by *tags*. Each tag appears within
brackets, for example, <tag>. There are two types of tags: Container tags
come in matched pairs to mark the beginning and ending of an element.

Example: <P> marks the start of a paragraph of normal body text;
</P> marks the end of the paragraph.

In fact, aside from some identifying material at the top, the entire
HTML document is bracketed between <HTML> and </HTML> tags.
They denote the beginning and end of the HTML code the browser is
expected to recognize.

There are also open, or empty, tags. These are tags that issue one-time instructions to the browser, such as a command to draw a horizontal line at this point. In HTML, the line automatically extends across the page. Once you tell it to start, you need not tell it to stop.

Identifying the Document

The <HEAD> element is not displayed in the final output, but it is important to identifying the document:

```
<HEAD>
    <TITLE>Comparison document</TITLE>
    <META NAME = "GENERATOR" CONTENT = "Mozilla/3.01Gold
(Win95; I) [Netscape]">
    </HEAD>
```

Within this element are a couple of other elements. The <TITLE> element identifies the document in places like the Netscape Properties display in Fig. 10-6. The title and other <HEAD> elements can appear in this Properties window.

Where the <BODY> Is Hidden

With these preliminaries out of the way, we can get to the heart of the document, between the <BODY> tags. Here, hidden between the various HTML codes, is the actual text.

Each of the headings has its own pair of beginning and ending tags:

```
<H1>Heading 1 </H1>
<H2>Heading 2 </H2>
<H3>Heading 3 </H3>
```

A paragraph can be assigned to any of several *styles* that govern its formatting and other characteristics. If you are accustomed to assigning style tags in a word processor or desktop publisher, HTML styles are much the same. The drop-down menu in Fig. 10-7 lists some of the styles you might find in an HTML document.

HTML styles do not offer quite as much control over appearance, though, since each browser decides how it will display each particular style. You can be reasonably sure that the Heading 1 style, or <H1>, will be displayed more prominently than <H2>, which should be bigger than <H3>, and so on.

Figure 10-6
The title and other
<HEAD> elements
can appear in this
Properties window.

Figure 10-7
Some of the styles
available in an HTML
document.

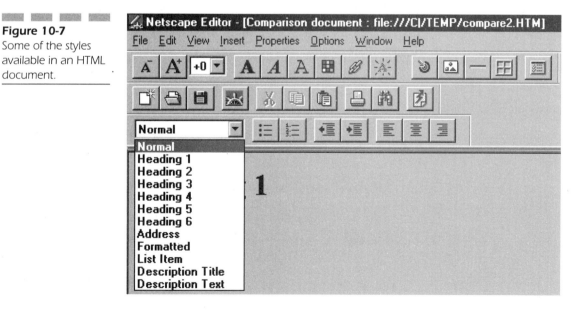

Finally, the body text, with the <P> paragraphs, appears in a style called Normal.

```
<P>Body type </P>.
```

More Realistic—and More Complex

This example page has a couple of things going for it: It loads quickly, and it is easy to explain and understand. Unlike graphics-laden pages that have given the web a well-deserved reputation for sluggishness, these few lines of text would load almost instantly.

Let us look at a page that is slightly more complex: Genentech's introduction to its Access Excellence program. This page (Fig. 10-8) displays a few graphics, but it is mostly text. All in all, it is a tasteful presentation to its intended audience of educators.

The HTML code for this page is considerably more complex (Fig. 10-9). It features various forms of text, plus some graphics. It is not necessary that you understand all the tags in this example. It would take a full book in its own right to explain HTML in detail. The purpose here is to

Figure 10-8
This page sports a few graphics and a large amount of text.

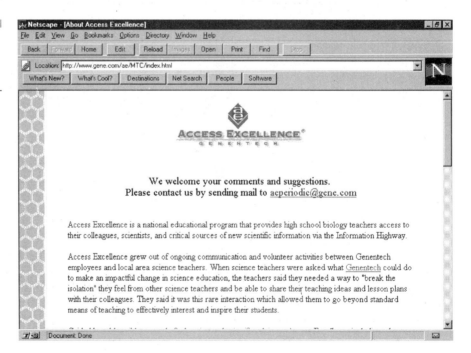

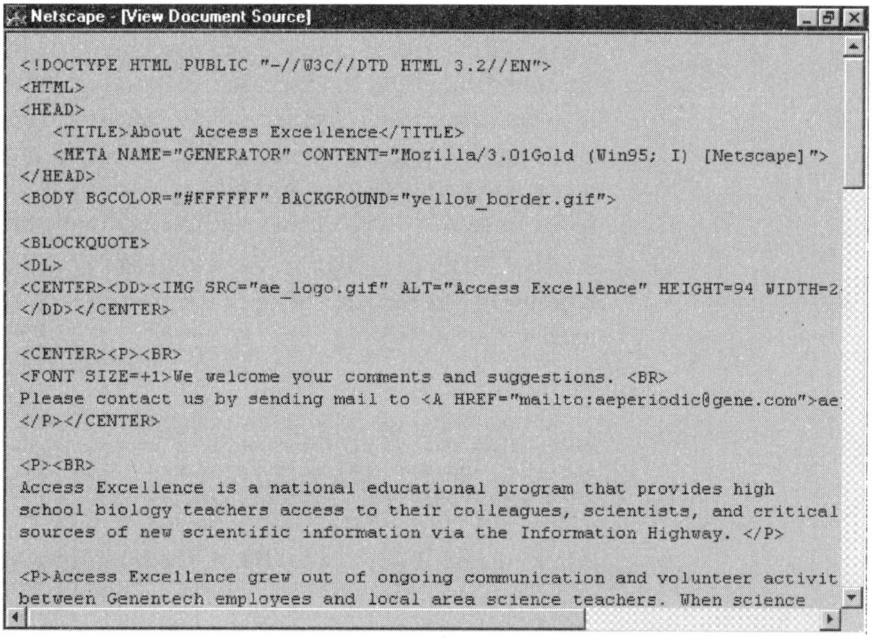

Figure 10-9
HTML code for the Access Excellence page.

```
Netscape - [View Document Source]
<!DOCTYPE HTML PUBLIC "-//W3C//DTD HTML 3.2//EN">
<HTML>
<HEAD>
    <TITLE>About Access Excellence</TITLE>
    <META NAME="GENERATOR" CONTENT="Mozilla/3.01Gold (Win95; I) [Netscape]">
</HEAD>
<BODY BGCOLOR="#FFFFFF" BACKGROUND="yellow_border.gif">

<BLOCKQUOTE>
<DL>
<CENTER><DD><IMG SRC="ae_logo.gif" ALT="Access Excellence" HEIGHT=94 WIDTH=2
</DD></CENTER>

<CENTER><P><BR>
<FONT SIZE=+1>We welcome your comments and suggestions. <BR>
Please contact us by sending mail to <A HREF="mailto:aeperiodic@gene.com">ae
</P></CENTER>

<P><BR>
Access Excellence is a national educational program that provides high
school biology teachers access to their colleagues, scientists, and critical
sources of new scientific information via the Information Highway. </P>

<P>Access Excellence grew out of ongoing communication and volunteer activit
between Genentech employees and local area science teachers. When science
```

Figure 10-10
An example of formatted text.

We welcome your comments and suggestions.
Please contact us by sending mail to aeperiodic@gene.com

demonstrate what you can do and to give you some understanding of how it happens.

For example, this line produces the text in Fig. 10-10.

```
<CENTER><P><BR>
<FONT SIZE = +1>We welcome your comments and suggestions.
<BR>
    Please contact us by sending mail to <A
HREF = "mailto:aeperiodic@gene.com">aeperiodic@gene.com</A></F
ONT><BR>
    </P></CENTER>
```

Some of the tags in this section and their results are

■ <**CENTER**>: Centers the text between the margins

■ <**BR**>: An empty tag calling for a line break.

■ <**FONT SIZE=+1**>: Increase the font size of this paragraph.

- **<A HREF="mailto:aeperiodic@gene.com">**. This is a long string with some advanced elements. The underlined part of the paragraph is a link. In this case, it happens to be an e-mail link. This is so because this tag identifies it as such, stating that when someone clicks on the link, they will generate an e-mail message to the person at the stated address. You will notice that the address appears twice, once within the *mailto* tag and again as part of the text.

- **</A></FONT>
</P></CENTER>**: These tags, which begin with slashes, are the opposite numbers of the container tags used at the beginning.

```
<P><BR>
Access Excellence is a national educational program that pro-
vides high school biology teachers access to their colleagues, sci-
entists, and critical sources of new scientific information via the
Information Highway. </P>
```

After another line break **
**, the body text begins.

An Optional Graphic

Above this text is this interesting material:

```
<IMG SRC="ae_logo.gif" ALT="Access Excellence" HEIGHT=94
WIDTH=245>
</DD></CENTER>
```

Here, the tags call for an image with the file name *ae_logo.gif*. The image is to appear in the stated dimensions, measured in pixels, or picture elements—the dots that make up your screen.

Believe it or not, some early Web browsers could not handle graphics. Today, there are people who speed up the Web by loading pages in text-only form. For these folks, the tag provides an alternative to the graphic image. If there is not a graphic, the text phrase *Access Excellence* will appear instead.

The Information You Publish

All this effort, of course, is directed at one ultimate objective: getting information to your employees and business partners and perhaps to other folks as well. Although the Web runs on HTML, you can use just about any text editor, from a desktop publisher to the Windows Notebook, to prepare the files. In any of these, you can type the HTML tags and other coding information that turns your text into a vibrant Web site.

You will do better, however, if you do not try to do all the coding yourself.

A High-Graphics Site

The Bank One home page (Fig. 10-11) is made up mainly of several rows of small pictures. The HTML code for one of these pictures is

```
<TD align="center"><IMG SRC="entertainment.gif" ALT="Ent.
Sports Partners" HEIGHT=35 WIDTH=110 ALIGN=CENTER></TD>
```

As with the illustration in the preceding example, the code calls for either the picture or alternative text. Pity the poor person who had to write all that code, for every picture in the site. Fortunately, nobody had

Figure 10-11
You do not have to know the code—just the editor.

Figure 10-12
How to really write
HTML.

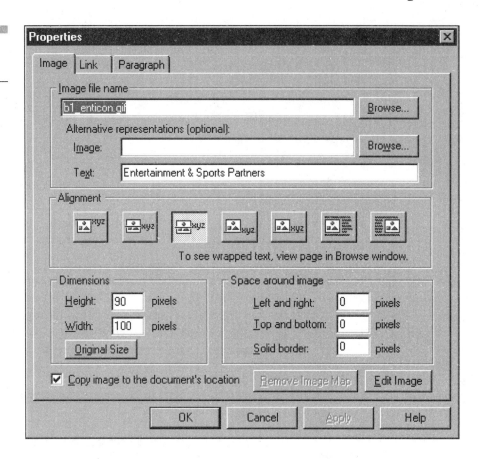

to. No doubt a Web editor did it. Figure 10-12 shows how the Netscape Gold Editor opens a window to let you specify the size, positioning, and other details of each picture. Why write code when you can fill in a form?

In this case, the near row and column alignment of the pictures was created by setting up a table. The HTML code for the table looks like this:

```
<CENTER><TABLE CELLSPACING=0 CELLPADDING=0 WIDTH="600" >
```

The easy way to set up a table looks like Fig. 10-13.

This is why this book does not pretend to be even a decent primer on HTML. It helps—and can help very greatly—to understand how to use HTML to control the appearance and content of a Web site. It can help even more, though, to become familiar with a modern HTML editor.

Figure 10-13
Setting up a table the
easy way.

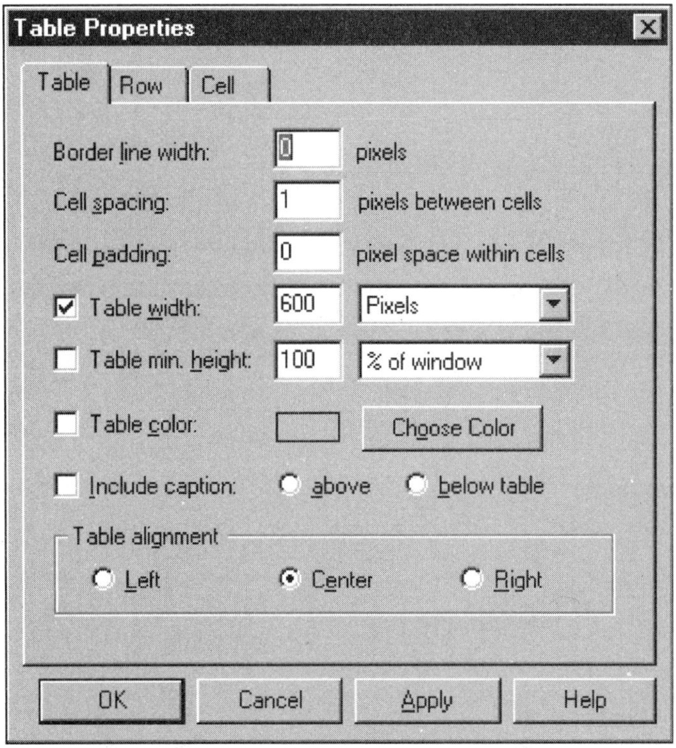

The Gold version of the Netscape browser comes with the editor that
was used for the preceding screen shots. There are many alternatives.
With a good tool at hand, you can focus less on learning all the fine
details of HTML programming and concern yourself with something
that really is more important: creating a rich and richly rewarding Web
site.

Text is not Everything

You can have pictures on your Web site, of course. In most cases, this is
probably a necessity to keep the page from declining into boredom.
And yes, you can relieve the boredom of waiting for the page to load by
playing some sound. The home page for the Microsoft Internet Explorer
plays the mindless, repetitive type of music you might associate with
some of the less imaginative computer games. Other sites do better. Full-
motion video is also a possibility, but at this point it is only a remote
possibility. Many folks do not have the bandwidth to handle it; your

graphics could well end up on someone's browser looking one notch worse than a low-grade silent movie.

Links and CGI

The heart of HTML is its ability to build links to other pages and to other parts of the same page. Consider the very simple page in Fig. 10-14.

It consists mainly of some simple formatted text and some graphic lines to replace the homely horizontal rules of HTML. Like any good home page, however, it also includes links to other pages. The HTML code for these links is

```
<DL>
<DD><IMG SRC="bullet1.gif" HEIGHT=7 WIDTH=5> <A
HREF="http://westtech.com/products/">Products
  and services<BR>
  <IMG SRC="bullet1.gif" HEIGHT=7 WIDTH=5></A> <A
HREF="http://westtech.com/info/">Corporate
  Information<BR>
  <IMG SRC="bullet1.gif" HEIGHT=7 WIDTH=5></A> <A
HREF="http://www.westtech.com/pr">Press
  room</A><BR>
  </DD>
  </DL>
```

Figure 10-14
A simple home page.

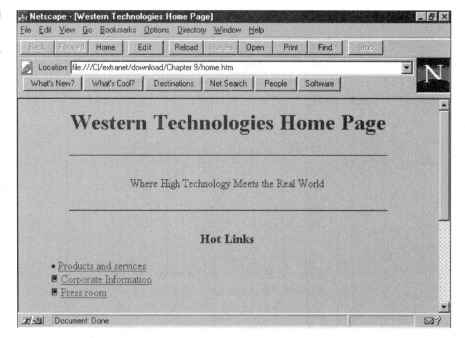

Although Web contents are displayed in pages, you cannot turn these pages like you can in a conventional book. On the other hand, you can go directly to nearly any page you like, as long as your know where to find it. The book's index can help you find the number of the page you want to find. In HTML, links take you to other, related pages.

In this case, there are links to four common types of corporate Web pages: a listing of products and services, a few pages of information on the corporation and its leaders, and a collection of recent press releases.

Actively Interactive

HTML is a programming language of sorts: It tells the browser what to do with your stuff. Sometimes, though, you need something more versatile. One of the more versatile things you may find useful is the Common Gateway Interface (CGI).

One of the keys to the Web has been its interactive nature. By and large, people do not just read the stuff they find there. They interact with it. Links are one way to provide interactivity. They give the individual the power to jump to whatever page seems interesting or worthwhile. Even so, HTML is a read-only type of process. Jumps just give you a choice of what to read. CGI lets you write as well as read. You can enter your own information, or information requests, into the system.

There are a growing number of ways to do this. Java and its companion JavaScript are major examples. Nevertheless, CGI has an established place in the Web. Whenever you fill in a form on a Web page, you probably are using CGI.

CGI Assists in a Search

A typical search program is an example. You enter the text you want to find and, perhaps, some description of the place you expect to find it: the whole Web down to one section of a corporate Web site. Thus you type in the words and click on the location. You click on the *Send* button. Then GCI takes over.

CGI probably does not have to work for very long. It does not actually conduct the search. It triggers the program that conducts the search. When the results are in, the server typically inserts the information, in the form of HTML statements, into the waiting blanks of a prepared results-reporting page.

How It Works

The Web's HTTP servers are designed primarily to serve up HTML documents. CGI files are programs, not documents. The Web server needs some way to identify them. The programs' location is a key. Most Web servers store CGI programs in a special directory, often named *cgi-bin*. The Web server knows that files stored in the cgi-bin directory are to be executed, not just dispatched to the browser for display.

CGI programs can be written in any of several languages, including DOS batch files, BASIC, C, and scripting languages such as Perl. The CGI program must be activated at the proper time and pass along any necessary information generated by a user or the operating environment. The CGI program then processes whatever data that happens to be. Once the program accomplishes this process, it must return some output to the user via the user's Web browser. This means that the program has to turn the output into an HTML document.

Staying in Good Form

The first requirement is that you get the data to the CGI program. This is usually the job of an HTML form. The form can have one of more text input fields, and perhaps some multiple choice fields. Drop-down selection lists are also common on HTML forms. For example, when you want to download a product from the Netscape Web site, you can open various lists and select the product, identify your operating system, and enter other specifications for the program you want. One necessary component is a button on which to click to submit the completed form. CGI can do nothing with the information until it is received. There also may be a *Clear* button to erase the current entries and start over.

The HTML tag to designate a form is, logically enough, <FORM>. <FORM> and its counterpart, </FORM>, begin and end the form section.

When you create a form, you also describe the script it uses and the method it will use. To do this, it uses two attributes:

▪ The ACTION attribute points the form to a URL that will accept and process the forms information. If you do not specify an action, the information will return to the same URL it came from.

▪ The METHOD attribute tells the form how to send its information back to the script. The more common method is POST, which sends all the information from the form separately from the URL. The other option is GET, which tacks the information from the form to the end of the URL. Whichever method you choose, make sure the CGI program is prepared to accept it.

With these attributes included, a FORM statement might look like this:

```
<FORM ACTION="/cgi-bin/product_script" METHOD="POST">
```

This tells the browser to run the CGI script product_script and to return the results using POST.

Prompting for Input

A line like this is the signal to make an entry:

```
<INPUT TYPE="TEXT" NAME="PRODUCT" SIZE="15" MAXLENGTH="30">
```

The Text input type tells the browser that this is a text field, as opposed to other kinds of data. The name, which you can assign, suggests that the person who encounters this field should enter a product name. The remaining entries mean that the browser will display a text box 15 characters long and that the entry is limited to a maximum of 30 characters. The last 15 characters, if present, will scroll across the box.

Many forms also have radio buttons and check boxes. These are similar: Each has spots you can select, much like answering a multiple choice question. The most visible difference is that the radio buttons are round and the check boxes are square. The most important difference is that you can select only one item in a list of radio buttons. You can select as many check boxes as you like. Consider an HTML entry like this:

```
<INPUT TYPE="RADIO" NAME="PLATFORM" VALUE="Windows NT">
Windows NT>
```

Here, we have a radio button that, when checked, associates the name PLATFORM with the value Windows NT. All the radio buttons in this series will have the same name; each will have a different value, such as Unix or Windows 95. Because all these radio buttons have a common name, when you select one, any other selection in the group is canceled.

Looking Good on Screen

Many people who use desktop publishers and word processors are accustomed to applying style tags to describe how a particular element should look. Since each browser has its own idea of how to present things, using HTML tags is a little different: do not try to use them to describe how things should look. Use them to identify what things are. Since each browser reflects its maker's ideas of how things ought to be, each browser will respond somewhat differently to the tags it encounters in an HTML document. There are ways to force browsers to display your favorite typeface or size, but most carry extreme performance penalties ordinary customers may not be willing to endure. If you want to emphasize a block of text, for example, it is better to assign an <EMPHASIZED> tag than to specify that it appear in bold or italic type.

Using tags for identification has a specific benefit: If a browser recognizes the tag, it will act on it more or less appropriately. You can count on the browsers in common use to display your text in an attractive, readable form. And if you limit your use of nonstandard HTML, you can be assured that nearly any browser will respond to your tags in an appropriate fashion.

This does not mean that every browser will display your work in the spectacular fashion with which you designed it. Accept the idea that a browser will make your work look passably decent or even better.

It also pays to check your finished pages on all the browsers in common use. This will help prevent unpleasant surprises.

On Good Authority

Journalist Pierre Salinger was embarrassed not long ago by something he picked up on the Internet. For some time, the Internet had been circulating a paper that stated that the Pan Am flight that went down off Long Island had been hit by a Navy practice missile. Salinger picked it up and widely proclaimed it as factual, when it was really just a rumor making the rounds of cyberspace back fences.

Beyond the red face of a public figure who jumped to a conclusion is a serious problem: the credibility of information you find on the Internet. Much of the information that makes the rounds is crude and unsubstantiated, circulated by people with axes to grind or who get careless or simply do not care. Another class consists of obsolete information that has not been brought up to date. It is easy to be fooled by this type of pseudoinformation. For all the scorn heaped on the established news media, they do have an extensive process of checking information to make sure that it is accurate and timely. Just about anyone can post anything on the Internet. The usual controls are absent.

This means that self-control is essential. It is one thing to be fooled by inaccurate information. It is much worse to circulate such stuff yourself. You must take personal responsibility for making sure that the information you post is accurate and that it stays that way.

To this end, nothing replaces basic self-discipline. Some folks are not really very good at this. There are some other things you can do as well to help extranet clients assess the value and credibility of what they find on your site. These measures supplement self-discipline; they do not replace it:

- Include in each document the date that it was last modified. This helps people screen outdated information.

- Give each document a link to the home page. People can follow the link to examine the document's source. If your site contains the credentials of the people responsible for creating the page, provide links to these biographies as well.

- Provide a MAILTO: link to an e-mail address where people can send their comments, questions, and, sometimes, corrections.

Keep it Organized

Visitors to an extranet are looking for information, not excitement—at least this is the usual case. While the site should look good, the real objective is to provide easy access to information. Therefore, along with the good looks it inherited from you, the site also should display the workings of an organized mind.

One sign of good organization is that your links are meaningful. A good link should flow naturally into the text. This link does not:

```
The bibliography lists several other sources of
information. Click here to see the bibliography.
```

Try this instead:

```
The bibliography lists several other sources of
information.
```

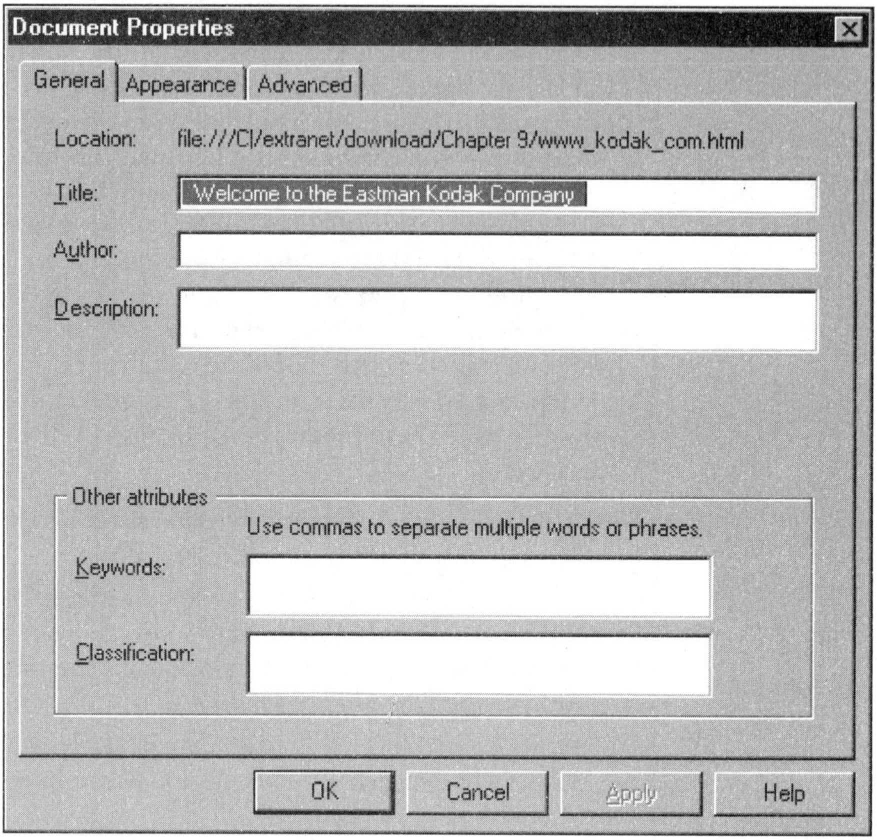

Figure 10-15
Applying a title to a
document.

Remember, too, that the terms you choose for a link should help readers understand what they can expect to find there. A suggestion: When
you create an HTML document, you can give it a title separate from a
headline or other contents. Figure 10-15 shows how to display or apply a
title in the Netscape Gold editor. The page known in URL as
www.kodak.com appears under the title, "Welcome to the Eastman
Kodak Company." The HTML code looks like this:

```
<TITLE>  Welcome to the Eastman Kodak Company  </TITLE>
```

Applying a descriptive title has two benefits:

- You can use the title as a link. If you title a document "Eastern
  Technologies Product Catalog," you also can use a link that says: See
  the Eastern Technologies Product Catalog.

Figure 10-16
Kodak's home page displays a large graphic, but its pages are planned to minimize loading time.

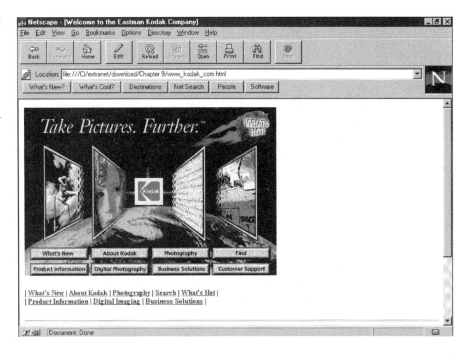

■ You make it easier for business partners and prospects to find your site again. If they use their browsers to set bookmarks for your site, which you certainly hope they do, the bookmark will display your title rather than a semimeaningless URL. When they decide to revisit your site, the title will be right there, in words they should be able to understand. As a bonus, the title in Fig. 10-15 also appears in the title bar of the page display in Fig. 10-16.

Getting a Head

HTML includes a sequence of heading styles, <H1>, <H2>, <H3>, and so on. The Heading 1, or H1, style is intended for entries on the magnitude of document or chapter titles. Each subsequent heading level is usually shown a little smaller or with less emphasis. Proper use of these headings can help you organize your site in an easy-to-follow outline form.

These rules will help you use these styles to best effect:

■ Use the heading styles in order. If you use <H1> as the page title, make the next heading <H2>, not <H3>.

- Use the heading styles only for legitimate headings and subheadings. Do not assign a heading style to a paragraph just because it produces the particular typeface and style you want to use. Remember, different browsers have different ways of presenting things. What looks great in your browser might look totally out of place in another. What you can trust most browsers to do is to present the heading styles in a manner that clearly indicates the relation of each numbered style to the others.

- Do not add bold, italic, or emphasis to a heading style. Again, trust the browsers to display the headings in an appropriate manner, even if it is not exactly what you had in mind.

Provide the Right Emphasis

Like the standard generalized markup language (SGML) of which it is a part, HTML is intended as a language that describes the contents of documents. Few HTML tags are intended to give you direct control over how the page will look. The major exceptions are in character highlighting.

There are two types of character highlighting styles: physical and logical. When you use a physical style, you directly specify that the text will appear in italics or boldface. True to HTML principles, logical styles describe the purpose of the text, such as "emphasis," "citation," or "strong."

As a general rule, use logical styles. Again, you must trust individual browsers to display different kinds of text in appropriate ways. When you use physical styles, you are trying to second-guess the browsers. This can be a mistake. For example, when you specify italic type but there are a few browsers that do not display text in italics, you can only guess what a customer with one of these browsers will see, instead of the display you intended. It is better to describe your text in logical styles and then to allow the browsers to give appropriate display characteristics to the selected styles.

Using Graphics

You would think a company as visually oriented as Eastman Kodak would put up a Web site loaded with graphics. Well, yes and no. Kodak's home page (Fig. 10-16) features a large image-mapped graphic with links assigned to various parts of the picture. This is the kind of page you might expect from a company that employs 17 graphic artists to create and maintain its Web site.

Nevertheless, Kodak has published strict guidelines for Web page construction. Among them:

- Any graphic must load within 10 seconds, even on a 14.4-kB/s modem, the slowest in general Internet use.
- No page can consume more than 60 kb.

Both requirements have the same objective: to minimize the amount of time a patron must spend waiting for a Kodak Web page to load.

This will become important to Kodak customers and dealers, because the company is developing its Web site to include extranet functions. An early goal has been to integrate the Web site with an Oracle database using Oracle's Universal WebServer. This will make information in the database available to trading partners via the Web. This information includes product catalogs and environmental reports, previously available via GCI scripts. The plan includes the use of Oracle certificate servers to verify the identities of authorized business partners.

User-friendly Images

Downloading speed is only one way that the way you use images can attract or repel business partners. Another problem is the use of many small in-line images when text tags would do much the same job. Web-page authors interested in typographic control often try to use small in-line images to present favored typefaces, colored bullets, more attractive rules, and other custom typographic elements.

Many small images are nearly as great a problem as a few large ones. Each smaller image requires less time to load, of course, but there is a tradeoff: Each new image file requires that the browser establish a new contact with the server that is supplying the images. Sometimes it may take longer to make the connection than to transmit the image itself.

Image size can be another problem. At SOHO modem speeds, a large image can take an eternity to load. Those who are impatient but truly dedicated may opt for the text-only version of your home page. This deprives both parties of whatever effects the images were supposed to create.

You can at least provide your text-only patrons with some appropriate text to be displayed in place of the images. You then can at least use the text to get across some of the information you are trying to communicate.

Figure 10-17

An editor's view of the
big Kodak graphic.

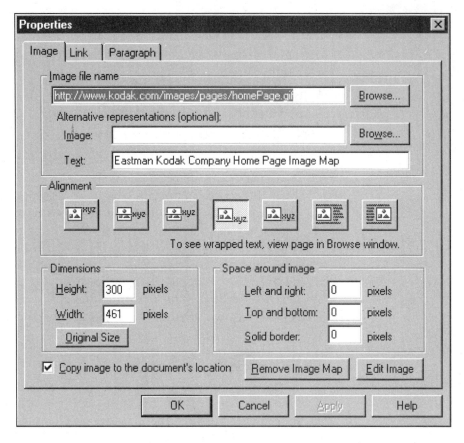

You can do this by adding an ALT attribute to your HTML image specifications. Take this example:

```
<IMG SRC="whatsnew.gif" ALT="What's New">
```

This is the basic command to insert a picture, in this case named *whatsnew.gif*. However, it also specifies a text statement that will appear when the picture does not. As the ALT statement specifies, the text reads, "What's New."

This is another instance where the right HTML editor can make it easy to get the right code into the document. Figure 10-17 shows the properties of the big graphic on the Kodak home page, including a text alternative.

There are other ways as well to make images easier on your patrons:

- Use Joint Photographic Experts Group (JPEG) images instead of Graphic Interchange Format (GIF) whenever possible. These are the two types of image files HTML accepts. In general, JPEG images load faster.

- Use fewer colors. Full-color-scale images like the Kodak home page deserve full-blown color treatment. However, if you are presenting a two- or three-color logo, it makes sense to use fewer colors. This reduces file size and speeds loading.

- Your pages may have a common graphic element such as the corporate logo in every upper left corner. You can do this with a single image, with each page carrying a reference to the same image. After all, it makes little sense to manage 24 duplicate images for 24 pages. Furthermore, browsers create local caches of the pages and images they have loaded recently. When a reader goes to a new page, the same image often will be loaded from the local cache rather than being retransmitted over the network. The image will load much more quickly.

Aligning Images

Figure 10-17 also shows how to use alignment characteristics. Across the middle of this dialog box is a group of small icons from which you can specify the alignment of the image relative to its accompanying text. You also can determine whether the text will wrap around the graphic and, if so, how.

You can use tables for an even more precise alignment. The Bank One home page back in Fig. 10-11 uses several midsized graphics arranged in a grid pattern. Some of the code that generates this table and inserts the images is shown in Fig. 10-18.

Figure 10-18
The HTML code for
images in a table.

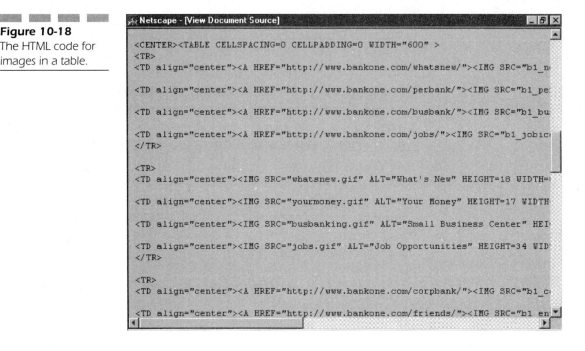

```
Netscape - [View Document Source]                                    _ □ X

<CENTER><TABLE CELLSPACING=0 CELLPADDING=0 WIDTH="600" >
<TR>
<TD align="center"><A HREF="http://www.bankone.com/whatsnew/"><IMG SRC="b1_n

<TD align="center"><A HREF="http://www.bankone.com/perbank/"><IMG SRC="b1_pe

<TD align="center"><A HREF="http://www.bankone.com/busbank/"><IMG SRC="b1_bu

<TD align="center"><A HREF="http://www.bankone.com/jobs/"><IMG SRC="b1_jobic
</TR>

<TR>
<TD align="center"><IMG SRC="whatsnew.gif" ALT="What's New" HEIGHT=18 WIDTH=

<TD align="center"><IMG SRC="yourmoney.gif" ALT="Your Money" HEIGHT=17 WIDTH

<TD align="center"><IMG SRC="busbanking.gif" ALT="Small Business Center" HEI

<TD align="center"><IMG SRC="jobs.gif" ALT="Job Opportunities" HEIGHT=34 WID
</TR>

<TR>
<TD align="center"><A HREF="http://www.bankone.com/corpbank/"><IMG SRC="b1_c

<TD align="center"><A HREF="http://www.bankone.com/friends/"><IMG SRC="b1_en
```

11

Linking with Other Applications

When Imation Corporation became an independent entity—it formerly was part of 3-M Corporation—the spin-off found itself with a variety of database resources, including mainframe, Oracle, and Notes varieties. Imation (Fig. 11-1) faced an old problem: providing access to this information stored in different, incompatible forms.

To meet the need for universal access, Imation chose a universal client: a Web browser front end. The challenge then became to link the browser to the diverse database resources.

This is a challenge more and more companies are facing these days, particularly as intranets evolve into extranets. Much of the information you want to distribute is in legacy database form—even client/server and Notes databases can claim legacy status where the Web is concerned. You do not want to convert all this material to HTML, for many good reasons that only begin with the workload involved. The good news is that you do not have to.

Figure 11-1
The Imation home page (http://www.imation.com).

Linking the New with the Old

Imation has implemented or is planning several applications that link Web browsers with its database access. Most early projects have been internal, but many have external possibilities as well. They include

- Giving employees the ability to update their own personnel directory information. When employees move or marry, they can enter the changes themselves, using the Web browser to open their records in an Oracle database.

- A Notes-based work-flow application that lets employees file expense accounts automatically and then transfers the reimbursements directly to the employees' bank accounts. A logical extension of this process could be to handle accounts and payments with external vendors and customers.

- A database that keeps employees posted on how the company's stock is doing. This could readily become a resource available to any interested investor.

- A set of Oracle-based marketing tools that let marketing professionals develop predictive models and other forms of analysis to evaluate marketing programs.

Goodbye CGI

Until recently, CGI, the Common Gateway Interface, has been the most common way to make the connection between a Web page and an underlying database. CGI still is important and widely used, but its limitations have become increasingly obvious. CGI is often compared with the DOS batch files: simple and easy to use but unsophisticated. Furthermore, the interpreted languages used in CGI scripts can produce bottlenecks in high-volume applications.

Several alternatives have been developed. Among them

- Open Database Connectivity (ODBC), which brings to Web browsers the database access already enjoyed by some more conventional database applications
- Java and JavaScript
- Using a Web server API.
- CGI extensions called *Fast CGI*

The Common Gateway

CGI is a set of specifications for passing information between a client Web browser, a Web server, and a CGI application. Someone using a client Web browser can start a CGI application by filling out an HTML form or clicking on a link in an HTML page. The CGI application can accept the information the client Web browser supplies and do almost anything that can be programmed. Then it can return the results of the application in an HTML page, or it can post the information to a database. Because simple CGI applications are often written using scripting languages such as Perl, CGI applications are sometimes called *scripts* (Fig. 11-2).

The Client Sends a Request

A client browser can make a CGI request to a server by either of two methods:

- *GET:* The client appends data to the URL it passes to the server.
- *POST:* The client sends data to the server by way of an HTTP mes-

Figure 11-2
Exchanging informa-
tion by CGI.

CGI data exchange

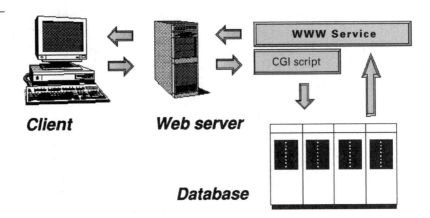

sage data field. This method generally allows you to send larger amounts of data.

The client initiates a CGI process by clicking on

- A hypertext link that runs the script directly
- The *Submit* button in an HTML form
- An in-line object retrieved with the GET method
- A search object that uses the HTML tag *ISINDEX*

The Server Relays the Request

The URL that the client browser sends to the server contains the name of the CGI script to be run. The server runs the script and passes information to the database application by means of environment variables. It then launches the application.

Returning Data

The application then performs its processing. The application responds by sending the resulting data back to the server in a format the client can receive. Often, this means sending it to a standard output stream (STD-

OUT). The server takes the data it receives from STDOUT and adds standard HTTP headers. It then passes the HTTP message back to the client.

The Open Database

Microsoft's Internet Information Server links Web servers and ODBC databases, using Open Database Connectivity (ODBC) drivers provided the product. With these, you can

- Create Web pages with information contained in a database
- Insert, update, and delete information in the database based on user input from a Web page
- Perform other Structured Query Language (SQL) commands

How It Works

Web browsers submit requests to the server using HTTP. The Internet server responds with a document formatted in HTML. Access to databases is accomplished through an IIS component called the Internet Database Connector (IDC).

The IDC uses two types of files to control access to how the database is accessed and construction of the output Web page:

- IDC   (.idc)
- HTML extension (.htx) files

The IDC files contain the necessary information to connect to an ODBC data source and execute an SQL statement. An IDC file also contains the name and location of the HTML extension file.

The HTML extension file is a template for the HTML document that is returned to the Web browser after the database information has been merged into it by the IDC.

A Sample Query

Suppose you have a Web page with one hyperlink that triggers an SQL query using an ODBC driver. The results are returned in the form of another Web page.

When someone clicks on the hyperlink, a new URL is sent to the server. In the HTML code, the URL precedes the hyperlink text:

```
<A> REF="http://easttech/samples/dbapps/query.idc".Search
Database,</A>.
```

The IDC file for the IDC to use (query.idc) is given a reference in the URL. On IIS, the process is

1. The URL is received by the Internet Information Server.

2. The Internet Information Server loads a link library that is called *Hpodbc.dll* and provides it with the remaining information in the URL. IDC files are mapped to Httpodbc.dll. Httpodbc.dll loads and obtains the name of the IDC file and other items from the URL passed to the Internet Information Server.

3. Httpodbc.dll reads the IDC file, which contains several entries in the format: *field: value.* For example, the ODBC data source might be specified by

```
Datasource: Web SQL
```

And the HTML extension file is specified by

```
Template: sample.htx
```

4. The file might then continue with an **SQLstatement:**

```
SQLStatement:
SELECT partno, description, price
  from catalog
  where account = wholesale
```

5. The IDC connects to the ODBC data source and executes the SQL statement.

6. The IDC retrieves the requested information from the database and merges it into the HTML extension file.

7. The IDC sends the merged document back to the Internet Information Server, which returns it to the client. After all the data have been merged into Sample.htx, the complete HTML document is sent back to the client. The resulting Web page is displayed in the browser.

Advanced Database Manipulation

This was the simplest kind of query, defined completely in the IDC file. You can build more powerful Web pages through the use of parameters. *Parameters* are the names and values of HTML form controls, such as <INPUT>, and names specified directly in URLs. These names and values are sent by Web browsers and can be used in SQL statements on the server.

This query might produce only a selection of wholesale catalog items. By using a parameter, you could build a Web page that asks customers to identify themselves as wholesale, retail, or some other class. You then could display the product information appropriate to that class of customer.

The Web page must prompt the user for the customer type, perhaps by displaying a drop-down list of available categories. The specification is then assigned to a variable, perhaps called *customer_type*. The parameter should have the same name as the input variable on the HTML page.

The query then could read:

```
SQLStatement:
SELECT partno, description, price
  from catalog
  where account = %cust_type
```

Netscape's Server Side

In addition to CGI scripts, a Netscape server can run several types of what the company calls *server-side applications.* These run on the server as distinguished from client-side applications that run on the browser. These applications include

- Java applets
- Applications constructed using LiveWire, Netscape's implementation of JavaScript programs
- Plug-in programs that use the server plug-in API

All but the plug-ins run in conjunction with the server, providing extra programs for clients to take advantage of. These can include search tools, group scheduling programs, and others, including games if you like. Plug-ins replace the server's features with new ones, such as a different way to control access or different logging mechanisms.

Java applets, LiveWire applications, and CGI programs have different strengths and uses. Java is a full-featured programming language intended for creating network applications. LiveWire programs are written in JavaScript, a scripting language based on Java; it is easier to learn than an entire programming language and is useful for creating programs quickly. CGI programs can be written in C, Perl, or other programming languages; all use a standard way to accept and return information.

The LiveWire

In its most recent incarnations, Netscape LiveWire and its upscale partner, LiveWire Pro, have been boosted into position as multipurpose Web site construction and management tools. For the purposes of this discussion, the most important of these multiple purposes is database management. An Informix-OnLine Workgroup database, included in LiveWire Pro, helps you develop databased Web applications.

LiveWire applications are written in JavaScript, which provides dynamic client/server interaction. Web site developers can create server-side programs that let Web clients browse, search, and update relational databases from Web browsers. The LiveWire Database Connectivity Library works with Informix, Oracle, Sybase and, through ODBC, dozens of other databases from the desktop to mainframes.

The Windows NT version of LiveWire Pro adds Crystal Reports Professional, a report design and data analysis tool for Windows systems. Crystal Reports offers cross-tabs, graphing, and data drill-down.

A database connectivity library processes SQL client/server connections to Informix, Oracle, and Sybase databases. It also

- Supports ODBC links to databases with ODBC drivers
- Uses a conventional database cursor model
- Supports SQL Pass through for database-specific SQL statements and commands
- Provides cross-platform and cross-database functionality using cursor access methods
- Supports triggers and stored procedures

The Crystal Reports Professional Version includes easy visual forms builder and data analysis tools. It also

■ Offers predefined report template and style libraries with full customization

■ Provides cross-tabs

■ Simplifies analysis with table and graph drill-down

■ Includes dozens of graph styles and formats

■ Integrates HTML report generation

Oracle Gets Involved

When it comes to linking Web browsers with relational databases, Oracle naturally has gotten involved. On one hand, Oracle has been a guiding force for the Network Computer, which depends almost entirely on Web connections. On the other, Oracle has been bringing out a line of Web/database products, including a server designed to work with other Web servers.

Oracle WebServer gives customers a common platform to develop and deploy Web applications on Microsoft, Netscape, and Oracle servers. Built on Oracle's Web Request Broker technology, WebServer can host applications even in a distributed corporate intranet or an extranet involving multiple companies. These installations often include a variety of Web servers. WebServer also includes an integrated Java Virtual Machine that supports open database access through Java Database Connectivity (JDBC).

Web Request Broker is a component of Oracle's Network Computing Architecture (NCA), an open software platform that allows customers and third-party developers to build "cartridges" that plug into a client, Web server, application server, or database. WebServer provides a framework to build cartridges that interoperate with the client and the database, as well as across various HTTP servers. This interoperability is possible through native connections to the Netscape Server API and Microsoft's Internet Information Server API.

The Web Request Broker links Web servers to live applications and databases that can dynamically generate HTML-formatted data in real time. Through its open API, the Web Request Broker extends a Web server's functions and lets you create applications that can use multiple platforms.

No More Mainframes

The Burlington Coat Factory Warehouse Corporation abandoned its mainframes several years ago in favor of Oracle's client/server databases. More recently, Burlington has been anticipating the emerging Network Computer technology which uses a minimal amount of local computing resources and relies on the Web as a host.

While waiting, Burlington has been connecting its Oracle databases and its TCP/IP network using integration products also from Oracle.

Developer Companion

A companion product, Developer/2000 for the Web, enables software developers to extend existing client/server applications to HTTP networks without manual code changes. This could mean that an estimated 5 million existing Oracle-based applications could instantly be made available for network computers and PCs or to workstations with Java-enabled browsers.

The new Web-based applications will look familiar to those who have used earlier products, providing the same functions and data-entry screens as the existing applications. Developer/2000 for the Web is the application development component for NCA, which allows all PCs, network computers and other clients to work with all Web servers, database servers, and applications servers over any network. Developer/2000 for the Web applications separate presentation, application, and database access logic and run them as Java applets or cartridges on the client and server.

Electronic Commerce

Oracle also has been busy in the related field of electronic commerce, with a line of products designed to let you sell your wares, accept orders, and process secure payments in an extranet or Web situation. These products, developed in many cases by Oracle's own business partners, include

- Project Apollo, a merchant server designed to allow businesses to quickly establish a commerce presence on the Web

- The Oracle Payment Server, a server that comes both integrated with Project Apollo or as a stand-alone product that delivers a choice of payment methods

- Oracle Security Server, authentication software designed to recognize and authorize consumer identity and payment information

- Strategic relationships with Cybercash, Hewlett-Packard, Quark, and VeriFone designed to quickly move retailers to the Web

Also based on the Network Computing Architecture, Oracle's electronic commerce products allow consumers and corporations to securely use any client over any network to access any server, allowing for the execution of secure electronic commerce transactions.

Apollo Details

Project Apollo is a Web cartridge that allows any business to establish a commerce presence using a Web site and set up electronic storefronts with integrated transactions. The Apollo server manages product browsing, personalized marketing and promotions, order entry, inventories, payment processing, and order fulfillment. Combined, these features let merchants expand their sales channels and open up to Internet customers and extranet business partners.

Integrated with Project Apollo is the Oracle Payment Server, an electronic payment system that enables secure commerce transactions that can use multiple, concurrent payment mechanisms. Both Apollo and the Oracle Payment Server will support electronic payments from electronic payment leaders CyberCash, First Data, VeriFone, and other vendors.

The system is designed to showcase a business' product line, allow immediate purchases and instant payments through secure electronic transactions, and integrate with a merchant's existing business processes to complete the transaction.

The Apollo Merchant Server functions as a cartridge that plugs into the Oracle Web Request Broker and works with Oracle Universal Server. The Apollo architecture allows you to customize the commerce site, so businesses can tailor the look and feel of the storefront, and supports multiple payment processing, order entry, and inventory management systems. Apollo also uses database technology to track items selected by the customer and to maintain shopper profiles, allowing merchants to custom tailor Web site content and special promotions or discounts based on individual shopping preferences. Additionally, consumers can search for items based on key words and themes and rank the relevancy of results through the Oracle ConText Option.

Securing Transactions

The Oracle Payment Server is an electronic payment system for secure Internet commerce transactions. The Payment Server technology is integrated with the Apollo Merchant Server to enable retail payment processing. It also can function as a stand-alone payment server for other types of businesses that require payment mechanisms. For example, if you want to sell directly from your extranet, you would need a separate payment system but may not need not a complete merchant server, which is used for direct on-line retailing.

The Payment Server provides a link between the merchant, the financial institution, and the payment vendor to ensure that a payment transaction is completed. With Payment Server, merchants and other businesses can employ applications that use multiple payment mechanisms, such as electronic checks and credit cards. For example, a single application might process electronic coin transactions using the CyberCash cartridge while processing credit card transactions using the VeriFone cartridge.

Tapping into the Mainframe

Web products will be increasingly able to tap into client/server databases. But what about those mainframe repositories which are still usefully hanging around? If you are to share information with business partners, these old-timers likely hold some information it would be profitable for you to share.

The good news is that these tools also exist, and they can be expected to develop further as time goes on and demand increases. The bad news, and it is not really that bad, is that the development pace has lagged behind that for client/server database access.

Companies like OpenConnect Systems (http://www.oc.com) and Teubner and Associates (http://www.teubner.com) now market software that

Figure 11-3
WebConnect brings
the mainframe to the
Web almost intact.

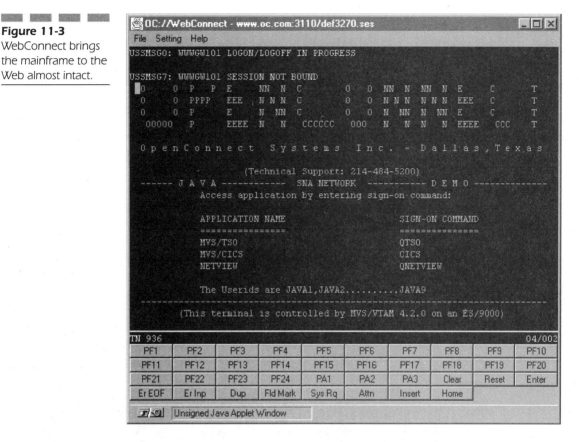

Figure 11-3
WebConnect brings
the mainframe to the
Web almost intact.

spans the gap between mainframe systems and Web browsers. These two sources are typical of different approaches to the same task. OpenConnect's WebConnect uses Java applets to maintain the familiar mainframe look and feel (Fig. 11-3).

More products, increasingly sophisticated, have probably appeared by the time you read this. In fact, Teubner is an example. A demonstration of its basic Corridor Web-to-mainframe software displays the type of legacy artwork in Fig. 11-4. A Gold version of the same software can produce the more Web-like display in Fig. 11-5.

One reason is low cost. Although dumb terminals connected to mainframes do not cost much, it costs even less to outfit existing PCs with browser software. The connection software does not cost that much more, particularly when you break it down by individual users. Furthermore, the Web browsers are available to telecommuters and mobile workers. And if you need further proof, active Java applications make the interface much more appealing and useful than the cluttered green

Figure 11-4
When did you last draw pictures like this?

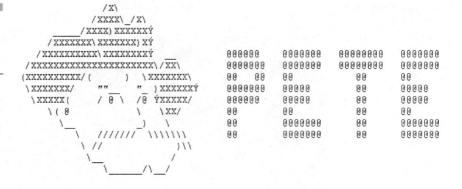

THE
OKLAHOMA STATE UNIVERSITY
AUTOMATED LIBRARY SYSTEM

Figure 11-5
An updated mainframe's browser displays Web-like graphics.

screens of standard mainframe practice. In fact, one of the things that many users have told IS in their companies is that they would like the ability to customize the appearance of their screens.

More fundamentally, an estimated 75 percent of the real-time transaction systems in the world still run on mainframes. This is not automatically available to browsers and extranets, but there are ways to make it available.

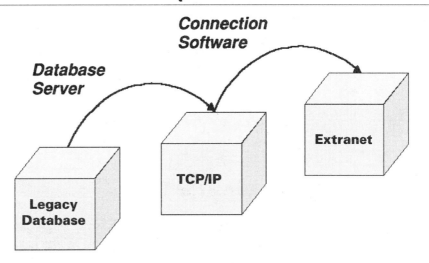

Figure 11-6
Legacy data converted to HTML.

Two Ways, in Fact

There are two ways to give browsers access to mainframe hosts, more specifically IBM mainframe hosts. You can use the mainframe's native mode, or you can convert everything to HTML. There is the usual mix of advantages and drawbacks.

The big drawback to the native approach is that it requires its own special kind of browser. The usual Web browser will not do. If you take the HTML approach, on the other hand, the mainframe screens are changed to HTML format and made available on a Web server. Once on the server, any Web browser can reach and read them (Fig. 11-6).

Converting to HTML

To further subdivide things, there are two kinds of HTML conversion:

- A static approach in which you have what amounts to read-only access to data made available by an administrator
- A dynamic approach in which you query a mainframe database and the results are returned to the browser, much like in the client/server systems

There are places in an extranet where you might want to consider the static approach. Say you want to post confidential product planning specifications for use by a vendor's design staff. The limited access of a static approach helps maintain security and ensures that someone does not take it on themselves to rewrite the specifications.

In this case, the design specs would be pulled off the mainframe and converted to HTML. Then, authorized users could use their browsers to look up the information; all they need do is enter its URL. Of course, you would have to maintain access control to make sure that this information goes only to the people who are authorized to see it.

Exceeding the Limits

There are other times when you want to go past the limits imposed by the static approach. For example, you might have a discussion group that brings together the interests of your own organization, your customers, and your suppliers. This group might negotiate daily changes to the specifications. This means that the database information must be updated just as often. You can not simply store it on a server and forget it.

You can achieve this kind of access through embedded scripts that activate mainframe commands. Again, this process is much like using scripts to retrieve client/server database material.

First, a Systems Network Architecture (SNA) gateway into the mainframe host retrieves a standard host screen with embedded data. This screen is converted on the fly to HTML format and is presented on the browser screen.

On the client end, an individual can enter the URL of an HTML server. That server is connected to a second server that performs the HTML conversions. The system can use CGI scripts or other methods to generate HTML pages in response to queries. One possible drawback to this method is that HTML and script language might not be able to issue the range of commands available in the mainframe environment.

Going Native

The native approach would avoid HTML and use its own kind of browser to emulate a 3270 terminal. This kind of browser would replace the usual terminal emulator and include the technology necessary to maintain a connection to the mainframe.

The biggest question concerning this approach is, Why bother? The most cogent answer is to note that the preceding paragraph refers to prospective, not present products. This approach might pay off if you have a specialized need. There also have been suggestions that with two vendors currently dominating the Web browser market, smaller firms might enter this kind of niche market. This still leaves open the question of who their customers and their applications might be.

Maintaining Security

Maintaining security is one possibility. A well-maintained mainframe is a relatively secure computing environment, particularly in the area of access control. Those who tap mainframe data usually must supply the usual combination of an ID and a password.

However, this is where Web browsers create a weak spot. Both the market leaders maintain caches of recently retrieved Web pages on their systems' hard disks. The object is to speed access if you return to the same page, but the information you thought was surely resting on the mainframe also may be in vulnerable PC directories. However, the browser vendors could easily add HTML extensions to cover this problem.

In fact, the vendors of mainframe-browser connections have already done so. Most, if not all, have hooks to a set of Netscape security application program interfaces (APIs). These include the Netscape Security API (NSAPI), a set of functions and header files that helps you take other security measures. One of these is setting up encryption using Secure Sockets Layer (SSL). Some products also support the Internet Security API (ISAPI), which is Microsoft's take on the same idea.

Making CGI Faster

One of the main drawbacks of GCI is that, as an interpreted, batch-oriented language, it lacks the performance to handle large applications or high-volume service. Another problem is that each time you invoke a CGI script, you must retrieve it fresh from the server and run it from the beginning. There is no stored logic you can readily repeat.

The responses discussed so far have concentrated mainly on finding a substitute for CGI. At least one vendor, however, Open Market Corporation (Cambridge, MA), has concentrated on producing a set of extensions that turn CGI into FastCGI. FastCGI keeps a script running as a process outside the Web server; it issues "tickets" to clients who want to use the CGI program to get to a database.

There is one big problem: lack of recognition by the major makers of Web servers and other software. As this was written, neither Netscape nor Microsoft seemed ready to support the necessary CGI extensions. Instead, they were trying to induce developers to use their respective server APIs.

12

Basic Network Security

By definition, a local area network (LAN) covers a local area. An extranet represents the opposite extreme. Your connections to business partners—in fact, within your own organization—can extend to other parts of the country and even other countries.

The nature of an extranet means that many familiar rules of computer security must be rewritten or at least heavily edited. Mainframe techniques built around securing central locations are clearly insufficient to secure a virtual computer that can encompass entire organizations. Standard LAN techniques can do a good job of securing local networks based on nearby servers, but securing the extranet requires that you expand your vision by several multiples.

Nevertheless, securing an extranet also can be a great deal like securing any other kind of network. The basic techniques of computer security are still valid. The extranet simply requires that you adopt and adapt these, sometimes stretching them a little. It will not be easy, but you can do it. In fact, you must do it. Extranets will continue to spread, with or without your participation.

Building a Security Plan

To meet the challenge of extranet security, start with a good plan. Include these elements:

- Adapt familiar methods to new needs. Just because you decentralize the network, you need not decentralize security management.

- Control file access. The types of controls available over a LAN are even more important as the network expands.

- Set priorities. Concentrate first on the most likely areas of loss.

- Audit the program. Keep track of who is or is not behaving as they should.

- Make effective use of encryption. You need not encrypt everything that travels across your extranet, but you should plan to encrypt any form of sensitive information.

- Keep it simple. Here is another built-in contradiction, but it is important. Encourage people to use their security measures by making them easy to use.

Spread the Word

With many members of top management, security is still a hard sell. This seems to be particularly true of those who control the finances. Even those who understand a need for security may not appreciate the scope required by the expansion of extranets. It is up to you to make them understand.

Start with some ammunition. The Communications Fraud Control Association estimates that unauthorized access to computer and telephone systems costs victims $500 million a year. This is in the United States. Worldwide, the estimated loss is more than $2 billion. When the University of Texas conducted a survey of computer losses, it found that 43 percent of the firms that suffer a major loss never reopen. This is true whether the loss is due to criminal activity or to natural disaster. Even among the firms that do manage to reopen, 90 percent are out of business within 2 years. This is not to say that the computer losses caused all these failures, but they certainly did not help.

This is essentially a selling job; technicians and security experts are not always good at it. Still, it is necessary. If you are convinced that certain security measures are necessary, it is part of your job to transfer those convictions to the people who make the final decisions.

Do not forget the rest of the organization. Selling security to the people at the keyboards can be as important as selling it to the people in corner offices. You cannot maintain a full security program without their cooperation. Ideally, they should become participating partners in protecting the resources for which they are responsible. You are no longer in an environment where you can control everything. You must get users to take charge of their own working environments. In particular, users need to learn to protect their own passwords. Carelessness in creating and protecting passwords is one of the biggest sources of loss.

Then there is the matter of your extranet business partners. Their management and their employees must be as well-educated as your own. And they are outside of your direct control.

Do Not Change Everything

Decentralized computing need not mean decentralized security. In fact, it is even more important that security be centrally managed. Training, planning, and management should all be consistent throughout the organization. Often, you will have to teach users to help maintain the security system. They should have the advantage of consistent, easy procedures.

You also may need a larger security staff. There are limits to your dependence on user cooperation. Someone has to manage computer security wherever the need exists. Spreading yourself too thin is a real possibility.

Set Priorities

You cannot do everything at once. Attack the most urgent needs first.

Usually, that will mean controlling access to the Web site. Use keys, passwords, and other basic security techniques to ensure that only authorized users can get into the system.

Establish the basic classes of network access:

- The network supervisor, who needs access to all functions, including the security system.

- Administrative users. This should be a small group given sufficient rights to maintain and support the extranet.

- Trusted users, who need and can use access to sensitive information.

- Vulnerable users, who do not need access beyond the strict confines of their responsibilities.

Access control is a balancing act. Authorized users should find it easy to gain access. Anyone else should find it very difficult. Striking this balance will always be a major challenge, and there is no magic formula. Just knowing that balance is necessary can help you achieve it.

Checking Up

Creating the system is one thing; making it work is another. Auditing is the process of making sure your security measures work as well as you had hoped. Without being unduly intrusive, you want to make sure you know who is doing what with the network. The system should provide information like this that you can use to oversee the extranet:

- A log of all attempts to gain access to the system. This is one of the best ways to determine if your system is under attack. The more often you check this log, the more effective it can be.

- A chronologic log of all network activity. Log every event, including identification of the users and workstations involved.

- Flags to identify unusual activity and variations from established procedures.

In addition, let people know you are keeping track. Do not hold it over their heads, but letting people know you are watching is the kind of security that helps keep honest people honest.

Encryption Has a Larger Role

The value of encryption in an extranet setting is that information obtained improperly will still be useless. Encryption can be a costly process that inhibits system performance. This limits its value in securing LANs and individual systems, but expanded networks can make it more worthwhile.

The basic standard: Encrypt all sensitive information that travels along the network.

Major Security Functions for Extranets

The National Institute for Standards and Technology (NIST) has developed what it calls *Minimal Security Functional Requirements for Multi-user Operational Systems*. The security precautions it lists are not always unique to extranets, but NIST has developed a useful checklist of the functions you should consider in planning a security system. The major functions are:

- *Identification and authentication.* Uses a password or some other form of identification to screen users and check their authorization.
- *Access control.* Keeps even authorized users from gaining access to material they should not see.
- *Accountability.* Links the activities on a network to the user's identity.
- *Audit trails.* Determines whether a security violation has occurred and what, if anything, was lost.
- *Object reuse.* Ensures that resources can be secured in the hands of multiple users.
- *Accuracy.* Guards against errors and unauthorized modifications.
- *Reliability.* Protects itself against monopolization by any user.
- *Data exchange.* Promotes secure transmission over communication channels.

Identify the User

In the extranet, as in most other installations, user identification is necessary but not sufficient. An identification and authentication system usually relies on passwords, although it can use other clues such as badges and biometric measurements. None of the rest of the security system will work unless you can first make sure that you can determine whether a would-be user is authorized to be there.

Gaining entry should not be enough. Once someone is admitted, the system still should govern each person's access to information. Use privilege control management to make sure that a user has access to what he or she needs to do the job, but nothing else. You often can do this by assigning predefined sets of privileges to particular job responsibilities.

Right the First Time

Ensuring accuracy can be one of the toughest challenges in extranet security. No one should be allowed to modify Web pages except under carefully controlled conditions. Be sparing with your use of this privilege. This is even more important if your extranet makes use of database resources.

The Role of Encryption

The most important role for encryption in an extranet is to protect passwords, credit card numbers, and other information whose disclosure would provide further access to the network. Include the password generation and recording systems.

You also can use encryption to preserve the confidentiality of information transmitted between browsers and servers. It also can help guard against such threats as wiretapping, electronic eavesdropping, misrouting, substitution, modification, and injection of messages. You also can use encryption algorithms to create digital signatures, which can help verify the identity of message senders and recipients.

Protecting Identity Verification

When passwords or other information known to an authorized user are entered into a system, it is possible for someone to intercept this information by wiretap or some other means. The penetrator then can use the information to impersonate the authorized users.

Encryption can be used to protect the information from the point where it leaves the browser or server and is transmitted to its destination. If you already are using encryption to protect transmitted information, this same capability may be suitable for protecting verification information.

The encryption process used to protect the verification information must provide for the information to be coded differently with each transmission. Otherwise, a penetrator might record the encrypted information from a point in its transmission path and fool the system simply by injecting the same encrypted information without ever having to decrypt it. Encryption systems generally have provisions for achieving the required variability.

When a personal attribute is used to verify an identity, a set of measured values is obtained, digitized, and used for comparison with a reference profile. This information, in clear form, can be used by a skillful penetrator to simulate the data obtained from an authorized user. To guard against this, the device that measures the attribute should be safeguarded against tampering so that the measured information cannot be taken while it is in the clear. Encryption can be used to protect this information during transmission.

Verification systems based on personal attributes are configured in a variety of ways. In one configuration, the measuring device sends the measured values to a central system where the reference profile is stored and where the comparison takes place. In this case, the measured values should be encrypted for transmission to the central system.

In another configuration, the reference profile is sent to the measuring device, with the comparison taking place in the device. In this case, the reference profile should be encrypted to prevent a penetrator from being able to inject a reference profile of his or her own.

Also, the device will produce a pass/fail signal, based on the results of the comparison, and this will be transmitted elsewhere, such as back to the central system that controls network access. This pass/fail signal also should be encrypted. Otherwise, a penetrator might be able to simulate this signal and produce a false pass response without ever having to deceive the measurement device.

Generally, the personal attribute sensing device will be either an integral part of a remote terminal or will be closely associated with such a terminal. Precautions should be taken to ensure that equipment enclosures are tamper protected and that there are no exposed leads that would let a penetrator tap sensitive information.

Digital Signatures

One form of authentication is the *digital signature*, in which the sender of a message attaches a coded identification to the message, enciphered in such a way that only the intended recipient can decipher it and verify the identity of the sender. One way to do this is based on using individual station identifiers in the process of encrypting keys, which in turn are used to encrypt messages between the stations. Because of the hardware arrangements and operating procedures used with this system, it is possible for a sender to encipher a signature or any other message in such a way that only the prearranged recipient can decipher it correctly.

Digital signatures also can be achieved through public key encryption. In such a system, the encryption key differs from the decryption key, and knowledge of the encryption key does not result in knowledge of the decryption key. In a public key system, users may freely publicize the keys for encrypting messages that are to be sent to them; they keep secret the corresponding decryption keys.

The encryption and decryption procedures for some public key systems are inverses of each other. In normal practice, a message would first be enciphered for transmission and then be deciphered on receipt to recover the information. However, the procedures in these systems may be applied in the reverse order, first using the decryption procedure to conceal the information and then using the encryption procedure to recover it.

A secure digital signature can be achieved this way: Assume that user A wants to send a secure digital signature to user B. User A first passes the signature through user A's own private decryption procedure, which in effect leaves it in unintelligible form. User A then enciphers the signature in this form using user B's public encryption procedure for privacy and sends it to user B.

User B first deciphers the signature using user B's secret decryption procedure. User B then applies user A's public encryption procedure and recovers the digital signature. In practice, it is preferable to apply this process to entire messages rather than just to the authenticating signature to keep a valid signature from being attached to a falsified message.

Range of Capabilities

Once the identity of a user has been established and authenticated, he or she may be granted access to the network and may request the use of various available resources. These resources consist of various entities such as host computers, areas of main memory, files, programs, auxiliary memory devices, and instructions. They often are referred to as *objects*.

Users must have proper authorization to be granted access to these objects. Each user has an associated set of access privileges to which he or she is entitled. This may be called the *capability profile*.

Similarly, each object comes with a set of requirements for its use, which may be called an *access requirement profile*. An access request is authorized when the requester's capability profile matches the objects' access requirements profile.

An object can have many ways in which it can be used, such as reading data from a file, writing data into a file, carrying out a transaction, executing a program, compiling a program, or invoking various operating system routines. Thus there is a range of capabilities associated with an object, not all of which may be authorized for use by every user. You can visualize this situation as a three-dimensional array, with users along one dimension, objects along another, and capabilities along the third.

Levels of Access Control

You also can visualize access control and privacy protection in three levels: memory, procedure, and logical. Access control at the memory level regulates access to memory in terms of units of memory. Concern at this level is with defined regions of memory rather than with its contents. This protection applies to the contents only while they remain in the defined region. Protected regions of memory typically are defined by the means of memory-bound registers or storage protection keys that control access to the bounded memory regions.

Access control at the procedure level regulates access to procedures, where a *procedure* is a set of programs and associated data. Access control at this level is concerned with the conditions under which programs can pass control from one to another. That is, the execution programs must be monitored in terms of calls, returns, and the passing of parameters.

Access Authorization Principles

Access control can be governed by a set of principles like these:

- *Least privilege.* No requester has any access privileges that are not required to perform the function—in other words, a need-to-know standard. As a corollary to this, access to resources should be compartmentalized whenever this separation adds to security.

- *Least common mechanism.* There are minimal shared or common mechanisms, other than those which expressly are there for security purposes.

- *Reference monitor approach.* Access control is always invoked, isolated from unauthorized alteration, and accredited as being trustworthy.

- *Object versus path protection.* Protection can be provided to the object itself, the path to the object, or both. The network aspects are almost entirely path-oriented protection.

Composite Authorizations

Nearly every computer transaction involves several entities. These could include a person, a terminal, a host computer, and a process. Each of these entities must be authorized either to receive, process, or transport the information being handled.

The logical intersection of these authorizations will establish the level of information that can be sent by this sequence of entities, but a further step-by-step authorization check also is necessary to ensure that only the proper entity or entities are the ultimate recipients of the information. For example, one entity may be authorized to process but not to copy the information.

In some instances, the request will be connected to a host that will, in turn, need access to other resources on the requester's behalf. Authorization is a larger problem than authentication, since the latter is strictly binary at each intermediate requester. In contrast, the authorizations of each intermediate requester may differ, as may the authorization needs, when information is processed at different nodes along the chain.

You can take either of two approaches:

- Continually subsetting the authorizations as necessary so that the final privileges are the intersection of those of the original requester and all intermediate nodes. This will ensure that no intermediate node gets any information for which it is not authorized.

- Handling the authorization on a pairwise basis so that the *n*th level will provide any requested information for which the (*n*-1)th level is authorized and leave the burden of further controls on passing of data to the host. This procedure allows the use of statistical programs, in which specific details are lost in favor of summaries. For example, the system might respond with the average value of a group of data but not with a specific value within the group. Of course, you still would be vulnerable to a cleverly devised statistical request.

Access to the Authorization Mechanism

The authorization mechanism is called on whenever a user presents an access request for an object. The mechanism therefore must be readily accessible for frequent use.

There also will be occasions when the mechanism must be modified to reflect changes in status for users and objects. This mechanism has a critical security function, and it must be protected properly from unauthorized modifications.

Guarding the Gates

One of the most vulnerable spots in a network is the system that administers the passwords. On many LANs, including both Ethernet and Token Ring systems, the passwords are transmitted in plain text that anyone with a little gumption and knowledge can intercept and use. The same is true of passwords transmitted by remote login and file-transfer protocols. An invader can capture such a password to gain access to the network. Once inside, the invader also usually knows how to obtain the necessary privileges to see and modify even the most sensitive files.

Furthermore, someone who gains access to one machine on the network often can find easy access to others. A server can be set up to automatically accept commands from a designated group of "trusted" workstation, or another server. An invader who gains access to one of the trusted machines then can use that authorization to gain access to the server.

Larger networks compound the problem because they usually involve multiple networks and protocols, each with its own passwords buzzing around the network. You have to assume that anything transmitted on the network—including the passwords—is open to interception.

Junkyard Dog

A major challenge in securing an extranet, then, is to protect the password system. You must ensure that someone who uses a password is truly authorized to use it.

One of the primary standards for authenticating identities is Kerberos. Developed at the Massachusetts Institute of Technology (MIT) to protect its own network, Kerberos is named for the mythical three-headed dog that supposedly guards the gates to Hades. The MIT implementation can do much the same job on any network that uses the Transmission Control Protocol/Internet Protocol (TCP/IP). Kerberos uses encryption technology to require that a user and the system prove their identities to each other before they exchange data. It also helps keep unauthorized parties from eavesdropping on the data exchange.

Tickets and Keys

In uncounted spy novels, two figures meet in a dark place and exchange cryptic remarks. "How about them Bucs?" asks one. "Only if it rains in Cleveland," replies the other. This exchange constitutes a password and countersign—the exchange of shared secrets. In this way they confirm each other's identities.

Kerberos also relies on shared secrets called *keys*. Used in conjunction with a parallel system of tickets, the system lets a user prove his or her identity to a server, using a Kerberos server as a third-party intermediary.

A key is a string of characters used to encrypt a message. Kerberos uses several types of keys. Client and server keys are both persistent; they stay in effect until someone changes them. There is also a session key that changes after every communication session. This key is known only to three entities, the client, the server, and Kerberos itself.

The user takes on the role of client. Before it can gain access to the system, the client must establish its password. The Kerberos server stores the password in encrypted form. The encrypted client password becomes the client key.

Like an airline traveler, the client must obtain a ticket to each network destination it wants to visit. To obtain a ticket, the client enters a password at its workstation. In response, client software forwards the client's request to a key distribution center (KDC) on the Kerberos server. The KDC responds with a message encrypted in the client key, the key that was derived from the client's password. By decoding the message successfully, the client verifies that it is indeed who it says it is. In this exchange, only the encrypted messages travel across the network. In particular, the client's password never has to make that perilous trip.

The Travel Agent

Having decoded the message, the client forwards the ticket request and proof of identity to a ticket-getting service (TGS), which functions something like a network travel agency. The request includes encrypted proof of the client's identity. The TGS uses a combination of the client's key and its own to obtain a ticket for each machine to which the client requires access. Then TGS returns the ticket to the client system, this time with proof of the server's identity encrypted in the combined client and server key. This information and a time stamp are enclosed within the ticket.

The client then can use the ticket to gain access to the desired resources. To further verify its identity, the client must submit a key matching the one encoded inside the ticket. The ticket also must be used within a short time after it was issued. Usually, software on the client's workstation will handle this process automatically.

The client also can ask for assurance that the server is authentic, not an impersonator. To do this, the client can issue a challenge, which can be a time stamp or a random number encrypted in the combined client and server key. An authorized server will decode this information, increase the time or number by one, encrypt the new signal, and return it. The client then can encrypt the return message and compare it with the expected response.

It Does Not Do Everything

Like any dog, Kerberos can be a loyal, reliable servant. However, while you can train it to recognize its master, there are things it never can do. Specifically, Kerberos is an authentication service. It verifies identities. It can determine who someone is, but it has nothing to say about what that person can do. This is a job for an access control and privilege system.

Kerberos also has this in common with all other security measures: Even the best are not perfect. The exchange of encrypted messages make useful interception difficult, but there are ways an expert, determined invader can overcome the system. It also does nothing to protect passwords from that ever-present peril, human carelessness.

Securing Unix and Open Systems

Sooner or later, the extranet will take you to the world of Unix and open systems. Some professionals worry that involving open systems in a network will leave it open to security risks. This is possible, but as with LANs, Unix does offer the tools to build secure networks. The main requirement is that you use them.

Unix security is not as easy as securing some other kinds of networks. There are several reasons:

- Netware's security features are familiar and widely used. Many network managers are less familiar with the Unix counterparts.

- Unix is often found in open systems that offer remote, direct dial-in access.

- There are no generally accepted standards under Unix for access control, setting privileges, or auditing the system. Some standards are being developed, though.

- The people who know Unix tend to know it very well. If motivated to do so, they know how to exploit its weaknesses.

What Can You Do?

One way you can make Unix more secure is to institute mandatory access controls. These can be similar to those imposed under Netware, with access rights assigned both to users and to files. Users should not have the authority to change either.

You also can subdivide access to the Unix root, which governs its access-control system. Unix file systems are organized much like DOS directories: a tree system with a root directory at the top. Within the Unix root directory are the privileges to conduct 20 to 30 functions. Only a few people need access to them all. Allot these privileges carefully, according to each user's need.

Unix security also responds to many universal techniques, the most important of which is proper password administration. If your system is connected to the Internet, forbid the use of the file-transfer program FTP. In particular, avoid the variety known as *anonymous FTP*. It provides direct, anonymous access to the files on remote computers. It is also a good idea to limit yourself to only one connection with outside systems.

Securing the Telephone Line

Telephony is one of those concocted words that makes you wonder, where did it come from and how can we send it back? Unfortunately, it is now a vital part of a network manager's vocabulary.

For better and for worse—and it truly is some of both—the variety of devices now connected to the typical extranet includes the telephone. This is particularly important, because the phone is the most popular route for invading a computer network.

Large-scale networking has always depended heavily on telephone lines. The wide area network (WAN) is usually based on telephone services. When you link the LANs and WANs in your organization, you may connect your network to the public telephone system. An extranet makes the phone connection almost inevitable.

Furthermore, new products are blurring the line between voice and data communication. Both serve the same body of clients, in the same locations, and both use wiring to do it. Add the digital technology in the newest Private Branch Exchanges (PBXs), and the underlying technology is similar.

Unfortunately, there is another common trait: exposure to fraud. In fact, Paul Merenbloom, a network manager and *Infoworld* columnist, identifies four vulnerable spots that could compromise a phone system:

- Direct inward system access (DISA)
- Unsecured voice mailboxes
- Unsecured systems
- Insider information

As telephone systems and computer networks are linked together, these same four threats can imperil the extranet.

Direct-dial Trouble

DISA is a popular system because it saves companies money on long-distance phone charges. It is popular with another group, too: hackers who can use it not only to invade your system but also to get there at your expense. Several telephone equipment suppliers are now advising their customers to discontinue their DISA services.

Hackers also have learned to use unsecured voice mail systems as a way to gain illicit access to a company's internal telephone system. Many voice mail systems let a caller press the zero to leave messages and get assistance. In some of these systems, pressing the zero plus a trunk access code puts the caller in a position to make outward calls from your telephones. Naturally, the phone company bills you for the calls.

What You Can Do

In ways like these, networks become the unwitting tools of phone fraud, but there are several things you can do:

- Get a list of all the test mailboxes used by the vendor. Change their passwords.
- If you can avoid it, do not allow outward dialing for a voice mailbox. If you truly need this service, program the PBX to limit the exchanges and area codes to which calls can be made.
- Make all passwords at least five digits long. Six or more is better.
- Change passwords every 60 to 90 days.
- When you create new voice mail accounts, avoid the temptation to use the box number as the initial password. This is much too obvious.
- Do not assign numbers to unused mailboxes. This may seem like a convenience for future expansion, but it is also a heavily traveled invasion route.

Securing the Client/Server Database

The word went out some time ago that a popular database server used in client/server applications was not really suited for client/server duty. It offered no way to centrally manage the security of each server installation. You could set up individual security schemes on each server, but in one organization that maintained database files on 16 different servers, this was turning out to be a critical problem. Just as frustrating, while the maker of one component of the client/server system said it was willing to work on a solution, the makers of other components were busy denying responsibility.

If any one thing characterizes the client/server database, it is its split personality. The system is centered on a database server, where you can store large bodies of information in a database management system (DBMS). At each workstation, a separate application runs as a client. When an employee needs information from the database, he or she enters the request into the front-end client system. The client then passes the request to the back-end server, usually using structured query language (SQL). The server processes the request and sends the requested information back to the client side, where the employee can work with it. The client and server software can and often do come from different vendors.

From a security standpoint, client/server has a great many advantages. The main body of data remains in a central server. The only data that travel over the network are in response to clients' requests. Although the main object of this feature is to minimize network traffic, it also has the effect of minimizing exposure. Furthermore, SQL has a substantial built-in security system comparable with those in network operating systems. You can use SQL commands to identify users, control access, and grant and revoke varied types of privileges to use selected parts of the database. Although SQL is primarily a data-management language, it has more commands to govern access control than to manage data.

Nevertheless, the client/server system also has shown its weaknesses. The SQL security commands work only one database at a time. If your data are distributed among several servers, the administrative burden is also multiplied. Furthermore, the multivendor environment makes it hard to bring about solutions. The organizations involved in the dispute mentioned earlier had to deal with three different parties: those responsible for the client system, the server system, and the operating system. The division can be an internal problem, too. Often, database security and network security are in the hands of two different people.

Principles of Database Security

The typical user of a client/server database must pass through two levels of security: at the network and at the DBMS. This is not as good an idea as it might seem. For the user, it can be the kind of awkward, difficult experience many people try to avoid and evade.

At the operating system level, the employee, as usual, must enter a password or provide some other form of identification. Connected with this password is a set of privileges to conduct certain kinds of operations on certain categories of data.

DBMS Security

If the network's security scheme grants the user access to the database server, the DBMS security kicks in. Just like the network operating system, a DBMS controls access by setting up a system of user accounts.

Again, the user must enter a password and gain acceptance at the server. In some systems, the DBMS processes the password already entered to gain entrance to the network, but other installations require a second password. Using the same password is a big convenience for administrators and a benefit to the users as well. It does have the effect, though, of removing one level of security. Someone who breaks into the network then can have unchallenged access to the database.

Database Privileges

In most DBMS systems, you can grant privileges on two levels: system privileges and database object privileges. System privileges govern your access to the DBMS as a whole. For example, the DBMS usually will have a provision that lets an authorized user create a new table. Other system privileges include the ability to create, alter, and drop the accounts of database users or to create or drop various database objects including the database itself.

This is a powerful feature you can use to administer the overall security of a database server. With most systems, you can create custom accounts to conduct specific management jobs such as authorizing users, organizing the database, and backing up files. With different administrators for different functions, you can create a system of finely tailored access privileges.

Object Privileges

An SQL database is a collection of tables. Not all the data have to be in the same table; the essence of a relational database is to relate multiple tables. Everything, though, is in some form of a row and column format.

Someone in the organization owns the table. Initially, the owner is the person who created it. In practice, this usually will be the network administrator. If you own a particular asset, you may grant other users the privileges of access to your data. You can grant privileges for any table or view you have created. A view is a selected portion of a database table. These privileges come in several varieties:

- *Select* lets the newly privileged user see but not alter, the data in your table or view.

- *Insert* lets the user add new rows or records to the table. A personnel clerk would use this privilege over the roster table to add new employees to the list.

- *Update* grants permission to edit existing data.

- *Delete* confers authority to delete existing rows or records, as you would do to the roster table when an employee leaves the company.

- *Alter* gives the user permission to change the structure of the table, such as by adding, deleting, or renaming columns.

- *Index* grants the authority to create an index. This is a database management function that has no direct bearing on security.

- *References* controls the ability of one table to refer to data in another.

- *Execute* controls the ability to execute a procedure.

Granting Privileges

As owner of a table, you can grant varying powers to individual users. For the purpose of an SQL database, every individual has both a user name and a password. First, you must identify an authorized user. This SQL command does this

```
SQL>    GRANT RESOURCE
2       TO ADDIE
3       IDENTIFIED BY SHEPHERD;
```

(The SQL> and the subsequent line numbers are prompts provided by the SQL database system; these vary from system to system. The semi-colon is the standard closing punctuation for an SQL command.) The individual is now known by the user name ADDIE, and her password is SHEPHERD. You can assign user names and passwords to the other employees as well.

Having given Addie her identity, as far as the database system is concerned, you can grant her whatever privileges you care to delegate. If Addie is a department head, she needs the privileges necessary to manage a table that contains her departmental employee records. If that table is named ROSTER, you can

```
SQL>     GRANT ALL
2        ON ROSTER
3        TO ADDIE;
```

This command gives Addie the full list of privileges, including reading, adding, deleting, and altering the structure. You might want to grant one further type of authority by using this command instead:

```
SQL>     GRANT ALL
2        ON ROSTER
3        TO ADDIE
4        WITH GRANT OPTION;
```

Now, Addie has the authority to grant access privileges to other users. She can grant only the privileges she has herself. For example, she might want to give her office clerk the authority to view the roster table and to add and subtract new employees as they join and leave the company. The command would go like this:

```
SQL>     GRANT SELECT, INSERT, DELETE
2        ON ROSTER
3        TO MISTY;
```

Thus the employee with this user name could view, add, or remove employee records. She could not change any of the data, though.

In addition to privileges over tables, some SQL databases let you assign privileges over individual columns. This is a dubious advantage, though, particularly if holders of the privilege use it with less than absolute care. For example, you can invite all manner of trouble if someone who holds privileges over only a column or two tries to insert a new row into the table. The results vary; none are good. Usually, you can use a view to meet the same objectives, with less uncertain results.

The View as a Security Device

In an SQL database, the view is important for many reasons, not the least of which is security. By assigning privileges, you can individually control the actions each employee is authorized to take with your data. You can use the view to control the data on which those actions can be taken.

An SQL query usually retrieves selected elements from one or more database tables. For example, a table called ROSTER might contain employees' names, job assignments, and department numbers. A second table called DEPTS could contain the department numbers and the supervisors' names. You could retrieve the names and specialties from the first table and then use the department numbers from the first table to look up the supervisors' names in the second. The SQL query would go something like this:

```
SQL>    SELECT NAME, SPECIALTY, SUPERVISOR
2       FROM ROSTER, DEPT
3       WHERE ROSTER:DEPTNO = DEPT:DEPTNO;
```

The result, reported back to the client station, would be a virtual table that uses selected parts of the source tables: the names, specialties, and supervisors. It offers a look at only the data requested by the query.

The view makes this virtual table permanent. It stores and names the query that created it. You can then use the view's name in an SQL query, just like you would use a table's name. You also can grant privileges for its use.

The view's value in security is its ability to provide a precisely defined look at data. Say, for instance, the ROSTER table has a column that lists every employee's salary. You probably do not want these data to be open to general viewing, even by people who are privileged to see other elements of the data. Accordingly, you create a tight scheme of limited access to ROSTER. Then you can be much more liberal in granting access to a view that omits the less sensitive data.

Managing Privileges

It is easy enough to set up a system of privileges for a few people, but the job gets harder as the number of privilege holders increases. An extended extranet could become a rat's nest of different rights to do different things to different resources. The job of managing all these varied permissions easily can outstrip the ability to handle it. When this happens, the access-control system can easily become a liability instead of an asset.

There are two ways you can get a handle and keep a firm grip: grouping and role playing. Many operating systems and DBMS installations let you establish groups of people who all have the same permission requirements. Often, these are employees in a single department or a particular job specialty. Instead of creating an individual account, you establish an account under a group name. Then you assign a set of privileges to the group. Once the group has been established, you need not go through the process of establishing privileges for each employee. Instead, you assign the employee to the privileges by assigning the employee to a group that has the proper assortment.

Most database servers come with a preinstalled group called *public*. Every user is in the public group and enjoys whatever privileges you may assign to that group. Naturally, you will want to keep them limited. If you want to grant added privileges to an individual employee, you can assign that employee to a more privileged group or grant the privileges directly to the employee.

The role system is a variation on grouping. Instead of granting privileges based on an individual's overall responsibilities, it grants them on the basis of whatever activity the individual happens to be performing at the moment.

To create a role system, you start by defining the roles. Usually, these are defined by application. When a user starts a particular application, the system grants a set of privileges associated with it. If the user is authorized to work with that application, the user enjoys the privileges associated with that application.

The advantage of a role system is that the grants of privileges are dynamic. An application's privileges are available only to people who are actively working with the application. The privileges expire when the user leaves the application. The drawback is that you must control access to privileged applications tightly.

Managing Resources

In addition to managing access to the system, DBMS security must control the use of system resources. If available, use the resources of your DBMS to establish interval controls. These limit the length of time an individual can claim access to the central processing unit (CPU) without interruption or the number of disk activities allowed per transaction.

Without these limits, a user—deliberately or by accident—could throw the system into an endless loop that would deny everyone else access to the database. Users who interrupt a transaction could leave critical assets locked and unavailable to anyone else. Just a single complex transaction could impede the system's performance for other users.

Only a few DBMS servers have interval controls to prevent this, but if you have them, use them.

Getting Together on Security

There is no standard pattern for client/server DBMS installations. There is one scheme that is in wide use, though, as organizations move away from their large systems through client/server databases toward TCP/IP networks. This is a transitional system with a server-based DBMS handling new and downsized applications. Meanwhile, a large-system DBMS continues to store legacy applications and larger databases.

Although SQL is supposed to be standardized, in practice, it comes in many variations. This is particularly true of the security commands, which vary widely from system to system. Different systems have different combinations of security features and use different commands to invoke them. Then there is this added complication: Network security and database security are often administered by different people.

On one hand, security over the database installations is often the responsibility of the database administrator. Not only must this person maintain security on a variety of systems and platforms, but he or she also is responsible for the entire database system, not just its security. Furthermore, the administrator may have to deal with a separate official, who is likely to be a security professional, with responsibility for network security.

There are few management tools available to establish unified management over this doubly diverse field. There are few standards to guide you too. Instead, an organization in this position usually develops an ad hoc security plan that administers each DBMS separately. The typical plan follows these two basic steps:

- Determine what you need.
- Then figure out how you can get it done.

Facing Frustration

This can be a frustrating experience. For example, one New York City bank maintains two DBMS systems. One is an IBM DB/2 installation running on a mainframe. The other is the Microsoft/Sybase SQL Server running on a LAN. Each DBMS has its own security system, and the LAN operating system presents a third. These systems present no common platform from which to administer a single security scheme.

Situations like this are difficult—and common. The bank has responded with a plan that seeks to make maximum use of all the security features each system has to offer. For example, it is able to use the DB/2 security system down to the table level, where the LAN system picks up the load. There is a similar working relationship using SQL Server security. This means, however, that an employee who has the rights to see information from both databases must penetrate three security schemes: the network's, the server's, and the mainframe's.

This approach to security is not entirely a bad thing. Implementing security one DBMS at a time helps promote a granular approach that fine-tunes each user's access rights. Still, this type of system can produce a great deal of confusion for users and, more important, for the people who have to maintain the security system. Faced with this situation, administrators often are tempted to take shortcuts. With multiple checkpoints available, they decide to enforce security more rigidly at one point than at the others.

Typically, they exert their tightest controls at the LAN and then assume that anyone who can cross that point successfully is also entitled to use the database. This plan is weak because there are so many ways to evade LAN security.

Draw the Line

An alternative is to impose security most strongly at the system level. Again, you make the assumption that anyone who can pass the main security barrier is entitled to use the database. This is where large systems still have an advantage. Compared with LANs, their security systems are strong enough that the basic assumption is safer.

Action Item: Wherever you decide to draw the line, you must draw it somewhere. Determine the point at which you want to exert your main access control, and set up your main line of defense there. You can still set up additional security checkpoints further into the system, but their roles should be to back up the initial screening.

Pick and Choose

A second point is to be selective in what you try to control. Only a few highly sensitive databases require row-by-row oversight, and most of these belong to the government. Refer again to your initial assessment, and review your most serious protection needs. Then concentrate your efforts and assets on meeting those identified needs. You can pick from the security measures listed in Table 12-1 (see next page).

Local-area networks (LANs)

- Encrypt passwords that are transmitted over the network.
- Associate passwords with time stamps and adapter addresses.
- Provide screen locking.
- Require that users sign on again if the server becomes unavailable.
- Require that users sign off when leaving their workstations.
- Forbid sign-ons while the system is being maintained.

File access control

- Define file access rules for both physical and logical drivers and at the subdirectory and file levels.
- Make sure file-level security will support filename wild cards.
- Access rules should not have to be rewritten if you move groups of files or directories.
- Limit the number of current users at the subdirectory and file levels.
- Limit LAN administration to a single server.
- Report all access attempts to the resource owner.

Server security

- Prevent all input to the server without a valid ID. Impose this requirement on the mouse as well as the keyboard.
- Maintain backups of the entire server operating system as well as data files.
- Run scheduled, unattended backups of the server.
- Use disk mirroring for quick recovery.
- Establish scheduled server-controlled backups of the workstations.

Securing multiple servers

- Do not require that employees use unique IDs and passwords for each server. Provide a one-stop logon.
- Maintain local control of remote access.
- Give the administrator the power to determine whether the access rules for a particular file will apply to copies of that file or to information extracted from it.

CHAPTER 13

Developing a
Security Policy

Only a few people may be making money on the Intranet, but this does not keep others from trying. Some engage in electronic commerce. Others engage in electronic theft.

This means that your information assets could be vulnerable. And the big drawback of an extranet is that even controlled outside access could make your information very vulnerable indeed. Of course, the objective of extranet security is to give only the right people the right kind of access to your intranet assets. While this line is easy enough to draw, you need something more to keep some people from jumping across it.

A business owner who suspected an employee of stealing left a packet of cash in plain view on a counter. When it was not there the next morning, the owner was sure he had caught the thieving employee red-handed. No such luck. It seems someone else had walked in and taken advantage of the unguarded stash. Not only did the owner lose the bait money, but the loss also failed to produce any evidence against the suspected employee.

Dangerous Ideas About Security

Most businesspeople are not that careless about either their cash or their information assets. Nevertheless, some people come surprisingly close, and too many people seem unaware of the security issues they face. They express attitudes like these:

- Sending credit card information across the Intranet is no more dangerous than handing your credit card to a waiter after a meal.
- Can you point to even one instance where someone has really been burned?
- We have a good firewall. What else could we possibly need?

To be sure, sending your credit card information over the Intranet really is no more dangerous than the well accepted practice of handing a card to a waiter. But it is no safer either. And this type of analysis addresses only one small corner of Intranet security. It says nothing at all about the problems of letting the good guys in while keeping the bad guys out.

It is also true that there have been few if any reported instances of successful Internet theft. However, if Internet security follows the pattern of other forms of computer security, victims are notoriously reluctant to report their losses. Furthermore, if few people are yet making large sums of money on the Web, it stands to reason that few criminals are making big scores either. If the money is not there, it can be very hard to steal.

Now, about the firewall. These products are becoming better and more sophisticated all the time, as I will discuss in Chap. 14. The problem with firewalls is that people rely on them too much. Protecting your assets requires a thorough, well-planned security program. A firewall probably will be an important part of that program. However, it is not the whole thing.

Why You Need a Security Policy

Security is very subjective, and only one organization—yours—can determine the best security policy for your yourself and your organization. Although corporate culture may be an overused oxymoron, there is still something to the idea.

Each business is different. Each has its own attitudes, assets, and technology. Each has different requirements for storing, sending, and communicating information in electronic form. No single security policy is best for any given organization. Furthermore, businesses change. As your business evolves to adapt to changing market conditions, your security policy must evolve to meet changing technology conditions.

Not long ago, the Computer Security Institute (CSI, San Francisco) and the Federal Bureau of Investigation (FBI) got together to survey some of the nation's leading organizations. Responses came from 428 major corporations, financial institutions, health care centers, government agencies, and major universities. The results were as follows:

- The threat of computer crime over the Intranet is real and serious.
- The surveyed businesses and institutions are seriously underprepared.

For example, even many password-protected applications have trap doors left open for maintenance and other purposes. For example, the program may come with a well-known default maintenance password that customers are expected to change. Many do not. These openings usually can be secured, such as by changing the maintenance password to something known only to selected members of your own organization. However, large numbers of the survey respondents had failed to take such simple steps. Many did not even know where the openings to their systems were. Such companies are taking unnecessary chances with their information and their reputations.

It Takes Money

Up-to-date security costs money. Not a lot, but enough that management will rightly be concerned with the return on a security investment. Security can be a hard sell, particularly if there have been no serious losses so far.

Furthermore, you probably are hard-pressed to keep up with the rush of legitimate technology, not to mention the increasingly sophisticated attacks used by serious invaders. Respondents to the CSI/FBI survey reported that their defenses were being probed increasingly by a diverse array of attacks, including brute force, password guessing, data diddling, and forcing service shutdowns. A separate study, conducted at Michigan State University, showed that more than 40 percent of the respondents not only had been the targets of computer crime but also had suffered at least 25 attacks each.

However, no doubt the person who left open the proverbial barn door offered the excuse that the horse had never been stolen before. And if you do not believe that unauthorized access attempts are a threat, just listen to the spiel of a security product sales representative. Even when you allow for exaggeration, the number of attacks clients suffer, and their increasing sophistication, should remove any sense of assurance you might have felt.

In the News

Although countless victims of computer crime try to hide their losses and vulnerability, the last few years have seen several highly publicized incidents:

- In 1994, General Electric, IBM, and NBC were attacked on the same holiday weekend. The attack caused major service disruptions.
- In 1995, Citibank was hit by Russian invaders who used a laptop personal computer to transfer $10 million to their own bank accounts.
- Employees of the Social Security Administration were accused of passing personal information on about 11,000 people to a credit card fraud ring. The information included the individuals' Social Security numbers and mothers' maiden names, both used often for identification in credit and bank transactions.

These are just the major reported cases. In the CSI/FBI survey, fewer than 17 percent of the respondents had reported security incidents to law enforcement. The reason given by most: They wanted to avoid negative publicity.

Admitted Losses

CSI, a member research organization that provides public service information, is only one among many authorities who acknowledge that most computer security violations are kept quiet. You probably never hear about the most amazing stories.

Another authority who feels the same way is Martha Stansell Gamm, the U.S. attorney who prosecuted hacker Kevin Mitnick. Gamm estimates that for every reported case, nearly 500 are kept quiet. CSI says that of 8923 attacks on proprietary information in 1993, only 19 were reported.

Pause, if you like, to ponder how these authorities seem to have such detailed reports of unreported cases. Nevertheless, it is well established that most victims of computer crime do try to hide their misfortunes. The upshot is that many other organizations lack a keen awareness that the same kinds of things could happen to them.

Gamm cited Boeing's disclosure that its supercomputer in Seattle had been attacked and how follow-up monitoring showed that it was being used as a springboard site to attack the federal district court system. Judges' rulings were altered, but the courts' system administrator apparently was unaware that attacks were taking place.

The National Center for Computer Crime Data (Santa Cruz, CA) states that the annual loss from computer network crime is $550 million a year in the United States alone. The Yankee Group, an industry consulting firm, estimates that when you include losses in productivity, confidence, and competitive advantage, the total financial loss for such security breaches is closer to $5 billion annually.

The trade publication *Information Week* and the accounting firm Ernst and Young conducted a survey of industry network managers. They found that 16 percent of those responding reported network break-ins, sabotage, or stolen data. At least 20 respondents said their security losses came to more than $1 million.

In one survey, 30 respondents admitted that security violations have caused financial loss. The total loss among this group was $66 million. This included a single $50 million loss when a system was penetrated, but there were three others of $1 million or more.

When the U.S. Senate conducted hearings on computer security, it received one survey report that had covered a small number of small security firms. Nevertheless, these respondents said their clients had suffered losses of more than $800 million in a single year.

Companies are experiencing different types of losses. Examples include

- Service interruption, where attackers effectively shut down your network gateway to the outside world

- Theft of on-line corporate assets or interception of sensitive e-mail or data as they are transmitted

- Fraudulent misrepresentation of data or people

Do Not Let the Scare Stores Scare You

Security consultants are fond of telling such stories, of course. Do not let them scare you out of an extranet or into a hasty reaction. Proceed, but do it carefully. You cannot take security for granted.

For example, AT&T, among others, accepts credit applications over its extranet. Browser security encrypts the transaction—in Netscape Navigator, the broken key in the lower left corner of the screen becomes a solid key when its Secure Sockets Layer (SSL) is active.

Security First Network Bank uses the Intranet to give customers remote electronic access to their accounts. In addition to the solid-key assurance, a second screen assures them of a verified contact with the bank. Then the customer must be identified by personal identification number (PIN) or credit card number. Verification services such as VeriSign (Mountain View, CA) or Veriphone (Redwood City, CA) can do the necessary verification for banks, retailers, and others who conduct business over the Web.

Safe Transactions Available

With SSL and verification services available, many types of transactions can be made adequately secure. However, different applications expose you to different kinds of risks. This means that they require different kinds of security.

This means that when you consider a security plan, you also must consider the kind of business you want to conduct. The security needs appropriate to banking and credit card transactions are not the same security needs you would have if you were opening a limited selection of business information to external business partners. You would need yet another security plan if you plan to offer an on-line mall type of business.

For example, an on-line mall selling items at retail, using credit card transactions, usually risks only the loss of the single transaction, and there is a ceiling even on this. A bank, on the other hand, could face a very large liability if someone transfers money illegally or obtains the credit card records of several thousand customers.

Some Do It Safely

These are examples of organizations that have learned to use Web commerce safely. There are many other examples of those who have not. Many companies unknowingly increase the vulnerability to their computer network, all in the name of improving productivity:

- By adding a remote access e-mail gateway so that employees can use their e-mail while away from the office, companies may unwittingly provide a side door into their computer network, particularly if they do not use strong authentication measures.

- By adding a World Wide Web site and ftp server so that their customers can instantly retrieve product information and software, companies may unwittingly provide an electronic tunnel to other, nonpublic corporate data.

- By embracing electronic document interchange (EDI), a company could be allowing criminals access to both inventory and checkbook.

There Are Reasons for Doing This

In each of these cases there is a good reason to take the security risks. Indeed, too much security can be as counterproductive as too little security. As companies come to rely on internetworking to lower the costs of doing business—e-mail for communications, World Wide Web sites for information publishing, ftp for software update distribution, EDI for supplier-vendor transactions, and extranets for other business partner relations—the productivity gains become too compelling to ignore.

First, Secure the Inside

You need a security policy to establish an enterprise-wide standard for important elements like these:

- How both internal and external users interact with a company's computer network

■ How the corporate computer architecture and topology will be implemented and where computer assets will be located.

The policy must balance the seriousness of possible threats against the value of personal productivity and corporate assets that need different levels of protection.

Needed: A Broader Focus

One of the problems in establishing a security plan is a tendency to concentrate on one or two problems at the expense of many others. Historically, the problem of recreational hackers has gained a lot of attention. Meanwhile, a large majority of computer-based crime is committed by people inside the organization.

Where extranet security is concerned, there is a new version of the traditional tunnel vision. People are concerned primarily about firewalls and encryption. The best you can say is that they are now isolated on two subjects instead of one. Nevertheless, both the traditional single concentration and the more modern dual focus have one thing in common. They are concerned with protecting the system from outsiders, not insiders.

To be sure, if you are thinking of extending your intranet into an extranet, your main concern will be with controlling external access. You must police yourself carefully, though, to make sure you have a comprehensive security program that protects you against internal as well as external threats.

The Threat from Within

If the internal part of the system is not secure, the system itself is not secure. There are not as many dishonest employees as the most cynical seem to believe, but there are enough to cause some worry. It does little good to protect against hacking from outside while an employee quietly taps the system and makes off with thousands or millions.

Furthermore, if someone from the outside does want to invade your system, the easiest route could be to find your way into an ill-protected internal system. Either way, from inside or outside, the network's perimeter is a likely point of attack.

One of the most vulnerable spots in many networks is the link that carries data between a Web server and a legacy database. It is very easy for a knowledgeable person to slip past a firewall to tap this vulnerable source of illicit information.

At the familiar bottom line, if your network is insecure to begin with, there is no real point in securing the extranet portion of it. On the other hand, if you start with a secure network, it is fairly easy to extend that security externally.

Learn the Layout

The best way to start developing a security plan is to get a complete, detailed picture of your network. This may not be easy. Many organizations literally do not know how many Internet connections they have or where to find them.

The most common practice is to manage a network as a single entity. This is an invitation to trouble. It means that you must secure the entire network against every possible kind of attack. You will be managing the forest, oblivious to the decay in individual trees. Instead, split the network into smaller parts of a size you can handle.

Start by establishing a logical series of domains: production, sales, business partners, finance, and other major business activities. You could then assess where each domain is now connected to the outside world and get a handle on where the connections are. At the same time, determine the types of access the people in each group should have: perhaps a multisite internal information exchange for product design and a controlled-access extranet connection for the business partners.

This exercise can be time-consuming, but it can help you learn where the access points are and should be. You will have a better idea of what kind of extranet access needs to be controlled, and you can go a long way toward identifying internal systems that may be weak.

Accent the Positive

Be as positive as you can in selling the security plan to management—and to the employees whose cooperation is vital to make the security system work. Avoid scare tactics or anguished wailing. Electronic commerce is going to happen with or without you, and a great deal of it will take place over extranet connections. Be honest about identifying the risks, but also be prepared with constructive suggestions that can point to solutions.

Take control of extranet activities or, better, get management to do so. All extranet commerce should have management's specific approval. A healthy dose of freelance content is welcome on an intranet, but the interaction you have via the extranet should be defined and controlled carefully.

Assess Your Situation

A security assessment is a vital baseline for security planning. A thorough assessment will give you the means to spell out the threats you face and the places where you are most vulnerable. Conduct the assessment with the objective of incorporating extranet commerce into the overall security program.

Other Measures

Other elements of a security program include the following:

- Establish formal agreements with the business partners who will have access to the extranet. Try to anticipate the disputes and misunderstandings that could arise. Establish areas of responsibility. And do not automatically expect that existing agreements with partners, even those written for EDI transactions, will be adequate for the extranet. Look at the specific details of extranet commerce, and make sure your agreements acknowledge them.

- Make sure the trading partners have secured their own networks. Just as extranet communication creates a seamless chain between multiple customers and suppliers, it also can create a seamless link of vulnerability.

- Use the tools you have available. Back in the 1920s, a boat encountered a surprise storm and sank. In the lawsuit that ensued, a court held the ship's owners responsible for the loss. Had they used a weather radio, they would have known the storm was coming. Although marine radio was a new technology at the time, the judge believed the ship should have been so equipped. The same principle applies to security. If a protective tool, no matter how new, can help secure your network, it deserves at least strong consideration.

- Keep track of intrusion attempts. Firewalls and other security installations usually have these services available. Even when the attempts are unsuccessful, it pays to know their origins so that you can continue to be prepared for them.

- Store important data away from the Internet. As transactions come into the system, make sure they are encrypted, and route them to safe storage elsewhere.

- Do not erect difficult barriers for authorized users. After all, you do want them to use the extranet. Obtrusive security will discourage the very type of activity for which you created the extranet. More seriously, authorized people who encounter difficult barriers will tend to find ways around them. As they do so, they blaze trails for less welcome visitors to follow.

- Be prepared for the worst. Despite your best-executed plans, you will sometimes suffer losses. Establish clear procedures for dealing with cases of fraud. And when natural disaster strikes, make sure you have a recovery plan in place.

The Security Challenges of an Extranet

The Internet and related technology present a list of challenges that seems to grow nearly as fast as the Internet itself. One of the first is that the main vehicle of Internet communication, Transmission Control Protocol/Internet Protocol (TCP/IP), was not designed to add security to communication. It can be used to solve security problems, but it does not do so automatically.

If it is going to help secure your extranet, TCP/IP will need some help, including

- *Access control.* It is not enough just to admit people who can present the proper identification. You also should authenticate them, to make sure they are who they say that they are. And once admitted, they should have only the most carefully tailored forms of access to your information.

- *Easy login.* Here is where ease of use is important for authorized users. The security system should be all but invisible to those who legitimately use your network. It is worthwhile, too, for both their convenience and yours, to have a single system of access control throughout the network.

Protection You Cannot Buy

Many information services (IS) people have become accustomed to thinking of products as "solutions." They imagine that they can secure their networks by buying the right combinations of hardware and software. As the ancient maps put it, "This way lie demons."

A security consultant tells of a client who asked his firm to try to penetrate the intranet security barrier it placed on its Internet connection. And the consultant failed. It seems the client had done a great job of securing that one Internet connection, but it did not realize that marketing and other groups had set up their own connections. There were 14 in all. Using these openings, the consultant infiltrated the intranet successfully and downloaded strategic plans and product designs.

This is an example of the "set it, forget it" style of security. You assume that once you have installed a firewall or some other security measure, you are permanently safe. Consultants who specialize in attacking supposedly secure networks have one of the easier jobs in information technology. Extranets will only make life easier for them, and potentially harder for you.

The Unknown Web Sites

Even in an intranet environment, it is hard enough to secure computers known to be attached to a corporate network. In many cases, Web servers have been put up without the knowledge of the information technology (IT) department. The presence of unknown and unsanctioned Web servers is a significant security risk. Typically, a desktop personal computer is turned into a server and attached to the wide-area network (WAN), but it is not physically segregated. It is a potential entry point to sensitive corporate information.

Even servers and other hardware installed with department knowledge and permission can become vulnerable points. IT managers might inadvertently leave loopholes open when they set up a firewall's routing table, when they make applications hypertext markup language (HTML) aware, or when they set up the Secure Sockets Layer (SSL) on the servers.

The Irony of Firewalls

Unsecured servers are primarily an intranet problem, but this problem leads to an ironic fact of extranet security. Firewalls, the very devices meant to secure internal webs, often prove vulnerable because IT managers make so many access allowances that the brick walls ends up with yawning gaps. Such was the case at a Fortune 500 company that asked a consultant to find out if the firewall was enforcing the policy it was supposed to be.

In this case, the firewall was letting in everything. It was not filtering any traffic. By the time various people had built in their own exceptions, the firewall was essentially a workstation acting as a router.

This kind of thing can happen easily. If 5000 employees with browsers decide they need to run audio clips off the Internet, they can pressure IT to open a port on the firewall. IT, however, may not have had a chance to thoroughly test the audio application for security weaknesses.

Self-fulfilling Description

It is significant that many companies define an intranet as the portion of their network behind a firewall. This view may be rather limited and simplistic, but it points out the trust companies place in the technology.

Intranet builders install firewalls on the corporate web's perimeter and limit entry to remote clients with appropriate names and passwords. Firewalls are available with a range of capabilities from a variety of vendors large and small.

First-generation firewalls use packet filtering techniques that examine the source and destination addresses of inbound TCP/IP packets. They check them against a list of accepted addresses and allow or reject entry as appropriate.

Second generation firewalls, called *proxy servers* or *application-level filters*, are meant to address that problem and are particularly important for securing intranets. As proxies for Web servers, these application layer firewalls have the authority to communicate with the system that is requesting access. Besides verifying the validity of user names and passwords, these products examine the data being transmitted. An HTML proxy, for instance, knows what valid HTML data look like and can determine if access should be provided.

There is also a category of third generation firewalls that use a stateful multilayer technique (SMLT) for screening packets. Rather than examining packets using a proxy, SMLT firewalls use data parsing software that takes a snapshot of an entire packet. These firewalls compare packets with the known states of friendly packets. The technique saves processing time that can bog down proxy server firewalls.

There is nothing absolute about these classifications. Many current products are hybrids of one or more types. Furthermore, there are those who maintain that SMLT firewalls do not constitute a distinct class. Of course, this claim comes primarily from companies that do not market SMLT firewalls.

Access Control

Increasingly, IT managers are using firewalls like these to control access to the information on intranets. Many companies would prefer to not have human resources or key accounting functions visible to everyone in the company. A firewall can be a highly selective means of access control.

For example, at J.P. Morgan & Company, an information security services team helps business managers assess the risk associated with data they want to put on the financial firm's intranet. If the information is meant for only part of the company population, the security team might recommend that the information be hosted on a private Web rather than the corporate intranet. The company then will use a firewall to segment the Web server.

Configuration Woes

Whether you are buying a firewall to restrict external access or segment an intranet, make sure it is one that you can understand and configure. Improper configuration is one of the most common sources of firewall leaks. The easier a product is to set up, the more effective it can be.

The risk of configuration problems also dictates that you test a firewall frequently to make sure that there are no vulnerabilities. If a firewall is installed incorrectly or is managed imperfectly, some of the holes that were supposed to be plugged will be left open. Intranet administrators can use outsiders to test their firewalls, or they can do it themselves using commercial software.

Openings in TCP/IP

Transmission Control Protocol/Internet Protocol (TCP/IP) is another source of vulnerability. It is so universal that plenty of people know how to manipulate all its features and failings. Because extranets run TCP/IP, they can be more difficult to secure than other corporate networks. TCP/IP promotes open communication and ease of sharing information. This is the polar opposite of maintaining security and minimizing access.

Lockheed Martin Corporation appreciates that self-evident truth. The challenge of building an intranet and providing universal access to information has required that the company shift from the mainframe mindset of protecting everything to the open Unix philosophy. This was particularly hard for a security-conscious company in the defense industry

To protect the data on its intranet, Lockheed uses secure Web servers, public and private keys, "smart" cards, encryption, and internal and external firewalls. Further plans include encrypted tunneling, which allows remote connections to the intranet over a secure Internet link.

The Java Threat

Lockheed Martin also does not allow the use of JavaScript on the intranet because of security problems found in the programming language. Neither does Amoco, the Chicago-based petrochemical firm. Amoco's security managers have blocked imported Java applets from the intranet, but employees can develop their own scripts. A Java script can have Trojan horse characteristics, but this is much less likely with internally developed scripts.

More Peril from Cached Data

The Java weaknesses represent just one example of problems associated with emerging Web technologies. Cached data are another potential weak spot. The typical browser caches 5 to 10 MB of the most recently accessed data on the computer's hard drive. The Microsoft Internet Explorer, for example, reserves about 10 percent of the hard drive for the cache. On a 1GB drive, this is 100 MB of potentially sensitive data waiting to be stolen.

For peak security, configure the server so that pages are not cached, and do not allow browsers to maintain caches. Figure 13-1 shows a typical configuration screen you can use to manage a browser cache.

Even supposedly secure forms of technology are potentially vulnerable. For example, the standard Secure Hypertext Transfer Protocol (S-HTTP) authentication and access control scheme used by Web servers provides no way to end an authenticated session without shutting down the browser. This is something many people do not do routinely. Since there is no easy way to log out, they leave sessions open. Their user names and passwords, plus all the associated privileges, get attached to a session and communicated with each request from the point of logon.

Figure 13-1
The Netscape configuration screen is typical of available features to control a browser cache.

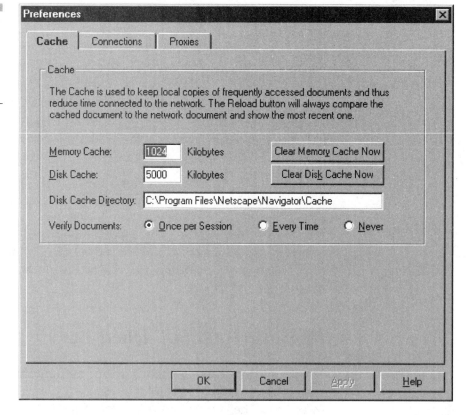

Human, Not Technical, Solution

There are technical solutions to all these problems. As the TCP/IP, Java, and S-HTTP problems illustrate, intranets do introduce new elements of risks. But the market has responded with products that compensate. More significant is that these problems illustrate a generally poor state of corporate network security. Extranets, particularly those which integrate with internal database systems, create new needs for security. It requires that you apply more thought to the problem and rely less on even the best products to protect you by themselves.

Elements of a Security Policy

There are many strong tools you can use to secure a computer network. By themselves, the software applications and hardware products that secure a business' computer network do not constitute a security policy, but they are essential elements in the creation of security. They are tools, and like a more primitive tool, the hammer, their effect depends on how they are used.

These tools have been evolving for the last two decades, roughly the same length of time people have been trying to break into computer networks. These tools can protect your computer network at many levels, and a well-guarded enterprise deploys many different types of security technologies.

Physical Security

The most obvious element of security is often the most easily overlooked: physical security, or controlling access to the most sensitive components in your computer network, such as a network administration station or the server room. Since network and data access is controlled from these places, physical security deserves strong consideration in any security policy. No amount of planning or expensive equipment will keep your network secure if someone can just walk in and use your central control consoles. Even without evil intent, an untrained person may unknowingly provide unauthorized outside access or override protective configurations.

The next level of computer security is operating system security. The guidelines for operating system security generally have been established by the Department of Defense. Other countries and other federal organizations have set their own standards. In the past few years, certified secure operating systems like Unix and Windows NT have been introduced in commercial operating systems. These provide discretionary access control such as read and write permissions for files and directories, plus auditing and authentication controls.

Firewalls and Access Control

A firewall is the point at which your private company network and a public network such as the Internet connect. A firewall system is a hardware/software combination that guards this perimeter, controlling access into and out of your company's network. In theory, firewalls allow only authorized communications between the internal and external networks. In practice, new ways are constantly being developed to get past these systems. If properly implemented, though, firewalls are very effective at keeping out unauthorized users and stopping unwanted activities on an internal network.

Firewall systems protect the network in several ways:

- They allow e-mail and other applications such as ftp and remote login to take place as desired. Meanwhile, they limit other kinds of access to the internal network.

- They provide an authorization mechanism that offers reasonable assurance that only specified users or applications can gain access through the firewall.

- They usually provide a logging and alerting feature that tracks designated usage and signals at specified events.

- They offer address translation that masks the actual name and address of any machine communicating through the firewall.

- They are adding new functions such as encryption and virtual private networks. Encryption is the coding or scrambling of data and keeps unintended users from reading the information. Virtual private networks employ encryption to provide secure transmissions over public networks such as the Internet.

Custom Controls

Firewalls also can be used within an enterprise network to compartmentalize different servers and networks, controlling access within the network. For example, an organization may want to separate the accounting and payroll server from the rest of the network and only allow certain individuals to see that information.

One thing to remember: All firewall systems exact a performance penalty, large or small. As a system repeatedly checks or reroutes communication packets, they do not flow through the system as efficiently as they would if the firewall was not in place.

Password Mechanisms

Passwords are the accepted way to identify and authenticate the people who try to gain entry to a computer system. In simple terms, passwords verify that a user is he or she says he or she is. Unfortunately, there are a number of ways in which a password can be compromised:

- Someone wanting to gain access can "listen" for a user name and password as an authorized user gains access over a public network.

- Someone wanting to gain access can mount an attack on your access gateway, entering an entire dictionary of words (or license plates or any other list) against a password field.

- Someone may give his or her password to a coworker or may leave it out in a public place.

Fortunately, there are password technologies and tools that can assist in making your network more secure:

- One-time password generation assumes that a password will be compromised. Before someone goes beyond the internal network, the system generates a list of passwords that will work only one time with a given user name. When logging on to the system remotely, a password is used once and then will no longer be valid.

- Some operating systems provide such features as password aging and password policy enforcement. Password aging requires that individuals create new passwords every so often. Good password policy dictates that there be a minimum number of characters and a mix of letters and numbers. The operating system will not accept a password that does not meet these rules.

- ■ "Smart" cards provide extremely secure password protection. Unique passwords, based on a challenge-response scheme, are created on a small credit card device. The password is then entered as part of the logon process and validated against a password server, which logs all access to the system. As you might expect, these systems can be expensive to implement.

- ■ Single sign-on overcomes an irony in system security: As a user gains more passwords, these passwords actually become less secure. Many enterprises require different passwords for access to different parts of the system. As users acquire more passwords—some people have more than 50—they cannot help but write them down or create easy-to-remember passwords.

A single sign-on system is essentially a centralized access control list that determines who is authorized to access different areas of the computer network. There is also a mechanism for providing the expected password. A user need only remember a single password.

Encryption and Privacy

Encryption mechanisms rely on keys or passwords. The longer the password, the more difficult the encrypted data are to break. The Data Encryption Standard (DES) uses a 56-bit key length, and some keys are hundreds of bits long.

There are two kinds of encryption mechanisms: private and public key. Private key encryption uses the same key to encode and decode the data. Public key encryption uses one key to encode the data and another to decode the data. The name *public key* comes from a unique property of this type of encryption mechanism: One of the keys can be public without compromising the privacy of the message or the other key. Public key encryption mechanisms rely on a certificate authority, a trusted store and dispenser of public keys.

Still, the best privacy is physical security. While encryption is a reasonable option for most commercial uses, the strongest method of privacy for the most sensitive data relies on keeping the data off the network, under lock and key.

Good Stuff In, Garbage Out

Encryption is the coding of data through an algorithm or transform table into hard-to-decipher garbage. You can encrypt data stored on a server, or you can apply the encryption as data pass through a network. Encryption is a way to ensure that private data remain private and that only intended users can see the information.

There are many forms of encryption, but the most popular forms are

- DES, or the Data Encryption Standard, has been endorsed by the National Institute of Standards and Technology since 1975 and is the most commercially available encryption standard. As recently as 1994, it was reaffirmed for federal use for another 5 years. DES is subject to federal export control restrictions. Programs that use DES generally are not available for export from the United States.

- RSA encryption is a public key encryption system that is a patented technology in the United States and thus not available without a license. However, the algorithm was published before the patent was filed, and RSA encryption may be used in Europe and Asia without a royalty. RSA encryption is growing in popularity and has a record of resisting brute force attacks.

- An emerging encryption mechanism is Pretty Good Privacy (PGP), with which you can encrypt information stored on your system and send and receive encrypted e-mail. PGP also provides tools and utilities for creating, certifying, and managing keys.

Authentication and Integrity

Authentication simply means knowing that someone is who he or she says he or she is. When using resources or sending messages, it often can be important that people are identified accurately.

Integrity involves knowing that the data you send or receive have not been altered along the way. Message integrity is maintained with digital signatures.

A *digital signature* is a block of data at the end of a message that attests to the authenticity of the file. Digital signatures perform both authentication and message integrity functions. Digital signatures are available in PGP and when using RSA encryption.

Kerberos is an add-on system that can be used with any existing network. Kerberos validates a user through its authentication system and uses DES when communicating sensitive information—such as passwords—on an open network. In addition, Kerberos sessions have a limited life span, requiring people to login after a predetermined amount of time and preventing would-be intruders from gaining entry by replaying captured sessions.

Turning Hacker Tools to Your Advantage

Security is, by definition, a defensive activity. Nevertheless, some security experts suggest that you take the offensive once in a while.

Hackers use many tools to probe your system for weaknesses. You can do the same thing and discover system weaknesses before they do. Then you can take action to correct the situation.

Among the best known of these tools is SATAN (Security Analysis Tool for Auditing Networks), which is publicly available on many Web sites. According to the National Computer Security Institute, many companies are using SATAN on their own network to uncover vulnerabilities.

Developing a Security Policy

The first rule for any extranet security policy should be that anything not expressly permitted should be prohibited. The policy should start by denying all access to all network resources and then expressly permit access for which there is a specific justification. Implemented in this way, your security policy should not allow any inadvertent actions or procedures.

Good Password Procedures

A good starting point for a security policy is a list of proper password policies. A thorough password policy would state that you should not

- Use your login name in any form as a password. This includes reversed, capitalized, and doubled forms.
- Use your first, middle, or last name in any form or use your spouse's or child's name.

- Use any other easily obtained information. This includes license-plate numbers, telephone numbers, Social Security numbers, the make of your automobile, or the name of your street.
- Use a password of all digits or all the same letter.
- Use a word found in English or foreign-language dictionaries, spelling lists, or other lists of words.
- Use a password shorter than six characters.

The policy also should contain a list of things password holders should do:

- Use a password with both upper- and lowercase letters.
- Use a password with some nonalphabetic characters like digits or punctuation.
- Use a password that is easy to remember so that you do not have to write it down.

Define Your Expectations

The goal of a security policy is to define what the organization expects. The policy should state your standards of proper computer and network use, and it should define procedures to prevent and respond to security problems. This means that you cannot limit yourself to discussing technology and procedures. You also must consider what the organization and its various components want to accomplish.

In particular, consider the goals and direction of the organization. For example, a defense contractor may have much different security concerns than a book publisher. In addition, departments within the organization will have different requirements. The network security policy also must mesh with existing policies, rules, regulations, and laws.

Since you probably intend to make an extranet available to business partners, you also must consider their needs. The policy should address any local problems that might arise from activities at the partner's site. The reverse is also true: The policy should describe what to do when something on your end creates problems in your partners' systems.

The diverse needs of your organization also should be reflected in the makeup of the policymaking body itself. Policywriting must be a joint effort by a representative group, usually including:

- Decision makers, who will be responsible for enforcing the policy

- Technicians, who will implement the policy
- Employees, who must make use of the policy

In short, involve or at least represent everyone who will be responsible for making the security policy work. A security policy that cannot be enforced, implemented, or used in everyday operations is useless.

The Development Process

Developing a security policy involves several steps:

- Identifying the organizational assets that should be protected
- Identifying the threats to these assets
- Evaluating the risk these threats entail
- Evaluating and selecting the tools and techniques available to meet the risks
- Developing a policy

The completed policy should include an auditing procedure that conducts timely reviews of network and server use. The policy also should provide for an appropriate response to a violation or breakdown. This response mechanism should be in place before any incident occurs. Finally, the policy should be communicated to everyone who uses the computer network, whether employee or business partner, and the policy should provide for regular reviews of its effectiveness.

Identifying Organizational Assets

The first step is to draw up a list of all the things that need to be protected. Organize the list so that you can update it easily and regularly. If yours is like most organizations, you will add and subtract equipment all the time. Items to be considered include

- *Hardware:* CPUs, boards, keyboards, terminals, workstations, PCs, printers, disk drives, communication lines, terminal servers, routers
- *Software:* source programs, object programs, utilities, diagnostic programs, operating systems, communication programs
- *Data:* during program execution, stored on-line, archived off-line, backups, audit logs, databases, in transit over communication media

- *People:* the individuals who run and use the systems
- *Documentation:* on programs, hardware, systems, and local administrative procedures
- *Supplies:* paper, forms, ribbons, magnetic media

Assessing the Risk

Risk analysis determines what you need to protect, what you need to protect it from, and how to protect it. Among other things, it is a great antidote to the tendency to focus excessively on outside threats and pay too little attention to the greater threats from inside. You examine all your risks and rank them by level of severity. You also must make cost-effective decisions on what you want to protect. Possible risks to your network include

- Unauthorized access
- Unavailable service, which can include some or all network services, corruption of data, or a slowdown due to a virus
- Disclosure of sensitive information, especially that which gives someone else a particular advantage, or theft of information such as credit card information

Once the list has been assembled, develop a scheme to balance the risk against the importance of the resource. This will help determine how much effort you should expend to protect the resource.

Defining a Policy for Acceptable Use

Tools and applications form the technical foundation of a security policy, but they are only part of the solution. How users interact with the network is just as important. A policy for acceptable use should consider

- Who is allowed to use the resources?
- What is the proper use of the resources?
- Who is authorized to grant access and approve usage?
- Who should have system administration privileges?
- What are the users' rights and responsibilities?
- What are the rights and responsibilities of the system administrator compared with those of employees and external contacts?

- What do you do with sensitive information?

For example, you may want to cover the following topics when defining the users' rights and responsibilities:

- Guidelines on resource consumption: whether individuals are restricted, and if so, what the restrictions are.
- A definition of abuse in terms of system performance.
- Whether individuals are permitted to share accounts or let others use their accounts.
- The extent to which people should go to protect their passwords.
- How often users should change their passwords, and any other password restrictions or requirements.
- Whether you provide backups or expect others to create their own.
- Disclosure of information that may be proprietary.
- A statement on electronic mail privacy. This is governed by the Electronic Communications Privacy Act. The company should state whether it considers electronic mail private to each employee or views it as the property of the organization?
- Your policy concerning mail or postings to mailing lists or discussion groups. It should include guidelines on subjects like obscenity or harassment and on how to properly represent the organization in messages and discussions.
- A policy on electronic communication, covering such subjects as mail forging.
- Who will interpret the policy. This could be an individual or a committee. No matter how well written, the policy will require interpretation from time to time, and this body would serve to review, interpret, and revise the policy as needed.

Auditing and Review

To help determine if there is a violation of your security policy, take advantage of the tools included with your computer and network. Most operating systems store numerous bits of information in log files. Check these files periodically. This is often the first line of defense in detecting unauthorized use of the system.

Compare lists of currently logged-in users and past log-in histories.

Most people typically log in and out at about the same time each day. An account logged in outside the usual time may be an intruder.

Many systems maintain accounting records for billing purposes. You can use these records to determine usage patterns for the system; unusual accounting records may indicate unauthorized use of the system.

Also check any system logging facilities such as the Unix syslog utility, for unusual error messages from system software. For example, a large number of failed log-in attempts in a short period of time may indicate someone trying to guess passwords.

Operating system commands that list currently executing processes can be used to detect people who access programs they are not authorized to use, as well as to detect unauthorized programs that have been started by an intruder. By running various monitoring commands at different times throughout the day, you make it hard for an intruder to predict your actions.

You would have to be very lucky to catch a violator in a first act. However, by reviewing log files, you have a very good chance setting up procedures to spot the violation later.

Modern computers and software make review even more important than in the past. It is getting astoundingly easy to break into network sites through available point-and-click packages. Security is a dynamic process. Periodically assemble the core team or a representative part of it. Review how well things are working, identify the latest threats and security tools, and assess the risk to new assets and business practices. This is the only way an organization can stay secure and productive.

Communicating the Policy

The security policy should include a formal process to communicate the policy to everyone affected. Plan and conduct an educational campaign to make people aware of how the organization expects computer and network systems to be used and how to protect themselves from unauthorized users. This is particularly important when the policy extends to external parties.

Everyone should be informed about what is considered proper or improper use of their accounts and workstations. The best time to do this is when the account is established. In the case of an external client, a notice can be put on-line when the account is opened.

People should know how to detect unauthorized access to their account. If the system opens by displaying displays the last login time, people should be told to check that time make sure it agrees with the last actual use. Ideally, the security policy should strike a balance between protection and productivity.

Responding to Violations

When you identify a security violation, there are several ways you can respond. Some are better than others. If you plan your responses for different scenarios well in advance, without the distraction of dealing with an actual event, you will have the benefit of unhurried thinking.

You need to define how you would react to each specific type of violation. You also just develop a clearly defined series of actions based on the kind of party who violates your security policy. For example, an employee who violates the policy could be subject to disciplinary action. But what would you do should a business partner be responsible for the violation? This is a more difficult question, probably to be negotiated with the outside party. Whatever decision you reach, your policy should reflect it.

When a policy violation is detected, make sure you clearly determine how and why the violation occurred. This exercise often suggests the appropriate corrective action. Ideally, your policy will already specify the right response.

Responding to External Attacks

If you detect a violation and determine that it comes from outside the organization, there are several elements of your security plan that should go into effect. Your security plan should contain the answers to these questions:

- What outside agencies should be contacted, and who should contact them?
- Who should talk to the press?
- Under what circumstances do you contact law enforcement and investigative agencies?
- If a connection is made from a remote site, is the system manager authorized to contact that site?

■ What are your responsibilities to your business partners and other Internet sites?

Whenever your computer security is threatened, you may well find yourself between two conflicting types of responses. If management fears that the site is unacceptably vulnerable, it may choose a *protect and proceed* strategy. The primary goal of this approach is to protect and preserve facilities and to provide normal operations as quickly as possible. You will try to actively interfere with the intruder's processes, prevent further access, and begin immediate damage assessment and recovery. This process may involve shutting down the facilities, closing off access to the network, or other drastic measures. This approach may still leave you vulnerable unless you are able to identify the intruder quickly. Otherwise, the intruder may return via a different path or may attack another site.

The alternate approach, *pursue and prosecute,* adopts the opposite approach. Here, the primary objective is to let intruders continue their activities until you can identify them. Prosecutors and law enforcement agencies generally prefer this approach. A drawback is that this approach relies primarily on criminal prosecution. There is little here to protect you from civil litigation, particularly if a connected business partner suffers loss.

Prosecution is not the only outcome possible if the intruder is identified. If the culprit is an employee or a student, the organization may choose to take disciplinary action. The computer security policy needs to spell out the choices and how they will be selected if an intruder is caught.

Your selection between these alternatives should be one of the decisions you make in advance. You do not have to universally adopt one or the other. Your strategy choice might depend on the circumstances. Whatever your choice, make it on the basis of thorough evaluation, and notify all affected parties in advance of what they can expect from you.

When to Protect and Proceed

These factors tend to favor a protect and proceed policy:

■ Assets are not well protected.

■ Continued penetration could result in great financial risk.

■ Successful prosecution is unlikely.

■ The user base is unknown.

- Users are unsophisticated and their work is vulnerable.
- The site is vulnerable to lawsuits if others' resources are undermined.

When to Pursue and Prosecute

These factors favor a pursue and prosecute policy:

- Assets and systems are well protected.
- Good backups are available.
- The risk to the assets is outweighed by the disruption caused by present or future penetrations.
- This is a strong attack that occurs often.
- The network regularly attracts intruders.
- You are willing to accept any risk to your assets by allowing the penetration to continue.
- The intruder's access can be controlled.
- Your monitoring tools are sufficiently well developed to make the pursuit worthwhile.
- The support staff is clever and knows enough about the operating system, related utilities, and systems to make the pursuit worthwhile.
- Management is willing to prosecute.
- System administrators understand what kind of evidence would lead to successful prosecution.
- There is established contact with knowledgeable law enforcement officials.
- You have someone who is well versed in the relevant legal issues.
- You are prepared for possible civil action if data or systems become compromised during the pursuit.

Following Up

Even after you believe that a system has been restored to a safety, other holes and traps could be lurking in the system. It is important that you follow up on the incident and your response. Monitor the system closely for items that may have been missed during the cleanup stage.

Keep a detailed security log during the recovery phase. It can be valuable for two reasons:

■ To record the procedures you used to make the system secure again. This should include command procedures such as shell scripts that can be run periodically to recheck the security.

■ To maintain a record of important system events. This is a reference resource you can use when you to determine the extent of the damage from a particular incident.

After an incident, write a report describing the incident, method of discovery, correction procedure, monitoring procedure, and a summary of lessons learned. This will aid in a clear understanding of the problem. Remember, it is hard to learn from an incident if you do not understand the source.

14

Build a Better Firewall

The first rule of firewalls is not to depend on them. A firewall suggests heavy duty security like moats and drawbridges—places that are hard to penetrate.

It may be no accident, though, that one of the leading classes of computer viruses is called a *Trojan horse*, after the deceptive device that sneaked an army into a walled city. The biggest problem with firewalls is a tendency to take them for granted—to assume that once a firewall is in place, it provides all the protection you require, and you need not worry about it any further.

Both assumptions are wrong. A firewall is not the only protection you need. It is rightfully at the heart of any security program, but it cannot serve as the entire program. You need other forms of protection to back it up. In an extranet in particular, a firewall is only the first half of a firewall-encryption tandem.

And firewalls require constant worry. A firewall is a kind of filter, letting pass only the messages that meet the conditions you specify. Since the conditions are subject to constant change, you must keep changing the specifications constantly. A firewall is not a set-and-forget installation.

Firewalls Get Better

Not long ago, the typical firewall was a rough-edged Unix product using a single, simple technology limited to a few basic kinds of protection and with ease of use well down in the list of design priorities. The current crop of firewall products illustrates how far the field has come and how quickly. The best now offer sophisticated, customizable access control schemes that let you determine in fine detail who will be allowed to pass and under what conditions. Many of these same products take advantage of graphic interfaces to make it easier to manage all the choices you must make. More important, these interfaces make it harder to make mistakes that can leave costly holes in your primary security barrier. And for a growing number, the most important platform is Windows NT.

Table 14-1 describes a group of typical firewall products. Also see Appendix A for details on these products, features, specifications, and design philosophies.

These updated products originated in a young, fast-growing market, and they offer varied approaches to their tasks. At the same time, though, they reflect the evolution of a maturing market. While a typical firewall product was based on a single technology previously, today's most sophisticated offerings use hybrid technologies to extend an administrator's range of options. It is now possible to say, if you wish, that one group of users can have full access to the network, while another group must use Lotus Notes and then only during business hours.

With this wider range of options comes greater complexity. Fortunately, many firewall products now provide graphic interfaces to help you make the many decisions that face a firewall manager. Although there will continue to be many Unix firewalls, Windows NT is becoming a popular platform, and some allow administration from lighter-weight workstations like those which run Windows 95.

Class Structure Breaks Down

One indication of the industry's growth is that the products are becoming harder to classify. Not long ago firewalls could be grouped into three major classes depending on the type of access control they used: packet filtering, application gateways, and circuit level gateways. Today, most products are hybrids that sprawl across the conventional classes. In

TABLE 14-1

Typical firewall products.

Product	Vendor	Product Type	Platforms
ANS InterLock 3.0	ANS, 1875 Campus Commons Drive, Suite 220, Reston, VA 20191	Application-layer gateway	Sun Solaris
Black Hole	Milkyway Networks Corporation, San Jose, CA, 408-566-0800, e-mail: rmedrano@milkyway.com, fax: 408-566-0810, http://www.milkyway.com	Application-level gateway.	SPARC
Borderware Firewall Server 3.0.1	Border Network Technologies, Toronto, Ontario, 416-368-7157	Packet filter, application proxy	Maintenance module kernel; Pentium processer
Centri Firewall 3.1	Global Internet, 755 Page Mill Road, Suite A-101, Palo Alto, CA 94304, Palo Alto, CA 94304, 800-682-5550, http://www.globalinternet.com	Application gateway; packet filtering operation	Windows NT
Connect:Firewall	Sterling Commerce, 5215 N. O'Connor Blvd., Suite 1500, Irving, TX 75039, 800-700-5599, fax: 972-868-5100, e-mail: connect@csg.stercomm.com	Application proxy server	Windows NT, Solaris 25
CyberGuard Firewall 3.0	CyberGuard Corp., 2101 W. Cypress Creek Rd., Fort Lauderdale, FL 33309, 800-666-4273 or 954-973-5478	Hybrid packet and application filter	Intel Pentium and Pentium Pro; Concurrent Computer Night Hawk
Digital Firewall	Digital Equipment Corp., Maynard, MA, 508-493-5111	Packet filter, application proxy, network address translator	Digital Unix
Eagle	Raptor Systems, Inc., 69 Hickory Drive, Waltham, MA 02154, 800-932-4536 or 617-487-7700, http://www.raptor.com	Application-level firewall	Windows NT on Intel of Digital Alpha; Unix

TABLE 14-1

Typical firewall products. *(Continued)*

Product	Vendor	Product Type	Platforms
Firewall/Plus	Network-1 Software & Technology, Inc., 909 3rd Ave, New York, NY 10022, 800-NETWRK1 or 212-293-3068, http://www.network-1.com	Frame, packet, and application filtering; Windows NT version uses stateful inspection	DOS, Windows NT; Windows 95 pending
Firewall-1 2.1	Checkpoint Software Technologies, Redwood City, CA, 415-562-0400, http://www.checkpoint.com	Stateful inspection	Gateway; Sun Solaris for SPARC and Intel; HP-UX; Windows NT. Management module also operates on Windows 95
Gauntlet 3.1	Trusted Information Systems Inc., 2277 Research Blvd, Rockville, MD 20850, 301-527-9555, http://www.tis.com	Application proxy	BSD/OS, HP-UX SunOS
Interceptor 2.0	Technologic, Inc, 1000 Abernathy Road, Suite 1075, Atlanta, GA 30328, 770-522-0201, http://www.tlogic.com	Application level gateway in a proxy-based firewall	Intel
NetSP Secure Network	IBM www.ibm.com	Packet filter, application proxy	AIX on RS/6000
Gateway 2.1 PrivateNet	NEC Technologies, Internet Business Unit, 110 Rio Robles Drive, San Jose, CA 95134, 408-433-1226, fax: 408-433-1230, e-mail: info@privatenet.nec.com, http://www.privatenet.nec.com	Circuit- and application-level proxies	Bundled sytem based on BSD/OS on a Pentium system

fact, you will not even find widespread agreement on what constitutes a product category. In addition, new categories are arising all the time.

Packet Filters

In packet filtering, a router examines each incoming Internet Proctocol (IP) packet, checking its source or destination addresses and services against a list of accepted addresses. Packet filtering is generally the easiest type of control to administer—and to penetrate. Setting up the rules for granting access can be a time-consuming, error-prone process that demands that you identify every type of packet you *do not* want to admit. Mistakes can leave serious weaknesses in your shield.

These firewalls act more as a deterrent than a security stronghold. Hackers can easily substitute friendly addresses, a process called *spoofing*, and gain access to the intranet. In most products today, packet filtering appears as an option or as part of a hybrid package.

Application Gateways

Application gateways use special-purpose software that restricts traffic to a particular application such as your e-mail system or Lotus Notes. The gateway uses a specialized code for each application instead of general-purpose code for all network traffic.

These filters tend to be more secure because you will usually need to provide access rules for only a few applications. Furthermore, application gateways have an established reputation for success. Some authorities cite the limited number of applications to be accommodated as an ease-of-maintenance factor. Others consider application gateways hard to implement because each application requires its own approach. When a new user service arises, you must go through the process again to accommodate the new application. Application gateways also tend diminish performance, although not usually by enough to offset their advantages.

Proxy servers make up a class of products in their own right, but they can serve readily as firewalls and are sometimes placed in the application-server class. (In fact, proxies can include circuit-level gateways as well.) Acting as proxies for Web servers, application-layer firewalls can communicate with a system that requests access. In addition to checking the validity of user names and passwords, these products examine the data being transmitted. A hypertext markup language (HTML) proxy, for instance, knows what valid HTML data look like and can determine if access should be provided.

A proxy server maintains replicated copies of Web pages for easy access by a designated class of users. You can readily set up a proxy server with public-access material and route visitors to this information. Store more sensitive material safely away from this access point.

Circuit-Level Gateways

Circuit-level gateways connect an outside TCP/IP port to an internal destination such as a network printer. Circuit-level gateways function as intelligent filters that can distinguish a valid Transmission Control Protocol (TCP) or User Datagram Protocol (UDP) session. They do not identify the application being used.

Affairs of State

Yet another firewall class has arisen recently. It is called *stateful inspection,* or, more formally, the *stateful multilayer technique* (SMLT). This process examines the status of a message packet and checks it not only against the organization's security policies but also against a recorded history of similar transmissions.

In many implementations, state information is stored, so messages from similar sources can be examined in context. For example, an SMLT firewall can extract information from the application used by a previous authorized user and apply it again to allow access only to this user's authorized services. SMLT applies itself at the lowest levels of the Open Software Interconnect (OSI) networking protocol stack and screens transmissions before they make contact with the operating system.

This classification structure is breaking down, in part because it has never been recognized universally. Among more substantive reasons, new forms of technology are appearing constantly, and today's products are usually hybrids. Even when a product is based on a single type of technology, it often includes others as supplementary features or as options. These hybrids offer more choices for setting access control rules.

The Real Test

The real test of a firewall is how effectively it blocks unwanted access attempts. To effectively protect your most critical assets from outsiders, a firewall should offer

■ *Flexible access control.* You should be able to fine-tune the rules by which you admit or reject would-be visitors. The products that do this best are hybrids of the available standard technologies. The most effective firewalls offer extremely fine-grained control options.

■ *Ease of use.* Administration is an ongoing responsibility. A good firewall makes it easy to set up useful access controls and avoid costly mistakes. A graphic user interface is a major ease-of-use factor, although it does not offer absolute assurance. In any event, look for a product that makes it easy to set up and monitor control rules.

■ *Error response.* A firewall should not just turn away unauthorized visitors. It should report the attempt and should do its best to identify the source. The best sound immediate alarms and file detailed reports.

Controlling Access

Access control is a basic function. A firewall is usually placed between internal local-area networks (LANs) and wide-area networks (WANs) and external networks such as the Internet. Its main purpose is access control. In effect, a firewall creates a kind of "Checkpoint Charlie," where users must stop to have their credentials checked. The firewall identifies people, applications, IP addresses and other characteristics of the incoming call. The firewall then checks this information against access rules you have programmed into the system.

The best firewalls let you determine, in very fine detail, what combinations of people, programs, systems, and times are acceptable and which are not. The more control options you have, the more control you can exercise.

Supporting Good Decisions

Of course, having more control means making more decisions, with the ever-present possibility that a bad decision could leave an exploitable opening. Where a firewall is concerned, ease of use is more than a mere convenience. It should help you through the decision-making process.

A firewall is not a plug and play device. Someone must write and maintain the internal rules that identify the types of people, addresses, or applications that are allowed or rejected. Maintaining these rules and keeping them up to date are continuing responsibilities.

A good firewall should give its manager a clear, easy way to establish and enforce access rules and to maintain the system. And when in doubt, a firewall's default decision should be to reject a transmission unless specifically authorized.

Responding to Errors

Logging is another important management function. Effective security requires that you identify and record all attempts to pass the firewall, even the unsuccessful ones. Knowing the source of an attempted invasion can give you a big boost in trying to defend against it. Furthermore, the notification should be immediate. Some products will send telephone or e-mail messages or will signal your pager. Although e-mail notification may be quick initially, the message will sit unread until someone checks the mail. The pager usually gets quicker attention.

Building Internal Firewalls

Several years ago, the Federal Bureau of Investigation (FBI) estimated that 80 percent of all computer crime is committed by insiders. If so, this means that a firewall between you and the outside world will be effective only 20 percent of the time.

Among the firms to heed this advice has been Atlanta-based Bell-South, itself the victim of a highly publicized hacker attack. BellSouth has installed firewalls to help ward off future attacks, but it has gone further. It also has installed internal firewalls to protect against the threat from within.

If you are considering an extranet, you are naturally concerned about the ability to control access from outside. But remember, an extranet still has a great deal of intranet about it—it is merely an intranet with external connections. This means that you also must pay attention to the much more likely threat of an invasion from inside.

Trusted Domains

BellSouth has erected its firewalls between separate operating units. It has created a system of trusted domains that lets people share information within their groups but keeps them from exploring the information in departments other than their own. In a further development of this theme, the company has been installing firewalls that separate its financial information from other parts of the network.

The multiple firewalls also provide extra layers of external protection. Even if someone reaches one part of the network, there still are other obstacles to cross within the organization.

The Price of Security

The added security of internal firewalls does come at a price. By segregating small pieces of the organization, the firewall system makes collaboration and information sharing more difficult. These are the very reasons many organizations install intranets in the first place. These are also the reasons extranets have extended communication and collaboration to business partners.

Still, it is more than wise to consider the inside threat in any security plan. Furthermore, some firewall vendors are describing their internal products as a form of enabling technology rather than an obstacle.

For example, you can establish firewalls at two locations and create a direct link between them, encrypting the data that pass over the link. This technique, called *tunneling*, provides what one vendor describes as the equivalent of a virtual private network that can share information in a secure environment. You can use tunneling to provide secure communication with branch offices and external business partners.

Packet filtering

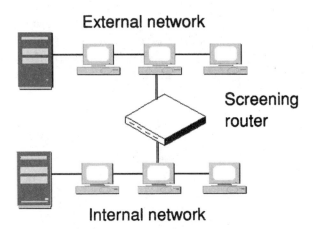

How Packet Filtering Works

Although packet filtering is seen as early firewall technology, it still has a role in a present-day firewall. This is why many more advanced products include packet filtering as an additional service or as part of a hybrid.

Packet-filtering systems route packets of information between internal and external hosts but are particular about how they do it. They grant access only to certain types of packets. You can define which packets are accepted, and your selections should fit your own security policy. Packet filtering uses a type of router called a *screening router* in a configuration like that in Fig. 14-1.

A screening router relies on the fact that each packet has a set of headers that contains information like

■ The source and destination addresses

■ The message protocol

■ The source and destination ports

■ The message type.

The router might also apply some knowledge of its own, including the interfaces with which the packet arrives and departs.

The servers for particular Internet services use a relatively short list of port numbers. The router can check a packet's port number with a list of authorized numbers and grant or deny access accordingly. You can use this capacity to

- Block all incoming connections from external systems, except for the SMTP connections that carry e-mail.
- Block all connections for sources you do not trust or, conversely, allow connections only with sources you do trust.
- Allow e-mail and File Transfer Protocol (FTP) services but block others.

The Difference Between Routers

A screening router and an ordinary router are much the same, but they have key differences. An ordinary router looks at the destination address of each packet and forwards the packet by the best route it can find. The decision about how to handle the packet is based solely on its destination. One of only two things can happen: The router can find the destination and send the packet on its way, or it can return the packet with an address-unknown message.

A screening router takes a closer look at the packet's full contents. It does not stop with determining whether it can route a packet toward its destination. The screening router also determines whether it is a good idea. It bases this decision on the rules derived from your security policy.

In theory, a screening router alone could serve as a barrier between your internal and external networks. In practice, you need more complete protection. As your sole source of security, a screening router could be overwhelmed easily. Furthermore, it provides only a limited number of options for implementing your security policy.

The screening router concentrates almost exclusively on the contents of packet headers. While this information can help identify a packet and support a go—no go decision, good security management requires a much more fine-grained approach to screening communication.

Application and Circuit Filters

Application and circuit filters, grouped into the supercategory of *proxy servers*, are specialized applications that run on firewall hosts. This often

Figure 14-2

Proxies act as stand-ins for protected servers.

Proxy systems

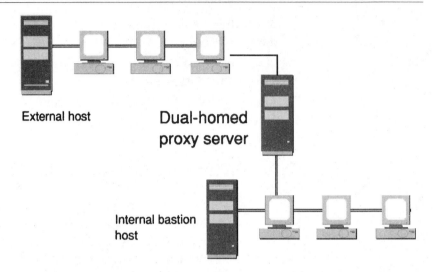

External host   Dual-homed proxy server

Internal bastion host

is dual-homed host that has separate connections for internal and external networks (Fig. 14-2).

Proxy services separate someone on the internal network from someone on the outside. Instead of talking to each other directly, each talks to a proxy. The proxy handles all communication between the internal and external parties.

Ideally, this takes place transparently. In practice, a proxy server presents the illusion that the user is dealing directly with the real server. To the real server, the proxy server presents the illusion that the real server is dealing directly with a user.

Proxy services are effective only when used in conjunction with a mechanism that restricts direct communication between the internal and external hosts. Either a dual-homed host or packet filtering can serve the need. If internal hosts can communicate directly with external hosts, people will discover this and will bypass the proxy services.

How Proxy Services Work

A proxy service is a client/server installation. The proxy server runs on the host system. A proxy client talks to the proxy server rather than to a real server outside the firewall.

It would be possible to use any client application as a proxy client. The main requirement is that employees be taught how to use the application in this way—and that they follow the instructions.

The proxy server evaluates requests from the proxy client and decides which to accept or reject. Again, the decision is based on business rules programmed into the server. If a request is approved, the proxy server contacts the real server on behalf of the client and relays requests from the proxy client to the real server. It also relays responses from the real server to the proxy client.

The proxy server does not always just forward users' requests. The proxy server can control what users do, based on your organization's security policy. For example, a file transfer protocol (FTP) proxy might refuse to let users export files, or it might allow users to import files only from certain sites. More sophisticated proxy services might allow different responses to different hosts.

Stateful Inspection

Stateful inspection or the stateful multilayer technique (SMLT) is the newest type of firewall technology (at least at this writing). It is based on a premise that it is not enough to examine data transmission packets in isolation. The most effective firewall uses state information derived from past communications and other factors as an essential factor in deciding whether to accept a current communication attempt.

Depending on the nature of the communication, SMLT can examine

- A *communication state* using information derived from past communications. For example, the outgoing PORT command of a File Transfer Protocol (FTP) session could be saved. An incoming FTP transmission then could be compared with the saved information.

- An *application state*, which takes its information from other applications. For example, a previously authenticated user who has used a particular service would be allowed access again, but only for the same service.

SMLT firewalls also can manipulate information, performing logical and mathematical inspections on any data within a packet, not just the header information.

How SMLT Works

An SMLT firewall intercepts packets at the network layer of the TCP/IP stack. It then can analyze all the data derived from all communication layers. Stateful inspection can incorporate content and context information, which is stored and updated continually. This process provides a cumulative collection of data with which to evaluate later communication attempts. It also has the ability to create virtual session information for tracking connectionless protocols.

Firewalls Brick by Brick

A firewall can be put together in any of several ways. Authors D. Brent Chapman and Elizabeth D. Zwicky describe these possibilities:

- A dual-homed architecture has interfaces to two or more networks, which can be internal or external.
- A screened host system is attached only to an internal network.
- A screened subnet architecture adds a perimeter network to the screened host.

A Firewall with a Second Home

A dual-homed-host architecture is built around a host computer that has two or more network connections. This type of host could serve as a router between the networks, but for the sake of security, one of your first acts should be to disable the routing function. When you do this, IP packets from one network are not routed directly to another, and you can exercise more control over what passes through this portal (Fig. 14-3).

Systems inside and outside the firewall can communicate with the dual-homed host, but they cannot communicate directly with each other. IP traffic between them must stop for a security check.

Dual-Homed Host Architecture

Dual-homed hosts can provide a very high level of control. If you allow no packets to pass between external and internal networks, you have the

Figure 14-3
A dual-homed host is
build to reject
imposters.

Dual homes add control

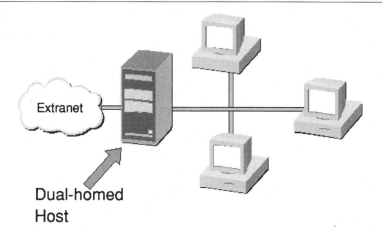

Dual-homed
Host

basis of a fail-safe access-control system that defaults to rejecting the transmission. Nothing passes unless you say it can pass.

However, this is the easier part of the job. It then is necessary to translate your security policy into rules that allow access only to the accepted packets.

While a dual-homed host is attached to multiple networks and has routing turned off, a screened host architecture provides a host that is attached to only the internal network, using a separate router. The primary security is provided by packet filtering.

A screened host is part of the internal network and works with a screening router. The packet filtering on the screening router is set up so that the screened host is the only system on the internal network that can have an outside connection. Even then, only certain types of connections are allowed. Any external system that tries to reach an internal system must go through this host (Fig. 14-4).

Packet filtering allows the host to open certain connections, as determined by your policy. The packet-filtering configuration in the screening router may

- Allow other internal hosts to open connections to hosts on the Internet for certain services
- Disallow all connections from internal hosts, forcing those hosts to use proxy services

You can mix and match these approaches for different services; some

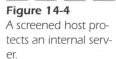

Figure 14-4
A screened host protects an internal server.

Screened host

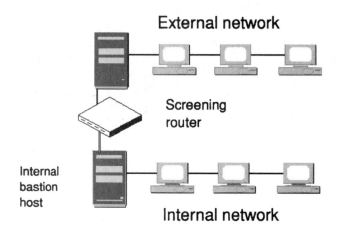

may be allowed directly via packet filtering, while others may be allowed only indirectly via proxy.

Because this architecture lets packets move from external sources to internal networks, it may seem less reliable than a dual-homed-host architecture. In practice, the dual-homed-host architecture can be prone to unexpected failures that let unwanted packets cross the barrier. In addition, it is easier to defend a router, which provides limited services, than it is to defend a host. For most purposes, the screened-host architecture provides both better security and better usability than the dual-homed-host architecture.

Nevertheless, there are some disadvantages to the screened host architecture. The major one is that if an attacker manages to break into the host, there is nothing left in the way of network security between the host and the internal network. The router also presents a single point of failure; if the router is compromised, the entire network is wide open.

Screened Subnets

The screened-subnet architecture adds an extra layer of protection to a screened-host architecture. This protection comes in the form of a perimeter network that further isolates the internal network from the outside (Fig. 14-5).

Figure 14-5
A screened subnet
provides an added
layer of protection.

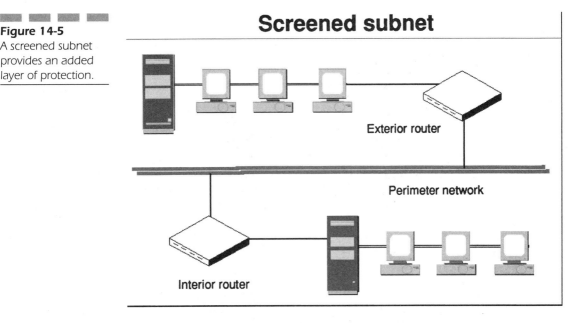

By their nature, firewall hosts are the most vulnerable machines on
your network. Even when well defended, they are open to attack simply
because they are in the path of any attack that arrives. Should this happen in a screened host architecture, your internal network is wide open
to attack. There are few other defenses between it and your other internal machines.

By isolating the firewall host on a perimeter network, you can reduce
the impact of a successful attack on this host. The intruder has gained
some access but still has other barriers to cross.

A basic screened subnet uses two screening routers, each connected to
the perimeter net. One is between the perimeter net and the internal
network, and the other is placed between the perimeter net and the
external network. To break into the internal network with this type of
architecture, an attacker would have to get past both routers. There is no
single point of vulnerability.

Some organizations go so far as to create a layered series of perimeter
nets between the outside world and their interior networks. Less trusted
and more vulnerable services are placed on the outer perimeter nets, far-
thest from the interior network. The additional barriers do not make an
attack on internal resources impossible, but they do make it much more
difficult.

This does require that there be meaningful distinctions in the access rules at different layers of the system. If the same rules apply to all layers, an entry into one is as good as an entry into all of them.

The Bastion Host

The perimeter network is one major component of a screened-subnet system. The other is a so-called bastion host, the outpost that is the main point of contact for communication with the outside world. This host uses both packet and proxy filtering to connect to and accept connections with external networks. One of a bastion host's main jobs is to act as a proxy server for various services.

The Interior Router

Another major component is the interior router, also called a *choke router*. It protects the internal network from both inside and outside.

The interior router does most of the packet filtering for your firewall. It allows selected services to pass outward to external contacts. Limit these services to those you feel your site can provide safely using packet filtering rather than proxies.

The services the interior router allows between your bastion host and your internal net are not necessarily the same services the interior router allows between external and internal networks. Reducing the number of available services also reduces the number of machines and services that can be attacked from the bastion host should it be compromised.

Which services you allow depend on your specific needs, but allow only those which you actually need. In addition, restrict these services to those found on specific internal hosts. The remaining services and hosts are those you can protect with the interior router, even if the bastion host falls.

An Exterior Router

The exterior router, or access router, is the last piece of architectural protection. Often, it simply repeats the packet filtering rules of the internal router.

It is reasonable to ask, then, what purpose the exterior router serves. It does add a small dose of redundancy, which never hurts. It also can take on one task that is not done anywhere else: It can block incoming packets that have falsified source addresses. These forged packets often carry fake internal addresses when they really come from outside. An exterior router, operating at the perimeter, can help identify and repel these fakes.

Firewalls and the Extranet

When building an extranet, controlled access is important. You want to admit only authorized business partners. And you want to provide this access only to particular types and classes of information. These considerations become important parts of the business rules you must encode into your firewall.

Joint Venture Firewalls

When two organizations decide to work together, they must be able to share systems, information, and other resources for the duration of the project. However, they need not share all their resources all the time. Undertaking some common activity does not mean that you and your partners have decided to merge your organizations or to open up all your operations to each other.

In fact, even while you and your partners trust each other for the purposes of working together, you still want to protect most of your systems and information. This is not just a matter of trusting your partner. It is also a question of whether you trust your partner's security system. Every connection with an external business partner is a potential connection for an unwanted outsider. An intruder into your partner's system might find a route into your system as well. This can be a problem even among the best of partners.

Maintain Good Relations

Consider your connections with an outside vendor. Several of your joint activities depend on information transfer, including questions of design, production, shipping, and payment.

An external vendor probably is not a direct competitor, but a vendor also may have your competitors as customers. The vendor is probably aware of the need to protect your confidential information; your contract with the vendor should help build this awareness. A vendor interested in keeping you as a customer will try to protect your information to the best of its ability.

However, what if the vendor's best is not good enough? A leak could be as simple as a routing slip-up, when data you did not intend to transmit find their way to a business partner's network. The partner will probably be completely unaware of the error and thus will see no reason to protect it.

This happens more often than you might expect. One company discovered routes on its network for a competitor's internal network. More surprisingly, someone was using these routes. It turned out that the shortest route between the company and the competitor was through a common outside vendor.

In this case, the information being carried was not confidential; had it not taken this route, it would have gone through the Internet. Even so, the incident revealed a vulnerable point. The outside vendor itself had no Internet connection, and no one had considered the possibility of cross connections with other clients who did have Internet links.

In such a situation, an internal firewall can limit your exposure. It provides a way to share some resources while protecting most of them.

Questions to Ask

Before you set out to build an internal firewall, be sure you have a clear picture of what you want to share, protect, and accomplish. Ask these questions:

- What do you want to accomplish by linking your network with some other organization's network? The answer will determine which services you need to provide and, by implication, which services should be blocked.

- Are you interested in simply exchanging files and e-mail? If so, you may not need a full interconnected extranet.

- Do you want to create a full work environment for a joint project? This would be a hookup in which team members from both organizations can work together and yet still have access to protected home systems. If so, you might need two firewalls, separating each

organization's private networks from a jointly used net between
the firewalls.

■ Are you looking for something between these extremes? Determine exactly what your objectives are and what your security concerns you must meet. The answers will determine what firewall
   technologies will be useful to you.

Sharing a Perimeter

A shared perimeter network is a another approach to joint networks
with business partners. Each party can install its own router on a
perimeter net between the two organizations. In some configurations,
these two routers might be the only systems on the perimeter net, with
no bastion host. In this case, you may not need local-area network (LAN)
technology but can use direct high-speed connections.

This is highly desirable with an outside vendor. Your partners may
not be networking wizards, and they may try to economize by connecting multiple clients to the same perimeter network. If the perimeter net
is an Ethernet or something similar, any client that can get to its router
on that perimeter network can see the traffic for all the clients on that
perimeter network. At least some of that traffic will be yours. Using a
point-to-point connection instead of a shared multiclient perimeter net
will prevent them from doing this, even by accident.

By the same token, you might not need to place a bastion host on a
perimeter network. This decision depends on what services you want
the firewall to provide and the degree to which each organization trusts
the other. If you trust your partners—and if you trust your partners'
security—you will rarely need a bastion host on a perimeter net for
relationships with vendors and customers. Instead, the partners can agree
to send data using a single selected protocol. You then can use a
screened host to filter that protocol. .

On the other hand, if the partners are not quite as trusting, each may
want to place a bastion host at their connection with the perimeter net.

A Firewall Needs Good Backup

Firewalls have tended to seem more secure than they really are. One reason is that they need complementary security technology like access

control. The other is that a firewall also needs procedural backup in the form of continued oversight and maintenance.

Even the highest-technology firewall is vulnerable to internal complacency. A consultant who tests firewalls by trying to get past them reports that in 8 years he has been stopped cold only once. More typically, he manages to roam around a target system for many weeks before his activities are discovered.

One reason for this is that although a good firewall can detect and report unauthorized access attempts and make logs of all activity, system administrators often fail to monitor the logs. Invaders could be crawling all over their systems, and they would recognize the problem belatedly if at all.

Another reason is that careless administrators leave yawning gaps in their security walls. For example, Unix systems come with several default user IDs for installation and maintenance. Once the system is in service, administrators are supposed to change the default IDs and passwords to something only authorized technicians know and use. Perhaps 20 percent, tops, actually do this. Although default IDs usually grant only limited privileges, outsiders can use them to get into the system and look at things like the password files. They then can find and use IDs that grant a much broader range of access. Once they gain access to the Unix root account, they have access to just about anything they want to see.

Know the Floor Plan

If you are going to close all the doors and windows to your network, it is important to know where these are. The default passwords are just one portal. There are many others. Hackers can find their way into your system through anything that connects one computer to another.

This includes bridges, routers, and gateways. You should know exactly how many TCP/IP hosts your network supports. Each is a potential entry point, and if you leave even one unprotected, you might as well open them all. After you have identified the danger points, you can do something about them.

Performance Issues

Believe it or not, system performance is a security issue. Firewalls unavoidably slow down transmission speeds. If your extranet produces an increase in traffic—which, after all, is the objective—the traffic might slow to a rush-hour crawl. Low performance will cause both internal and external patrons to complain, and perhaps to look for short-cuts. At a minimum, information service (IS) will be under pressure to reduce security to improve performance. Giving in to this pressure will have obvious repercussions.

One IS manager has helped avoid a bottleneck by upgrading the CPU in the firewall server. This manager is also installing proxy servers to cache heavily used information and relieve some of the traffic burden.

15

Making the World Safe for Electronic Commerce

Even the people who supply parts to keep old cars on the road have Web sites these days. If you need a head gasket for your 1949 Hudson Commodore Six, you can probably find it at some parts firm's Uniform Resource Locator (URL).

There is nothing like the sense of triumph an automobile collector feels on locating a long-sought part—unless it is the pang of fear that comes with committing your credit card number to the Internet. You worry about whether the card number will be intercepted and even about whether you can trust the dealer with your card number. Never mind that credit card numbers have been stolen routinely from trash cans and that face-to-face contact does not make a merchant more or less honest. Still, there is something about the Internet that makes people fear the financial risk of doing business on-line.

To a large extent, this is simply fear of the unknown. Many people still are unfamiliar with the Internet, and with this uncertainty comes a healthy dose of caution.

Nevertheless, ordinary parts-buying citizens have company in their concern with some of the nation's largest corporations. If you are worried about doing credit card business with them, they are also worried about the security implications of doing credit card business with you. And their worry can be magnified when they think about doing business with each other in an on-line version of electronic document interchange (EDI). Although the Internet is not as insecure as often believed, neither is its security as rock solid as EDI partners would like it to be. When Ernst and Young conducted a survey of 1300 information technology (IT) managers, few said they were yet engaging in any form of electronic commerce. However, 86 percent said they would do so if they felt the Internet was more secure.

This could happen soon, if it has not already. Consider these developments:

- The credit card giants MasterCard and Visa have agreed on a single standard for electronic connections with their payment systems. Called *Secure Electronic Transactions* (SET), the system provides a secure interface over open networks among financial institutions and credit card issuers. The agreement ended a brief duel of competing standards between the two major card issuers.

- RSA Data Security (Redwood City, CA), developer of the widely used public key encryption technology, is now supporting SET throughout its product line. In fact, SET uses encryption technology developed by RSA just for the purpose.

- VeriFone, the company that provides many of the cardswipe readers to local merchants, has been working on client, server, and gateway components that will allow Web servers to become part of the transaction process.

- VeriSign, a company started by RSA and backed by many financial institutions and would-be Web users, has developed a system of digital certificates, or *digital IDs* as VeriSign calls them. These can be used to ensure the validity of public keys. VeriSign provides digital IDs to corporations and individuals, acts as a certifying authority, and sells certificate-issuing hardware to third-party vendors. For example, a bank could use this technology to create certificates for their cardholders.

Making Direct Contact

Although the credit card industry has long used its own systems to process long-distance electronic transactions, developments like these are bringing the Web into the picture. An automated, Web-based sales system, tied directly to the credit card and banking systems, can reduce delivery times, make purchasing easier, and cut the overhead needed for processing. As these methods are developed for credit card transactions, they also can be extended to other forms of electronic commerce, including EDI.

Without these benefits, when a merchant takes a credit card order, from the Internet or any other source, it must travel through a closed, private network to the credit card processing systems. With SET implemented in a Web commerce server, merchants have secure, direct interfaces to the credit card processors via the Internet.

In addition to the efficiencies of more direct contact, this gives many organizations the opportunity to revamp their business process and integrate the Web into their electronic commerce. For example, a merchant could automate the processing between its Web server and the financial payment system. It also could use triggers and stored procedures to generate invoices, update general ledger accounts, adjust inventory records, and maintain a current record of all transactions with the customer.

Back-End Security

Securing over-the-Internet transactions is only part of the picture. Security analysts also point to a big danger of stolen or corrupted data on the corporate database. This asset faces many possible points of attack, of which the Internet is only one. Use a system of roles and privileges to restrict access, maintain a security auditing procedure, and take all the other recommended steps to maintain conventional security over this data gold mine.

Securing EDI

Electronic data interchange (EDI) in many ways is the ultimate in electronic commerce. It goes beyond retail credit card transactions into what is often the higher order of transactions between businesses. In some businesses, like automobile manufacturing, EDI is an established practice. As a result of the quality movement a few years back, automobile makers learned to involve themselves not only in their own work but also in the work of suppliers back down the chain. You cannot build a quality car without quality parts, and one way to get such parts was to become directly involved in their design and manufacture.

EDI is part of this process. It involves the electronic transmission of invoices, purchase orders, payments, and all the other records—paper or electronic—that accompany business-to-business transactions. EDI is based on standards. There are well-established definitions for electronic versions of the standard forms and for the data-entry fields in each. Nevertheless, most EDI systems tend toward the proprietary; the systems are often package deals of products and services from a single source, often a value-added network (VAN).

Reliability the Key

EDI over the Internet is attractive, of course. It can look particularly good to small suppliers of large corporations. Often, the big customer dictates that the small supplier must use EDI. The Internet promises an inexpensive way to meet the need.

If security is important in retail transactions, it is just as vital in EDI. Furthermore, EDI needs a high degree of reliability—more than the Web is currently prepared to offer.

This may change with the help of a few more acronyms. The Internet Engineering Task Force (IETF) has formed a working group called *EDI Over Internet* (EDIINT) to work on practical EDI products for the Web. These products should be available soon, if they are not on the market already.

The Internet EDI products will implement the basic technologies businesses need to conduct secure, protected electronic commerce of all kinds over the Internet. It will not be limited to EDI. This could reduce the costs of EDI significantly. Some estimates say EDI via Internet should cost only 10 percent of the current cost of using a VAN.

Others say, however, that the major cost reductions will come to large businesses, not the small, financially challenged firms that need to expand into EDI. It is the larger firms that bear most of the cost of VAN services; the most expensive item for a small business is an EDI translator. Nevertheless, intranet service also should help small firms avoid the costs of these translators.

The Multimedia Purchase Order

Internet transmission also will allow more economical transmission of large files. Electronic purchase orders can include not only the usual text product descriptions but graphics, images, and video, transmitted as attachments to the usual EDI transactions.

One early EDIINT accomplishment has been to standardize EDI messaging. This is considered a key to progress in other areas. Still, Internet and EDI experts have identified two dozen major issues that must be solved before people can conduct business over the Internet in a secure, reliable fashion. The most urgent of these fall into three categories:

- Detecting and eliminating duplicate messages
- Managing cryptograph keys
- Maintaining secure communication between trading partners

Duplicate Bridge

Duplication is a problem only in a few circumstances, but these can be critical circumstances. It usually becomes a factor when two companies are using the Simple Mail Transfer Protocol (SMTP) in a transaction that requires a quick reply. This can be a problem, for example, when a supplier is trying to maintain a just-in-time (JIT) schedule, delivering products as they are needed and avoiding the extremes of either shortages or oversupply. JIT requires that manufacturers have quick, clear communication with their suppliers that so the suppliers can make and ship products at exactly the right time. Duplicate messages in this setting can create enough confusion to stop an assembly line.

Obviously, these duplicates must be detected and rejected. The main question is at what level of the communication stack to do it. A related issue here is whether it can be done appropriately in a messaging system, with its store-and-forward configuration.

Keepers of the Keys

There is no shortage of standards organizations and similar bodies looking into the problems of key management. Most proposals in this area are based on X.509, a subspecies of the X.500 communication standard, that sets a standard for issuing certificates. This is the easy part. The real question is: Once you have issued a certificate, how can you revoke it if necessary? This problem might arise, for example, when a ranking manager leaves the purchasing department.

Securing the Channel

Of course, secure communication over the Internet is still the most visible problem. EDI, like all forms of electronic commerce, faces problems like these:

- Nonrepudiation of delivery and receipt, a process that creates a type of electronic certified mail
- Electronic signatures, to verify that a message came from its indicated source
- Encrypting messages to keep them confidential
- Maintaining the integrity of a message's content

All these issues must be resolved before many electronic merchants will consider the Internet safe enough for business.

There is no shortage of standards. Among them are

- The U.S. government's Message Security Protocol (MSP)
- Secure Multipurpose Internet Mail Extensions (S/MIME)
- Pretty Good Privacy/MIME (PGP/MIME)
- Multipart Object Security Standard (MOSS)

All offer answers to *most* of the identified problems. Only the government's MSP standard addresses the delivery receipt issue.

EDIINT has been focusing on S/MIME and PGP/MIME, with added standards to cover the delivery issue. Nonrepudiation is a long word to describe the receipt and delivery notifications already familiar to e-mail users. When you receive a delivery notification, you know that the message has been delivered to the recipient's mailbox. A read receipt goes further and notifies you when the recipient opens and reads the message. A further level of notification carries enough of the original message's content to make sure the response you receive is to the message you intended.

Maintaining Integrity

It is also important to know that the message you sent is the same as the message that was received. A message digest processor can produce a short, distinct electronic information block made up of key bits and pieces of the message. Usually, 128 bytes is the length. This information block is transmitted along with the message and the digital signature of the message originator. The recipient opens the message, retrieves the contents, the 128-byte block, and the signature. The recipient then can put the message contents through its own processor. If this processor returns the same 128 bytes, the messages match.

The Role of Cryptography

For many of us, cryptography dates back to the secret codes of childhood. Those who go back far enough can recall drinking endless glasses of chocolate drink to collect enough labels to send off for a secret recorder. Somewhat younger folks may have eaten bowls of Cap'n Crunch cereal for the decoder rings inside. One who surely remembered was the notorious hacker of recent history who adopted the captain's name.

Cryptography really is this universal, and sometimes it is even this simple. In much more sophisticated form, cryptography joins with firewalls to form the two-legged foundation of extranet security.

Cryptography is found in many Internet products and standards. They include Secure Electronic Transactions (SET) and Secure Multipurpose Internet Mail Encoding (S/MIME). These standards are the basis of a variety of security services including not only encryption but authentication, message integrity verification, and digital signatures.

Cryptography is actually a group of technologies that include

- *Encryption.* This is the processing of transforming data into an unreadable form. (This assumes, of course, that the document was readable in the first place.) A Netscape white paper compares an unencrypted Internet message with a postcard. Anyone who encounters it can read it. Encryption is the electronic equivalent of a sealed envelope.

■ *Decryption.* This is the reverse process. It transforms the encrypted material into a readable form again.

■ *Authentication.* This process identifies an individual, organization, or system to ensure that visitors are who they claim to be.

■ *Digital signatures.* These are electronic keys that identify a sender. They are equivalent to written signatures.

■ *Signature verification.* This is also an inverse function. It verifies that a digital signature is valid.

Why You Need Encryption

Every time a message passes through your system, it makes you a little more vulnerable to a security violation. This is true even of seemingly innocent communications such as outgoing e-mail messages.

The reason: A knowledgeable person with improper intent can use even outgoing messages to gain information that is useful in trying to penetrate your system. They can intercept not only the message contents but also key addressing and routing information that can help them eavesdrop on your messages, plant phony messages, or gain direct access to your system. They can burst through your defenses with as little as a single domain name or IP address.

Encryption not only encodes your messages; it also conceals this vital routing information. There is no such thing as foolproof encryption. Anything one human mind can encode, another eventually can decode. The best you can hope for is to make decoding so difficult and time-consuming that fewer people are willing or able to make the effort. There are encryption schemes that can do this, particularly when you couple them with firewalls, authentication, and other measures in an overall security problem.

No Overkill Here

Although some may think of encryption as overkill, this is certainly not the case in an extranet. Here you are dealing with information you want to make available only to selected outside parties. Furthermore, you want to protect internal information even while allowing some external access.

You should seriously consider encryption if any of these factors apply—and most will certainly apply to an extranet:

- You send sensitive data over public wide-area links. Communication with trading partners will almost certainly involve this type of connection.

- You send sensitive data via Internet e-mail. This could be a problem in some extranets if partners use e-mail to collaborate and exchange information.

- You use EDI or other forms of electronic commerce.

- You process things like order entries and status reports.

- You provide automated access to personnel files.

- Sensitive data are stored on-line.

- You oversee newsgroup-style distribution of sensitive data. This is possible if business partners cooperate on sensitive projects like future product designs.

The Politics of Encryption

There are few barriers to the use of basic encryption in an extranet. The major browser and server vendors have incorporated useful encryption into their products. All you need to do is exercise the right hypertext markup language (HTML) commands to activate it.

The much bigger problem involves the politics of encryption. For some time, two forces have made coded messaging an increasingly heated issue. On one side are federal intelligence and law enforcement agencies who want the power to intercept and read encrypted messages on much the same bases as they now can tap telephone lines. They present the specter of drug dealers, child pornographers, and foreign intelligence agents using encrypted messages to evade detection and prosecution. On the other side is an alliance of business and privacy interests dedicated to preserving the privacy of encrypted communication even—and particularly—from the government. They want strong encryption to be made widely available, although they favor it for different reasons. The business interests want to promote secure electronic commerce. The privacy interests are concerned with protecting private messages from electronic surveillance.

To the likely dismay of partisans on each side, each has a valid point. In a *Newsweek* column on the subject, Steven Levy used the analogy of two doomsday clocks. One, the cryptoanarchy clock, measures the danger that a powerless government will have to stand by while messages of all kinds fly around the world in a scrambled form. Spies and criminals could use the system at will and without fear of discovery.

The other is the insecurity clock. It measures the increasing amount of information that is passing into computerized form. The electronic versions of our medical records and financial transactions are vulnerable to violations of personal privacy. Meanwhile, computerized electric power grids and air traffic control systems are seriously vulnerable to sabotage.

Matter of Priorities

Levy believes the tolling of the second clock is more serious, but the government has chosen to place its emphasis on the first. The first reaction, a few years ago, was the "clipper chip," an idea advanced by the National Security Agency (NSA). NSA wanted to install this chip in electronic devices; it would contain a code with which the government, with a court-sanctioned warrant, could decode the messages that passed through the chip.

This approach and others like it have since been discredited and largely abandoned. However, the government is still keeping an active interest, in the form of a key recovery system that still allows government access to encrypted communication, but with stronger controls to prevent abuse. The government has offered it as a compromise; the other side has not been quick to accept it as such.

Restricted Exports

An allied issue is that of export restrictions. The government regulates encryption schemes in the same manner as arms and munitions and heavily restricts the export of all but the weakest schemes. The longer an encryption key, the harder it is to crack. Prevailing Internet standard encryption schemes call for 64-bit keys, and many security experts say that this is a practical minimum. Current federal policy is to forbid the general export of products that use keys longer than 40 bits. The government does allow some exceptions, but often at the usual price: letting the government or some other third party hold one of the keys.

Neither side seems ready to compromise, or at least not very far. As Levy suggests, however, "Instead of fighting the crypto revolution, we should embrace it. Why not try to fully exploit the protection this technology offers us, while at the same time figuring out strategies to mitigate its inevitable abuses?"

The Keys to the System

Much extranet security relies on public key cryptography. Surprisingly, if you are only going by the names, public key cryptography is more secure than so-called secret key cryptography.

The secret codes of youth are examples of secret key cryptography. You encode a message using a key. Then you give the key to anyone else you authorize to read the message. *Anyone else* might include thousands of kids who send in labels or fish in cereal boxes (Fig. 15-1). In the business world, life gets a lot more complicated. The big problem is the familiar one of sharing a secret. It often does not stay a secret for long. You cannot share your keys with any large number of customers or suppliers without the risk that someone will get the key who should not have it.

Another problem is one that might be familiar from more recent experience. Many of us already find ourselves having to remember an overload of passwords, PIN numbers, the combinations to post office boxes, and the codes that open garage doors. Business partners have long

Figure 15-1
The basic encryption process.

Encryption at its most basic

Breakfast menu: cereal and chocolate drink.

Vtrslgsdy zrmi: vrtrsa smf vjpvpayr ftoml

lists of other keys to remember, including the ones you give them. It is more than a lot of folks can recall, so the holders of these various keys jot them down on places like the backs of business cards. The security risks should be obvious. Therefore, the best way to ensure the security of your extranet transactions is to give away a key to the system.

Your Key, My Key

This is the basis of the pubic key system. It uses two keys, one public and the other private. Your public key is just that—available to the general public. You need not worry about protecting it. It is the private key that you hold in confidence. When you want to send information to a business partner, you encrypt it using the partner's public key. After all, this is the only key you should know. When the partner gets the message, it can be decrypted using the partner's private key. Only the partner needs to have the key; even you need not know it to send the message. There is never a need to exchange secret information (Fig. 15-2).

Random Keys

If the public key system has a drawback, it is lack of speed. Encrypting and decrypting a message can take time. But if you marry the public

Figure 15-2

A public key locks the information; a private key unlocks it.

Two keys fit the same lock

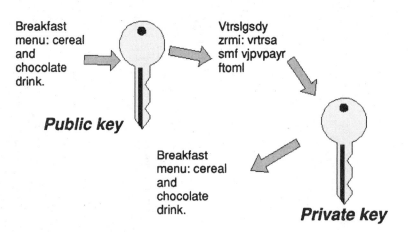

key system with the secret key system, you have a system that is both secure and reasonably quick. Instead of encrypting the full message, you encrypt the keys.

Now, if you want to send an encrypted message, you can generate a random string of digits. These can be used as a key to encrypt the message. Then you encrypt the generated key with the recipient's public key and send it along with the message. When the partner picks up the message, the partner's public key can decrypt the private key. The decrypted private key then can be used to decrypt the message. Of course, most exchanges over an extranet are more complex than this, but the general principle is the same.

Public Key Certificates

Another version of the pubic key system is the digital certificate, also called a *public key certificate,* among other names. A certificate is the digital counterpart to an employee's ID badge or a driver's license. Like these documents, they confirm your identity.

In network service, you can configure a server to grant access only to people who present certain kinds of certificates. In the same way, you can configure a client workstation to recognize only servers that present the proper electronic credentials.

A certificate is typically a small file with a few fields like those in Table 15-1.

TABLE 15-1

Fields of a Typical Public Key Certificate

Field	Description
Subject's distinguished name (DN).	An identifier that uniquely identifies the certificate holder
Issuer's DN	An identifier that uniquely identifies the authority that issued the certificate
Subject's public key	The certificate holder's public key
Issuer's signature	An electronic key that serves as a signature
Valid period	Dates between which the certificate is valid
Serial number	A number that uniquely identifies the certificate

TABLE 15-2

Public Key Technology Can Control Many Locks

Requirement	Technology Applied	Typical Use
User authentication while protecting IDs and passwords	Digital certificates	A Secure Sockets Layer (SSL) handshake exchanges client and server signatures and their corresponding signatures
Single-person login	Digital certificates	Servers can be configured to require digital certificates instead of ID and password matches
Message privacy, including store and forward operations like electronic mail	Public key encryption, optionally used with symmetric key technology to improve performance	SSL protects the session key used to encrypt and decrypt a data stream with public key encryption
Message integrity	Message authentication codes calculated using message digest algorithms	SSL calculates message authentication codes using a message digest algorithm and a key negotiated during the SSL handshake
Access control for confidential documents	Digital signatures	Matches the contents of access-control lists (ACLs) to certificates, or requires that a patron present a particular certificate

How Cryptography Helps

Public key technology, in its various forms, can be applied to many of the security needs of an extranet. Table 15-2 spells these out.

Presenting Secure Sockets

The Secure Sockets Layer (SSL) occupies a mainstream position in current extranet security. SSL is an industry standard protocol that makes substantial use of public key technology.

You will find SSL on the Internet, on intranets, and of course, it has a place in an extranet. Network projects from major vendors make use of SSL.

SSL uses public key techniques to provide three basic services:

- *Message privacy.* SSL uses a combination of public and symmetric key encryption to help keep messages safe from eavesdroppers. All traffic between an SSL client and an SSL server is encrypted using a key that is created during a process known as an *SSL handshake.* Encryption makes life more difficult for those who would eavesdrop on your messages using devices such as IP packet sniffers. Although packet sniffers can still capture the traffic, the encryption makes it much more difficult for them to read what they intercept.

- *Message integrity.* This service ensures that SSL session traffic does not alter a message while in transit. If an extranet is to support electronic commerce, you must make sure that no one tampers with the message as it travels between client and server.

When a certificate is presented for acknowledgment, SSL must determine that it comes from a legitimate owner, not an impostor. To do this, SSL requires that the presenter also provide a digital signature for the data exchanged during the handshake. The data exchanged at that point includes the entire certificate.

Signatures are attached to protocol data, including the certificates, to prove legitimate ownership. This helps prevent someone from impersonating you or a trusted partner by presenting a stolen certificate. The certificate alone does not authenticate your identity. It takes a combination of the certificate and the correct private key.

The SSL Handshake

A lot goes on during the brief exchange of information called an *SSL handshake*. When you click on a link or a button, the request to see the next page typically goes to an SSL-capable server. This server accepts your connection request on a different port than it accepts standard HTTP requests.

When a request reaches the special port, it initiates the handshake that verifies the SSL session. During the handshake, several things happen. First, the client and server exchange certificates to prove their identities. At your option, the exchange can validate not only certificates but also their issuers, in a chain that can extend back to an original certificate established by the first issuer. Certificates are verified by checking their validity dates and verifying that each bears the signature of a legitimate certificate-granting authority.

Next, the client generates a random set of keys that will be used to encrypt the transmission and calculate the message access code (MAC). The keys are encrypted using the server's public key and transmitted to the server. A separate set of keys is used for server-to-client communication—this is a total of four keys.

Finally, the algorithm to encrypt the message is determined, and so is the hash function for integrity.

Version 3 Improvements

The newest version of SSL, version 3, has several improvements over version 2:

- Fewer messages exchanged during a handshake, for faster operation
- Support for a greater number of key exchange and encryption algorithms
- Increased support for cryptography-capable "smart" cards
- A list of trusted certificate authorities (If the requested certificate does not come from one of these authorities, the request is rejected. This frees the user from having to choose a certificate for each occasion.)

Netscape Implements Public Keys

Almost from its beginnings, Netscape has touted its use of SSL to

- Encrypt communication using an algorithm negotiated with the server during the SSL handshake
- Check message integrity on communication delivered from the server
- Verify the server's identity on the basis of the public key certificate presented by the server during the SSL handshake

In addition, depending on the Navigator version you are using, the browser also can

- Read and edit the list of trusted certificate authorities (CAs). Users select Security Preferences from the Options menu to view and remove trusted CAs. New CAs can be added over HTTP. This gives you more control over which servers you trust by controlling the list of trusted certificate authorities. System administrators can configure a version of Navigator with the company-approved list of CAs before they distribute Navigator.

- Accept site certificates. If you connect to a server that presents a certificate signed by an unrecognized certificate authority, you may still choose to trust this site certificate. This option gives you more flexibility because you can choose to trust a server directly. Pretty Good Privacy, a popular secure e-mail solution, uses a similar technique.

- Check that certificates match their host's domain name. Navigator checks the server certificate's common name against the URL and displays a warning if the names do not match. If you wish, you still can choose to communicate with the suspicious server. This feature forecloses a potential person-in-the-middle attack where an impostor presents a stolen certificate.

- Generate and manage multiple key pairs. A special HTML tag called Keygen causes Navigator 3 and up to generate a key pair, prompt the user for a password to protect the private key, and deliver the public key as part of the HTML form data. This feature enables Navigator to perform public key operations such as digital signatures with its own key pair.

■ Manage multiple client-side certificates. You can manage a local database of client certificates delivered over HTTP. Certificates are stored in the local file system. No encryption is necessary because these certificates contain public information. This feature enables Navigator to perform strong authentication via SSL, laying the foundation for single-user login, which simplifies the login process and reduces the cost of maintaining servers.

■ Present certificates during the SSL handshake. Navigator's implementation of the SSL 3 protocol enables servers to ask for a certificate signed by a particular CA. Navigator searches its local database to present the necessary certificate. This feature simplifies the user interface. Earlier versions of the SSL protocol required the user to select a certificate from the certificate database rather than automatically finding the certificate the server needs.

■ Let you decide whether SSL documents should be cached. Users select Network Preferences from the Options menu to toggle caching of SSL documents. Caching SSL documents improves performance; not caching SSL documents may be required for more secure environments.

■ Provide fine-grained control over SSL 2 and SSL 3. You can select Security Preferences that toggle SSL 2 and SSL 3 on or off. You also can switch particular encryption algorithms on or off. This feature gives you fine-grained control over Navigator's encryption capabilities.

On the Server Side

SSL 3 is the encryption technology of choice for Netscape's SuiteSpot family of servers; those which have not yet implemented this standard are expected to do so shortly. All servers in the suite can

■ Communicate privately using an encryption algorithm negotiated with an SSL client such as Navigator. The traffic that is carried depends on the server. For example, Enterprise Server 2.0 carries HTTP data; Netscape News Server 2.0 carries Network News Transport Protocol (NNTP) data; and Netscape Mail Server 2.0 uses SSL to encrypt communication between Navigator and the Mail

Administration Server, enabling administrators to manage the server securely from any network node.

■ Use a message digest function, also negotiated with the client during the SSL handshake, to perform message integrity checks on data coming from the client.

■ Authenticate itself to clients using a digital certificate.

The server family is also soon expected to allow client authentication based on certificates rather than on the more conventional name-password combinations, IP addresses, or domain-naming service (DNS) names. Netscape cites several advantages to this approach:

■ *No passwords flow across the network.* Certificates are public information, so users can be authenticated without sending sensitive information such as a password over the network.

■ *The system is easier to use.* Users do not have to remember separate user name and password pairs for every Web server they visit. They simply log in to Navigator, and Navigator sends the necessary certificate to establish the user's identity.

■ *Authentication is stronger.* Certificates are a stronger form of authentication because they are based on what the user has (the certificate) as well as what the user knows (the password that protects the private key corresponding to the certificate).

■ *Administration costs less.* Certificate-based authentication can reduce the cost of server administration. Rather than managing separate access-control lists (ACLs) at every server, servers can be configured to grant access to users who present certificates signed by an approved list of certificate authorities.

Serving Certificates

Netscape Certificate Server is part of the SuiteSpot family with the task of creating and managing certificates. It lets administrators issue, revoke, renew, and otherwise manage X.509 public key certificates.

Certificate Server handles certificate requests from both client and server software. The format of the certificate signing request is slightly different for clients and servers.

Browser clients request certificates using HTML and HTTP. First, the client connects to a published URL where certificate requests are received. On request, the server delivers an HTML form that asks for identifying information such as the user's name, an authentication code such as mother's maiden name, and administrative information such as a phone number.

The HTML form also contains a special keyword called *<keygen>*. This tag tells Navigator to generate a public-private key pair. In the process, Navigator prompts the user to select a key length and provide a password to protect the private key database. Meanwhile, the public portion of the key pair is installed as a field in the HTML data form. To protect against replay attacks in which someone steals a public key and attempts to get a spurious certificate generated for that public key, the public key is signed and accompanied by a random-string challenge issued by the server as part of the tag.

After the applicant submits the form data, a certificate issuer logs in to Netscape Certificate Server, presenting a client certificate as a credential. The server's administrative tools are used to formulate a certificate based on the information in the posted form data. When satisfied with the user's identity, the certificate issuer provides a certificate and sends an e-mail message alerting the user that the certificate is ready.

The e-mail message contains a URL that the user can use to receive the certificate. The user clicks on a highlighted URL in the mail message to download the certificate. Navigator recognizes the certificate by a special MIME type and prompts the user to type a nickname to identify the certificate in the certificate database. Users can confirm the installation of their certificate by choosing Security Preferences from the Options menu.

When the request comes from a server, the server administrator logs in to the Server Manager and selects the Encryption button. Following the on-screen directions and using a supplied command-line utility, the administrator creates a key pair and enters a password to protect the private key file. The administrator clicks on the Request Certificate button and fills in the requested information, including the server's distinguished name, the file containing the key pair, and the e-mail address of the certificate authority.

The server software packages the information and sends by e-mail a standard certificate request formatted according to a Public Key Cryptography Standard published by RSA Laboratories. The server administrator retrieves the e-mail message containing the certificate request and cuts and pastes the request into a form published by the Certificate Server. When satisfied with the server's identity, the certificate issuer issues a certificate and sends the certificate back to the server administrator via e-mail.

Certificates: Build or Buy?

Companies that want to build a certificate infrastructure have two choices for managing it:

- Purchase a Certificate Server to create and manage their own certificate infrastructure. For most environments that require centralized directory management, a Directory Server also would be required.
- Outsource certificate management to an external vendor. Some certificate vendors also offer on-line directory services for getting up-to-date certificate information.

The do-it-yourself approach lets you tightly control your certificate management policies. It also allows more creativity with certificate contents and uses. You also can fine-tune your certificate policy to match your overall security policy. On the other hand, home-grown certificates can take longer to create and implement than those from a service provider.

The outsourcing approach takes advantage of the provider's professional expertise. It also gives you an opportunity to gain some of that expertise yourself so that eventually you can begin issuing your own certificates. You also have the advantage of the provider's understanding of the technical, legal, and business issues associated with certificate use.

There are also some actual or potential drawbacks. You may have less flexibility than you expected in managing certificates. You also may find yourself creating two directory standards, one for managing internal users, groups, and ACLs, and a separate directory for certificate information. Also, external vendors usually charge per certificate.

Internal and External Roles Differ

X.509 certificates can be used on an intranet or over the Internet. However, certificates may serve much different purposes when used inside or outside an organization.

Particularly in an extranet, you might want to install a server certificate that attests to your server's identity. You want to assure people who connect to your site that it is actually your site and not a sham put up by some impostor. In this case, consider outsourcing your certificate services to an external certificate authority (CA).

The outside firm will enhance the reliability of your certificates because you must first convince the outside firm. An external CA might require that you send a letter from your board of directors, submit a copy of your articles of incorporation, or pass credit or other third-party checks to be performed. Only after it is satisfied that you are indeed you will the CA issue a server certificate you then can install on your public server. The essential service that a CA provides is authentication: The CA must take some pains to verify your identity before issuing you a certificate.

The more lax a CA is, the less useful a certificate issued by that CA is. This public authentication service is crucial for thwarting Internet impostors. Without this service, there is no reliable way of knowing whether servers are actually operated by who they claim to be.

Certificate server products are not designed to issue certificates used in this fashion. Purchasing Certificate Server to issue certificates for this purpose would defeat the trust in the public key certificate model. Essentially, it would enable you to authenticate yourself. Your certificates would not enjoy the trust of a reputable certificate authority that takes careful steps to verify an entity's identity before it issues a certificate.

Client Certificates

What you can do is to issue client certificates to trusted business partners. Client certificates have several advantages over traditional user names and passwords. Some of these were mentioned earlier: Certificates are public information, so no sensitive information such as a password flows over the network. Your partners need not remember separate user name and password pairs for every Web server they visit.

There are further advantages in extranet service:

- Certificates are a stronger form of authentication because they are based on what the user has (the certificate) as well as what the user knows (the password that protects the private key corresponding to the certificate).

- Certificates can contain special information that gives hints as to how to customize the site for a particular user. For example, the certificate might contain attributes such as Native language = English or Account Number = 1238X018 or Clearance = Top Secret. These attributes can control which language in which the Web server presents its documents, what parts of the site a user can see, or some other customization.

If you want to issue certificates to business partners, you can create your own or rely on an external service provider. The criteria for making this decision are similar to the ones shown in the list above.

Certificates Inside the Organization

Inside an organization, certificates typically are used to provide services such as secure e-mail, single-user login, strong authentication, and access control. To provide these services, you can

- Issue one or more certificates to each authorized employee. You can use a variety of techniques to authenticate users, ranging from automated checks in an internal database to calling employees and having them give some private information such as their mother's maiden name. You also can ask employees to present their employee badges in person.
- Issue certificates to your various Web, mail, news, catalog, directory, and proxy servers to enable SSL's authentication, encryption, and message integrity services.
- Manage a directory containing certificates so that employees can send and receive encrypted e-mail.
- Manage and distribute user, group, and access-control lists in a directory server.
- Configure servers to update user, group, access-control, and certificate data (including certificate revocation lists) from central directory or certificate servers.

APPENDIX A

Netscape Commerce Server

The Commerce Server is part of the Netscape SuiteSpot, an integrated family of servers for building and running a full-service intranet. Netscape describes SuiteSpot not as a monolithic system, in which you would be required to run and manage all intranet services on all servers, but as a set of flexible components that can be deployed across your intranet in any way you want.

The SuiteSpot Server components are tied together through a common management architecture, a common directory services architecture, and a common security architecture, making it easy for you to centrally manage your secure distributed intranet server environment.

Enterprise Server 2.0 provides the following capabilities:

- *Content publishing and management.* Together with Navigator Gold, Enterprise Server 2.0 makes it easy for users on your intranet to publish and manage multimedia content.

- *Web publishing.* Enterprise Server 2.0 contains optimized automatic caching technology, symmetric multiprocessor support, support for popular HTTP performance extensions, and advanced memory and process management features, including full support for Windows NT threads. Enterprise Server 2.0 also enables a staging server, onto which content in progress is placed until the content is ready to be rolled out to the production server.

- *Integrated full-text searching.* All content managed by Enterprise Server 2.0 can be indexed automatically and made available for full-text searching. Enterprise Server 2.0 integrates the Verity Topic full-text search engine and supports advanced capabilities such as incremental indexing of documents, multiple arbitrary collections, and add-on support for many document types, such as Adobe PDF.

- *Integrated version control.* All content managed by Enterprise Server 2.0 can be subject automatically to version control. Each time a document is updated, a new version is created, and all old versions are

389

accessible instantly. Enterprise Server 2.0 makes it easy to compare any two versions or to revert back to a previous version at any time. Groups of people can work on the same document by using the locking feature, which lets one person check out the document and prevents others from changing it until it is checked back in.

■ *Single-server autocataloging.* Enterprise Server 2.0 can build automatically a browsable catalog of the contents it is managing. This catalog makes it easy to view content by author, by creation date, and so on. This is a single-server version of the full functionality of Catalog Server, covered below.

■ *Open live content and application development environment.* Enterprise Server 2.0 makes it easy to create live content and applications that dynamically generate content tied into relational databases, legacy systems, user preferences, or programmed application logic. Server-side Java allows enterprises to write and test a complex application once and then to deploy it on any Enterprise Server 2.0 immediately.

■ *Java application platform.* Enterprise Server 2.0 has an integrated Java run-time engine, allowing dynamic content and applications to be created using the Java programming language. High-performance Java server extensions can generate content on the fly and call out to external C/C++ libraries. Code written in Java is automatically cross-platform, so a Java application can be run on any server operating system without requiring any changes.

■ *JavaScript interpreter.* JavaScripts can be embedded in HTML documents and run automatically by Enterprise Server 2.0, making it easy to create dynamic content, personalize content to an individual user, or pull data from a relational database or legacy system into the document on the fly. JavaScript is natively cross-platform, so scripts run the same across all server operating environments without changes. JavaScripts run on the server can even create JavaScripts that Navigator will run once the document has been transferred to the client.

■ *Relational database access layer.* JavaScripts run on Enterprise Server 2.0 can access any relational database system transparently, including CA/Ingres, Informix, Microsoft, Oracle, and Sybase databases. ODBC support is included. JavaScripts within HTML documents can read data from relational database tables or modify data in tables.

- *User state tracking layer.* JavaScripts run on Enterprise Server 2.0 can identify individual users and track them across pages, making personalized content creation and detailed user behavior tracking easy.

- *NSAPI, CGI, and WinCGI interfaces.* Through the high-performance native NSAPI interface, the industry-standard CGI interface, and the Windows-specific WinCGI interface, Enterprise Server 2.0 is easy to extend and augment with custom platform-native functionality by programmers using common development environments such as C++, Perl, and Visual Basic.

- *Management services.* In addition to the native HTML server management interface that Enterprise Server 2.0 shares with all SuiteSpot servers, Enterprise Server 2.0 also includes support for SNMP Version 1 and Version 2 event monitoring so that you can monitor the status and activity of Enterprise server from any SNMP-based management system. The HTML server management interface makes possible the remote management of a server from anywhere on the network via Navigator. Enterprise Server 2.0 also supports configuration rollback, so you can revert to a previous configuration as a one-step process. Finally, Enterprise Server 2.0 features advanced, flexible logging and reporting capabilities that can be used to pinpoint exact user behavior patterns.

- *Security services.* Enterprise Server 2.0 provides full support for the SSL 3.0 security protocol, including user and server authentication via X.509 certificates, plus two-way encryption and data integrity assurance. Enterprise Server 2.0 allows the manager to set access-control privileges for users and documents. Users can be authenticated using X.509 certificates, user names and passwords, domains, hosts, IP addresses, and group membership.

- *Visual development environment and site management.* LiveWire Pro is a powerful, extensible visual development environment for creating live on-line applications—applications that are easier to build and more portable than those built using proprietary alternatives. Once a live on-line application is created, it can be deployed on any Enterprise server. LiveWire includes database connectivity to Informix, Oracle, Sybase, and any ODBC-compatible relational database. LiveWire Pro adds an integrated Informix database and Crystal Reports Professional software. Additionally, LiveWire includes an easy-to-use graphic site manager for creating and managing Web sites and their content.

LiveWire 1.0

LiveWire 1.0 provides the following capabilities:

- *Application development services.* LiveWire 1.0's JavaScript compiler enables application developers to quickly and easily create live on-line applications using server-side JavaScripts and HTML pages ready to run on any Enterprise server. Server-side JavaScripts can track users and user state, even across usage sessions.

- *Database connectivity.* With LiveWire 1.0 Connectivity Library, developers can create server-side direct SQL and ODBC connections to databases from CA/Ingres, Informix, Microsoft, Oracle, and Sybase, as well as dozens of other databases, from desktop to mainframe.

- *Enterprise-wide site management.* LiveWire 1.0 Site Manager provides a visual site management environment with a graphic view of an entire Web site, and it allows drag-and-drop site restructuring with automatic link reorganization. Wizards make site creation even faster and easier, and a site importer copies the contents of remote Web sites to a local file system for management and revision.

LiveWire Pro 1.0

LiveWire Pro 1.0 adds the following capabilities to the LiveWire feature set:

- *Informix on-line database.* LiveWire Pro 1.0 adds an Informix database licensed for a single developer and unlimited end users. It is designed for quick configuration and maintenance yet maintains full compatibility with Informix's scalable database architecture, which supports multiprocessor and parallel processing systems.

- *Crystal Reports Professional Version 4.5.* Included with LiveWire Pro 1.0 (Windows NT version only), Crystal Reports is the most popular report-design and data-analysis tool for Windows systems and makes it easy to dynamically create rich HTML reports.

- *Catalog Server answers the question, "How do I find information on the Net?"* Catalog Server automates functions that used to be performed by IT departments in an expensive, time-consuming, entry-by-entry manner—or could not be done at all. Catalog Server automatically creates and maintains a catalog of corporate documents and other electronic information on many servers scattered throughout an enterprise and across the World Wide Web. With Catalog Server, it is easy for enterprises to build their own Yahoo-style browsable indices, as well as to make an entire intranet searchable all at once. Catalog Server will be a premier implementation of such open standards as the Harvest Broker-Gatherer architecture and the Summary Object Interface Format (SOIF) standard for catalog and metadata interchange.

Catalog 1.0

Major Catalog features include the following:

- *Automated cataloging.* Catalog Server allows organizations to present a single, comprehensive overview of all electronic information. Much of this functionality is automated, with turnkey capabilities, providing out-of-the-box "What's New" and "What's Popular" listings as well as easy sorting by category, date, and author. Users can specify the sources and types of information they want to collect, and they also can specify filters. For example, a user could construct an index for all information with the keywords *sales* and *Europe.* This functionality is made possible by an automated catalog agent *robot* that discovers resources on a network and automatically generates the catalog information.
- *Navigation tools.* Users can easily find any information they need, using flexible Java-based user interfaces.
- *Searching.* With a Verity search engine, users will be able to execute both full-text and structured relational-style queries against the catalog. Catalog will support a wide variety of query types, including Boolean, wildcard, phrase, and free text, and will support range, adjacent, and soundex queries and thesaurus searches. Catalog also will provide search services utilizing the Verity search engine and supporting both full-text and structured relational-style queries and indexing.
- *Browsing.* Users will be able to navigate information through browsing trees that categorize information in a logical visual hierarchy—Yahoo-style.
- *Customized views.* Users will be able to create their own personal views of information. For example, engineers can browse the latest

technical information organized by topic, and salespeople can analyze a catalog that profiles by competitors. Catalog also will provide the flexibility for either users or companies to modify the look and functionality of catalog views, with flexible taxonomy, layout, and search menu.

- *Application development services.* Development APIs allow Catalog Server 1.0 to be extended in various ways, including by modifying the robot itself. For example, administrators will be able to plug in new modules that teach Catalog Server how to interact with specialty types of data sources (e.g., legacy systems).

- *Minimal network traffic.* Catalog Server 1.0 will transmit only summarized indexing information across the network, in contrast to existing search systems that require huge downloads and lead to high network costs.

- *Mail Server* is a native open-systems e-mail server that provides both state-of-the-art client/server e-mail functionality and robustness and support for industry-leading Internet e-mail standards and protocols. The result is a robust, reliable, scalable e-mail solution that provides all the capabilities you need from an industrial-strength client/server e-mail system and the ability to run across both your intranet and the Internet, plus the ability to interoperate seamlessly with all proprietary legacy e-mail systems that provide gateways for Internet standards.

Mail Server 1.1

Mail Server 1.1 offers the following capabilities:

- *Fast, reliable, scalable architecture.* Netscape's messaging architecture is several times faster than that of Notes or Exchange. This architecture also offers excellent reliability, with more than two decades of proven results and automatic notification of any unaddressable mail. Mail Server's scalability to thousands of users per server and use of Navigator as the universal client holds costs several times below those of Notes or Exchange.

- *Interoperability.* Interoperability with proprietary e-mail systems is automatic, since all proprietary e-mail systems either have or are providing gateways for open Internet standards such as SMTP.

There are also third-party products that help with interoperability, for example, Internet Message Associates (cc:Mail), Retix (Notes), and Innosoft (DEC, IBM, HP).

- *Management services.* Like all SuiteSpot servers, Mail Server 1.1 includes easy point-and-click administration via Navigator. Among other management features are support for multiple domains per server and addresses per user and NIS integration. Consequently, Mail Server 1.1 can take full advantage of all the available information in a network.

- *User management features.* Several aspects of e-mail management may be passed down to users, including automatic replies and user profile information.

Mail Server 2.0

Mail Server 2.0 adds

- *New end-user capabilities.* Improved off-line access capabilities with support for IMAP4. Users gain the flexibility to download messages selectively or download parts of messages, optimizing speed and memory use; create off-line mail for later upload; and synchronize local and server-stored mail. These capabilities also improve the user experience for those using remote access over slow-speed modems. Mail Server 2.0 also will extend end-user mailing list and alias management.

- *Security services.* Added SSL 3.0 support to enable secure remote administration and prevent network-based attacks. Additional security enhancements include support for multiple levels of password security, providing organizations with greater access flexibility, minimally privileged process, restricted access, storage of users in a separate database, and S/KEY single-session key encrypting client/ server communications, including passwords.

- News Server 1.1 accepts news feeds from public Usenet servers and is compatible with multiple news readers. With News Server 1.1, users can create electronic discussion groups, which enable people to participate in remote dialogs by posting and reading messages about topics of interest. Discussion groups support multiple conversations, or threads, on a given subject, displaying postings in the context of the prior discussion. As a result, readers can follow an entire discussion right from its inception, even if they join well after the discussion has started.

- *Encrypted access.* News Server provides encryption and protected password authentication, using SSL.

- *Easy setup and administration.* Remote management and encryption allows News Server 1.1 to be administrated from anywhere within an organization, via an HTML-based point-and-click interface.

News Server 2.0

News Server 2.0 includes these features:

- *Management services.* Administration improvements include support for name and password authentication on first connect, semipublic discussion groups, integration with SuiteSpot's administration interface, and report and log file access.

- *Performance and replication.* News Server 2.0 provides dramatic architectural improvements over previous versions of the server, including support for multithreading to provide greater scalability and faster performance. Threads let you take advantage of the latest multiprocessor systems, which provide outstanding scalability. Also, because News Server 2.0 supports new techniques for moving data between servers, discussion group replication speed is doubled.

- *Directory Server* ties together vital information such as user names, e-mail addresses, security keys, and contact information in a searchable, structured directory. Consequently, end users and servers will know automatically all information about all users instantly— which will make finding people easy and improve network management with single-step user account creation, modification, deletion, and lockout for all services. Because the directory services are based on the open Internet standard LDAP, corporations benefit from cross-platform availability. Further, LDAP compatibility will be built into many of the products, allowing tight integration with services such as messaging and security. Finally, as an Internet standard, LDAP will blur the distinction, with appropriate access control, between Internet and intranet directory information.

Directory Server 1.0

Directory Server 1.0 has features that include

■ *Directory services.* Directory Server provides the backbone for universal directory services in an enterprise. Its standards-based hierarchical naming supports the X.500 naming model, allowing portions of the "name space" to be delegated so that administration can be distributed. Directory Server 1.0 also routes queries for unknown addresses automatically to other LDAP-compliant servers, supplying a seamless service that incorporates both corporate and global Internet information. Designed for the Internet, Directory Server 1.0 easily supports 100,000 corporate users.

■ *Replication services.* The LDAP protocol provides sophisticated replication capabilities that include selective replication and query routing to deliver optimal performance and high availability, allowing scalability across components supplied by multiple vendors.

■ *Management services.* Directory Server 1.0 provides the encrypted, cross-platform, distributed, point-and-click installation, configuration, and maintenance that is common to all SuiteSpot servers.

■ *Bulk administration.* Administration can be driven from external sources such as a human resources database. The result is maximum installation and management efficiency.

■ *HTTP and LDAP client access.* This provides an easy-to-use and configurable interface in HTML that may be accessed by any HTTP client, in addition to providing LDAP access for Internet-compliant e-mail clients.

■ *Security services.* Directory Server 1.0 offers advanced access control with flexible, read/write access control to individual entries or name subtrees. Secure Sockets Layer (SSL) 3.0 and X.509 certificate handling are built in, providing authentication, message encryption, and message integrity services using a widely accepted Internet channel security standard. Integration with Certificate Server and Navigator makes encrypted and authenticated intranet- and Internet-wide e-mail a reality.

■ *Certificate Server* issues digital public key certificates, enabling encrypted communication with rich functionality over the corporate intranet or public Internet. Certificates allow organizations to provide secure e-mail and the ability for each user to login once to use multiple servers.

Certificate Server 1.0

Certificate Server 1.0 includes

- *Standards-based security.* Certificate Server 1.0 is based on open standards such as SSL, X.509v3, HTML, HTTP, PKCS, and LDAP. Only standards-based solutions offer the flexibility and interoperability that has become a requirement as networks span all systems inside and outside the corporate firewall.

- *Certificate creation.* Certificate Server 1.0 issues and signs public key certificates using an easy-to-use graphic interface.

- *Client-side certificates.* Client certificates allow users to login once to Navigator, which then automatically presents certificates establishing identity to subsequent servers. This feature increases user convenience and prevents sensitive information such as passwords from being sent over the network.

- *Server-side certificates.* Certificates also can be used to validate servers; for example, a user who connects to http://www.some-well-known publisher.com can be confident that the server is actually operated by that well-known publisher rather than by some impostor because the server presents a certificate to prove its identity.

- *On-line certificate requests and delivery.* Certificate Server 1.0 works seamlessly with Navigator and other SuiteSpot servers to issue certificates on demand over the network.

- *Certificate management.* Certificate Server 1.0 will provide a range of administration and management tools, based on a familiar graphic interface, that allow easy management of increasingly rich certificate implementations. Certificate Server will include sample templates with example documentation, forms, and JavaScript applets that demonstrate typical certificate management policies.

- *Certificate database.* Certificate management data will be stored conveniently in an included internal database, an unlimited run-time version of Informix On-Line Server. Certificate Server also will provide native support for Sybase and Oracle databases.

- *Certificate hierarchies.* To support flexible security policies, Certificate Server will add support for certificate hierarchies. This allows, for example, the certificate authority for the whole organization to delegate the ability to issue certificates to another organizational unit.

- *Directory services.* Certificate Server uses LDAP to provide interfaces between Directory Server and Certificate Server 1.0. This centralized certificate and user information management allows a single user login, enterprise-wide replication, and high-performance lookup.

Proxy Server 2.0

Proxy Server 2.0 includes the following

- *Replication services.* Proxy Server 2.0 stores frequently accessed documents automatically in the cache, conserving network bandwidth and improving response times for users. Proxy Server 2.0 provides replication on command by providing automatic cache refresh at specified intervals to ensure freshness and availability for periods of heavy use, document protection that refuses to cache documents protected by access control or SSL encryption, and batch retrieval that downloads a site or group of URLs.

- *Content filtering and access control.* Proxy Server 2.0 provides fine-grained access control to documents, directories, or sites; for example, users may be excluded from non-business-related sites (e.g., penthouse.com) or granted access only to specific sites. Proxy Server 2.0 also works with third-party filtering services. Access control may be based on user name and password, named groups, and IP-, DNS-, and host-based wildcard expressions. Proxy Server also can filter content types, including MIME types, and provide for an API for plugging in virus-scanning software.

- *Security services.* Proxy Server 2.0 enhances network security by providing a central control point for all network traffic. All transactions are recorded in common or extended log formats, including referred field, user agent, and transaction completion status. Proxy Server 2.0 also facilitates encrypted communications through firewalls to remote Web servers. Instead of allowing external users to connect to Web servers and critical applications inside the firewall directly, Proxy Server 2.0 may be used to "reverse proxy" this information outside a firewall, improving security and providing an additional barrier between the Internet and mission-critical data.

- *Management services.* You can manage a network of Proxy Servers with Netscape's simple, remote administration and SNMP version1 or version2 and route Web traffic using Proxy Scripting and Navigator's Automatic Proxy Configuration feature. Proxy Server also provides configuration rollback, enabling administrators to tune configurations without major planning efforts or high-risk implementations (rollback to the previous, stable configuration is always available). Encrypted communication remote administration is made possible using SSL. Additionally, Proxy Server 2.0 provides transaction logging and analysis logging of all HTTP, FTP, and Gopher transactions in common or extended log formats, including referrer field, user agent, and transaction completion status.

Extranet Services

In addition to the core functions of Navigator and the SuiteSpot servers, Netscape provides several extended products that are geared specifically to extranet types of service. They are

- *Publishing system.* A suite of applications and tools for a comprehensive, transaction-oriented system for publishing information.
- *Community system.* A suite of applications and tools to let users communicate and collaborate in a transaction-oriented on-line service environment.
- *Merchant system.* A suite of merchandise management and transaction processing tools and applications.
- *Live payment.* The basic tools and applications to extend SuiteSpot into electronic commerce.
- *Wallet.* A system that organizes a customer's on-line payment activities under a simple but powerful user interface.

Publishing System 1.5

Netscape Publishing System allows businesses and organizations to quickly implement a comprehensive, transaction-oriented Web site for publishing information on the Internet or on an intranet. Publishing System complements and extends the content creation and publishing capabilities in SuiteSpot by adding support for transaction-oriented and commercial-grade publishing environments. Using Publishing System reduces a commercial site's development and deployment time by months. Major features include

- *Transaction services.* Publishing System makes it easy for businesses to register and bill customers and then disseminate electronic information.

- *Registration services.* Publishing System incorporates customizable registration templates, variable account types (user, corporate, or family), and encrypted credit card authorization and preset membership reports, which can be customized via SQL.

- *Billing services.* Publishing System makes the creation of customized billable products easy, automatically generating billing statements and providing encrypted credit card processing via SSL.

- *Access-control services.* Access for individual documents, articles, issues, or entire publications can be controlled easily and linked to the registration and billing process. The access-control services are scalable to thousands of simultaneous users.

- *User services.* Publishing System provides a variety of additional features to ensure that users of the site have the best experience possible. Full-featured searching is included with a robust commercial search engine for full content and attribute searching. Personalized content can be created automatically via user profiles and other user-supplied information.

- *Content creation.* Publishing System adds several enhancements to other Netscape products to make an even more powerful publishing environment. Content staging provides convenient updating between the staging server (inside the firewall) and production system, incorporating automatic synchronization of content and automatic archival, indexing, and backup. It also allows automated content creation by importing content from other systems and from news and satellite feeds; it then formats, tags, converts, and loads documents into the system. All major text, desktop publishing, graphic, and newswire formats are converted to HTML.

Community System 1.5

Community System lets users communicate, collaborate, and share information in an open, encrypted on-line services environment. Community System includes a chat server, bulletin board server, and mail server that are scalable onto multiple systems for increased audience capacity. Community System also provides organizations substantial control over the look and feel of the entire environment.

- *Versatile chat services.* Community System builds diverse communication environments beginning with text and extending to multimedia information—graphics, audio, and video. Moderated auditoriums and traditional private and group conference rooms can be incorporated easily. Easy-to-use bulletin board services allow for threaded discussions that link articles on different topics and support public and private bulletin board searching tools.

- *Commercial functionality.* Community System provides all the components necessary to operate as a full-fledged commercial on-line service. Flexible registration services allow custom login templates to collect additional information about a customer. User registration information is stored in an underlying RDBMS that can be used for later access control, promotions, and advertising. Granular access controls offer organizations the flexibility to control access to chat rooms, chat special events, and bulletin boards. Additionally, a range of payment options allows the creation of billable products and an incorporated credit card processor.

LivePayment

An easy-to-construct Internet storefront, LivePayment, makes it easy for you to sell goods and services on-line. It provides all the basic functionality required for a high-performance, encrypted Internet storefront and is used in concert with Enterprise Server and LiveWire Pro.

LivePayment includes extensible sample applications that make use of existing Netscape banking relationships, with no need to use dial-up modems or leased lines. Security is based on the open SSL industry standard security protocol and the evolving SET open payments protocol.

LivePayment includes a payment processor, a set of LiveWire Pro commands, and an administrative interface.

Transactions are processed in much the same way as a bank card authorization system verifies and charges a bank card in a manual transaction through a conventional retailer. The transmission of charges to the bank occurs as soon as the service or product is provided, allowing the fastest collection possible. Transactions are cleared directly over the Internet using an encrypted connection to a payments processor.

Merchant System

Netscape Merchant System provides a suite of merchandise management and transaction processing tools that facilitate on-line shopping and include all the back-office retail functions of an electronic shopping mall.

- *Merchant and Staging Servers.* The front-end component, Merchant Server, contains all the storefront and product content and is responsible for serving all consumer requests. Merchant Server enables easy content generation and display, employing templates and automatic display options (e.g., display only if in stock) and automated product loading so that hundreds of products can be updated at once and automatically placed into the correct locations in the Merchant Server's directory structure. Netscape Staging Server is an optional front-end server that enables merchants to load up, review, and update their storefront displays in a preproduction environment before approving the transfer of the information to Merchant Server for consumer viewing and purchase selection. Merchant Server also allows advanced merchandising and shopping capabilities, including intelligent search (automatically points to related items, such as CDs and televisions, after a search for entertainment centers), promotional pricing, and fixed and free-form attributes (sizes, personalized logos, and so on).

- *Transaction Server.* The back-end component, Transaction Server, processes all completed purchases, calculates the appropriate shipping and sales tax charges, and securely delivers the completed orders directly to merchants' fulfillment houses.

- *Future releases.* Primary areas of innovation will include a more personalized user experience that leverages user profile and behavior information, and uses Java and JavaScript to generate personalized and highly engaging pages automatically. Integration with legacy systems also will be improved, including customer databases and dynamic pricing systems, through more APIs. Scalability will continue to be improved so that more products, customers, and orders can be handled by the system. Additionally, the system will include flexible sales analysis tools to leverage all information collected during the shopping and transactions process.

Wallet

Wallet will help customers conduct commerce on the Internet by keeping a customer's on-line payment activities under one simple but powerful user interface—just like a real wallet. Wallet lets consumers keep all their electronic financial instruments, such as credit cards, debit cards, electronic checks, receipts, and payment history, in one place.

Wallet complements the user authentication and certificate storage capabilities that are being built into Navigator's core feature set, and Wallet itself will be built into a future version of Navigator.

TABLE A-1

Server Products Summarized

Product	Source	Software	Hardware	Platforms
Internet Alpha Server	Digital Equipment Corp., 508-493-5258	X	X	Unix
Web Alpha Server	Digital Equipment Corp., 508-493-5258	X	X	Windows NT
Internet Connection Server	IBM, 919-254-6262	X	X	OS/2, Unix
Internet Information Server 1.0	Microsoft Corp., 708-622-0220	X		Windows NT
Enterprise Server 2.0	Netscape Communications Corp., 415-254-1900	X		Windows NT, Unix
FastTrack Server 2.0	Netscape Communications Corp., 415-254-1900	X		Windows NT, Unix
WebSite 1.1	O'Reilly & Associates, 707-829-0515, http://www.softwareora.com	X		Windows NT, Windows 95
WebForce Series	Silicon Graphics, Inc., 800-800-7441	X	X	Unix
Netra Internet Server	Sun Microsystems, Inc., 415-786-7737	X	X	Unix

405

APPENDIX B

Netscape Navigator

Netscape describes its Navigator as a universal client for accessing all the resources on an intranet. Three releases are either pending or in widespread current use.

Navigator Navigator 2.0 has enjoyed wide use on all platforms including Windows 3.1, 95, NT, Macintosh, and Unix. Its features include

- *Extensible, open platform.* Navigator 2.0 integrates live content and programmed applications on demand, ranging from lightweight JavaScripts and Java applets to stand-alone applications.

- *Java.* Navigator 2.0 incorporates support for the open cross-platform programming language Java, allowing graphics rendering, real-time two-way interaction with users, live information updating, and instant interaction with servers over the network.

- *JavaScript.* JavaScript provides flexible lightweight scripting and programmability, with an integrated API that allows cross-platform scripting of events, objects, and actions within HTML pages.

- *Navigator Plug-Ins.* Navigator Plug-Ins allow additional capabilities to be built into Netscape Navigator. For example, any Adobe Acrobat file can be viewed directly within Navigator 2.0. Plug-Ins are available from many vendors, encompassing functional areas like document and multimedia viewing, personal productivity, and collaboration.

- *Platform-specific APIs.* Navigator 2.0 supports platform-specific APIs such as OLE on Windows and AppleEvents on Mac. Navigator 2.0 can embed OLE objects and embed itself into OLE containers; further, an OLE automation vocabulary makes Navigator 2.0 controllable from other Windows desktop applications.

- *Communication interfaces.* Navigator 2.0 integrates communications with information sharing and navigation.

- *E-mail client.* Navigator 2.0 offers Simple Mail Transfer Protocol (SMTP) and Post Office Protocol 3 (POP3) e-mail functionality,

407

including drag-and-drop mailbox and message management, a graphic personal address book, viewing of rich media including embedded URL hyperlinks and complete HTML pages, MIME attachments with automatic viewing, and off-line reading and sending.

- *Discussion group client.* Navigator 2.0 also has a graphic user interface to public or private encrypted threaded discussion groups, including sorting and listing of messages, MIME-compliant messages with attachments, and posting of multimedia messages.

- *Functional, dynamic layout.* Content designers are able to flexibly present information that can be understood and used easily. For example, OLE objects, such as a download-ready Microsoft Power-Point presentation, can be embedded directly on an HTML page. Also, servers can "push" regularly updated information, such as stock quotes.

- *Ease of use.* Navigator 2.0 includes a configurable user interface and toolbar, manageable bookmark facility, and context-sensitive help, allowing users to exploit Navigator's capabilities out of the box and reducing corporate support costs.

- *Security services. Navigator* 2.0 has built-in security services, including support for HTTP and NNTP over the standard Secure Sockets Layer (SSL) security protocol, which allows encrypted transfer of Web pages, forms, data, and threaded discussion groups. Additional security capabilities include the validation of server security certificates.

The Gold Card

Navigator Gold 2.0 is a premium Navigator for the intranet environment. Navigator Gold 2.0 makes it easy for end users to generate and publish their own HTML-based content to the intranet. Navigator Gold 2.0 provides an intuitive editing environment, allowing "what you see is what you get" (WYSIWYG) and drag-and-drop results.

Navigator Gold 2.0 also includes a collection of editable home page templates, background color schemes, and graphic images, as well as more advanced functionality such as the ability to use Java applets and create and edit client-side or server-side JavaScripts.

Navigator Gold 2.0 includes automated wizards that walk users through the process of creating their own personalized pages. After a page is created, it can be published at the push of a button onto the intranet or Internet, and links can be managed easily. Consequently, server managers no longer need to post everything themselves but can grant access selectively to users to post their own content.

Navigator Dial-Up Kit

A Navigator Dial-up Kit allows enterprises to provide easy-to-use remote access for their users. Dial-up Kit makes getting started with Navigator on a dial-up connection as easy as answering a few questions in the Account Setup Wizard. Once the settings for your service have been pre-configured, all you need to do is enter a user name, password, and phone number. Dial-Up Kit software has been tested with a wide variety of servers and modems to ensure that your users will be able to connect easily to your intranet remotely.

Navigator 3.0

New functionality in the core Navigator 3.0 includes

- *Platform enhancements.* Netscape continues to provide the leading intranet applications platform. Netscape ONE, including the Java, JavaScript, and Navigator Plug-In standards, is the most widely supported intranet application development standard, and Navigator 3.0 adds additional critical functionality for developers.

- *LiveConnect.* Through LiveConnect, JavaScript, Java, HTML, and Plug-Ins are seamlessly integrated into a more powerful application development environment. For example, a sales manager can click on a single button that sends a JavaScript message to query a legacy database, and a Plug-In can then be used automatically to chart the resulting data.

- *JavaScript.* Navigator 3.0 improves JavaScript with support for dynamic images and loaded plug-in detection, which makes it easy to provide an intuitive user experience that blends Java, JavaScript, and Plug-Ins.

- *Java platform support and interoperability.* Navigator 3.0 expands Java support to the Macintosh, Windows 3.1, IBM AIX, and BSDI platforms.

- *Navigator Plug-In enhancements.* Navigator 3.0 is the first supporter of the next generation of the widely used Navigator Plug-In architecture, which allows Plug-Ins to expose properties and methods via LiveConnect to JavaScripts and Java applets.

- *Collaboration.* Internet-enabled collaboration becomes a reality because anyone using Navigator 3.0 can communicate with anyone else anywhere on the intranet or Internet, even over slow-speed modems.

- *Internet phone.* Navigator 3.0 incorporates CoolTalk, a full-featured Internet telephone that has full-duplex sound, a speed dialer, caller ID, call screening, and mute. CoolTalk includes an integrated phonebook, making it easy to locate other CoolTalk users, and an answering machine that can record missed calls.

- *Chat and shared whiteboard.* Navigator 3.0 provides real-time collaboration via an integrated whiteboard with rich painting, drawing, and highlight tools and built-in chat capabilities. The whiteboard can be used simultaneously with CoolTalk for remote collaboration.

- *Multimedia three-dimensional (3D) environment.* Navigator 3.0 provides leading-edge multimedia and 3D capabilities for publishing and viewing rich on-line content. These capabilities are useful for viewing audio and video broadcasts or archives, for interacting with 3D computer-aided design or architectural models, or for visualizing complex data sets or databases.

- *Integrated audio and video.* LiveAudio and LiveVideo capabilities allow users to view video and hear audio directly from Web pages using standard audio and video formats. Users do not have to wait to download a viewer or to launch a separate application to see a video clip or listen to a sound clip.

- *Built-in QuickTime support.* Navigator 3.0 provides built-in streaming QuickTime video and audio playback on Windows and Macintosh.

- *Integrated 3D.* Live3D lets users travel through animated interactive 3D worlds with our VRML 2.0 viewer integrated with Java. Live3D can be used to improve navigation through complex data, to view complex objects such as architectural diagrams and CAD models from multiple viewpoints, and to make presentations and on-line content more engaging and compelling.

- *Security services.* Navigator 3.0 supports public key security certificates, or "digital passports," that allow individual users to be authenticated remotely. This allows strong access control across the enterprise and onto the Internet and can eliminate the need for user passwords. Additional security improvements in Navigator 3.0 include SSL 3.0 support, personal passwords when multiple people use the same Navigator, and user control over caching of secure information.

Administration Kit

Administration Kit, a new product released with Navigator 3.0, makes it easy for corporate customers to specify and permanently lock Navigator settings, such as proxy configurations, default home pages, customized help menus, and customized directory buttons. This provides improved security, administrative control, and ease of use, reducing the cost of ownership and ensuring a uniform corporate standard that easily can be revised and updated centrally. The ability to lock preferences reduces the corporate support costs that result when users attempt to change these settings on their own.

Administration Kit provides a cross-platform solution for configuring Navigator within the intranet. Identical configuration files can be used to create custom Navigator versions for all available platforms. One copy of the toolkit may be used multiple times to configure Navigators for multiple distinct requirements throughout the organization.

Still to Come

Galileo is the code name for a Navigator product that was scheduled for release late in 1996. Its new features include

- *Communication and collaboration.* With Galileo and Orion (next-generation SuiteSpot, described below), Netscape's open standards-based solution will match proprietary groupware alternatives like Lotus Notes in functionality.

- *E-mail and discussion group enhancements.* Both e-mail and discussion groups have complete WYSIWYG and drag-and-drop editing of messages in HTML, allowing users to create rich text and graphic messages without extensive training or support. Users will find it easier to process and filter their messages, with automatic sort and response to messages and with full-text and metadata searches of received messages. Galileo provides full support for the IMAP mail-

box access protocol for synchronized on-line/off-line mailboxes
and fast access to messages over slow links.

- *Secure e-mail.* Galileo incorporates S/MIME support for encrypting
and authenticating e-mail.

- *Directory services.* LDAP directory services are integrated with the
Galileo address book, allowing users to find information about
people easily (e-mail addresses, security keys, etc.) on a corporate
network and on the Internet.

- *Off-line and mobile support.* The product offers full off-line support
for e-mail and discussion groups, including reading, filing, and
composing new messages. Galileo's IMAP e-mail protocol support
will allow users to download only what they need, even parts of
messages, for convenient off-line access, especially over slow-speed
modems.

- *Java.* New Java features include security enhancements that allow
differential privileges at different levels of assigned trust. Trusted
applets may receive increased functionality, including the ability to
connect to other servers or to read or write to local drives. Galileo
will improve Java run-time performance in several ways, including
integration of Borland's market-leading Java AppAccelerator just-
in-time compiler.

- *Java class libraries.* Java class libraries allow on-line applications to
leverage functionality that is stored on the client. Third-party
developers and companies will be able to build sophisticated, network-based applications with minimum demand on network
resources and optimal performance.

- *Layout and presentation.* The product provides more flexible layout
and presentation capabilities, incorporating three-dimensional (3D)
layered frames with richer content (e.g., audio and video), broader
font selection, and multiple columns. Additionally, the improvements to Java and the inclusion of Java class libraries will make it
practical to write entire user interfaces in Java. This will be far
more flexible than traditional HTML and will allow developers to
provide users with a more dynamic and interactive application
experience.

- *Forms.* The browser implements new forms functionality with
computation and validation capabilities. These will be easy to create via templates and editing controls. Companies will be able to
post sophisticated internal electronic forms that are less expensive

and more functional than traditional alternatives. An example is a 401k form that automatically calculates monthly contributions on-line and that prompts for missing or invalid entries.

- *Automatic Plug-Ins.* Plug-Ins are loaded automatically, so users do not have to find and download them.

- *Customization enhancements.* Users have improved control of Navigator's preferences, including the ability to customize many aspects of the user interface.

- *Administration kit.* Corporate IT departments have broader control of user settings plus a greater ability to centrally update and manage Navigator components, such as Plug-Ins. Administrator-defined configuration data, such as Proxy Server values, can be stored centrally and retrieved by Navigator at startup. This reduces the effort to modify these configuration parameters and to redeploy them to users. JavaScript can be used to provide dynamic configuration capabilities, including lookups from LDAP directories or other databases. More extensive resource configuration (menu items, button values, and so on) will be exposed so that the Navigator user interface will be better tuned for the application and user. Other management and monitoring capabilities will be designed into Navigator and the Administration Kit, making Navigator installation easier to manage in the context of other applications and systems.

Internet Explorer 3.0

Overview

Internet Explorer 3.0 is built as a set of ActiveX controls. At its heart is the component object model (COM), an object model that lets programmers mix and match languages as they program ActiveX objects. This architecture distributes Internet capabilities to the whole desktop. Any application can incorporate Internet functions by using Internet Explorer as an ActiveX control. In the same manner, Internet Explorer can take advantage of any other ActiveX-enabled applications.

Internet Explorer 3.0's component-based architecture is designed to make it extensible. Additional functions can be inserted without having to fundamentally change the code. Users only need to download the addition to update Internet Explorer and not another full-sized product.

Internet Explorer 3.0 includes these features:

■ HTML support including HTML 3.2 and Cascading Style Sheets

■ Web interactivity with programming and scripting language support

■ Multimedia with Active Movie

■ Additional security using Authenticode code authentication, CryptoAPI 1.0, and more

■ True collaboration using NetMeeting for multipoint communication

■ Personalization for the individual and the administrator with a customizable toolbar, ratings, and the Internet Explorer Administration Kit

When downloading Internet Explorer from the Microsoft Web site, you can choose which features to download. The program uses only the disk space and RAM needed to accommodate the chosen features.

HTML and Style Sheet Support

HTML is the backbone of the Internet. Through the help of Internet standards committees such as the W3C (http://www.w3.org/pub/www/) and the IETF (http://www.ietf.org/), HTML provides a set of guidelines that define the latest capabilities for the Internet.

However, Microsoft and Netscape have taken different approaches to HTML. Internet Explorer 3.0 and Navigator 3.0 both support all HTML 2.0 and some later standards, including these:

■ Frames let you open several panes within the browser window or embed a single frame along an edge of the page. Frames let you display many levels of information without requiring that a visitor leave your site. Both browsers support various options for the frame borders as well.

■ Tables give you control over the display of text, graphics, and background colors, making Web content more readable and visually interesting.

■ HTML 2.0.

■ Multimedia features let you run video and in-line sound in a Web page.

Internet Explorer 3.0 goes further by fully supporting W3C and IETF HTML specifications, including HTML 3.2, and more. Specifically:

- *Enhanced frames.* Includes frames-within-frames, floating frames (a frame can be inserted anywhere that a graphic might be), and non-scrolling frames.

- *Enhanced tables.* Beyond simply supporting background colors, Internet Explorer 3.0 also supports background images, wrapped text, and cell groupings within tables.

- *HTML and STYLE specifications.* These are among the first post-3.2 HTML specifications proposed by the W3C. This covers SPAN, DIV, and STYLE elements and linking of style sheets to HTML documents—it is the glue that binds style sheets to HTML.

- *Cascading Style Sheets (CSS), level 1.* Style sheets bring desktop publishing capabilities to the Web.

- *Embedding style information via STYLE attribute* (contained in the "HTML and Style" specification, an adjunct to CSS). This allows for in-line style information. Authors now have easy access to a variety of style attributes.

- *Linked style sheets.* For advanced authors, style information can be placed in external documents and reused across an array of HTML documents, a valuable tool for administratively defined intranet and Web publishing. The Webmaster can change the look and feel of an entire Web site with changes to a single style sheet.

- *Full font control.* Easier control of font families, weighting, and typographic measurement units (centimeters, inches, pixels, percentages, em spaces, etc.) for sizing.

- *Full white-space control.* Allows for setting margins in typographic units around all edges of elements. This is a first step toward realizing real desktop publishing-style pages.

- *Full background control* (nontiled). Allows the Web author to place an image behind an object, say, a table cell, in a variety of ways. Beyond the standard full tile, an image can be tiled vertically or horizontally or positioned directly anywhere on the page.

- *Backgrounds.* Background colors and image capabilities can be added to tables, paragraphs, or anywhere else they might enhance a Web page.

- *Typographic space control.* Allows for setting interline and intraline spacing (leading).

- *Indenting.* Easily indent a line or paragraph of text on an HTML page.

- *Negative margins.* Elements can float over other elements on a page.

- *CSS layout.* An experimental specification from W3C for handling frames, floating frames, multicolumn layout, two-dimensional direct placement of elements, and ordering and overlapping of elements, all in a rich and well-architected HTML syntax.

- *HTML layout control.* Supports and facilitates using new HTML extensions as pioneered between Microsoft and the W3C.

- *<OBJECT> tag support.* The first of the post-3.2 HTML specifications from the W3C, this tag is the W3C standard implementation for all EMBED and APPLET functionality and much more. It lets downlevel browsers see substitute content in place of the object, applet, or plug-in that an updated browser would prefer.

- *Scrolling marquees.*

Bringing Interactivity to the Web

While important to the viewing of static Web pages, HTML provides only some of the Web's potential for dynamic Web pages and Internet interactivity. More powerful Web content demands applications such as ActiveX controls or Netscape Plug-Ins to extend beyond HTML. Scripting these software applets together provides for interactivity and a dynamic Internet experience.

As corporations move to extranets, intranets, and the Internet, it becomes increasingly important that they are also able to make use of their existing knowledge and investment in tools and software.

Internet Explorer 3.0 and Navigator 3.0 both support:

- *Java applets,* software components created using the Java language

- *Just-in-time Java compiler* for greater performance

- *JavaScript*

- *Plug-ins* developed by third-party vendors to extend Web viewing functions

Customers have requested a browser that supports cutting-edge Web technology while making use of existing information and code. Internet Explorer 3.0 satisfies these demands using ActiveX.

- *Java.* Using ActiveX technologies, Java applets can communicate or be scripted with any ActiveX controls, regardless of the language in which they were created. And because of Internet Explorer's COM architecture, the same Java applets can be used in the browser or any other COM-based application.

- *ActiveX controls.* These are fast and lightweight software components based on Component Object Model (COM) technology, a technology that lets Webmasters and developers create live objects for Web pages or applications. ActiveX controls can be created in a wide variety of languages, including Java. And because they use existing technology, ActiveX controls can be used both on Web pages and on any stand-alone application that is an ActiveX component container.

- *ActiveX scripting.* This feature provides flexibility to developers for tying together software components. Microsoft Internet Explorer 3.0 supports JScript, Microsoft's JavaScript-compatible scripting language, as well as VB Script and any other ActiveX-enabled scripting language. This provides developers with the ability to choose from a variety of scripting languages, including custom languages.

- *ActiveX documents.* These are Microsoft's answer to the common use of the Internet and intranet for disseminating existing information. Rather than forcing users to port existing documents from their original forms into HTML format, support for ActiveX Documents enables you to open richly formatted documents, such as an Excel spreadsheet or chart, directly in the browser. For example, a finance intranet page might use ActiveX Documents support to place an Excel spreadsheet or chart on its internal Web site. Intranet users could then open the document in its native Excel format and have full editing and control capabilities through the use of the Excel toolbar.

- *Any just-in-time Compiler.* The Microsoft Just-In-Time Java Compiler provides the fastest way to run Java applications in a Web page, but Internet Explorer is extensible to use *any* JIT compiler.

Rather than only support Java, JavaScript, or LiveConnect and rely on existing technologies being recreated in these languages, Internet Explorer supports a variety of programming and scripting languages so that users can evolve their technologies to the Internet.

Multimedia on the Internet

Multimedia is another important chapter to the active content story. Internet multimedia provides the opportunity for Web developers and authors to provide stimulating content in a dynamic fashion.

Netscape Navigator 3.0 and Internet Explorer 3.0 both support

- AIFF, AU, MIDI, and WAV audio formats
- AVI video format
- In-line (streamed) sound support (Navigator needs the RealAudio plug-in)
- QuickTime video playback (Navigator needs the Apple QuickTime plug-in), 3D animation, and VRML

In addition, Internet Explorer 3.0 supports

- MPEG audio format
- MPEG video format
- Any ActiveX-controlled in-line (streamed) sound
- In-line (streamed) video
- Active Movie Streaming Format (ASF) allows synchronization of visuals with audio
- Active Movie, which supports MPV, MPA, MPE, MPEG, AU, AIF, AIFF, SND, MID, RMI, Wav + AVI, MOV, and QuickTime formats in a single control and is open and extensible for future technologies
- ActiveX scripting support and HTML layout control for more and better multimedia development possibilities

Multimedia performance is directly linked to integration with hardware, the operating system, and the browser itself. Internet Explorer uses DirectX technologies where available to ensure that hardware is optimized for various forms of multimedia. It is tightly integrated with all operating systems. And most important, Internet Explorer's component-object architecture and Active Movie allow multimedia to be fundamentally integrated with the browser for the best multimedia performance on the Internet.

Secure Communication and Interaction

Internet Explorer 3.0 provides comprehensive security through the Microsoft Internet Security Framework. It lets Web users communicate privately, download code they can trust, and identify themselves to others across the Internet. Users can conduct transactions and participate in consumer services on the Internet with the same privacy and security as in the real world.

Netscape Navigator 3.0 and Internet Explorer support

- *Server and client authentication.* This process uses a digital certificate to identify the user to Web servers. Conversely, server authentication ensures that end users are communicating with their intended parties.

- *SSL 2.0/3.0.* A Netscape-developed protocol intended to provide secure communication over a TCP/IP connection.

Beyond these features, Internet Explorer supports

- *Code signing with Authenticode.* This feature provides accountability for software and software components downloaded from the Internet, including Java applets and other ActiveX controls. Internet Explorer 3.0 lets you identify who published the software before it is downloaded and verify that it was not tampered with.

- *CryptoAPI 1.0* provides the underlying security services for the Microsoft Internet Security Framework and specifically for secure channels and code signing. The delivery of CryptoAPI through Internet Explorer 3.0 lets developers integrate strong cryptography into their applications.

- *PCT 1.0,* Microsoft's integrated protocol for secure TCP/IP communication.

Communicating and Collaborating on the Web

The Web provides the opportunity for unparalleled communication and collaboration. Other than communicating through the medium of

Web page publishing, features such as Internet telephones, data and video conferencing, mail, news, chat, and application sharing are integral to complete communications.

Navigator 3.0 and Internet Explorer 3.0 both offer the following features:

- *Internet Mail and News,* including quick access through the browser UI for easy access to mail and news functions

- *Point-to-point communications* using a whiteboard for two collaborators

- *Point-to-point Internet telephone service*

In addition, Internet Explorer provides

- *Full HTML support in Mail and News.* Internet Mail and News users can create and read mail and news messages in HTML. Any URL automatically becomes a link, with only a double-click required to send the default browser to the site.

- *Sophisticated mail organization and composition.* Includes automatic mail sorting using the Inbox Assistant, mail prioritization, integrated spell checking, and drag-and-drop attachments and text. In addition, the address book will import from other sources and has group management features that are easier than creating an alias.

- *Off-line and cached mail and news.* You can mark individual articles, threads, or entire newsgroups for download. Internet Mail and News caches articles while you read on-line. Cache management ensures that the cache is used efficiently and as defined by the user.

- *Comic chat.* A graphic chat client.

- *Application sharing.* A user can share any application with other users, and all can see, contribute to, and discuss the changes that are made, regardless of whether they have the shared application on their machines.

- *Multipoint communication.* Multipoint chat, whiteboard, and application sharing allow the user to hold meetings with three or more people, where everyone receives the transferred files, can draw on the whiteboard, and see and can control the shared applications. This is a true community or collaborative experience, not just a simple point-to-point call.

- *Industry standards.* NetMeeting adheres to T.120 protocols, the International Telecommunications Union standards for data conferencing used by telephone companies, PTTs, bridge manufacturers, video conferencing vendors, software vendors, and service providers worldwide.

- *Industry support.* Over 120 companies, including Sprint, AT&T, and BT, have announced their support for Microsoft's H.323/T.120/RTP/RTCP/RSVP approach. As of the original release of NetMeeting, 18 companies had announced products that are or will be compatible with NetMeeting, including Intel, PictureTel, MCI, and Creative Labs. Many more promise to come.

Personalizing the Internet Experience

The ability to personalize one's Internet experience makes accessing pertinent information even easier, whether it be through providing various localized versions or personalizing the look and feel of the browsing environment.

Navigator 3.0 and Internet Explorer 3.0 both offer

- *History and Favorites (bookmarks) menu*
- *Customizable, personal home page*
- *Localization in a limited amount of languages*

In addition, Internet Explorer provides

- Use of the *mail/news reader* of choice.
- *Greatest download flexibility.* Users can choose which components and features they download. This provides flexibility valuable for users with limited RAM and hard-drive resources or who have specific uses for their Web browsing that does not require certain features.
- *Customizable toolbar configuration and buttons.* Configure the Internet Explorer toolbar in any manner, and customize the quick link buttons to point to Web sites of your choice.
- *Ratings (PICS) support,* which allows the user (or parent or administrator) to limit access to sites with optional degrees of language, nudity, sex, or violence as defined by the Recreational Software Advisory Council (RSAC).
- *On-the-fly character set change* by clicking on an icon in the lower right corner of the user interface.
- *At least 25 localized versions.*

The Internet Explorer Administration Kit (IEAK) allows corporate administrators and organizations to

- Customize Internet Explorer 3.0 for distribution with corporate logos, favorites, and toolbars.
- Configure server settings for mail, news, User Location Services, proxy address, ports, and exceptions.
- Configure toolbar, favorites, Active Movie, and custom command folder in a per-user or group-defined manner.

APPENDIX C

LEADING FIREWALL PRODUCTS

The firewall market is a crowded place; it is almost impossible to find and list every product that is currently available. Here is a representative list of products and their features. *Note:* The material in this appendix is derived from material provided by the manufacturers and is current as of the time this was written. As you know, products and technology are subject to rapid change.

ANS InterLock

ANS InterLock service provides access-control, intrusion-detection, and cost-accounting functions to help organizations protect and manage Internet and intranet resources. This dual-homed, application-level gateway provides proxy support for FTP, Gopher, HTTP, LPR/LPD, NTP, NNTP, Real Audio, SSL, Telnet, TN3270, X-Windows, TCP, and UDP. Access and authorization functions let administrators control use of each application protocol according to user, group, service, time, day of seek, the pair of hosts or networks, and the direction of the connection.

The method used to authenticate each user can be tailored to address specific access scenarios. The system can support authentication using Unix passwords, SecurID, and SafeWord DES Gold Card.

Firewall functions include address remapping to protect proprietary network information, an integrity watcher demon for self-monitoring, and a full-featured audit log thresholder for real-time response to attacks. Detailed auditing information, cost or use/abuse controls, and accounting reports are provided for all services.

The product is available as a turnkey service including configured hardware and software, 7 × 24 support, and software upgrades or as a software product with a service contract option.

Black Hole

Black Hole (Milkyway Networks) incorporates hardened kernel and security. Features include

- NATO-like certification
- Strong Virtual Private Network (VPN) and key management using X.500 and X.509 key certificates
- Full and multiple network address
- Protection for multiple Web servers, File Transfer Protocol (FTP) servers, and many other servers
- Multiple virtual addresses on the outside can be hard-linked to the servers' addresses on the protected service network (The servers on the service network are still hidden but yet accessible directly from the internet. The same can be applied for any server on the private network.)
- One-step access for Telnet and FTP. (No need to configure browser or other client applications.)
- Flexible security groups (user, service, network) providing the ability to group entities into meaningful groups
- GUI for installation and configuration
- Ubiquous port monitoring (This is like a security system that monitors every inch of the house as opposed to the one that monitors only the windows and the doors.)
- Full user authentication
- All services can be set up to require authentication (The user can authenticate using a browser to activate other services.)
- Can be used as an Internet as well as an intranet firewall

Centri

Centri Firewall (Global Internet) serves as the only connection between the Internet and your internal network via protocol-specific proxies for the World Wide Web and other popular applications. Centri controls access and protects against potential security holes posed by new Internet technologies. This proejct is designed from the ground up for the Windows NT operating system.

Other features include

- Trusted Information Systems (TIS) Gauntlet technology used under license

- Enhanced network security under Windows NT (These security enhancements are made possible through a license from Microsoft Corporation, which has granted Global Internet an ongoing source license to key portions of the underlying Windows NT operating system.)

- Installation and administration using a graphic user interface designed for Windows NT, which allows you to modify proxy rules and redefine options

- Transparent operation of the most popular Internet applications including the World Wide Web (HTTP, SHTTP, HTTPS), e-mail (SMTP), Telnet, FTP, Netnews, and Plug proxy (for customization)

- Key TIS Gauntlet application proxies (The proxy services provide a transparent gateway with greater security than router-based packet filtering firewalls.)

- A packet filtering option providing faster communication with external hosts and flexibility for custom configurations (Combined with proxy services, this option provides you with the choices needed to balance security requirements with performance needs.)

- Network Address Translation to conceal IP addresses from external hackers (This also allows you to efficiently use fewer for-fee registered IP addresses. Port Mapping allows multiple users to use the same IP address concurrently, providing more flexibility for growth.)

- WWW caching for fast access to frequently used Web sites and URLs (Caching allows you to keep copies of Web site information locally on your server for faster access.)

- Web filters to control unauthorized Web surfing (Filtering helps to maintain employee productivity by disallowing access to Web sites that are not required for business purposes. You also can use filtering to prevent the download of Java applets.)

- Secure password authentication to support industry standard encryption techniques to safeguard passwords

- Commercial-grade DNS and SMTP Sendmail servers at no extra charge (These bundled products MetaInfo provide additional configuration options and eliminate your dependency on external service providers for mail delivery.)

- Audit logging providing 24-hour-a-day security auditing of your network connections (This facility logs all activity, periodically conducts automated sweeps for significant events, and summarizes significant security events.)

- Automated reporting allowing tracking of network activity (All security events are logged, giving you the ability to import your audit logging information into an Excel spreadsheet or another application to create customized usage pattern reports, break-in attempt reports, and other unusual activity analysis for reports to management.)

- Operation on the Intel hardware

FireWall-1

Check Point FireWall-1 3.0 is based on the company's stateful inspection architecture and offers integrated content security, connection control, and multiple encryption schemes delivered in an open security platform.

FireWall-1 3.0 also provides an array of security and management features to enable network managers to define and manage a fully integrated and comprehensive security policy from a central security console, including advanced network management, expanded authentication and encryption capabilities, improved user interface options, and additional application support.

Content Security

The content security features enable intelligent inspection of communication content and protect users from various hazards, including computer viruses, malicious Java applets, and undesirable Web content. FireWall-1's content security features are comprised of the Content Vectoring Protocol (CVP), an open protocol for integrating external and third-party content inspection programs, plus integrated content inspection capabilities for antivirus protection, URL screening, and Java security.

CVP and Antivirus Protection

The Content Vectoring Protocol (CVP) integrated into FireWall-1 3.0 provides an open specification to enable the integration of external and third-party content screening software in a plug-in manner. The CVP was developed in conjunction with content security vendors, including Cheyenne Software, Integralis, McAfee Associates, Symantec, and Trend Micro Incorporated to simplify deployment of antivirus products in tandem with Check Point FireWall-1 (see related release). The CVP also provides a plug-in interface for Check Point's FTP, HTTP, and SMTP security servers.

FireWall-1 3.0 also provides integrated antivirus capabilities via Cheyenne Software's InocuLAN antivirus software, which is bundled with FireWall-1 3.0, to offer users an integrated solution to screening transmission contents for harmful computer viruses.

URL Screening

FireWall-1's URL screening capabilities preserve valuable company bandwidth and add another level of network control by allowing network managers to restrict access to specific Web pages. This enables network managers to define flexible corporate security policies. In addition, the URL screening can be leveraged to record the types of URLs accessed for internal analysis needs, increasing the management capabilities of the FireWall-1 security platform.

Java Security

FireWall-1's Java security enables network managers to block Java applets entirely or allow Java applet traffic through the firewall, protecting against the most common and known Java network attacks. Check Point's Java security capabilities were developed based on technical input from Sun JavaSoft and Netscape Communications.

Connection Control

FireWall-1 extends its leading policy enforcement capabilities with the ConnectControl product module, offering additional features including application-independent load balancing and high availability/fault tolerance.

FireWall-1's load-balancing capabilities allow the network manager to transparently increase server capacity for a given application, such as Web access or FTP, by representing a series of replicated servers supporting that application as a single logical IP host name. FireWall-1 Connect-Control then dynamically balances the load for optimal performance, distributing client requests across the servers and in a manner transparent to the clients. Additionally, servers may be located in a single geographic location for all applications, or for Web traffic, servers can be distributed in multiple geographic locations to improve service to users in globally dispersed locations.

FireWall-1 3.0's high availability is designed to offer uninterrupted network connectivity by allowing multiple FireWall-1 installations on the network to share state tables. As a result, if one network connection fails, a backup firewall can take its place to maintain secure corporate Internet connectivity. In addition, this state table synchronization also provides a solution for firewalling enterprises that have asymmetric routing in their networks. FireWall-1's high availability ensures continuous Internet and intranet access to and within the corporation.

Enterprise Management

The data collection and analysis capabilities of FireWall-1 3.0 include network usage reporting and accounting. These features have been provided by extending the range of information captured at the inspection modules, such as the amount of data downloaded or session length, and enabling these data to be exported, allowing more detailed data manipulation and reporting for such uses as internal chargeback or billing.

FireWall-1 3.0 offers a motif-based interface across Unix environments. FireWall-1's enhanced address translation increases network flexibility and security by enabling network administrators to translate source and destination IP addresses simultaneously, to hide the source address and translate the destination address, for example. Graphic user interface support for address translation configuration and management is also integrated in the new version. Additionally, a new view within the user interface dynamically displays all live sessions, enabling network managers to monitor all open connections in real-time.

Encryption and Authentication

FireWall-1 3.0 widens its security capabilities and includes encryption and authentication capabilities to offer additional technology choices for implementing secure wide-area networks. FireWall-1 currently offers support of leading encryption technologies including Diffie-Hellman for key management, RSA for digital signature schemes, as well as DES, the recognized standard encryption technology, and Check Point's proprietary, exportable encryption algorithm, FWZ1. With Version 3.0, FireWall-1 is also the industry's first firewall to support three encryption schemes—FWZ, Check Point's proprietary encryption scheme, SKIP (Simple Key Management for Internet Protocols), an emerging encryption standard, and manual IPSec.

Check Point has expanded the range of authentication methods available to today's network manager by including compatibility with the RADIUS protocol standard to allow interoperability with emerging third-party RADIUS authentication servers. Check Point also has added support for AssureNet's (formerly Digital Pathways) authentication servers.

In addition, FireWall-1 offers transparent client and user authentication, allowing users to be transparently challenged for user and password information without requiring them to be aware of firewall locations in the network. This simplifies network access while allowing the full power of authentication to enable network access based on user information.

Enhanced Application Support

FireWall-1 3.0 adds support for numerous Internet multimedia applications including Netscape's CoolTalk, Xing Technology's StreamWorks, and Microsoft NetMeeting. FireWall-1 is designed to allow administrators to easily customize the firewall to incorporate new and custom applications. Many Internet audio and video technologies are based on connectionless protocols such as UDP and dynamically allocated channels. This makes it difficult or impossible for most firewalls to support these technologies securely. FireWall-1's Stateful Inspection implementation secures UDP-based applications by maintaining a virtual connection on top of UDP communications.

FireWall-1's programmable INSPECT engine, at the core of the Fire-Wall-1 technology, enables extensible Stateful Inspection and allows Check Point to provide support for new and custom applications quickly and easily.

CyberGuard

The CyberGuard Firewall features a Multi-Level Secure (MLS) architecture. Customers with internal networks that hold sensitive data can use the CyberGuard Firewall to prevent security breaches.

The CyberGuard Firewall is a bastion host with packet filtering, multi-homed gateway, circuit gateway, and application gateway. The Cyber-Guard Firewall can be customized to allow two-way, incoming-only, or outgoing-only communication while blocking high-risk commands.

Functioning as a multihomed gateway, the CyberGuard Firewall provides multilevel agents for protocols including Telnet, FTP, and rlogin. A development environment is provided for the implementation of other applications.

CyberGuard Firewall also can be configured to translate all internal addresses to the firewall's address. From the external network, the firewall appears to be the only machine in your company connected to the Internet.

Additional information hiding can be accomplished by using the CyberGuard Firewall as a domain-name system (DNS) server. With split DNS, one server works with external or nontrusted interfaces; the other server works with internal or trusted interfaces. Each server listens to all interfaces that are on its side of the firewall. This setup prevents external hosts from viewing or breaking into the internal system. Together with address translation, this permits the use of unregistered Internet Protocol (IP) addresses within an organization.

The screening router, a basic firewall component, can block traffic between networks or specific hosts on the IP port level. It provides the limited computer intelligence required to make necessary permit or deny determinations.

The CyberGuard Firewall offers filtering on source address, destination address, service, and protocol. You can set the connection timeout, audit packets, enable replies, force port matching, validate source addresses, and reestablish timed-out connections.

The CyberGuard Firewall also operates as an application gateway. The secure architecture ensures that proxies are protected from compromise and from each other. Proxies are provided for frequently used services:

- *Enhanced pass-through (EPT)*. An enhanced pass-through proxy listens for connections from external clients on a specified port, connects the client with the least-busy internal server associated with that port, and passes data between the client and server. Only connection requests directed at the firewall are permitted.

- *File Transfer Protocol (FTP)*. The FTP proxy intercepts FTP communications through the firewall and transfers and manipulates files and directories on the systems. Each user who is going to FTP through the firewall must have a login account on the firewall.

- *Gopher Protocol*. The Internet Gopher Protocol provides a menu-driven interface to aid searching for and retrieving files on other systems.

- *Hypertext Transfer Protocol (HTTP)*. HTTP is the underlying protocol used for World Wide Web client/server communication. The HTTP proxy intercepts transactions for Web browsers and similar services between the internal and external connections of the firewall in both directions.

- *Network News Transport Protocol (NNTP)*. The NNTP proxy passes news articles between systems. By replacing the originating internal host names in outbound news article header lines, it conceals the internal network architecture.

- *RealAudio 2.0 Protocol*. RealAudio 2.0 is a client/server application that allows for the delivery of streaming audio on the Internet. It enables a user (client) with a RealAudio player to hear audio clips and real-time (including live) audio broadcasts from Internet sites that are running a RealAudio server.

- *Remote login (rlogin)*. The remote login proxy permits users to log into hosts on the other side of the firewall without revealing internal addresses. Each user who is going to remotely log into or through the firewall must have a login account on the firewall.

- *Simple Mail Transfer Protocol (SMTP)*. The SMTP proxy exchanges mail between systems. It hides the internal network architecture by replacing internal domain names in outbound mail headers.

- *SOCKS.* The SOCKS Internet-secure proxy server allows hosts to use SOCKS clients. SOCKS clients are modified programs, such as FTP and Telnet; they connect to the SOCKS proxy server for more secure Internet access and then behave as usual.

- *Telnet Network Login (Telnet).* Like the rlogin proxy, the more generic Telnet proxy permits users to log into hosts on the other side of the firewall without revealing internal addresses. Each user who is going to Telnet into or through the firewall must have a login account on the firewall.

- *X Window System (X11).* The X11 protocol allows remote access to graphic resources. To protect X11 connections, the X11 proxy intercepts and examines all X11 traffic coming across the firewall.

- *Simple Network Management Protocol (SNMP).* SNMP allows administrators to manage, monitor, and maintain local or remote TCP/IP-based computer networks.

Mandatory Access Controls

Beyond user-specified permission bits and access-control lists (ACLs), these are the optional administrator-specified access restrictions on user processes, files, directories, and other objects based on security levels. The CyberGuard Firewall enforces mandatory separation of network traffic from administrative data. The enforcement scheme is adopted from the policy used with government-classified documents.

Reporting and Auditing

To aid in the identification and pursuit of attacks, the CyberGuard Firewall keeps an audit trail of all relevant events. This includes the ability to audit all violations of the security policy.

The administrator can set up an alarm for each auditable event. The alarm condition can be comprised of complex logical constructs, including thresholds and time concepts. The alarm can be directed to the console, a file, mail, window, or SNMP trap or can invoke a shell command.

Remote Administration

The CyberGuard Firewall configuration can be modified remotely through the Private Virtual Network (PVN) option or by utilizing a modem connected to the remote port. This allows administrators to manage multiple remote firewalls from a central location.

Graphical User Interface (GUI)

The CyberGuard Firewall provides an integrated graphic environment for setup, configuration, monitoring, and reporting. Based on the X Window System and Motif, the system hides internal mechanics from the user while presenting an easy-to-use, intuitive interface. No familiarity with the underlying operating system is necessary.

Firewall features configurable through the GUI include

- Defining proxy users
- Configuring packet-filtering rules and proxies
- Selecting audit trail alarms
- Enabling network address translation
- Setting up the split DNS

The CyberGuard Firewall is also available in a high-performance model, with throughput in excess of full, loaded Ethernet speeds.

FireWall/Plus

FireWall/Plus for Windows NT, the first and only multiprotocol and end-to-end network security firewall in the industry, is designed especially for the Windows NT operating system to protect networks from attacks. FireWall/Plus for Windows NT uses stateful inspection technology that operates at the application, circuit, frame (LAN), and packet levels. It simultaneously filters traffic at any layer of the communications architecture for any protocol or application. FireWall/Plus operates with the NT operating system in kernel mode and is able to intercept traffic before it arrives at the operating system level. Using Network-1's interception technologies at the lowest levels of the network path to and from NT, network attacks on the NT operating environment are defeated long before NT is affected.

FireWall/Plus for Windows NT is available in various configurations. These include a full-featured Enterprise Edition for use in a stand-alone configuration.

Through the use of real-time programming facilities, a high-speed stand-alone NT version of FireWall/Plus supports symmetric multiprocessing (SMP) facilities in the Digital Equipment Corporation 64-bit Alpha environment. The SMP Alpha version of FireWall/Plus is designed for those environments where very high-speed firewall facilities are required to deal with network interconnections to high-speed WAN, MAN, and LAN facilities that need serious security and serious speed at the same time. Using specialized object-oriented programming techniques, FireWall/Plus is capable of supporting multichanneled input-output (I/O) functions at high-speed on an SMP Alpha environment.

In addition, FireWall/Plus for Windows NT is being offered in a Server Edition for use as an intranet firewall that can reside on any fully functional Windows NT server. Implementation of FireWall/Plus on every server in a corporate network environment provides a full-functionality firewall on each system for extended application, packet, and frame filtering for any protocol used on the server. Where stand-alone firewalls protect network-to-network attacks, the FireWall/Plus Server Edition also protects against direct server attacks on either side of a stand-alone firewall system.

With FireWall/Plus on an NT server, network connections not allowed to the server are defeated by FireWall/Plus before access facilities are invoked. Transient, target-of-opportunity, dedicated, and covert network attack profiles are defeated by FireWall/Plus at the lowest network traffic level, increasing server network security dramatically and providing a full network audit trail of all activities to and from the server for any active protocol (e.g., IP, IPX, NetBEUI, SNA, AppleTalk, LAT, etc.). Server-to-server FireWall/Plus environments also include a full encrypted, multiprotocol tunneling capability that is beyond the normal server-to-firewall environments.

Gauntlet

The Gauntlet Internet Firewall is an application gateway firewall in which all communication between one network and another is initially turned off. The design philosophy behind the Gauntlet Internet Firewall is based on these points:

■ *Minimalism.* Simple is better than complex. This pertains to the methods and mechanisms used to implement security, the way a firewall is managed and used, and the network security paradigm embraced by a network security policy. That which is not expressly permitted is prohibited. The firewall blocks everything. All services are turned off. The administrator then selectively turns on the required services in a way that is considered safe. New services require review before they are allowed to be used.

- *Reductionism.* Simplicity is important with software as well. While you can never prove software to be bug-free, the smaller the piece of software is, the higher the level of assurance you can have that it is free of bugs. The goal for security-related software should be bug-free and trapdoor-free (or Trojan horse—free). These characteristics are measured by an assurance review, in which the software is examined independently.

- *Crystal box.* A crystal box is the opposite of a black box. With a crystal box approach, the source code and algorithms that implement security are examinable. In the case of the Gauntlet Internet Firewall, the code is examinable by any Gauntlet customer. The core functionality is examinable by anyone with FTP access to the Internet. The system does not depend on the secrecy of its algorithms, methods, or source code for security. A crystal box design means the Gauntlet Internet Firewall has benefited from experts in the firewall field who have examined it, used it, and commented on it.

- *No users.* Nearly all security breaches are caused by someone compromising a user account. Gauntlet is designed to have no user accounts or at most only one (for the firewall manager). Any interactive session on the firewall is treated as a significant security event that can be sent to trigger an alarm.

- *Auditable.* The firewall is configured to gather as much data as possible. It is easier to compress, consolidate, summarize, and delete log information than it is to capture extra information on an event that happened yesterday.

- *Controllable.* User identification is vitally important if users are to be allowed to connect through the firewall. Passwords used over an untrusted network are vulnerable to capture and reuse, so strong user authentication methods and mechanisms are employed.

- *Configurable.* A firewall is one of the methods and mechanisms used to implement a security policy. A security policy is based on input from a risk assessment and a business needs analysis. A firewall should not impose rules of its own but be configurable to implement an organization's security policy. It also must be flexible to change as the organization's security policy changes.

Product Default Operations

Following the minimalism tenet of its design philosophy, the Gauntlet Internet Firewall's initial state for all services is disabled. During the installation process, the installer defines trusted, untrusted, and unknown (and by definition, also untrusted) networks according to the network security policy of the site and a Gauntlet Internet Firewall Pre-Installation Questionnaire. The installation process walks the installer through defining the policies for electronic mail handling, setting up the domain-name system, and initializing access policies for the supported TCP/IP services.

Following the reductionism tenet, all software modules used for firewall security are written to be small, easily readable programs. Over 50 percent of the proxies are under 1000 lines of code. Only two programs are larger than 2000 lines of code. The average size is 1500 lines. The mean size is 971 lines. Also, following this tenet, application proxies are run in restricted environments when necessary, and no large program (not meeting system criteria) runs with system privileges.

In keeping with the crystal box tenet of the design philosophy, source code for all Gauntlet software is provided with each Gauntlet kit. Source code for application-level software is provided by default. Software source for operating system software is available under agreement due to having to pass on licensing requirements from the various operating system and other component vendors.

No user accounts are on the firewall, with the exception of the systems management account. Access is denied to this account except from the console. Access from other hosts on the trusted network may be granted through the configuration management system, using strong user authentication for the system manager.

Following the auditable tenet of the design philosophy, the Gauntlet Firewall provides detailed audit logs of sessions. All services accessed through the firewall are logged to the security log system. This is turned on by default at the highest level of logging. The following events are logged by default:

■ All operating system kernel warnings and errors

- All file system warnings and errors

- All attempted accesses to network services, whether successful, whether a supported service, including rejected source-routed addresses and ICMP redirects

- All successful network accesses, logging source and destination addresses, service, time of day, disconnection time of day, number of bytes transferred (if applicable), commands accessed (FTP), and URLs accessed (HTTP)

- All interactions with the user authentication server subsystem

Protection of the Firewall System

Gauntlet uses restricted file system access (chroot on Unix systems), restricted access, and modifications to the operating system kernel to secure the firewall system itself. The Gauntlet Internet Firewall employs a cryptographic system integrity checker and will notify the system management of any abnormality in firewall files.

Spoofproof

The Gauntlet Internet Firewall recognizes what computers and networks should be on each side of the firewall. Any attempt at spoofing—an attempt by a computer on one side of the firewall to be identified as a computer on the other side of the firewall—will be logged and the connection rejected.

As Internet use grows for business, the need for privacy in communications becomes more and more important. Packets on the Internet flow through many connections over many communication lines. There are many opportunities for those packets to be illegally observed, copied, or modified. In order to protect against these abuses, Gauntlet includes the ability to encrypt all data communication between one network protected by a Gauntlet Internet Firewall and another. Built on the de facto IP encryption standard swIPe and implementing the Data Encryption Standard, the encryption system allows organizations to communicate securely with each other over public networks, knowing that their data cannot be read or modified. The Gauntlet Internet Firewall also is offered with an optional DES hardware module for enhanced encryption performance.

Two or more offices of an organization, connected via a public network, have the option of extending their network security perimeters using the encrypting capabilities of the Gauntlet Internet Firewall. Because strong encryption is being used over the connection, network connections that circumvent the security controls normally enforced by the proxies of the firewall can be allowed. The offices in question should share the same security perimeter in all other ways—policy, procedures, and administrative control—for this option to be implemented without jeopardizing enterprise security.

TIS, with the Gauntlet Internet Firewall, is part of the RSADSI S/WAN initiative. The Gauntlet Internet Firewall is S/WAN-ready; when other IP products start to use the IPSEC emerging standard, the Gauntlet Internet Firewall will interoperate.

In addition, Commercial Key Recovery (CKR) capability in the Gauntlet Internet Firewall provides strong cryptographic protection that qualifies for export under U.S. government regulations. Thus users can extend their private networks beyond national borders without relying on weak encryption methods and without having to give their cryptographic keys to any government agency.

With the Gauntlet PC Extender, these privacy options can be extended to individual users. The Gauntlet PC Extender, a PC-based software product, offers an ideal method of enhancing security for telecommuters, mobile users, and users at specific desktops. Previously announced, the Gauntlet PC Extender is available as an option to the Gauntlet Internet Firewall and provides security from the PC to the firewall, from the PC through the firewall, and from PC to PC. It offers secure networking for employees who travel extensively, for those who perform some of their duties from home offices, or for those who need a high level of security at a particular desktop PC.

Product Features and Mechanisms

The Gauntlet Internet Firewall includes proxies for the following services:

■ Terminal services (Telnet, rlogin)

■ File Transfer (FTP)

■ Electronic mail (SMTP, POP3)

■ World Wide Web (HTTP)

- Gopher
- XWindows System (X11)
- Printer
- Remote execution (Rsh)
- RealAudio
- Sybase SQL
- ActiveX Guard

There is also a proxy that acts as a patch panel for simple services in a one-to-one or one-to-many configuration, called the *plug gateway*. Through this gateway, the Gauntlet Internet Firewall supports

- Finger
- Usenet News (NNTP)
- Whois

An authenticated circuit gateway allows the firewall manager to configure certain plug gateway services to be available on a per-user basis after users authenticate themselves to the firewall.

An authentication server supports the use of strong user authentication (identification) via security tokens or one-time password mechanisms.

The Gauntlet Internet Firewall terminal service supports Telnet, TN3270, and rlogin services. All use of these services from one side of the firewall to the other requires communication through the appropriate proxy. The proxies can be configured to be transparent if desired.

In nontransparent mode, the user connects to the proxy server on the firewall (e.g., Telnet firewall) and tells the proxy server what destination system to connect to. The user is not logging into the firewall; no user accounts are permitted on the firewall. The user is communicating with the proxy server. After this initial connection, all communications traffic is transparent to the user: It looks like there is a direct connection with no firewall in between.

In transparent mode, the user issues the command to connect to a machine on the other side of the firewall, and the connection is made. In both modes, all communication goes through the appropriate application gateway. Both modes are secure.

The rlogin service does not use the notoriously insecure rlogin daemon on the firewall. The rlogin service is similar to the Telnet service through the firewall but has the benefit of removing the requirement for a user who has already been authenticated to the firewall to issue a second login and password for the destination machine. The TN3270 service is provided through the Telnet proxy.

The rlogin proxy and the Telnet proxy run separately and are configured separately. A site may chose to allow one and not the other. In all cases—Telnet or rlogin, transparent or nontransparent—the network access tables are checked to make sure that the connection is allowed.

File Transfer Service

FTP also can be run in a transparent and nontransparent manner. The benefit of running FTP in the transparent mode, for people on the private side of a firewall, is that window-based applications (such as those for MS-Windows or Macs) that have no command line interface will work without modifications through a firewall.

Control for individual FTP commands is allowed (GET, PUT, DEL, etc.) to completely enforce the site's security policy.

Electronic Mail

The Gauntlet Internet Firewall acts as a mail gateway for Internet standard SMTP mail. Since many security incidents related to the Sendmail program have been reported over the past few years, the Gauntlet Internet Firewall does not allow Sendmail to run as a privileged process, nor is it allowed to accept SMTP connections from outside machines. Instead, the Gauntlet Internet Firewall includes a small (approximately 2000 lines versus Sendmail's 40,000) SMTP proxy. This process runs as an SMTP server on the Gauntlet Internet Firewall and gathers incoming mail. Sendmail is run as a nonprivileged process to parse addresses and determine how to deliver the mail.

The Gauntlet Internet Firewall hides internal e-mail addresses from the outside.

The Gauntlet firewall can be configured to act as a POP3 access point for external users wanting to access their electronic mail via the Internet standard Post Office Protocol Version 3. As described in RFC1725, the Post Office Protocol Version 3 (POP3) is intended to permit a workstation (or a PC) to dynamically access a mail drop on a server host in a useful fashion. Usually, this means that POP3 is used to allow a workstation to retrieve mail that the server is holding for it. The APOP user authentication mechanism, also described in RFC1725, is used to allow access to the electronic mail.

HTTP, SHTTP, SSL, and Gopher

HTTP, the protocol that implements the World Wide Web (WWW), sometimes erroneously referred to as Mosaic after the first WWW client program, and Gopher, are supported by the HTTP proxy in the Gauntlet Internet Firewall. This proxy allows the firewall administrator to set up access rules, just like the other firewall services. In addition, the access control file can be set up to specify what URLs (HTTP control commands) are allowed or not allowed in particular directions.

The HTTP proxy is another example of reductionism in practice, being 20 times smaller than the HTTP proxy used on most other firewalls. Is this other proxy insecure? Who knows. It is too big to examine.

Secure HTTP (S-HTTP) and Secure Socket Layer (SSL) for encrypted HTTP transactions are both supported.

The HTTP proxy has a Java Guard feature. If it is a site's security policy to not allow Java Scripts from being downloaded, the Gauntlet Internet Firewall can be configured to block them. (Based on examination and the reports and observations of others, Java is a powerful tool, easily exploited to attack remote systems.)

Strong authentication has been added to the HTTP proxy, allowing firewall administrators control over who can access the Internet via the World Wide Web.

The X Windows System service is well known for security problems. If a user allows access from a machine on the other side of the firewall to the user's X display, it is the same as turning over control of the keyboard and mouse to anyone else on the other machine. The X proxy of the Gauntlet Internet Firewall is used in conjunction with the Telnet or rlogin proxies. The firewall sets up a virtual display for the foreign host to display to. Every time a request is made to open a display, the virtual display server on the firewall answers and then directs a query window to the X server on the inside machine. Each time a connection is requested, the user must click on a yes or no button before the display is opened. When the connection ends, all open X connections are torn down at the firewall.

Printer

In some circumstances, users need to print information using printers connected to other machines on other networks. Users behind a firewall might want to print to printers on systems on the outside or behind other firewalls. Others might want to be able to print from a remote system, for example, a mobile PC, to a printer behind a firewall. The Gauntlet Internet Firewall includes a printer proxy that securely handles the transfer of print requests.

When the firewall receives requests for services on the standard printer port, it calls the lp proxy. The lp proxy checks its configuration information and determines whether the initiating host has permission to use lp. If the host has permission, the proxy logs the transaction and passes the request to the outside host. The lp-gw remains active until either side closes the connection.

Remote Execution

Administration and support activities can be easier when you can just execute a shell on a remote machine. The rsh service allows users to do this. The rsh program is not without risks: It runs programs on another machine and requires some privileges to login. The Gauntlet Internet Firewall includes the rsh proxy that securely handles the execution of rsh requests from machines on the trusted side of the network to machines on the untrusted side.

Plug Gateway

The plug gateway proxy is really a software patch panel. It allows for patching certain services through from one side of the firewall, from a particular port, to another (or the same) port on a system on the other side of the firewall. This proxy supports logging and all the options and access controls that any other proxy provides. This proxy was developed for NNTP Usenet News so that the news server could *look* like it was the firewall machine but actually be a machine on the inside of the security perimeter. Two obvious benefits of this are that (1) the firewall is not being loaded down with Usenet News operations and (2) the News administrator does not have to have access to the firewall.

The plug gateway is used by other services such as Webster and Whois.

The authenticated plug gateway, also called the *circuit gateway*, allows an authenticated connection between a client on one side of a network perimeter and an application server on the other side of the perimeter. It is used for plugged services. (Since the plug-gw is somewhat generic, it cannot provide strong user authentication itself.) After authentication to the proxy, the user chooses the desired service, and a connection between the client and the server is made through the proxy. Use of the proxy requires a standard, ASCII-based, Telnet client.

The user can start up multiple target client/server connections after the initial authentication to the proxy. The user also can abort existing client/server connections, obtain a list of existing client/server connections, and obtain a list of allowed services.

User Authentication

The network authentication server provides a generic authentication service for firewall proxies. Its use is optional, required only if the firewall interactive proxies are configured to require authentication. It acts as a piece of middleware that integrates multiple forms of authentication, permitting an administrator to associate a preferred form of authentication with an individual user. This permits organizations that already provide users with authentication tokens to enable the same token for authenticating users to the firewall. Several forms of challenge/response cards are supported, along with software-based one-time password systems and plain-text passwords. Use of plain-text passwords over the Internet is strongly discouraged due to the threat of password sniffing attackers.

The Gauntlet Internet Firewall supports the following devices:

- CryptoCard, from CryptoCard
- Digipass
- Fortezza from NSA (as an option)
- SafeWord AS from Enigma Logics
- S/KEY software from Bellcore (freely available)
- SecurID from Security Dynamics
- SecurNet Key from Digital Pathways
- Vasco

Transparency

One of the attractions of filtering router based firewalls is that they can be completely transparent to users; it seems that the firewall is not there for supported services. Indeed, this is the biggest security problem with filtering routers: The firewall *is not* really there for supported services.

The Gauntlet Internet Firewall is as transparent as a filtering router but retains all the superior security benefits of a proxy-based firewall. For all supported services, the Gauntlet Internet Firewall looks like it is behaving as an internetwork router. For example, on a private network connected to the Internet, the Gauntlet Internet Firewall can be configured to allow all authorized users on the private side of the network to use all permitted services through the firewall transparently. The user issues commands just as if there was no firewall in place. No modifications to client software are required; no special client software is needed.

Mail Gateway and Name Server

Since a firewall often acts as an internetwork gateway to an organization, the Gauntlet Internet Firewall includes an e-mail gateway and DNS set-up. Both the e-mail gateway and the name server hide internal addresses from the outside.

Network Address Translation

The Gauntlet Internet Firewall, by nature of its design as an application gateway—based firewall, translates all internal addresses to the firewall's address and is designed to hide internal addresses from the untrusted network.

Product Audit/Event Reporting and Summaries

The Gauntlet Internet Firewall provides detailed audit logs of sessions. All services accessed through the firewall are logged to the security log system. The location of the log files can be specified by the administrator of the firewall. Usually audit logs are sent to a secure machine (usually on a private side of a public/private network connection). Information such as time of connection, duration, number of bytes sent and received, source host, destination host, and user ID used (if applicable) is logged. Additionally, the system will log system anomalies (such as disk space shortages).

The Gauntlet Internet Firewall also includes a notification system for items that might need immediate attention. E-mail or some other similar mechanism is used to notify the firewall administrator of items that do not appear on the administrator's ignore list. This allows the administrator to specify the types of things to be ignored but ensures that something that has never been logged before—not on the ignore list—will be reported immediately.

The Gauntlet Internet Firewall philosophy about logging data can be summarized as, "Log as much as you can as often as you can. It is easy to compress, consolidate, or delete log information; it is impossible to get information from the past that was never logged."

Interceptor

Interceptor cites three key distinctions from other products:

- *RADAR.* Remote Administration, Diagnostics, and Reporting is described as a secure, platform-independent, Web-based graphic administration interface. With RADAR, authorized administrators can set up and modify Interceptor from any local or remote workstation that has an SSL-capable browser. All RADAR activities take place via a two-way encrypted channel. With RADAR, multiple Interceptor firewalls can be configured and managed from one desktop.

- *Granularity.* Interceptor supports rules and classes that allow you to control access to virtually all services and specific destinations by individual user. Access can be controlled by users right down to the individual URL level, including time-of-day and day-of-week controls. One example: A corporation only allows access to its internal intranet during normal business hours but lets employees surf the net after hours. Using RADAR's individual controls, exceptions can then be made as needed. For instance, the accounting group could be permitted to access the IRS site during the day.

- *Automatic vulnerability testing.* Interceptor has integrated the Internet Scanner from Internet Security Systems. On request, a complete external scan of the firewall will be conducted.

PrivateNet

The NEC PrivateNet system is an off-the-shelf, commercial firewall product combining hardware and software that provides security for TCP/IP networks. The PrivateNet system also can provide secure communications over public networks, such as the Internet, to reduce network costs through its Virtual Private Network (VPN) technology. The PrivateNet Firewall Security Server blends *two* technologies to create a secure Internet communications environment:

- Applications that originate their connections from within an internal network are managed by the SocksPlus proxy, NEC's advanced circuit-level proxy technology.

- Applications that originate their connections from outside the network are managed by security-hardened application-level proxy servers. Application services include Telnet, Email (SMTP), Web Server (HTTP), and NetNews (NNTP).

The PrivateNet system is suitable for securing a network from the Internet, as well as isolating subnetworks within a corporate network.

The PrivateNet system provides easy installation and configuration through CD-ROM—based software, friendly administration, user transparency, SOCKS 4.2 protocol compatibility, and parallel and serial firewall configurations.

The PrivateNet system has been designed to provide the technologies for both a firewall and a virtual private network. It offers a very high level of security while providing adequate access. Like most commercial firewall products, the PrivateNet system uses a number of different technologies to establish the required connectivity.

A firewall's primary purpose is to provide security. To do so, all components must be secure, and they must be tested both individually and in combination with the other components. The PrivateNet system is a complete system, including hardware, a security-hardened operating system, and firewall system software.

In addition, NEC is creating a referral program for Internet security consultants who want to team up with its national base of network product resellers to serve PrivateNet system customers. This referral program ensures customers access to experts in Internet security who can recommend an optimal security solution.

Like most other commercial firewall products, the basic assumption in the design of the PrivateNet system is that anything not explicitly allowed is denied. However, the design of the PrivateNet system goes further, making every attempt to provide an effective and secure firewall.

One example of this approach is that all software, including the operating system and other programs, is stored on a CD-ROM and is always loaded directly from the CD rather than from a hard disk. This allows a high degree of trust in the integrity of the software because it is not normally possible for someone to modify the content of the CD-ROM. This approach also provides a very easy upgrade path. Installing a new release is only a matter of shutting down the PrivateNet system, replacing the CD-ROM, and rebooting the system. There are no installation scripts to run or patches to apply.

The design of the firewall software is based on the philosophy that being small is good. The software that implements the firewall is split into small individual programs so that each can be verified easily and tested. In addition, different proxy technologies are applied to different levels of security requirements.

The operating system used for the PrivateNet system is a scaled-down and security-hardened version of BSD Unix 4.4 from Berkeley Software Design, Inc. NEC chose this platform believing that it is the best possible operating system today for Internet connectivity, as opposed to other common Unix implementations with bloated kernels, which are much more difficult to secure effectively.

The hardware is based on a Pentium PC. The machine is intended to run without an attached console, but a terminal or terminal server can be connected for configuration and monitoring. The machine is shipped with two Ethernet cards, allowing it to be installed in either a single- or dual-homed configuration.

The PrivateNet System Firewall Technology

The PrivateNet system uses two different types of technologies for two different levels of security. For connections originating from inside the organization, the PrivateNet system uses a circuit-level proxy. A circuit-level proxy provides a medium level of security while being both flexible and adaptable to the various access requirements of the organization. However, NEC believes that circuit-level proxies give an inadequate level of protection for access from the Internet to the inside of an organization's private network. Therefore, it provides application-level proxies for such access.

Circuit-level Proxy

A circuit-level proxy implements a generalized proxy mechanism that relays IP connections from the originating application through the firewall to its destination. Before completing the connection, the circuit-level proxy verifies that the connection is permitted in its configuration file. When the connection is verified and established, the circuit-level proxy program relays packets back and forth between the user application program and the Internet service to which it is connected.

The circuit-level proxy used in the PrivateNet system is based on the SOCKS 4.2 protocol, originally implemented by Dave Koblas and maintained by NEC since public release of the software. The SocksPlus proxy, NEC's commercial version of SOCKS 4.2, has been completely rewritten to avoid any intellectual property issues and to eliminate the shortcomings in the freeware version. The SocksPlus proxy

- Uses proper software layering, leaving it much less vulnerable to bad packet formats
- Can be configured to listen only to client connections on the inside network and properly identifies IP spoofing attacks originating from the outside but using an inside IP address
- Provides UDP support in addition to the TCP support found in the original SOCKS 4.2 implementation
- Provides encrypted data communication between the servers
- Supports parallel configuration, providing both high availability and load balancing between servers
- Does not require a configuration file at each client (The server information is obtained from DNS.)
- Does not accumulate log information at each client

The SocksPlus proxy uses its own improved protocol when communicating with the SocksPlus proxy clients and the SocksPlus proxy servers, but it is also fully backward compatible with existing SOCKS 4.2 servers and clients. This means that if a site is already using SOCKS 4.2, converting to the PrivateNet system is straightforward. However, such sites are encouraged to convert to the SocksPlus proxy to take full advantage of the improvements in the SocksPlus protocol.

The SocksPlus circuit-level proxy lets the user access standard Internet services such as Telnet, FTP, World Wide Web, and Archie. For Windows, NEC provides SocksPlus Windows client support. Using this utility, any Windows 3.X application client based on the standard Winsock.dll can be used without any modifications.

As for Unix, other network applications can be converted easily to operate with the SocksPlus proxy through a simple recompilation and relinking procedure. Existing SOCKS 4.2 clients are fully supported by the SocksPlus proxy.

Application-level Proxy

An application-level proxy implements a specific proxy mechanism for each application. It is a program that understands the application protocol and that can screen the traffic passing through the gateway with a comprehension of context not present in either circuit-level proxies or packet filtering.

The main advantage of an application-level proxy over a circuit-level proxy is its ability to understand the flow of information and make intelligent decisions about requests. For example, the PrivateNet system provides a proxy for electronic mail over Simple Mail Transfer Protocol (SMTP). An application-level proxy eliminates the possibility of someone extracting information about the local user population using SMTP commands such as EXPN (expanding a mail alias) or VRFY (verify the presence of a user). While NEC cannot remove these commands without violating the definition of the protocol, it can disarm the commands by not returning any useful information (they echo any argument given to them). Another example is the FTP proxy (available in a future PrivateNet system release), which will intercept and disallow commands considered dangerous, such as the DELETE command.

The disadvantages of this mechanism are that it is not transparent to the user, and it is necessary to design and implement an individual application-level proxy for each supported protocol. The PrivateNet system currently supports the following application-level proxies:

- A Telnet proxy with good user authentication based on the challenge/response system. SNK is available in Release 1.0, and other mechanisms will be added in future releases.
- An SMTP proxy, which acts as a security wrapper for sendmail.
- An NNTP proxy for support of network news.
- An HTTP proxy, primarily intended for support of HTTP servers on a screened subnet.
- An FTP proxy (in a future PrivateNet system release), intended for support of FTP servers on a screened subnet.

Connection Filtering

The access-control style used for both a circuit-level proxy and an application-level proxy is called *connection filtering* because filtering is performed at the time of connection. In other words, a proxy-based connection needs to be verified only when the connection is initially established, while packet filtering needs to verify each and every packet.

Because verification is performed only once per connection, it is possible to verify the connection thoroughly. When a connection request is received by an application-level proxy, the connection is verified based on a source/destination address and port number. In addition, more checks are performed. For example, it is verified that all connections arrived on the expected interface. If a connection request claims to originate from the internal network but arrives on the interface connected to the outside network, it is recognized by the system as a spoofing attempt. The system reports the attempt in the system log, and the connection is refused. Similarly, as a matter of routine, all name server lookups are validated by a reverse lookup. While this does not guarantee that name server spoofing does not take place, it does decrease the likelihood of a successful name server spoofing attack.

Address Hiding

One of the desirable side effects of proxies is that because all network traffic either originates or terminates at a proxy program on the firewall, internal networks are completely hidden from those outside. This means that a cracker cannot obtain information by scanning internal networks and that the internal networks do not need to be the official registered network addresses. While NEC does not advocate the internal use of network addresses that have been registered by somebody else, the Internet Engineering Task Force (IEFT) has set aside several networks guaranteed not to be registered by anyone else (see RFC 1587 for details) and that should not be routed by anyone else on the Internet. Using such addresses gives an organization all the address space it needs and helps protect the firewall from IP spoofing because the addresses are not supposed to be routed across the Internet.

User Authentication

Users from outside the PrivateNet system can Telnet to hosts in the internal network with the Telnet proxy. However, for security reasons, challenge/response is the only supported authentication method using nonreusable passwords. It is common practice for crackers on the Internet to run a packet sniffer, which intercepts and records traditional Unix login name and password pairs.

Nonreusable passwords employ a mechanism to ensure that a given password can be used only once. The current version of the PrivateNet system uses Digital Pathways' SNK calculator for this purpose.

Firewall-to-Firewall Connectivity

The PrivateNet system also supports connectivity to other PrivateNet systems within the same organization. This ensures that large organizations can install departmental firewalls that work in unison with the corporate Internet firewall.

When a client requests a connection to a destination host through several PrivateNet servers, each PrivateNet system verifies the request before forwarding it to the next PrivateNet system. After all servers verify that the connection is allowed, an acknowledgment is sent to the client. This strategy ensures that the client receives its acknowledgment only after all verifications have been conducted and the connection to the destination has been established.

Because the PrivateNet system is designed to encrypt communication between servers, it can be used to build encrypted tunnels or virtual private networks across the Internet, allowing transparent access for effective and secure long-distance service.

For geographically distributed organizations, it is possible to allow connections either through the application proxy mechanism or to perform server-to-server connection if the organization has standardized on the PrivateNet system.

Parallel Configuration

For network sites that require high performance and availability, multiple PrivateNet units can be connected in parallel and configured as a single firewall. This configuration ensures that the firewall is not overloaded. To distribute the networking load evenly between PrivateNet servers, the internal name server is set up in a round-robin configuration, enabling clients to switch back and forth between servers.

If a server becomes unavailable, any client attempting to connect through that server waits only a few seconds and then moves on to the next server. Therefore, when a firewall consists of multiple servers, high availability is ensured because the remaining servers continue to transparently service all client connection requests.

Raptor Systems Eagle

Raptor's Eagle is an application-level firewall. Acting as a security wall and gateway between a trusted internal network and untrustworthy networks such as the Internet, Eagle offers bidirectional Internet security—simultaneously prohibiting unwanted intruders from accessing the corporate network while also managing internal users' Internet access privileges.

The Eagle forms the basic component, or foundation, on which additional Raptor security products are layered. Eagle runs on the three major Unix platforms (Sun, Hewlett-Packard, and IBM workstations) and Windows NT. Eagle licenses are available for small, medium-sized, and large enterprises. Eagle provides these forms of security for the enterprise network.

User Authentication

Using the Eagle firewall, network administrators have the option to require users to be authenticated prior to accessing the corporate network. Authentication prevents one user from pretending to be another, referred to as *user spoofing,* and also allows the administrator to restrict network privileges on a per-user basis. Eagle provides three means of user authentication: multiuse passwords, SecureID "smart" card from Security Dynamics, and S/KEY single-use passwords from Bellcore.

Encryption

Raptor's EagleConnect virtual private networking technology is integral to all Eagle products. EagleConnect uses encryption to secure communications and prevent address spoofing. IP address spoofing occurs when a hacker accesses a corporate network by obtaining an IP address (so as to appear as a trusted system), thereby gaining fraudulent access. EagleConnect establishes a private "tunnel" between two systems, allowing Eagle users to communicate securely with each other. Data decryption occurs within one of Raptor's Eagle products as specified by the network administrator. EagleConnect provides a secure network path between two hosts, a host and a subnet, or two subnets—completely transparently, giving end users hassle-free network connectivity. Eagle products are fully compliant with DES and RC2 export encryption standards.

For additional security, Eagle incorporates autochecking of its own code to prevent unauthorized users from accessing or modifying the code.

Network Administrators Control Access

Eagle provides the network administrator with complete control over incoming and outgoing network access. No traffic can pass in or out of the gateway until a rule has been created to authorize its passage. Eagle provides the X Windows network security management facility that uses an intuitive GUI to simplify configuration and authorization procedures. Using the GUI to establish rules greatly reduces the chances of configuration errors and gives administrators the flexibility to manage access by individuals or groups of users, system names, domains, subnets, date, time, protocol, and service.

For example, an administrator might create a rule to allow users A, B, and C to Telnet to a specific machine outside the corporate network from 9 A.M. to 5 P.M. Monday through Friday or to create a rule allowing a specific user outside the corporate network to FTP files to a specified server.

Eagle provides network users with access to virtually all network services. For the most frequently used services, such as Telnet and FTP, proxy access occurs at the application level, providing a greater level of management control.

Unique Real-time Suspicious Activity Monitor Catches Hackers in the Act

The Eagle firewall includes a real-time suspicious activity monitor (SAM), a watch-dog feature that constantly monitors the network and lets administrators view network activity in real time. This process is called *active security* and differentiates Eagle from passive security approaches.

Eagle quietly gathers and logs information about where an attempted break-in originates, how it got there, and what the person appears to be doing. When the Eagle system reaches thresholds of activity set by the network administrator, it sends the administrator a real-time alarm in one of the following ways: via page, phone, fax, e-mail, system message, audible alarm, or SNMP alert. SAM helps the network administrator find a perpetrator and provides the reports and documentation necessary to take action and potentially prosecute, if desired. All activities are logged in one of seven severity levels ranging from *informational* to *emergency.* Log entries include information on connection attempts, service types, users, file transfer names and size, connection duration, and trace routes. With other systems, once a hacker has left the network, there is rarely an electronic footprint that will aid in their identification.

Solstice FireWall-1

Solstice FireWall-1 Version2.1 enables an enterprise to build its own customized security policy yet is installed and managed from a single workstation console. Solstice FireWall-1 Version 2.1 is designed to meet the rapidly evolving security needs of today's networks, while its flexibility, scalability, extensibility, and cross-platform support ensure that it will meet your needs as they evolve in the future.

Solstice FireWall-1 is based on Stateful Multilayer Inspection Technology (SMLT), delivering unmatched security, connectivity, and performance. It offers a combination of network and application-level security, providing security for any size enterprise while also enabling transparent access to the Internet's vast resources.

Installed on a gateway server, the Solstice FireWall-1 inspection module acts as a security router for traffic passing between a company's private networks and public networks, the Internet for example. All inbound and outbound data packets are inspected, verifying compliance with the enterprise security policy. Packets that the security policy does not permit are immediately logged and dropped.

Services Support

By incorporating dynamic, application-level filtering capabilities and advanced authentication capabilities, Solstice FireWall-1 enables connectivity for over 120 built-in services, including secure World Wide Web browsers and HTTP servers, FTP, RCP, MBone, and the entire UDP family.

Solstice FireWall-1 runs on Solaris on SPARC and Intel platforms and on Windows NT on Intel platforms. A management module running on one platform can manage inspection modules running on other supported platforms. The management module itself is now a client/server application, with a GUI client that runs on Windows 95 and Windows NT, as well as on all supported platforms.

Virtual Private Networks

The Solstice FireWall-1 encryption module enables virtual private networks and commerce over the Internet. By providing an additional layer of security and data integrity, Solstice FireWall-1 encryption capabilities ensure uncompromising and cost-effective communication or commerce between any two enterprises around the world.

Client Authentication

Client authentication permits only specified users to gain access to the internal network or to selected services as an additional part of secure communications between an enterprise's local network and corporate branch offices, business partners, and nomadic users. Client authentication works without modifying the application on either the client or server side.

Solstice FireWall-1 supports four different approaches for user authentication, including the Security Dynamics SecurID one-time password cards. Unknown users can be granted access to specific services such as Web servers or e-mail, depending on your corporate security policy.

Remote and Mobile Use

The new SecuRemote feature creates a virtual private network for Windows 95 users, connecting to their networks with dial-up connections over the Internet or the public switched phone network to any Solstice FireWall-1 system running VPN. SecuRemote will transparently encrypt any TCP/IP-based application without change to the application itself.

Anti-spoofing

Spoofing is a commonly used technique to gain access to a network from outside (the Internet, for example), by making packets appear to come from inside the network or firewall. Solstice FireWall-1 detects such packets and drops them and also can log and issue an alert.

Combined Network and User-level Security

Solstice FireWall-1 enables an organization to take full control over all its Internet and intranet TCP/IP traffic. Its leading-edge technology inspects each communication attempt and blocks all unwanted tries. A robust auditing and alerting mechanism identifies and flags any suspicious communication.

Solstice FireWall-1 provides centralized and granular control of all users, including authenticated and unknown users. Clients can be authenticated based on permitted servers or applications, allowed times and dates of communications, and authorized number of sessions. No modification of local servers or applications is required. Unknown users can be granted access to specific services such as Web servers or e-mail, depending on the corporate security policy.

The Solstice FireWall-1 encryption module uses in-place encryption. By maintaining the size of the encrypted data packets, communications lengths are not altered and packet fragmentation is eliminated. The highest network performance is achieved, and routing priorities and policies are preserved.

Sterling Commerce

Sterling Commerce's CONNECT:Firewall provides the physical component necessary to help satisfy an organization's Internet security requirements. CONNECT:Firewall offers these features:

- As a proxy server firewall, CONNECT:Firewall provides control over inbound and outbound applications. Through the use of CONNECT:Firewall's access control lists, users can be required to go through authentication at the proxy or be given transparent passthrough (outbound only). If additional authentication is required, the use of one-time passwords is supported via OPIE (One-time Passwords In Everything) or SecureID by Security Dynamics, Inc.

- Logging features are available with a strong set of alert notification functions, which provide real-time monitoring and notification of unacceptable activity.

- CONNECT:Firewall's Motif graphic user interface (GUI) helps make it easy to administer. Configuration changes can be made quickly and verified automatically for proper syntax, aiding in the reduction of human error.

APPENDIX D

SITE SECURITY HANDBOOK

Status of this memo: This handbook is the product of the Site Security Policy Handbook Working Group (SSPHWG), a combined effort of the Security Area and User Services Area of the Internet Engineering Task Force (IETF). This FYI RFC provides information for the Internet community. It does not specify an Internet standard. Distribution of this memo is unlimited.

Contributing Authors

The following are the authors of the Site Security Handbook. Without their dedication, this handbook would not have been possible.

Dave Curry (Purdue University), Sean Kirkpatrick (Unisys), Tom Longstaff (LLNL), Greg Hollingsworth (Johns Hopkins University), Jeffrey Carpenter (University of Pittsburgh), Barbara Fraser (CERT), Fred Ostapik (SRI NISC), Allen Sturtevant (LLNL), Dan Long (BBN), Jim Duncan (Pennsylvania State University), and Frank Byrum (DEC).

Editors' note: This FYI RFC is a first attempt at providing Internet users guidance on how to deal with security issues in the Internet. As such, this document is necessarily incomplete. There are some clear shortfalls; for example, this document focuses mostly on resources available in the United States. In the spirit of the Internet's "Request for Comments" series of notes, we encourage feedback from users of this handbook. In particular, those who utilize this document to craft their own policies and procedures.

This handbook is meant to be a starting place for further research and should be viewed as a useful resource, but not the final authority. Different organizations and jurisdictions will have different resources and rules. Talk to your local organizations, consult an informed lawyer, or consult with local and national law enforcement. These groups can help fill in the gaps that this document cannot hope to cover.

Finally, we intend for this FYI RFC to grow and evolve. Please send comments and suggestions to ssphwg@cert.sei.cmu.edu.

1. Introduction

1.1 Purpose of This Work

This handbook is a guide to setting computer security policies and procedures for sites that have systems on the Internet. This guide lists issues and factors that a site must consider when setting their own policies. It makes some recommendations and gives discussions of relevant areas.

This guide is only a framework for setting security policies and procedures. In order to have an effective set of policies and procedures, a site will have to make many decisions, gain agreement, and then communicate and implement the policies.

1.2 Audience

The audience for this work are system administrators and decision makers (who are more traditionally called *administrators* or *middle management*) at sites. This document is not directed at programmers or those trying to create secure programs or systems. The focus of this document is on the policies and procedures that need to be in place to support any technical security features that a site may be implementing.

The primary audience for this work are sites that consists of members of the Internet community. However, this document should be useful to any site that allows communication with other sites. As a general guide to security policies, this document also may be useful to sites with isolated systems.

1.3 Definitions

For the purposes of this guide, a *site* is any organization that owns computers or network-related resources. These resources may include host computers that users use, routers, terminal servers, PCs, or other devices that have access to the Internet. A site may be a end user of Internet services or a service provider such as a regional network. However, most of the focus of this guide is on those end users of Internet services.

We assume that the site has the ability to set policies and procedures for itself with the concurrence and support from those who actually own the resources.

The *Internet* is those set of networks and machines which use the TCP/IP protocol suite, connected through gateways, and sharing a common name and address spaces.[1]

The term *system administrator* is used to cover all those who are responsible for the day-to-day operation of resources. This may be a number of individuals or an organization.

The term *decision maker* refers to those people at a site who set or approve policy. These are often (but not always) the people who own the resources.

1.4 Related Work

The IETF Security Policy Working Group (SPWG) is working on a set of recommended security policy guidelines for the Internet.[23] These guidelines may be adopted as policy by regional networks or owners of other resources. This handbook should be a useful tool to help sites implement those policies as desired or required. However, even implementing the proposed policies is not enough to secure a site. The proposed Internet policies deal only with network access security. It says nothing about how sites should deal with local security issues.

1.5 Scope

This document covers issues about what a computer security policy should contain, what kinds of procedures are needed to enforce security, and some recommendations about how to deal with the problem. When developing a security policy, close attention should be paid not only to the security needs and requirements of the local network but also to the security needs and requirements of the other interconnected networks.

This is not a cookbook for computer security. Each site has different needs; the security needs of a corporation might well be different from the security needs of an academic institution. Any security plan has to conform to the needs and culture of the site.

This handbook does not cover details of how to do risk assessment, contingency planning, or physical security. These things are essential in setting and implementing effective security policy, but this document leaves treatment of those issues to other documents. We will try to provide some pointers in that direction.

This document also does not talk about how to design or implement secure systems or programs.

1.6 Why Do We Need Security Policies and Procedures?

For most sites, the interest in computer security is proportional to the perception of risk and threats.

The world of computers has changed dramatically over the past 25 years. Twenty-five years ago, most computers were centralized and managed by data centers. Computers were kept in locked rooms, and staffs of people made sure they were carefully managed and physically secured. Links outside a site were unusual. Computer security threats were rare and were basically concerned with insiders: authorized users misusing accounts, theft and vandalism, and so forth. These threats were well understood and dealt with using standard techniques: computers behind locked doors and accounting for all resources.

Computing in the 1990s is radically different. Many systems are in private offices and labs, often managed by individuals or persons employed outside a computer center. Many systems are connected into the Internet and from there around the world: The United States, Europe, Asia, and Australia are all connected together.

Security threats are different today. The time honored advice says "Don't write your password down and put it in your desk" lest someone find it. With worldwide Internet connections, someone could get into your system from the other side of the world and steal your password in the middle of the night when your building is locked up. Viruses and worms can be passed from machine to machine. The Internet allows the electronic equivalent of the thief who looks for open windows and doors; now a person can check hundreds of machines for vulnerabilities in a few hours.

System administrators and decision makers have to understand the security threats that exist, what the risk and cost of a problem would be, and what kind of action they want to take (if any) to prevent and respond to security threats.

As an illustration of some of the issues that need to be dealt with in security problems, consider the following scenarios (thanks to Russell Brand[2] for these):

- A system programmer gets a call reporting that a major underground cracker newsletter is being distributed from the administrative machine at his center to five thousand sites in the United States and western Europe.

Eight weeks later, the authorities call to inform you that the information in one of these newsletters was used to disable 911 in a major city for 5 hours.

- A user calls in to report that he cannot login to his account at 3 o'clock in the morning on a Saturday. The system staffer cannot login either. After rebooting to single user mode, he finds that the password file is empty. By Monday morning, your staff determines that a number of privileged file transfers took place between this machine and a local university.

Tuesday morning a copy of the deleted password file is found on the university machine along with password files for a dozen other machines. A week later you find that your system initialization files had been altered in a hostile fashion.

- You receive a call saying that a breakin to a government lab occurred from one of your center's machines. You are requested to provide accounting files to help track down the attacker.

A week later you are given a list of machines at your site that have been broken into.

- A reporter calls up asking about the break-in at your center. You haven't heard of any such break-in.

Three days later, you learn that there was a break-in. The center director had his wife's name as a password.

- A change in system binaries is detected.

The day that it is corrected, they again are changed. This repeats itself for some weeks.

- If an intruder is found on your system, should you leave the system open to monitor the situation, or should you close down the holes and open them up again later?
- If an intruder is using your site, should you call law enforcement? Who makes this decision? If law enforcement asks you to leave your site open, who makes that decision?
- What steps should be taken if another site calls you and says they

see activity coming from an account on your system? What if the account is owned by a local manager?

1.7 Basic Approach

Setting security policies and procedures really means developing a plan for how to deal with computer security. One way to approach this task is suggested by Fites et al.[3]:

- Look at what you are trying to protect.
- Look at what you need to protect it from.
- Determine how likely the threats are.
- Implement measures that will protect your assets in a cost-effective manner.
- Review the process continuously, and improve things every time a weakness is found.

This handbook will concentrate mostly on the last two steps, but the first three are critically important to making effective decisions about security. One old truism in security is that the cost of protecting yourself against a threat should be less than the cost of recovering if the threat were to strike you. Without reasonable knowledge of what you are protecting and what the likely threats are, following this rule could be difficult.

1.8 Organization of This Document

This document is organized into seven parts in addition to this introduction. The basic form of each section is to discuss issues that a site might want to consider in creating a computer security policy and setting procedures to implement that policy. In some cases, possible options are discussed along with the some of the ramifications of those choices. As far as possible, this document tries not to dictate the choices a site should make, since these depend on local circumstances. Some of the issues brought up may not apply to all sites. Nonetheless, all sites should at least consider the issues brought up here to ensure that they do not miss some important area.

The overall flow of the document is to discuss policy issues followed by the issues that come up in creating procedures to implement the policies.

Section 2 discusses setting official site policies for access to computing resources. It also goes into the issue of what happens when the policy is violated. The policies will drive the procedures that need to be created, so decision makers will need to make choices about policies before many of the procedural issues in the following sections can be dealt with. A key part of creating policies is doing some kind of risk assessment to decide what really needs to be protected and the level of resources that should be applied to protect them.

Once policies are in place, procedures to prevent future security problems should be established. Section 3 defines and suggests actions to take when unauthorized activity is suspected. Resources to prevent security breaches are also discussed.

Section 4 discusses types of procedures to prevent security problems. Prevention is a key to security; as an example, the Computer Emergency Response Team/Coordination Center (CERT/CC) at Carnegie-Mellon University (CMU) estimates that 80 percent or more of the problems they see have to do with poorly chosen passwords.

Section 5 discusses incident handling: What kinds of issues does a site face when someone violates the security policy? Many decisions will have to be made on the spot as the incident occurs, but many of the options and issues can be discussed in advance. At the very least, responsibilities and methods of communication can be established before an incident. Again, the choices here are influenced by the policies discussed in Section 2.

Section 6 deals with what happens after a security violation has been dealt with. Security planning is an ongoing cycle; just after an incident has occurred is an excellent opportunity to improve policies and procedures.

The rest of the document provides references and an annotated bibliography.

2. Establishing Official Site Policy on Computer Security

2.1 Brief Overview

2.1.1 Organization Issues

The goal in developing an official site policy on computer security is to define the organization's expectations of proper computer and network use and to define procedures to prevent and respond to security incidents. In order to do this, aspects of the particular organization must be considered.

First, the goals and direction of the organization should be considered. For example, a military base may have very different security concerns from a those of a university.

Second, the site security policy developed must conform to existing policies, rules, regulations, and laws that the organization is subject to. Therefore, it will be necessary to identify these and take them into consideration while developing the policy.

Third, unless the local network is completely isolated and stand-alone, it is necessary to consider security implications in a more global context. The policy should address the issues when local security problems develop as a result of a remote site as well as when problems occur on remote systems as a result of a local host or user.

2.1.2 Who Makes the Policy?

Policy creation must be a joint effort by technical personnel who understand the full ramifications of the proposed policy and the implementation of the policy and by decision makers who have the power to enforce the policy. A policy that is neither implementable nor enforceable is useless.

Since a computer security policy can affect everyone in an organization, it is worth taking some care to make sure you have the right level of authority on the policy decisions. Though a particular group (such as a campus information services group) may have responsibility for enforcing a policy, an even higher group may have to support and approve the policy.

2.1.3 Who Is Involved?

Establishing a site policy has the potential for involving every computer user at the site in a variety of ways. Computer users may be responsible for personal password administration. Systems managers are obligated to fix security holes and to oversee the system.

It is critical to get the right set of people involved at the start of the process. There may already be groups concerned with security who would consider a computer security policy to be their area. Some of the types of groups that might be involved include auditing/control, organizations that deal with physical security, campus information systems groups, and so forth. Asking these types of groups to "buy in" from the start can help facilitate the acceptance of the policy.

2.1.4 Responsibilities

A key element of a computer security policy is making sure everyone knows their own responsibility for maintaining security. A computer security policy cannot anticipate all possibilities; however, it can ensure that each kind of problem does have someone assigned to deal with it.

There may be levels of responsibility associated with a policy on computer security. At one level, each user of a computing resource may have a responsibility to protect his or her account. A user who allows his or her account to be compromised increases the chances of compromising other accounts or resources.

System managers may form another responsibility level: they must help to ensure the security of the computer system. Network managers may reside at yet another level.

2.2 Risk Assessment

2.2.1 General Discussion

One of the most important reasons for creating a computer security policy is to ensure that efforts spent on security yield cost-effective benefits. Although this may seem obvious, it is possible to be mislead about where the effort is needed. As an example, there is a great deal of publicity about intruders on computers systems, yet most surveys of computer security show that for most organizations the actual loss from "insiders" is much greater.

Risk analysis involves determining what you need to protect, what you need to protect it from, and how to protect it. It is the process of examining all your risks and ranking those risks by level of severity. This process involves making cost-effective decisions on what you want to protect. The old security adage says that you should not spend more to protect something than it is actually worth.

A full treatment of risk analysis is outside the scope of this document. Fites et al.[3] and Pfleeger[16] provide introductions to this topic. However, there are two elements of a risk analysis that will be briefly covered in the next two sections:

1. Identifying the assets

2. Identifying the threats

For each asset, the basic goals of security are availability, confidentiality, and integrity. Each threat should be examined with an eye to how the threat could affect these areas.

2.2.2 Identifying the Assets

One step in a risk analysis is to identify all the things that need to be protected. Some things are obvious, like all the various pieces of hardware, but some are overlooked, such as the people who actually use the systems. The essential point is to list all things that could be affected by a security problem.

One list of categories is suggested by Pfleeger[16] (p. 459); this list is adapted from that source:

1. Hardware: CPUs, boards, keyboards, terminals, workstations, personal computers, printers, disk drives, communication lines, terminal servers, routers

2. Software: Source programs, object programs, utilities, diagnostic programs, operating systems, communication programs

3. Data: During execution, stored on-line, archived off-line, backups, audit logs, databases, in transit over communication media

4. People: Users, people needed to run systems

5. Documentation: On programs, hardware, systems, local administrative procedures

6. Supplies: Paper, forms, ribbons, magnetic media

2.2.3 Identifying the Threats

Once the assets requiring protection are identified, it is necessary to identify threats to those assests. The threats can then be examined to determine what potential for loss exists. It helps to consider from what threats you are trying to protect your assets.

The following sections describe a few of the possible threats.

Unauthorized Access

A common threat that concerns many sites is unauthorized access to computing facilities. Unauthorized access takes many forms. One means of unauthorized access is the use of another user's account to gain access to a system. The use of any computer resource without prior permission may be considered unauthorized access to computing facilities.

The seriousness of an unauthorized access will vary from site to site. For some sites, the mere act of granting access to an unauthorized user may cause irreparable harm by negative media coverage. For other sites, an unauthorized access opens the door to other security threats. In addition, some sites may be more frequent targets than others; hence the risk from unauthorized access will vary from site to site. The Computer

Emergency Response Team (CERT; see below) has observed that well-known universities, government sites, and military sites seem to attract more intruders.

Disclosure of Information

Another common threat is disclosure of information. Determine the value or sensitivity of the information stored on your computers. Disclosure of a password file might allow for future unauthorized accesses. A glimpse of a proposal may give a competitor an unfair advantage. A technical paper may contain years of valuable research.

Denial of Service

Computers and networks provide valuable services to their users. Many people rely on these services in order to perform their jobs efficiently. When these services are not available when called on, a loss in productivity results.

Denial of service comes in many forms and might affect users in a number of ways. A network may be rendered unusable by a rogue packet, by jamming, or by a disabled network component. A virus might slow down or cripple a computer system. Each site should determine which services are essential and for each of these services determine the affect to the site if that service were to become disabled.

2.3 Policy Issues

There are a number of issues that must be addressed when developing a security policy. These are

1. Who is allowed to use the resources?

2. What is the proper use of the resources?

3. Who is authorized to grant access and approve usage?

4. Who may have system administration privileges?

5. What are the user's rights and responsibilities?

6. What are the rights and responsibilities of the system administrator versus those of the user?

7. What do you do with sensitive information?

These issues will be discussed below. In addition you may wish to include a section in your policy concerning ethical use of computing resources. Parker et al.[17] and Forester and Morrison[18] are two useful references that address ethical issues.

2.3.1 Who Is Allowed to Use the Resources?

One step you must take in developing your security policy is defining who is allowed to use your system and services. The policy should state explicitly who is authorized to use what resources.

2.3.2 What Is the Proper Use of the Resources?

After determining who is allowed access to system resources, it is necessary to provide guidelines for the acceptable use of the resources. You may have different guidelines for different types of users (i.e., students, faculty, external users). The policy should state what is acceptable use as well as unacceptable use. It also should include types of use that may be restricted.

Define limits to access and authority. You will need to consider the level of access various users will have and what resources will be available or restricted to various groups of people.

Your acceptable use policy should clearly state that individual users are responsible for their actions. Their responsibility exists regardless of the security mechanisms that are in place. It should be stated clearly that breaking into accounts or bypassing security is not permitted.

The following points should be covered when developing an acceptable use policy:

- Is breaking into accounts permitted?
- Is cracking passwords permitted?
- Is disrupting service permitted?
- Should users assume that a file being world-readable grants them the authorization to read it?
- Should users be permitted to modify files that are not their own even if they happen to have write permission?
- Should users share accounts?

The answer to most of these questions will be "no."

You may wish to incorporate a statement in your policies concerning copyrighted and licensed software. Licensing agreements with vendors may require some sort of effort on your part to ensure that the license is not violated. In addition, you may wish to inform users that the copying of copyrighted software may be a violation of the copyright laws, and is not permitted.

Specifically concerning copyrighted and/or licensed software, you may wish to include the following information:

- Copyrighted and licensed software may not be duplicated unless it is explicitly stated that you may do so.
- Methods of conveying information on the copyright/licensed status of software.
- When in doubt, *don't copy.*

Your acceptable use policy is very important. A policy that does not clearly state what is not permitted may leave you unable to prove that a user violated policy.

There are exception cases like tiger teams and users or administrators wishing for "licenses to hack"—you may face the situation where users will want to "hack" on your services for security research purposes. You should develop a policy that will determine whether you will permit this type of research on your services and, if so, what your guidelines for such research will be.

Points you may wish to cover in this area:

- Whether it is permitted at all.
- What type of activity is permitted: breaking in, releasing worms, releasing viruses, etc.
- What type of controls must be in place to ensure that it does not get out of control (e.g., separate a segment of your network for these tests).
- How you will protect other users from being victims of these activities, including external users and networks.
- The process for obtaining permission to conduct these tests.

In cases where you do permit these activities, you should isolate the portions of the network that are being tested from your main network. Worms and viruses should never be released on a live network.

You also may wish to employ, contract, or otherwise solicit one or more people or organizations to evaluate the security of your services, of which may include "hacking." You may wish to provide for this in your policy.

2.3.3 Who Is Authorized to Grant Access and Approve Usage?
Your policy should state who is authorized to grant access to your services. Further, it must be determined what type of access they are per-

mitted to give. If you do not have control over who is granted access to your system, you will not have control over who is using your system. Controlling who has the authorization to grant access also will enable you to know who was or was not granting access if problems develop later.

There are many schemes that can be developed to control the distribution of access to your services. The following are the factors that you must consider when determining who will distribute access to your services:

- Will you be distributing access from a centralized point or at various points?

You can have a centralized distribution point to a distributed system where various sites or departments independently authorize access. The tradeoff is between security and convenience. The more centralized, the easier to secure.

- What methods will you use for creating accounts and terminating access?

From a security standpoint, you need to examine the mechanism that you will be using to create accounts. In the least restrictive case, the people who are authorized to grant access would be able to go into the system directly and create an account by hand or through vendor supplied mechanisms. Generally, these mechanisms place a great deal of trust in the person running them, and the person running them usually has a large amount of privileges. If this is the choice you make, you need to select someone who is trustworthy to perform this task. The opposite solution is to have an integrated system that the people authorized to create accounts run or the users themselves may actually run. Be aware that even the restrictive case of having a mechanized facility to create accounts does not remove the potential for abuse.

You should have specific procedures developed for the creation of accounts. These procedures should be well documented to prevent confusion and reduce mistakes. A security vulnerability in the account authorization process is not only possible through abuse but is also possible if a mistake is made. Having clear and well-documented procedure will help ensure that these mistakes will not happen. You also should be sure that the people who will be following these procedures understand them.

The granting of access to users is one of the most vulnerable of times.

You should ensure that the selection of an initial password cannot be guessed easily. You should avoid using an initial password that is a function of the user name, is part of the user's name, or some algorithmically generated password that can be guessed easily. In addition, you should not permit users to continue to use the initial password indefinitely. If possible, you should force users to change the initial password the first time they log in. Consider that some users may never even log in, leaving their password vulnerable indefinitely. Some sites choose to disable accounts that have never been accessed and force the owner to reauthorize opening the account.

2.3.4 Who May Have System Administration Privileges?

One security decision that needs to be made very carefully is who will have access to system administrator privileges and passwords for your services. Obviously, the system administrators will need access, but inevitably other users will request special privileges. The policy should address this issue. Restricting privileges is one way to deal with threats from local users. The challenge is to balance restricting access to these to protect security with giving people who need these privileges access so that they can perform their tasks. One approach that can be taken is to grant only enough privilege to accomplish the necessary tasks.

Additionally, people holding special privileges should be accountable to some authority, and this also should be identified within the site's security policy. If the people you grant privileges to are not accountable, you run the risk of losing control of your system and will have difficulty managing a compromise in security.

2.3.5 What Are the Users' Rights and Responsibilities?

The policy should incorporate a statement on the users' rights and responsibilities concerning the use of the site's computer systems and services. It should be stated clearly that users are responsible for understanding and respecting the security rules of the systems they are using. The following is a list of topics that you may wish to cover in this area of the policy:

- What guidelines you have regarding resource consumption (whether users are restricted and, if so, what the restrictions are)
- What might constitute abuse in terms of system performance
- Whether users are permitted to share accounts or let others use their accounts

- How "secret" users should keep their passwords.

- How often users should change their passwords and any other password restrictions or requirements

- Whether you provide backups or expect the users to create their own

- Disclosure of information that may be proprietary.

- Statement on electronic mail privacy (Electronic Communications Privacy Act)

- Your policy concerning controversial mail or postings to mailing lists or discussion groups (obscenity, harassment, etc.)

- Policy on electronic communications: mail forging, etc.

The Electronic Mail Association sponsored a white paper on the privacy of electronic mail in companies.[4] Their basic recommendation is that every site should have a policy on the protection of employee privacy. They also recommend that organizations establish privacy policies that deal with all media rather than singling out electronic mail.

They suggest five criteria for evaluating any policy:

1. Does the policy comply with law and with duties to third parties?

2. Does the policy unnecessarily compromise the interest of the employee, the employer, or third parties?

3. Is the policy workable as a practical matter and likely to be enforced?

4. Does the policy deal appropriately with all different forms of communications and record keeping with the office?

5. Has the policy been announced in advance and agreed to by all concerned?

2.3.6   What Are the Rights and Responsibilities of System Administrators Versus Rights of Users

There is a tradeoff between a user's right to absolute privacy and the need of system administrators to gather sufficient information to diagnose problems. There is also a distinction between a system administrator's need to gather information to diagnose problems and investigating security violations. The policy should specify to what degree system administrators can examine user files to diagnose problems or for other purposes and what rights you grant to the users. You also may wish to make a statement concerning system administrators' obligation to maintaining the privacy of information viewed under these circumstances. A few questions that should be answered are

- Can an administrator monitor or read a user's files for any reason?
- What are the liabilities?
- Do network administrators have the right to examine network or host traffic?

2.3.7   What to Do with Sensitive Information

Before granting users access to your services, you need to determine at what level you will provide for the security of data on your systems. By determining this, you are determining the level of sensitivity of data that users should store on your systems. You do not want users to store very sensitive information on a system that you are not going to secure very well. You need to tell users who might store sensitive information what services, if any, are appropriate for the storage of sensitive information. This part should include storing of data in different ways (disk, magnetic tape, file servers, etc.). Your policy in this area needs to be coordinated with the policy concerning the rights of system administrators versus users (see Section 2.3.6).

2.4   What Happens When the Policy Is Violated

It is obvious that when any type of official policy is defined, be it related to computer security or not, it will eventually be broken. The violation may occur due to an individual's negligence, accidental mistake, having not been properly informed of the current policy, or not understanding the current policy. It is equally possible that an individual (or group of individuals) may knowingly perform an act that is in direct violation of the defined policy.

When a policy violation has been detected, the immediate course of action should be predefined to ensure prompt and proper enforcement. An investigation should be performed to determine how and why the violation occurred. Then the appropriate corrective action should be executed. The type and severity of action taken vary depending on the type of violation that occurred.

2.4.1 Determining the Response to Policy Violations?

Violations to policy may be committed by a wide variety of users. Some may be local users, and others may be from outside the local environment. Sites may find it helpful to define what it considers *insiders* and *outsiders* based on administrative, legal, or political boundaries. These boundaries imply what type of action must be taken to correct the offending party; from a written reprimand to pressing legal charges. Therefore, not only do you need to define actions based on the type of violation, but you also need to have a clearly defined series of actions based on the kind of user violating your computer security policy. This all seems rather complicated but should be addressed long before it becomes necessary as the result of a violation.

One point to remember about your policy is that proper education is your best defense. For the outsiders who are using your computer legally, it is your responsibility to verify that these individuals are aware of the policies that you have set forth. Having this proof may assist you in the future if legal action becomes necessary.

As for users who are using your computer illegally, the problem is basically the same. What type of user violated the policy, and how and why did they do it? Depending on the results of your investigation, you may just prefer to "plug" the hole in your computer security and chalk it up to experience. Or if a significant amount of loss was incurred, you may wish to take more drastic action.

2.4.2 What to Do When Local Users Violate the Policy of a Remote Site

In the event that a local user violates the security policy of a remote site, the local site should have a clearly defined set of administrative actions to take concerning that local user. The site also should be prepared to protect itself against possible actions by the remote site. These situations involve legal issues that should be addressed when forming the security policy.

2.4.3 Defining Contacts and Responsibilities to Outside Organizations

The local security policy should include procedures for interaction with outside organizations. These include law enforcement agencies, other sites, external response team organizations (e.g., the CERT, CIAC), and various press agencies. The procedure should state who is authorized to make such contact and how it should be handled. Some questions to be answered include

- Who may talk to the press?
- When do you contact law enforcement and investigative agencies?
- If a connection is made from a remote site, is the system manager authorized to contact that site?
- Can data be released? What kind?

Detailed contact information should be readily available along with clearly defined procedures to follow.

2.4.4 What Are the Responsibilities to Our Neighbors and Other Internet Sites?

The Security Policy Working Group within the IETF is working on a document entitled, "Policy Guidelines for the Secure Operation of the Internet."[23] It addresses the issue that the Internet is a cooperative venture and that sites are expected to provide mutual security assistance. This should be addressed when developing a site's policy. The major issue to be determined is how much information should be released. This will vary from site to site according to the type of site (e.g., military, education, commercial) as well as the type of security violation that occurred.

2.4.5 Issues for Incident Handling Procedures

Along with statements of policy, the document being prepared should include procedures for incident handling. This is covered in detail in the next section. There should be procedures available that cover all facets of policy violation.

2.5 Locking In or Out

Whenever a site suffers an incident that may compromise computer security, the strategies for reacting may be influenced by two opposing pressures. If management fears that the site is sufficiently vulnerable, it may choose a "protect and proceed" strategy. This approach will have as its primary goal the protection and preservation of the site facilities to provide for normalcy for its users as quickly as possible. Attempts will be made to actively interfere with the intruder's processes, prevent further access, and begin immediate damage assessment and recovery. This process may involve shutting down the facilities, closing off access to the network, or other drastic measures. The drawback is that unless the intruder is identified directly, he or she may come back into the site via a different path or may attack another site.

The alternate approach, "pursue and prosecute," adopts the opposite philosophy and goals. The primary goal is to allow intruders to continue their activities at the site until the site can identify the responsible persons. This approach is endorsed by law enforcement agencies and prosecutors. The drawback is that the agencies cannot exempt a site from possible user lawsuits if damage is done to their systems and data.

Prosecution is not the only outcome possible if the intruder is identified. If the culprit is an employee or a student, the organization may choose to take disciplinary actions. The computer security policy needs to spell out the choices and how such actions will be selected if an intruder is caught.

Careful consideration must be made by site management regarding their approach to this issue before the problem occurs. The strategy adopted might depend on each circumstance. Or there may be a global policy that mandates one approach in all circumstances. The pros and cons must be examined thoroughly, and the users of the facilities must be made aware of the policy so that they understand their vulnerabilities no matter which approach is taken.

The following are checklists to help a site determine which strategy to adopt: "protect and proceed" or "pursue and prosecute."

Protect and Proceed

1. If assets are not well protected.

2. If continued penetration could result in great financial risk.

3. If the possibility or willingness to prosecute is not present.

4. If user base is unknown.

5. If users are unsophisticated and their work is vulnerable.

6. If the site is vulnerable to lawsuits from users, e.g., if their resources are undermined.

Pursue and Prosecute

1. If assets and systems are well protected.

2. If good backups are available.

3. If the risk to the assets is outweighed by the disruption caused by the present and possibly future penetrations.

4. If this is a concentrated attack occurring with great frequency and intensity.

5. If the site has a natural attraction to intruders and consequently regularly attracts intruders.

6. If the site is willing to incur the financial (or other) risk to assets by allowing the penetrator continue.

7. If intruder access can be controlled.

8. If the monitoring tools are sufficiently well developed to make the pursuit worthwhile.

9. If the support staff is sufficiently clever and knowledgable about the operating system, related utilities, and systems to make the pursuit worthwhile.

10. If there is willingness on the part of management to prosecute.

11. If the system adminitrators know in general what kind of evidence would lead to prosecution.

12. If there is established contact with knowledgeable law enforcement.

13. If there is a site representative versed in the relevant legal issues.

14. If the site is prepared for possible legal action from its own users if their data or systems become compromised during the pursuit.

2.6 Interpreting the Policy

It is important to define who will interpret the policy. This could be an individual or a committee. No matter how well written, the policy will require interpretation from time to time, and this body would serve to review, interpret, and revise the policy as needed.

2.7 Publicizing the Policy

Once the site security policy has been written and established, a vigorous process should be engaged to ensure that the policy statement is widely and thoroughly disseminated and discussed. A mailing of the policy should not be considered sufficient. A period for comments should be allowed before the policy becomes effective to ensure that all affected users have a chance to state their reactions and discuss any unforeseen ramifications. Ideally, the policy should strike a balance between protection and productivity.

Meetings should be held to elicit these comments and also to ensure that the policy is correctly understood. (Policy promulgators are not necessarily noted for their skill with the language.) These meetings should involve higher management as well as line employees. Security is a collective effort.

In addition to the initial efforts to publicize the policy, it is essential for the site to maintain a continual awareness of its computer security policy. Current users may need periodic reminders. New users should have the policy included as part of their site introduction packet. As a condition for using the site facilities, it may be advisable to have them sign a statement that they have read and understood the policy. Should any of these users require legal action for serious policy violations, this signed statement might prove to be a valuable aid.

3. Establishing Procedures to Prevent Security Problems

The security policy defines what needs to be protected. This section discusses security procedures that specify what steps will be used to carry out the security policy.

3.1 Security Policy Defines What Needs to Be Protected

The security policy defines the *what's*: what needs to be protected, what is most important, what the priorities are, and what the general approach to dealing with security problems should be.

The security policy by itself doesn't say *how* things are protected. This is the role of security procedures, which this section discusses. The security policy should be a high-level document, giving general strategy. The security procedures need to set out, in detail, the precise steps your site will take to protect itself.

The security policy should include a general risk assessment of the types of threats a site is mostly likely to face and the consequences of those threats (see Section 2.2). Part of doing a risk assessment will include creating a general list of assets that should be protected (see Section 2.2.2). This information is critical in devising cost-effective procedures.

It is often tempting to start creating security procedures by deciding on different mechanisms first: "Our site should have logging on all hosts, call-back modems, and smart cards for all users." This approach could lead to some areas that have too much protection for the risk they face and other areas that are not protected enough. Starting with the security policy and the risks it outlines should ensure that the procedures provide the right level of protection for all assets.

3.2 Identifying Possible Problems

To determine risk, vulnerabilities must be identified. Part of the purpose of the policy is to aid in shoring up the vulnerabilities and thus to decrease the risk in as many areas as possible. Several of the more popular problem areas are presented in the following sections. This list is by no means complete. In addition, each site is likely to have a few unique vulnerabilities.

3.2.1 Access Points
Access points are typically used for entry by unauthorized users. Having many access points increases the risk of access to an organization's computer and network facilities.

Network links to networks outside the organization allow access into the organization for all others connected to that external network. A network link typically provides access to a large number of network services, and each service has a potential to be compromised.

Dial-up lines, depending on their configuration, may provide access merely to a login port of a single system. If connected to a terminal server, the dial-up line may give access to the entire network.

Terminal servers themselves can be a source of a problem. Many terminal servers do not require any kind of authentication. Intruders often use terminal servers to disguise their actions, dialing in on a local phone and then using the terminal server to go out to the local network. Some terminal servers are configured so that intruders can Telnet in from outside the network, and then Telnet back out again, again serving to make it difficult to trace them.[19]

3.2.2 Misconfigured Systems
Misconfigured systems form a large percentage of security holes. Today's operating systems and their associated software have become so complex that understanding how the system works has become a full-time job.

Often, systems managers will be nonspecialists chosen from the current organization's staff.

Vendors are also partly responsible for misconfigured systems. To make the system installation process easier, vendors occasionally choose initial configurations that are not secure in all environments.

3.2.3 Software Bugs

Software will never be bug free. Publicly known security bugs are common methods of unauthorized entry. Part of the solution to this problem is to be aware of the security problems and to update the software when problems are detected. When bugs are found, they should be reported to the vendor so that a solution to the problem can be implemented and distributed.

3.2.4 "Insider" Threats

An insider to the organization may be a considerable threat to the security of the computer systems. Insiders often have direct access to the computer and network hardware components. The ability to access the components of a system makes most systems easier to compromise. Most desktop workstations can be easily manipulated so that they grant privileged access. Access to a local area network provides the ability to view possibly sensitive data traversing the network.

3.3 Choose Controls to Protect Assets in a Cost-Effective Way

After establishing what is to be protected, and assessing the risks these assets face, it is necessary to decide how to implement the controls that protect these assets. The controls and protection mechanisms should be selected in a way so as to adequately counter the threats found during risk assessment and to implement those controls in a cost-effective manner. It makes little sense to spend an exorbitant sum of money and overly constrict the user base if the risk of exposure is very small.

3.3.1 Choose the Right Set of Controls

The controls that are selected represent the physical embodiment of your security policy. They are the first and primary line of defense in the protection of your assets. It is therefore most important to ensure that the controls that you select are the right set of controls. If the major threat to your system is outside penetrators, it probably does not make much sense to use biometric devices to authenticate your regular system users. On the other hand, if the major threat is unauthorized use of computing resources by regular system users, you will probably want to establish very rigorous automated accounting procedures.

3.3.2 Use Common Sense

Common sense is the most appropriate tool that can be used to establish your security policy. Elaborate security schemes and mechanisms are impressive, and they do have their place, yet there is little point in investing money and time on an elaborate implementation scheme if the simple controls are forgotten. For example, no matter how elaborate a system you put into place on top of existing security controls, a single user with a poor password can still leave your system open to attack.

3.4 Use Multiple Strategies to Protect Assets

Another method of protecting assets is to use multiple strategies. In this way, if one strategy fails or is circumvented, another strategy comes into play to continue protecting the asset. By using several simpler strategies, a system often can be made more secure than if one very sophisticated method were used in its place. For example, dial-back modems can be used in conjunction with traditional logon mechanisms. Many similar approaches could be devised that provide several levels of protection for assets. However, it is very easy to go overboard with extra mechanisms. One must keep in mind exactly what it is that needs to be protected.

3.5 Physical Security

It is a given in computer security that if the system itself is not physically secure, nothing else about the system can be considered secure. With physical access to a machine, an intruder can halt the machine, bring it back up in privileged mode, replace or alter the disk, plant Trojan horse programs, or take any number of other undesirable (and hard to prevent) actions.

Critical communications links, important servers, and other key machines should be located in physically secure areas. Some security systems (such as Kerberos) require that the machine be physically secure.

If you cannot physically secure machines, care should be taken about trusting those machines. Sites should consider limiting access from non-secure machines to more secure machines. In particular, allowing trusted access (e.g., the BSD Unix remote commands such as rsh) from these kinds of hosts is particularly risky.

For machines that seem or are intended to be physically secure, care should be taken about who has access to the machines. Remember that custodial and maintenance staff often have keys to rooms.

3.6 Procedures to Recognize Unauthorized Activity

Several simple procedures can be used to detect most unauthorized uses of a computer system. These procedures use tools provided with the operating system by the vendor or tools publicly available from other sources.

3.6.1 Monitoring System Use

System monitoring can be done either by a system administrator or by software written for the purpose. Monitoring a system involves looking at several parts of the system and searching for anything unusual. Some of the easier ways to do this are described in this section.

The most important thing about monitoring system use is that it be done on a regular basis. Picking one day out of the month to monitor the system is pointless, since a security breach can be isolated to a matter of hours. Only by maintaining a constant vigil can you expect to detect security violations in time to react to them.

3.6.2 Tools for Monitoring the System

This section describes tools and methods for monitoring a system against unauthorized access and use.

Logging

Most operating systems store numerous bits of information in log files. Examination of these log files on a regular basis is often the first line of defense in detecting unauthorized use of the system.

- Compare lists of currently logged in users and past login histories. Most users typically log in and out at roughly the same time each day. An account logged in outside the "normal" time for the account may be in use by an intruder.

- Many systems maintain accounting records for billing purposes. These records also can be used to determine usage patterns for the system; unusual accounting records may indicate unauthorized use of the system.

- System logging facilities, such as the Unix syslog utility, should be checked for unusual error messages from system software. For example, a large number of failed login attempts in a short period of time may indicate someone trying to guess passwords.

- Operating system commands that list currently executing processes can be used to detect users running programs they are not authorized to use, as well as to detect unauthorized programs that have been started by an intruder.

Monitoring Software

Other monitoring tools can be constructed easily using standard operating system software by using several, often unrelated programs together. For example, checklists of file ownerships and permission settings can be constructed (e.g., with ls and find on Unix) and stored off-line. These lists can then be reconstructed periodically and compared against the master checklist (on Unix, by using the diff utility). Differences may indicate that unauthorized modifications have been made to the system.

Still other tools are available from third-party vendors and public software distribution sites. Section 3.9.9 lists several sources from which you can learn what tools are available and how to get them.

Other Tools

Other tools also can be used to monitor systems for security violations, although this is not their primary purpose. For example, network monitors can be used to detect and log connections from unknown sites.

3.6.3 Vary the Monitoring Schedule

The task of system monitoring is not as daunting as it may seem. System administrators can execute many of the commands used for monitoring periodically throughout the day during idle moments (e.g., while talking on the telephone) rather than spending fixed periods of each day monitoring the system. By executing the commands frequently, you will rapidly become used to seeing "normal" output and will easily spot things that are out of the ordinary. In addition, by running various monitoring commands at different times throughout the day, you make it hard for an intruder to predict your actions. For example, if an intruder knows that each day at 5:00 P.M. the system is checked to see that everyone has logged off, he or she will simply wait until after the check has completed before logging in. But the intruder cannot guess when a system administrator might type a command to display all logged-in users, and thus he runs a much greater risk of detection.

Despite the advantages that regular system monitoring provides, some intruders will be aware of the standard logging mechanisms in use on systems they are attacking. They will actively pursue and attempt to disable monitoring mechanisms. Regular monitoring therefore is useful in detecting intruders, but does not provide any guarantee that your system is secure, nor should monitoring be considered an infallible method of detecting unauthorized use.

3.7 Define Actions to Take When Unauthorized Activity Is Suspected

Sections 2.4 and 2.5 discussed the course of action a site should take when it suspects its systems are being abused. The computer security policy should state the general approach toward dealing with these problems.

The procedures for dealing with these types of problems should be written down. Who has authority to decide what actions will be taken? Should law enforcement be involved? Should your organization cooperate with other sites in trying to track down an intruder? Answers to all the questions in Section 2.4 should be part of the incident handling procedures.

Whether you decide to lock out or pursue intruders, you should have tools and procedures ready to apply. It is best to work up these tools and procedures before you need them. Do not wait until an intruder is on your system to figure out how to track the intruder's actions; you will be busy enough if an intruder strikes.

3.8 Communicating Security Policy

Security policies, in order to be effective, must be communicated to both the users of the system and the system maintainers. This section describes what these people should be told, and how to tell them.

3.8.1 Educating the Users

Users should be made aware of how the computer systems are expected to be used, and how to protect themselves from unauthorized users.

Proper Account/Workstation Use

All users should be informed about what is considered the *proper* use of their account or workstation (proper use is discussed in Section 2.3.2). This can most easily be done at the time a user receives his or her account, by giving them a policy statement. Proper use policies typically dictate such things as whether or not the account or workstation may be used for personal activities (such as checkbook balancing or letter writing), whether profit-making activities are allowed, whether game playing is permitted, and so on. These policy statements also may be used to summarize how the computer facility is licensed and what software licenses are held by the institution; for example, many universities have educational licenses that explicitly prohibit commercial uses of the system. A more complete list of items to consider when writing a policy statement is given in Section 2.3.

Account/Workstation Management Procedures

Each user should be told how to properly manage his or her account and workstation. This includes explaining how to protect files stored on the system, how to log out or lock the terminal or workstation, and so on. Much of this information is typically covered in the "beginning user" documentation provided by the operating system vendor, although many sites elect to supplement this material with local information.

If your site offers dial-up modem access to the computer systems, special care must be taken to inform users of the security problems inherent in providing this access. Issues such as making sure to log out before hanging up the modem should be covered when the user is initially given dial-up access.

Likewise, access to the systems via local- and wide-area networks presents its own set of security problems that users should be made aware of. Files that grant "trusted host" or "trusted user" status to remote systems and users should be explained carefully.

Determining Account Misuse

Users should be told how to detect unauthorized access to their account. If the system prints the last login time when a user logs in, he or she should be told to check that time and note whether or not it agrees with the last time he or she actually logged in.

Command interpreters on some systems (e.g., the Unix C shell) maintain histories of the last several commands executed. Users should check these histories to be sure someone has not executed other commands with their account.

Problem Reporting Procedures

A procedure should be developed to enable users to report suspected misuse of their accounts or other misuse they may have noticed. This can be done either by providing the name and telephone number of a system administrator who manages security of the computer system or by creating an electronic mail address (e.g., "Security") to which users can address their problems.

3.8.2 Educating the Host Administrators

In many organizations, computer systems are administered by a wide variety of people. These administrators must know how to protect their own systems from attack and unauthorized use, as well as how to communicate successful penetration of their systems to other administrators as a warning.

Account Management Procedures

Care must be taken when installing accounts on the system in order to make them secure. When installing a system from distribution media, the password file should be examined for "standard" accounts provided by the vendor. Many vendors provide accounts for use by system services or field service personnel. These accounts typically have either no password or one that is common knowledge. These accounts should be given new passwords if they are needed or disabled or deleted from the system if they are not.

Accounts without passwords are generally very dangerous because they allow anyone to access the system. Even accounts that do not execute a command interpreter (e.g., accounts that exist only to see who is logged in to the system) can be compromised if set up incorrectly. A related concept, that of "anonymous" file transfer (ftp),[20] allows users from all over the network to access your system to retrieve files from (usually) a protected disk area. You should carefully weigh the benefits that an account without a password provides against the security risks of providing such access to your system.

If the operating system provides a "shadow" password facility that stores passwords in a separate file accessible only to privileged users, this facility should be used. System V Unix, SunOS 4.0 and above, and versions of Berkeley Unix after 4.3BSD Tahoe, as well as others, provide this feature. It protects passwords by hiding their encrypted values from unprivileged users. This prevents an attacker from copying your password file to his or her machine and then attempting to break the passwords at his or her leisure.

Keep track of who has access to privileged user accounts (e.g., root on UNIX or MAINT on VMS). Whenever a privileged user leaves the organization or no longer has need of the privileged account, the passwords on all privileged accounts should be changed.

Configuration Management Procedures

When installing a system from the distribution media or when installing third-party software, it is important to check the installation carefully. Many installation procedures assume a "trusted" site and hence will install files with world write permission enabled or otherwise compromise the security of files.

Network services also should be examined carefully when first installed. Many vendors provide default network permission files, which imply that all outside hosts are to be "trusted," and this is rarely the case when connected to wide-area networks such as the Internet.

Many intruders collect information on the vulnerabilities of particular system versions. The older a system, the more likely it is that there are security problems in that version that have since been fixed by the vendor in a later release. For this reason, it is important to weigh the risks of not upgrading to a new operating system release (thus leaving security holes unplugged) against the cost of upgrading to the new software (possibly breaking third-party software, etc.). Bug fixes from the vendor should be weighed in a similar fashion, with the added note that "security" fixes from a vendor usually address fairly serious security problems.

Other bug fixes, received via network mailing lists and the like, usually should be installed, but not without careful examination. Never install a bug fix unless you are sure you know what the consequences of the fix are—there is always the possibility that an intruder has suggested a "fix" that actually gives him or her access to your system.

Recovery Procedures—Backups

It is impossible to overemphasize the need for a good backup strategy. File system backups not only protect you in the event of hardware failure or accidental deletions but also protect you against unauthorized changes made by an intruder. Without a copy of your data the way they are "supposed" to be, it can be difficult to undo something an attacker has done.

Backups, especially if run daily, also can be useful in providing a history of an intruder's activities. Looking through old backups can establish when your system was first penetrated. Intruders may leave files around which, although deleted later, are captured on the backup tapes. Backups also can be used to document an intruder's activities to law enforcement agencies if necessary.

A good backup strategy will dump the entire system to tape at least once a month. Partial (or incremental) dumps should be done at least twice a week, and ideally they should be done daily. Commands specifically designed for performing file system backups (e.g., Unix dump or VMS BACKUP) should be used in preference to other file-copying commands, since these tools are designed with the express intent of restoring a system to a known state.

Problem Reporting Procedures

As with users, system administrators should have a defined procedure for reporting security problems. In large installations, this is often done by creating an electronic mail alias that contains the names of all system administrators in the organization. Other methods include setting up some sort of response team similar to the CERT or establishing a "hotline" serviced by an existing support group.

3.9 Resources to Prevent Security Breaches

This section discusses software, hardware, and procedural resources that can be used to support your site security policy.

3.9.1 Network Connections and Firewalls

A *firewall* is put in place in a building to provide a point of resistance to the entry of flames into another area. Similarly, a secretary's desk and reception area provide a point of controlling access to other office spaces. This same technique can be applied to a computer site, particularly as it pertains to network connections.

Some sites will be connected only to other sites within the same organization and will not have the ability to connect to other networks. Sites such as these are less susceptible to threats from outside their own organization, although intrusions may still occur via paths such as dial-up modems. On the other hand, many other organizations will be connected to other sites via much larger networks, such as the Internet. These sites are susceptible to the entire range of threats associated with a networked environment.

The risks of connecting to outside networks must be weighed against the benefits. It may be desirable to limit connection to outside networks to those hosts which do not store sensitive material, keeping "vital" machines (such as those which maintain company payroll or inventory systems) isolated. If there is a need to participate in a wide-area network (WAN), consider restricting all access to your local network through a single system. That is, all access to or from your own local network must be made through a single host computer that acts as a firewall between you and the outside world. This firewall system should be rigorously controlled and password protected, and external users accessing it also should be constrained by restricting the functionality available to remote users. By using this approach, your site could relax some of the internal security controls on your local net but still be afforded the protection of a rigorously controlled host front end.

Note that even with a firewall system, compromise of the firewall could result in compromise of the network behind the firewall. Work has been done in some areas to construct a firewall that even when compromised still protects the local network.[6]

3.9.2 Confidentiality

Confidentiality, the act of keeping things hidden or secret, is one of the primary goals of computer security practitioners. Several mechanisms are provided by most modern operating systems to enable users to control the dissemination of information. Depending on where you work, you may have a site where everything is protected, or a site where all information is usually regarded as public, or something in-between. Most sites lean toward the in-between, at least until some penetration has occurred.

Generally, there are three instances in which information is vulnerable to disclosure: when the information is stored on a computer system, when the information is in transit to another system (on the network), and when the information is stored on backup tapes.

The first of these cases is controlled by file permissions, access control lists, and other similar mechanisms. The last can be controlled by restricting access to the backup tapes (e.g., by locking them in a safe). All three cases can be helped by using encryption mechanisms.

Encryption (Hardware and Software)

Encryption is the process of taking information that exists in some readable form and converting it into a nonreadable form. There are several types of commercially available encryption packages in both hardware and software forms. Hardware encryption engines have the advantage that they are much faster than the software equivalent, yet because they are faster, they are of greater potential benefit to an attacker who wants to execute a brute force attack on your encrypted information.

The advantage of using encryption is that even if other access control mechanisms (passwords, file permissions, etc.) are compromised by an intruder, the data are still unusable. Naturally, encryption keys and the like should be protected at least as well as account passwords.

Information in transit (over a network) may be vulnerable to interception as well. Several solutions to this exist, ranging from simply encrypting files before transferring them (end-to-end encryption) to special network hardware that encrypts everything it sends without user intervention (secure links). The Internet as a whole does not use secure links; thus end-to-end encryption must be used if encryption is desired across the Internet.

Data Encryption Standard (DES)

DES is perhaps the most widely used data encryption mechanism today. Many hardware and software implementations exist, and some commercial computers are provided with a software version. DES transforms plain text information into encrypted data (or *ciphertext*) by means of a special algorithm and "seed" value called a *key*. As long as the key is retained (or remembered) by the original user, the ciphertext can be restored to the original plain text.

One of the pitfalls of all encryption systems is the need to remember the key under which a thing was encrypted (this is not unlike the password problem discussed elsewhere in this document). If the key is written down, it becomes less secure. If forgotten, there is little (if any) hope of recovering the original data.

Most Unix systems provide a DES command that enables a user to encrypt data using the DES algorithm.

Crypt

Similar to the DES command, the Unix crypt command allows a user to encrypt data. Unfortunately, the algorithm used by crypt is very insecure (based on the World War II Enigma device), and files encrypted with this command can be decrypted easily in a matter of a few hours. Generally, use of the crypt command should be avoided for any but the most trivial encryption tasks.

Privacy-Enhanced Mail

Electronic mail normally transits the network in the clear (i.e., anyone can read it). This is obviously not the optimal solution. Privacy-enhanced mail provides a means to automatically encrypt electronic mail messages so that a person eavesdropping at a mail distribution node is not (easily) capable of reading them. Several privacy-enhanced mail packages are currently being developed and deployed on the Internet.

The Internet Activities Board Privacy Task Force has defined a draft standard elective protocol for use in implementing privacy-enhanced mail. This protocol is defined in RFCs 1113, 1114, and 1115.[7-9] Please refer to the current edition of the *IAB Official Protocol Standards* (currently, RFC 1200[21] for the standardization state and status of these protocols.

3.9.3 Origin Authentication

We mostly take it on faith that the header of an electronic mail message truly indicates the originator of a message. However, it is easy to *spoof*, or forge the source of a mail message. Origin authentication provides a means to be certain of the originator of a message or other object in the same way that a notary public ensures a signature on a legal document. This is done by means of a public key cryptosystem.

A public key cryptosystem differs from a private key cryptosystem in several ways. First, a public key system uses two keys, a public key that anyone can use (hence the name) and a private key that only the originator of a message uses. The originator uses the private key to encrypt the message (as in DES). The receiver, who has obtained the public key for the originator, may then decrypt the message.

In this scheme, the public key is used to authenticate the originator's use of his or her private key, and hence the identity of the originator is more rigorously proven. The most widely known implementation of a public key cryptosystem is the RSA system.[26] The Internet standard for privacy-enhanced mail makes use of the RSA system.

3.9.4 Information Integrity

Information integrity refers to the state of information such that it is complete, correct, and unchanged from the last time in which it was verified to be in an "integral" state. The value of information integrity to a site will vary. For example, it is more important for military and government installations to prevent the disclosure of classified information, whether it is right or wrong. A bank, on the other hand, is far more concerned with whether the account information maintained for its customers is complete and accurate.

Numerous computer system mechanisms, as well as procedural controls, have an influence on the integrity of system information. Traditional access control mechanisms maintain controls over who can access system information. These mechanisms alone are not sufficient in some cases to provide the degree of integrity required. Some other mechanisms are briefly discussed below.

It should be noted that there are other aspects to maintaining system integrity besides these mechanisms, such as two-person controls and integrity validation procedures. These are beyond the scope of this document.

Checksums

Easily the simplest mechanism, a simple checksum routine can compute a value for a system file and compare it with the last known value. If the two are equal, the file is probably unchanged. If not, the file has been changed by some unknown means.

Although it is the easiest to implement, the checksum scheme suffers from a serious failing in that it is not very sophisticated, and a determined attacker could easily add enough characters to the file to eventually obtain the correct value.

A specific type of checksum, called a *CRC checksum*, is considerably more robust than a simple checksum. It is only slightly more difficult to implement and provides a better degree of catching errors. It too, however, suffers from the possibility of compromise by an attacker.

Checksums may be used to detect the altering of information. However, they do not actively guard against changes being made. For this, other mechanisms such as access controls and encryption should be used.

Cryptographic Checksums

Cryptographic checksums (also called *cryptosealing*) involve breaking a file up into smaller chunks, calculating a (CRC) checksum for each chunk, and adding the CRCs together. Depending on the exact algorithm used, this can result in a nearly unbreakable method of determining whether a file has been changed. This mechanism suffers from the fact that it is sometimes computationally intensive and may be prohibitive except in cases where the utmost integrity protection is desired.

Another related mechanism, called a *one-way hash function* [or a manipulation detection code (MDC)], also can be used to uniquely identify a file. The idea behind these functions is that no two inputs can produce the same output; thus a modified file will not have the same hash value. One-way hash functions can be implemented efficiently on a wide variety of systems, making unbreakable integrity checks possible. (Snefru, a one-way hash function available via USENET as well as the Internet, is just one example of an efficient one-way hash function.)[10]

3.9.5 Limiting Network Access

The dominant network protocols in use on the Internet, IP (RFC 791),[11] TCP (RFC 793),[12] and UDP (RFC 768,[13] carry certain control information that can be used to restrict access to certain hosts or networks within an organization.

The IP packet header contains the network addresses of both the sender and the recipient of the packet. Further, the TCP and UDP protocols provide the notion of a port, which identifies the endpoint (usually a network server) of a communications path. In some instances, it may be desirable to deny access to a specific TCP or UDP port or even to certain hosts and networks altogether.

Gateway Routing Tables

One of the simplest approaches to preventing unwanted network connections is to simply remove certain networks from a gateway's routing tables. This makes it impossible for a host to send packets to these networks. (Most protocols require bidirectional packet flow even for unidirectional data flow, thus breaking one side of the route is usually sufficient.)

This approach is commonly taken in firewall systems by preventing the firewall from advertising local routes to the outside world. The approach is deficient in that it often prevents "too much" (e.g., in order to prevent access to one system on the network, access to all systems on the network is disabled).

Router Packet Filtering

Many commercially available gateway systems (more correctly called *routers*) provide the ability to filter packets based not only on sources or destinations but also on source-destination combinations. This mechanism can be used to deny access to a specific host, network, or subnet from any other host, network, or subnet.

Gateway systems from some vendors (e.g., cisco Systems) support an even more complex scheme, allowing finer control over source and destination addresses. Via the use of address masks, one can deny access to all but one host on a particular network. The cisco Systems also allow packet screening based on IP protocol type and TCP or UDP port numbers.[14]

This also can be circumvented by "source routing" packets destined for the "secret" network. Source-routed packets may be filtered out by gateways, but this may restrict other legitimate activities, such as diagnosing routing problems.

3.9.6 Authentication Systems

Authentication refers to the process of proving a claimed identity to the satisfaction of some permission-granting authority. Authentication systems are hardware, software, or procedural mechanisms that enable a user to obtain access to computing resources. At the simplest level, the system administrator who adds new user accounts to the system is part of the system authentication mechanism. At the other end of the spectrum, fingerprint readers or retinal scanners provide a very high-tech solution to establishing a potential user's identity. Without establishing and proving a user's identity prior to establishing a session, your site's computers are vulnerable to any sort of attack.

Typically, a user authenticates himself or herself to the system by entering a password in response to a prompt. Challenge/response mechanisms improve on passwords by prompting the user for some piece of information shared by both the computer and the user (such as mother's maiden name, etc.).

Kerberos

Kerberos, named after the dog who in mythology is said to stand at the gates of Hades, is a collection of software used in a large network to establish a user's claimed identity. Developed at the Massachusetts Institute of Technology (MIT), it uses a combination of encryption and distributed databases so that a user at a campus facility can log in and start a session from any computer located on the campus. This has clear advantages in certain environments where there are a large number of potential users who may establish a connection from any one of a large number of workstations. Some vendors are now incorporating Kerberos into their systems.

It should be noted that while Kerberos makes several advances in the area of authentication, some security weaknesses in the protocol still remain.[15]

"Smart" Cards

Several systems use "smart" cards (a small calculatorlike device) to help authenticate users. These systems depend on the user having an object in their possession. One such system involves a new password procedure that requires a user to enter a value obtained from a "smart" card when asked for a password by the computer. Typically, the host machine will give the user some piece of information that is entered into the keyboard of the "smart" card. The "smart" card will display a response that must then be entered into the computer before the session will be established. Another such system involves a "smart" card that displays a number that changes over time but which is synchronized with the authentication software on the computer.

This is a better way of dealing with authentication than with the traditional password approach. On the other hand, some say it is inconvenient to carry the "smart" card. Startup costs are likely to be high as well.

3.9.7 Books, Lists, and Informational Sources

There are many good sources for information regarding computer security. The Annotated Bibliography at the end of this document can provide you with a good start. In addition, information can be obtained from a variety of other sources, some of which are described in this section.

Security Mailing Lists

The Unix Security mailing list exists to notify system administrators of security problems before they become common knowledge and to provide security enhancement information. It is a restricted-access list, open only to people who can be verified as being principal systems people at a site. Requests to join the list must be sent by either the site contact listed in the Defense Data Network's Network Information Center's (DDN NIC) WHOIS database or from the "root" account on one of the major site machines. You must include the destination address you want on the list, an indication of whether you want to be on the mail reflector list or receive weekly digests, the electronic mail address and voice telephone number of the site contact if it is not you, and the name, address, and telephone number of your organization. This information should be sent to security-request@cpd.com.

The RISKS digest is a component of the ACM Committee on Computers and Public Policy, moderated by Peter G. Neumann. It is a discussion forum on risks to the public in computers and related systems and, along with discussing computer security and privacy issues, has discussed such subjects as the Stark incident, the shooting down of the Iranian airliner in the Persian Gulf (as it relates to the computerized weapons systems), problems in air and railroad traffic control systems, software engineering, and so on. To join the mailing list, send a message

to risks-request@csl.sri.com. This list is also available in the USENET
newsgroup comp.risks.

The VIRUS-L list is a forum for the discussion of computer virus
experiences, protection software, and related topics. The list is open to
the public and is implemented as a moderated digest. Most of the information is related to personal computers, although some of it may be
applicable to larger systems. To subscribe, send the line

```
SUB VIRUS-L your full name
```

to the address listserv%lehiibm1.bitnet@mitvma.mit.edu. This list is also
available via the USENET newsgroup comp.virus.

The Computer Underground Digest "is an open forum dedicated to
sharing information among computerists and to the presentation and
debate of diverse views." While not directly a security list, it does contain discussions about privacy and other security related topics. The list
can be read on USENET as alt.society.cu-digest, or to join the mailing
list, send mail to Gordon Myer (tk0jut2%niu.bitnet@mitvma.mit.edu).
Submissions may be mailed to cud@chinacat.unicom.com.

Networking Mailing Lists

The TCP-IP mailing list is intended to act as a discussion forum for developers and maintainers of implementations of the TCP/IP protocol suite.
It also discusses network-related security problems when they involve programs providing network services such as Sendmail. To join the TCP-IP
list, send a message to tcp-ip-request@nisc.sri.com. This list is also available in the USENET newsgroup comp.protocols.tcp-ip.

SUN-NETS is a discussion list for items pertaining to networking on
Sun systems. Much of the discussion is related to NFS, NIS (formally Yellow Pages), and name servers. To subscribe, send a message to sun-nets-
request@umiacs.umd.edu.

The USENET groups misc.security and alt.security also discuss security issues. misc.security is a moderated group and also includes discussions of physical security and locks. alt.security is unmoderated.

Response Teams

Several organizations have formed special groups of people to deal with
computer security problems. These teams collect information about possible security holes and disseminate it to the proper people, track intruders, and assist in recovery from security violations. The teams typically

have both electronic mail distribution lists and a special telephone number that can be called for information or to report a problem. Many of these teams are members of the CERT system, which is coordinated by the National Institute of Standards and Technology (NIST) and exists to facilitate the exchange of information between the various teams.

DARPA Computer Emergency Response Team

The Computer Emergency Response Team/Coordination Center (CERT/CC) was established in December 1988 by the Defense Advanced Research Projects Agency (DARPA) to address computer security concerns of research users of the Internet. It is operated by the Software Engineering Institute (SEI) at Carnegie-Mellon University (CMU). The CERT can immediately confer with experts to diagnose and solve security problems, and also establish and maintain communications with the affected computer users and government authorities as appropriate.

The CERT/CC serves as a clearinghouse for the identification and repair of security vulnerabilities, informal assessments of existing systems, improvement of emergency response capability, and both vendor and user security awareness. In addition, the team works with vendors of various systems in order to coordinate the fixes for security problems.

The CERT/CC sends out security advisories to the CERT-ADVISORY mailing list whenever appropriate. They also operate a 24-hour hotline that can be called to report security problems (e.g., someone breaking into your system), as well as to obtain current (and accurate) information about rumored security problems.

To join the CERT-ADVISORY mailing list, send a message to cert@cert.sei.cmu.edu and ask to be added to the mailing list. The material sent to this list also appears in the USENET newsgroup comp.security.announce. Past advisories are available for anonymous FTP from the host cert.sei.cmu.edu. The 24-hour hotline number is (412) 268-7090.

The CERT/CC also maintains a CERT-TOOLS list to encourage the exchange of information on tools and techniques that increase the secure operation of Internet systems. The CERT/CC does not review or endorse the tools described on the list. To subscribe, send a message to cert-tools-request@cert.sei.cmu.edu and ask to be added to the mailing list.

The CERT/CC maintains other generally useful security information for anonymous FTP from cert.sel.cmu.edu. Get the README file for a list of what is available.

For more information, contact CERT Software Engineering Institute, Carnegie-Mellon University, Pittsburgh, PA 15213-3890, (412) 268-7090, cert@cert.sei.cmu.edu.

DDN Security Coordination Center

For DDN users, the Security Coordination Center (SCC) serves a function similar to CERT. The SCC is the DDN's clearinghouse for host/user security problems and fixes and works with the DDN Network Security Officer. The SCC also distributes the DDN Security Bulletin, which communicates information on network and host security exposures, fixes, and concerns to security and management personnel at DDN facilities. It is available on-line, via kermit or anonymous FTP, from the host nic.ddn.mil, in scc:ddn-security-yy-nn.txt (where *yy* is the year and *nn* is the bulletin number). The SCC provides immediate assistance with DDN-related host security problems; call (800) 235-3155 (6 A.M. to 5 P.M. Pacific Time) or send e-mail to scc@nic.ddn.mil. For 24-hour coverage, call the MILNET Trouble Desk at (800) 451-7413 or AUTOVON at 231-1713.

NIST Computer Security Resource and Response Center

The National Institute of Standards and Technology (NIST) has responsibility within the U.S. federal government for computer science and technology activities. NIST has played a strong role in organizing the CERT system and is now serving as the CERT system secretariat. NIST also operates a Computer Security Resource and Response Center (CSRC) to provide help and information regarding computer security events and incidents, as well as to raise awareness about computer security vulnerabilities.

The CSRC team operates a 24-hour hotline, at (301) 975-5200. For individuals with access to the Internet, on-line publications and computer security information can be obtained via anonymous FTP from the host csrc.ncsl.nist.gov (129.6.48.87). NIST also operates a personal computer bulletin board that contains information regarding computer viruses as well as other aspects of computer security. To access this board, set your modem to 300/1200/2400 bps, 1 stop bit, no parity, and 8-bit characters, and call (301) 948-5717. All users are given full access to the board immediately on registering.

NIST has produced several special publications related to computer security and computer viruses in particular; some of these publications are downloadable. For further information, contact NIST at the following address: Computer Security Resource and Response Center, A-216 Technology, Gaithersburg, MD 20899, (301) 975-3359, csrc@nist.gov

DOE Computer Incident Advisory Capability (CIAC)

CIAC is the Department of Energy's (DOE's) Computer Incident Advisory Capability. CIAC is a four-person team of computer scientists from Lawrence Livermore National Laboratory (LLNL) charged with the primary responsibility of assisting DOE sites faced with computer security incidents (e.g., intruder attacks, virus infections, worm attacks, etc.). This capability is available to DOE sites on a 24-hour-a-day basis.

CIAC was formed to provide a centralized response capability (including technical assistance), to keep sites informed of current events, to deal proactively with computer security issues, and to maintain liaisons with other response teams and agencies. CIAC's charter is to assist sites (through direct technical assistance, providing information, or referring inquiries to other technical experts), serve as a clearinghouse for information about threats/known incidents/vulnerabilities, develop guidelines for incident handling, develop software for responding to events/incidents, analyze events and trends, conduct training and awareness activities, and alert and advise sites about vulnerabilities and potential attacks.

CIAC's business hours phone number is (415) 422-8193 or FTS 532-8193. CIAC's e-mail address is ciac@tiger.llnl.gov.

NASA Ames Computer Network Security Response Team

The Computer Network Security Response Team (CNSRT) is NASA Ames Research Center's local version of the DARPA CERT. Formed in August of 1989, the team has a constituency that is primarily Ames users, but it is also involved in assisting other NASA centers and federal agencies. CNSRT maintains liaisons with the DOE's CIAC team and the DARPA CERT. It is also a charter member of the CERT system. The team may be reached by 24 hour pager at (415) 694-0571 or by electronic mail at cnsrt@amesarc.nasa.gov.

DDN Management Bulletins

The DDN Management Bulletin is distributed electronically by the DDN NIC under contract to the Defense Communications Agency (DCA). It is a means of communicating official policy, procedures, and other information of concern to management personnel at DDN facilities.

The DDN Security Bulletin is distributed electronically by the DDN SCC, also under contract to DCA, as a means of communicating information on network and host security exposures, fixes, and concerns to security and management personnel at DDN facilities.

Anyone may join the mailing lists for these two bulletins by sending a message to nic@nic.ddn.mil and asking to be placed on the mailing lists. These messages are also posted to the USENET newsgroup ddn.mgt-bulletin. For additional information, see Section 8.7.

System Administration List

The SYSADM-LIST is a list pertaining exclusively to Unix system administration. Mail requests to be added to the list to sysadm-list-request@sysadmin.com.

Vendor-Specific System Lists

The SUN-SPOTS and SUN-MANAGERS lists are discussion groups for users and administrators of systems supplied by Sun Microsystems. SUN-SPOTS is a fairly general list, discussing everything from hardware configurations to simple Unix questions. To subscribe, send a message to sun-spots-request@rice.edu. This list is also available in the USENET newsgroup comp.sys.sun. SUN-MANAGERS is a discussion list for Sun system administrators and covers all aspects of Sun system administration. To subscribe, send a message to sun-managers-request@eecs.nwu.edu.

The APOLLO list discusses the HP/Apollo system and its software. To subscribe, send a message to apollo-request@umix.cc.umich.edu. APOLLO-L is a similar list that can be subscribed to by sending SUB APOLLO-L your full name to listserv%umrvmb.bitnet@vm1.nodak.edu.

HPMINI-L pertains to the Hewlett-Packard 9000 series and HP/UX operating system. To subscribe, send SUB HPMINI-L your full name to listserv%uafsysb.bitnet@vm1.nodak.edu.

INFO-IBMPC discusses IBM PCs and compatibles, as well as MSDOS. To subscribe, send a note to info-ibmpc-request@wsmr-simtel20.army.mil.

There are numerous other mailing lists for nearly every popular computer or workstation in use today. For a complete list, obtain the file net-info/interest-groups via anonymous FTP from the host ftp.nisc.sri.com.

Professional Societies and Journals

The IEEE Technical Committee on Security and Privacy publishes a quarterly magazine entitled, *CIPHER*.I(EEE Computer Society, 1730 Massachusetts Ave., N.W., Washington, DC 20036-1903). The ACM SigSAC (Special Interest Group on Security, Audit, and Controls) publishes a quarterly magazine entitled, *SIGSAC Review* (Association for Computing Machinery, 11 West 42nd St., New York, NY 10036). The Information Systems Security Association publishes a quarterly magazine called *ISSA Access* (Information Systems Security Association, P.O. Box 9457, Newport Beach, CA 92658). *Computers and Security* is an "international journal for the professional involved with computer security, audit and control, and data integrity" ($266/year, 8 issues, 1990; Elsevier Advanced Technology Journal Information Center, 655 Avenue of the Americas, New York, NY 10010). The *Data Security Letter* is published "to help data security professionals by providing inside information and knowledgable analysis of developments in computer and communications security" ($690/year, 9 issues, 1990; Data Security Letter, P.O. Box 1593, Palo Alto, CA 94302).

3.9.8 Problem Reporting Tools

Auditing
Auditing is an important tool that can be used to enhance the security of your installation. Not only does it give you a means of identifying who has accessed your system (and may have done something to it), but it also gives you an indication of how your system is being used (or abused) by authorized users and attackers alike. In addition, the audit trail traditionally kept by computer systems can become an invaluable piece of evidence should your system be penetrated.

Verify Security
An audit trail shows how the system is being used from day to day. Depending on how your site audit log is configured, your log files should show a range of access attempts that can show what normal system usage should look like. Deviation from that normal usage could be the result of penetration from an outside source using an old or stale user account. Observing a deviation in logins, for example, could be your first indication that something unusual is happening.

Verify Software Configurations
One of the ruses used by attackers to gain access to a system is by the insertion of a so-called Trojan horse program. A Trojan horse program can be a program that does something useful, or merely something interesting. It always does something unexpected, like steal passwords or copy files without your knowledge.[25] Imagine a Trojan login program that prompts for username and password in the usual way but also writes that information to a special file that the attacker can come back and read at will. Imagine a Trojan editor program that, despite the file permissions you have given your files, makes copies of everything in your directory space without you knowing about it.

This points out the need for configuration management of the software that runs on a system not as it is being developed but as it is in actual operation. Techniques for doing this range from checking each command every time it is executed against some criterion (such as a cryptoseal, described above) or merely checking the date and time stamp of the executable. Another technique might be to check each command in batch mode at midnight.

Tools

COPS is a security tool for system administrators that checks for numerous common security problems on Unix systems.[27] COPS is a collection of shell scripts and C programs that can be run easily on almost any Unix variant. Among other things, it checks the following items and sends the results to the system administrator:

- Checks /dev/kmem and other devices for world read/writability
- Checks special or important files and directories for "bad" modes (world writable, etc.)
- Checks for easily guessed passwords
- Checks for duplicate user IDs, invalid fields in the password file, etc.
- Checks for duplicate group IDs, invalid fields in the group file, etc.
- Checks all users' home directories and their .cshrc, .login, .profile, and .rhosts files for security problems
- Checks all commands in the /etc/rc files and cron files for world writability
- Checks for bad root paths, NFS file systems exported to the world, etc.
- Includes an expert system that checks to see if a given user (usually root) can be compromised, given that certain rules are true
- Checks for changes in the setuid status of programs on the system

The COPS package is available from the comp.sources.unix archive on ftp.uu.net and also from the Unix-SW repository on the MILNET host wsmr-simtel20.army.mil.

3.9.9 Communication Among Administrators

Secure Operating Systems

The following list of products and vendors is adapted from the National Computer Security Center's (NCSC) Evaluated Products List (EPL). They represent those companies who have either received an evaluation from the NCSC or are in the process of a product evaluation. This list is not complete, but it is representative of those operating systems and add-on components available in the commercial marketplace.

For a more detailed listing of the current products appearing in the NCSC EPL, contact the NCSC at National Computer Security Center, 9800 Savage Road, Fort George G. Meade, MD 20755-6000, (301) 859-4458.

Evaluated product	Vendor	Evaluated	Class
Secure Communications Processor (SCOMP)	Honeywell Information Systems, Inc.	2.1	A1
Multics	Honeywell Information Systems, Inc.	MR11.0	B2
System V/MLS 1.1.2 on UNIX System V 3.1.1 on AT&T 3B2/500 and 3B2/600	AT&T	1.1.2	B1
OS 1100	Unisys Corp.	Security Release 1	B1
MPE V/E	Hewlett-Packard Computer Systems Division	G.0.3.04	C2
AOS/VS on MV/ECLIPSE series	Data General Corp.	7.60	C2
VM/SP or VM/SP HPO with CMS, RACF, DIRMANT, VMTAPE-MS, ISPF	IBM Corp.	5	C2
MVS/XA with RACF	IBM Corp.	2.2, 2.3	C2
AX/VMS	Digital Equipment Corp.	4.3	C2
NOS	Control Data Corp.	NOS Security	C2
TOP SECRET	CGA Software Products Group, Inc.	3.0/163	C2
Access Control facility 2	SKK, Inc.	3.1.3	C2
UTX/32S	Gould, Inc. Computer Systems Division	1.0	C2
A Series MCP/AS with InfoGuard Security Enhancements	Unisys Corp.	3.7	C2
Primos	Prime Computer, Inc.	21.0.1DODC2A	C2
Resource Access Control Facility (RACF)	IBM Corp.	1.5	

Candidate Product	Vendor	Evaluated	Class
Boeing MLS LAN M1	Boeing Aerospace		A1 M1
Trusted XENIX	Trusted Information Systems, Inc.		B2
VSLAN	VERDIX Corp.		B2
System V/MLS	AT&T		B1
VM/SP with RACF	IBM Corp.	5/1.8.2	C2
Wang SVS/OS with CAP	Wang Laboratories, Inc.	1.0	C2

Obtaining Fixes for Known Problems

It goes without saying that computer systems have bugs. Even operating systems, on which we depend for protection of our data, have bugs. And since there are bugs, things can be broken, both maliciously and accidentally. It is important that whenever bugs are discovered, a should fix be identified and implemented as soon as possible. This should minimize any exposure caused by the bug in the first place.

A corollary to the bug problem is: From whom do I obtain the fixes? Most systems have some support from the manufacturer or supplier. Fixes coming from that source tend to be implemented quickly after receipt. Fixes for some problems are often posted on the network and are left to the system administrators to incorporate as they can. The problem is that one wants to have faith that the fix will close the hole and not introduce any others. We will tend to trust that the manufacturer's fixes are better than those posted on the net.

Sun Customer Warning System

Sun Microsystems has established a Customer Warning System (CWS) for handling security incidents. This is a formal process that includes

- Having a well-advertised point of contact in Sun for reporting security problems
- Proactively alerting customers of worms, viruses, or other security holes that could affect their systems
- Distributing the patch (or work-around) as quickly as possible

Sun has created an electronic mail address, security-alert@sun.com, that will enable customers to report security problems. A voice-mail backup is available at 415-688-9081. A "security contact" can be designated by each customer site; this person will be contacted by Sun in case of any new security problems. For more information, contact your Sun representative.

Trusted Archive Servers

Several sites on the Internet maintain large repositories of public-domain and freely distributable software and make this material available for anonymous FTP. This section describes some of the larger repositories. Note that none of these servers implements secure checksums or anything else guaranteeing the integrity of their data. Thus the notion of *trust* should be taken as a somewhat limited definition.

Sun Fixes on UUNET

Sun Microsystems has contracted with UUNET Communications Services, Inc., to make fixes for bugs in Sun software available via anonymous FTP. You can access these fixes by using the ftp command to connect to the host ftp.uu.net. Then change into the directory sun-dist/security and obtain a directory listing. The file README contains a brief description of what each file in this directory contains, and what is required to install the fix.

Berkeley Fixes

The University of California at Berkeley also makes fixes available via anonymous FTP; these fixes pertain primarily to the current release of BSD Unix (currently, release 4.3). However, even if you are not running their software, these fixes are still important, since many vendors (Sun, DEC, Sequent, etc.) base their software on the Berkeley releases.

The Berkeley fixes are available for anonymous FTP from the host ucbarpa.berkeley.edu in the directory 4.3/ucb-fixes. The file INDEX in this directory describes what each file contains. They are also available from UUNET (see next subsection).

Berkeley also distributes new versions of Sendmail and Named from this machine. New versions of these commands are stored in the 4.3 directory, usually in the files sendmail.tar.Z and bind.tar.Z, respectively.

Simtel-20 and UUNET

The two largest general-purpose software repositories on the Internet are the hosts wsmr-simtel20.army.mil and ftp.uu.net.

wsmr-simtel20.army.mil is a TOPS-20 machine operated by the U.S. Army at White Sands Missile Range (WSMR), New Mexico. The directory pd2:<unix-c> contains a large amount of Unix software, primarily taken from the comp.sources news groups. The directories pd1:<msdos> and pd2:<msdos2> contains software for IBM PC systems, and pd3:<macintosh> contains software for the Apple Macintosh.

ftp.uunet is operated by UUNET Communications Services, Inc., in Falls Church, Virginia. This company sells Internet and USENET access to sites all over the country (and internationally). The software posted to the following USENET source news groups is stored here, in directories of the same name: comp.sources.games, comp.sources.misc, comp.sources.sun, comp.sources.unix, and comp.sources.x. Numerous other distributions, such as all the freely distributable Berkeley Unix source code, Internet Request for Comments (RFCs), and so on, are also stored on this system.

Vendors

Many vendors make fixes for bugs in their software available electronically, either via mailing lists or via anonymous FTP. You should contact your vendor to find out if they offer this service and, if so, how to access it. Some vendors that offer these services include Sun Microsystems (see above), Digital Equipment Corporation (DEC), the University of California at Berkeley (see above), and Apple Computer.[5]

4. Types of Security Procedures
4.1 System Security Audits

Most businesses undergo some sort of annual financial auditing as a regular part of their business life. Security audits are an important part of running any computing environment. Part of the security audit should be a review of any policies that concern system security, as well as the mechanisms that are put in place to enforce them.

4.1.1 Organize Scheduled Drills
Although not something that would be done each day or week, scheduled drills may be conducted to determine if the procedures defined are adequate for the threat to be countered. If your major threat is one of natural disaster, then a drill would be conducted to verify your backup and recovery mechanisms. On the other hand, if your greatest threat is from external intruders attempting to penetrate your system, a drill might be conducted to actually try a penetration to observe the effect of the policies.

Drills are a valuable way to test that your policies and procedures are effective. On the other hand, drills can be time-consuming and disruptive to normal operations. It is important to weigh the benefits of the drills against the possible time loss that may be associated with them.

4.1.2 Test Procedures
If the choice is made to not to use scheduled drills to examine your entire security procedure at one time, it is important to test individual procedures frequently. Examine your backup procedure to make sure you can recover data from the tapes. Check log files to be sure that information that is supposed to be logged to them is being logged to them, etc.

When a security audit is mandated, great care should be used in devising tests of the security policy. It is important to clearly identify what is being tested, how the test will be conducted, and results expected from the test. This should all be documented and included in or as an adjunct to the security policy document itself.

It is important to test all aspects of the security policy, both procedural and automated, with a particular emphasis on the automated mechanisms used to enforce the policy. Tests should be defined to ensure a comprehensive examination of policy features, that is, if a test is defined to examine the user logon process, it should be explicitly stated that both valid and invalid user names and passwords will be used to demonstrate proper operation of the logon program.

Keep in mind that there is a limit to the reasonableness of tests. The purpose of testing is to ensure confidence that the security policy is being enforced correctly, and not to "prove" the absoluteness of the system or policy. The goal should be to obtain some assurance that the reasonable and credible controls imposed by your security policy are adequate.

4.2 Account Management Procedures

Procedures to manage accounts are important in preventing unauthorized access to your system. It is necessary to decide several things: Who may have an account on the system? How long may someone have an account without renewing his or her request? How do old accounts get removed from the system? The answers to all these questions should be set out explicitly in the policy.

In addition to deciding who may use a system, it may be important to determine what each user may use the system for (e.g., is personal use allowed?). If you are connected to an outside network, your site or the network management may have rules about what the network may be used for. Therefore, it is important for any security policy to define an adequate account management procedure for both administrators and users. Typically, the system administrator would be responsible for creating and deleting user accounts and generally maintaining overall control of system use. To some degree, account management is also the responsibility of each system user in the sense that the user should observe any system messages and events that may be indicative of a policy violation. For example, a message at logon that indicates the date and time of the last logon should be reported by the user if it indicates an unreasonable time of last logon.

4.3 Password Management Procedures

A policy on password management may be important if your site wishes to enforce secure passwords. These procedures may range from asking or forcing users to change their passwords occasionally to actively attempting to break users' passwords and then informing the user of how easy it was to do. Another part of password management policy covers who may distribute passwords—Can users give their passwords to other users?

Section 2.3 discusses some of the policy issues that need to be decided for proper password management. Regardless of the policies, password management procedures need to be set up carefully to avoid disclosing passwords. The choice of initial passwords for accounts is critical. In some cases, users may never log in to activate an account; thus the choice of the initial password should not be guessed easily. Default passwords should never be assigned to accounts: always create new passwords for each user. If there are any printed lists of passwords, these should be kept off-line in secure locations; better yet, do not list passwords.

4.3.1 Password Selection

Perhaps the most vulnerable part of any computer system is the account password. Any computer system, no matter how secure it is from network or dial-up attack, Trojan horse programs, and so on, can be fully exploited by an intruder if he or she can gain access via a poorly chosen password. It is important to define a good set of rules for password selection and distribute these rules to all users. If possible, the software that sets user passwords should be modified to enforce as many of the rules as possible.

A sample set of guidelines for password selection is shown below:

- Do not use your login name in any form (as is, reversed, capitalized, doubled, etc.).
- Do not use your first, middle, or last name in any form.
- Do not use your spouse's or child's name.
- Do not use other information easily obtained about you. This includes license plate numbers, telephone numbers, Social Security numbers, the make of your automobile, the name of the street you live on, etc.
- Do not use a password of all digits or all the same letter.
- Do not use a word contained in English or foreign-language dictionaries, spelling lists, or other lists of words.
- Do not use a password shorter than six characters.
- Do use a password with mixed-case alphabetics.

- Do use a password with nonalphabetic characters (digits or punctuation).

- Do use a password that is easy to remember so that you do not have to write it down.

- Do use a password that you can type quickly, without having to look at the keyboard.

Methods of selecting a password that adheres to these guidelines include

- Choose a line or two from a song or poem, and use the first letter of each word.

- Alternate between one consonant and one or two vowels, up to seven or eight characters. This provides nonsense words that are usually pronounceable and thus easily remembered.

- Choose two short words and concatenate them together with a punctuation character between them.

Users also should be told to change their password periodically, usually every 3 to 6 months. This makes sure that an intruder who has guessed a password will eventually lose access, as well as invalidating any list of passwords he or she may have obtained. Many systems enable the system administrator to force users to change their passwords after an expiration period; this software should be enabled if your system supports it.[5]

Some systems provide software that forces users to change their passwords on a regular basis. Many of these systems also include password generators which provide the user with a set of passwords to choose from. The user is not permitted to make up his or her own password. There are arguments both for and against systems such as these. On the one hand, by using generated passwords, users are prevented from selecting insecure passwords. On the other hand, unless the generator is good at making up easy-to-remember passwords, users will begin writing them down in order to remember them.

4.3.2 Procedures for Changing Passwords

How password changes are handled is important to keeping passwords secure. Ideally, users should be able to change their own passwords online. (Note that password changing programs are a favorite target of intruders. See Section 4.4 on configuration management for further information.)

However, there are exception cases that must be handled carefully. Users may forget passwords and not be able to get onto the system. The standard procedure is to assign the user a new password. Care should be taken to make sure that the real person is requesting the change and gets the new password. One common trick used by intruders is to call or send a message to a system administrator and request a new password. Some external form of verification should be used before the password is assigned. At some sites, users are required to show up in person with ID.

There also may be times when many passwords need to be changed. If a system is compromised by an intruder, the intruder may be able to steal a password file and take it off the system. Under these circumstances, one course of action is to change all passwords on the system. Your site should have procedures for how this can be done quickly and efficiently. What course you choose may depend on the urgency of the problem. In the case of a known attack with damage, you may choose to forcibly disable all accounts and assign users new passwords before they come back onto the system. In some places, users are sent a message telling them that they should change their passwords, perhaps within a certain time period. If the password is not changed before the time period expires, the account is locked.

Users should be aware of what the standard procedure is for passwords when a security event has occurred. One well-known spoof reported by the Computer Emergency Response Team (CERT) involved messages sent to users, supposedly from local system administrators, requesting them to immediately change their password to a new value provided in the message[24] These messages were not from the administrators, but from intruders trying to steal accounts. Users should be warned to immediately report any suspicious requests such as this to site administrators.

4.4 Configuration Management Procedures

Configuration management is generally applied to the software development process. However, it is certainly applicable in a operational sense as well. Consider that since many of the system level programs are intended to enforce the security policy, it is important that these be *known* as correct. That is, one should not allow system level programs (such as the operating system, etc.) to be changed arbitrarily. At the very least, the procedures should state who is authorized to make changes to systems, under what circumstances, and how the changes should be documented.

In some environments, configuration management is also desirable as applied to physical configuration of equipment. Maintaining a valid and authorized hardware configuration should be given due consideration in your security policy.

4.4.1 Nonstandard Configurations

Occasionally, it may be beneficial to have a slightly nonstandard configuration in order to thwart the "standard" attacks used by some intruders. The nonstandard parts of the configuration might include different password encryption algorithms, different configuration file locations, and rewritten or functionally limited system commands.

Nonstandard configurations, however, also have their drawbacks. By changing the standard system, these modifications make software maintenance more difficult by requiring extra documentation to be written, software modification after operating system upgrades, and, usually, someone with special knowledge of the changes.

Because of the drawbacks of nonstandard configurations, they are often only used in environments with a firewall machine (see Section 3.9.1). The firewall machine is modified in nonstandard ways because it is susceptible to attack, while internal systems behind the firewall are left in their standard configurations.

5. Incident Handling

5.1 Overview

This section will supply some guidance to be applied when a computer security event is in progress on a machine, network, site, or multisite environment. The operative philosophy in the event of a breach of computer security, whether it be an external intruder attack or a disgruntled employee, is to plan for adverse events in advance. There is no substitute for creating contingency plans for the types of events described above.

Traditional computer security, while quite important in the overall site security plan, usually falls heavily on protecting systems from attack and perhaps monitoring systems to detect attacks. Little attention is usually paid to how to actually handle the attack when it occurs. The result is that when an attack is in progress, many decisions are made in haste and can be damaging to tracking down the source of the incident, collecting evidence to be used in prosecution efforts, preparing for the recovery of the system, and protecting the valuable data contained on the system.

5.1.1 Have a Plan to Follow in Case of an Incident

Part of handling an incident is being prepared to respond before the incident occurs. This includes establishing a suitable level of protection so that if the incident becomes severe, the damage that can occur is limited. Protection includes preparing incident-handling guidelines or a contingency response plan for your organization or site. Having written plans eliminates much of the ambiguity that occurs during an incident and will lead to a more appropriate and thorough set of responses. Second, part of protection is preparing a method of notification so that you will know who to call and the relevant phone numbers. It is important, for example, to conduct dry runs, in which your computer security personnel, system administrators, and managers simulate handling an incident.

Learning to respond efficiently to an incident is important for numerous reasons. The most important benefit is directly to human beings—preventing loss of human life. Some computing systems are life critical systems, systems on which human life depends (e.g., by controlling some aspect of life-support in a hospital or assisting air traffic controllers).

An important but often overlooked benefit is an economic one. Having both technical and managerial personnel respond to an incident requires considerable resources, resources that could be utilized more profitably if an incident did not require their services. If these personnel are trained to handle an incident efficiently, less of their time is required to deal with that incident.

A third benefit is protecting classified, sensitive, or proprietary information. One of the major dangers of a computer security incident is that information may be irrecoverable. Efficient incident handling minimizes this danger. When classified information is involved, other government regulations may apply and must be integrated into any plan for incident handling.

A fourth benefit is related to public relations. News about computer security incidents tends to be damaging to an organization's stature among current or potential clients. Efficient incident handling minimizes the potential for negative exposure.

A final benefit of efficient incident handling is related to legal issues. It is possible that in the near future organizations may be sued because one of their nodes was used to launch a network attack. In a similar vein, people who develop patches or work-arounds may be sued if the patches or work-arounds are ineffective, resulting in damage to systems, or if the patches or work-arounds themselves damage systems. Knowing about operating system vulnerabilities and patterns of attacks and then taking appropriate measures are critical to circumventing possible legal problems.

5.1.2 Order of Discussion in This Session Suggests an Order for a Plan

This section is arranged such that a list may be generated from the table of contents to provide a starting point for creating a policy for handling ongoing incidents. The main points to be included in a policy for handling incidents are

- Overview (What are the goals and objectives in handling the incident?)
- Evaluation (How serious is the incident?)
- Notification (Who should be notified about the incident?)
- Response (What should the response to the incident be?)
- Legal/investigative (What are the legal and prosecutorial implications of the incident?)
- Documentation logs (What records should be kept from before, during, and after the incident?)

Each of these points is important in an overall plan for handling incidents. The remainder of this section will detail the issues involved in each of these topics and provide some guidance as to what should be included in a site policy for handling incidents.

5.1.3 Possible Goals and Incentives for Efficient Incident Handling

As in any set of preplanned procedures, attention must be placed on a set of goals to be obtained in handling an incident. These goals will be placed in order of importance depending on the site, but one such set of goals might be

- Ensure integrity of (life) critical systems.
- Maintain and restore data.
- Maintain and restore service.
- Figure out how it happened.
- Avoid escalation and further incidents.
- Avoid negative publicity.
- Find out who did it. Punish the attackers.

It is important to prioritize actions to be taken during an incident well in advance of the time an incident occurs. Sometimes an incident may be so complex that it is impossible to do everything at once to respond to it. Priorities are essential. Although priorities will vary from institution to institution, the following suggested priorities serve as a starting point for defining an organization's response:

- Priority 1: Protect human life and people's safety; human life always has precedence over all other considerations.

- Priority 2: Protect classified and/or sensitive data (as regulated by your site or by government regulations).

- Priority 3: Protect other data, including proprietary, scientific, managerial, and other data, because loss of data is costly in terms of resources.

- Priority 4: Prevent damage to systems (e.g., loss or alteration of system files, damage to disk drives, etc.); damage to systems can result in costly downtime and recovery.

- Priority 5: Minimize disruption of computing resources; it is better in many cases to shut a system down or disconnect from a network than to risk damage to data or systems.

An important implication for defining priorities is that once human life and national security considerations have been addressed, it is generally more important to save data than system software and hardware. Although it is undesirable to have any damage or loss during an incident, systems can be replaced; the loss or compromise of data (especially classified data), however, is usually not an acceptable outcome under any circumstances.

Part of handling an incident is being prepared to respond before the incident occurs. This includes establishing a suitable level of protection so that if the incident becomes severe, the damage that can occur is limited. Protection includes preparing incident-handling guidelines or a contingency response plan for your organization or site. Written plans eliminate much of the ambiguity that occurs during an incident, and will lead to a more appropriate and thorough set of responses. Second, part of protection is preparing a method of notification so you will know who to call and how to contact them. For example, every member of the Department of Energy's CIAC team carries a card with every other team member's work and home phone numbers, as well as pager numbers. Third, your organization or site should establish backup procedures for every machine and system. Having backups eliminates much of the threat of even a severe incident, since backups preclude serious data loss. Fourth, you should set up secure systems. This involves eliminating vulnerabilities, establishing an effective password policy, and other procedures, all of which will be explained later in this document. Finally, conducting training activities is part of protection. It is important, for example, to conduct dry runs, in which your computer security personnel, system administrators, and managers simulate handling an incident.

5.1.4 Local Policies and Regulations Providing Guidance

Any plan for responding to security incidents should be guided by local policies and regulations. Government and private sites that deal with classified material have specific rules they must follow.

The policies your site makes about how it responds to incidents (as discussed in Sections 2.4 and 2.5) will shape your response. For example, it may make little sense to create mechanisms to monitor and trace intruders if your site does not plan to take action against the intruders if they are caught. Other organizations may have policies that affect your plans. Telephone companies often release information about telephone traces only to law enforcement agencies.

Section 5.5 also notes that if any legal action is planned, there are specific guidelines that must be followed to make sure that any information collected can be used as evidence.

5.2 Evaluation

5.2.1 Is It Real?

This stage involves determining the exact problem. Of course, many, if not most, signs often associated with virus infections, system intrusions, etc., are simply anomalies such as hardware failures. To assist in identifying whether there really is an incident, it is usually helpful to obtain and use any detection software that may be available. For example, widely available software packages can greatly assist someone who thinks there may be a virus in a Macintosh computer. Audit information is also extremely useful, especially in determining whether there is a network attack. It is extremely important to obtain a system snapshot as soon as one suspects that something is wrong. Many incidents cause a dynamic chain of events to occur, and an initial system snapshot may do more good in identifying the problem and any source of attack than most other actions that can be taken at this stage. Finally, it is important to start a log book. Recording system events, telephone conversations, time stamps, etc., can lead to a more rapid and systematic identification of the problem and is the basis for subsequent stages of incident handling.

There are certain indications or symptoms of an incident that deserve special attention:

- System crashes

- New user accounts (e.g., the account RUMPLESTILTSKIN has unexplainedly been created) or high activity on an account that has had virtually no activity for months

- New files (usually with novel or strange file names, such as data.xx or k)

- Accounting discrepancies (e.g., in a Unix system you might notice that the accounting file called /usr/admin/lastlog has shrunk, something that should make you very suspicious that there may be an intruder)

- Changes in file lengths or dates (e.g., a user should be suspicious if he or she observes that the .EXE files in an MS DOS computer have unexplainedly grown by over 1800 bytes)

- Attempts to write to system (e.g., a system manager notices that a privileged user in a VMS system is attempting to alter RIGHTSLIST.DAT)

- Data modification or deletion (e.g., files start to disappear)

- Denial of service (e.g., a system manager and all other users become locked out of a UNIX system, which has been changed to single user mode)

- Unexplained, poor system performance (e.g., system response time becomes unusually slow)

- Anomalies (e.g., GOTCHA is displayed on a display terminal or there are frequent unexplained beeps)

- Suspicious probes (e.g., there are numerous unsuccessful login attempts from another node)

- Suspicious browsing (e.g., someone becomes a root user on a Unix system and accesses file after file in one user's account and then another's)

None of these indications is absolute proof that an incident is occurring, nor are all of these indications normally observed when an incident occurs. If you observe any of these indications, however, it is important to suspect that an incident might be occurring and act accordingly. There is no formula for determining with 100 percent accuracy that an incident is occurring (possible exception: When a virus-detection package indicates that your machine has the nVIR virus and you confirm this by examining contents of the nVIR resource in your Macintosh computer, you can be very certain that your machine is infected). It is best at this point to collaborate with other technical and computer security personnel to make a decision as a group about whether an incident is occurring.

5.2.2 Scope

Along with identification of the incident is evaluation of the scope and impact of the problem. It is important to identify the boundaries of the incident correctly in order to deal with it effectively. In addition, the impact of an incident will determine its priority in allocating resources to deal with it. Without an indication of the scope and impact of the event, it is difficult to determine a correct response.

In order to identify the scope and impact, criteria should be defined that are appropriate to the site and to the type of connections available. Some of the issues are

- Is this a multisite incident?
- Are many computers at your site affected by this incident?
- Is sensitive information involved?
- What is the entry point of the incident (network, phone line, local terminal, etc.)?
- Is the press involved?
- What is the potential damage of the incident?
- What is the estimated time to close out the incident?
- What resources could be required to handle the incident?

5.3 Possible Types of Notification

When you have confirmed that an incident is occurring, the appropriate personnel must be notified. Who and how this notification is achieved are very important in keeping the event under control both from a technical and an emotional standpoint.

5.3.1 Explicit

First of all, any notification to either local or off-site personnel must be explicit. This requires that any statement (be it an electronic mail message, phone call, or fax) provides information about the incident that is clear, concise, and fully qualified. When you are notifying others who will help you to handle an event, a "smoke screen" will only divide the effort and create confusion. If a division of labor is suggested, it is helpful to provide information to each section about what is being accomplished in other efforts. This not only will reduce duplication of effort but also will allow people working on parts of the problem to know where to obtain other information that would help them resolve a part of the incident.

5.3.2 Factual

Another important consideration when communicating about the incident is to be factual. Attempting to hide aspects of the incident by providing false or incomplete information not only may prevent a successful resolution to the incident but also may even worsen the situation. This is especially true when the press is involved. When an incident severe enough to gain press attention is ongoing, it is likely that any false information you provide will not be substantiated by other sources. This will reflect badly on the site and may create enough ill-will between the site and the press to damage the site's public relations.

5.3.3 Choice of Language

The choice of language used when notifying people about the incident can have a profound effect on the way that information is received. When you use emotional or inflammatory terms, you raise the expectations of damage and negative outcomes of the incident. It is important to remain calm in both written and spoken notifications.

Another issue associated with the choice of language is the notification to nontechnical or off-site personnel. It is important to describe the incident accurately without undue alarm or confusing messages. While it is more difficult to describe the incident to a nontechnical audience, it is often more important. A nontechnical description may be required for upper-level management, the press, or law enforcement liaisons. The importance of these notifications cannot be underestimated and may make the difference between handling the incident properly and escalating to some higher level of damage.

5.3.4 Notification of Individuals

- Point of contact (POC) people (technical, administrative, response teams, investigative, legal, vendors, service providers), and which POCs are visible to whom

- Wider community (users)
- Other sites that might be affected

Finally, there is the question of who should be notified during and after the incident. There are several classes of individuals that need to be considered for notification. These are the technical personnel, administration, appropriate response teams (such as CERT or CIAC), law enforcement, vendors, and other service providers. These issues are important for the central point of contact, since this is the person responsible for the actual notification of others (see Section 5.3.6 for further information). A list of people in each of these categories is an important time saver for the POC during an incident. It is much more difficult to find an appropriate person during an incident when many urgent events are ongoing.

In addition to the people responsible for handling part of the incident, there may be other sites affected by the incident (or perhaps simply at risk from the incident). A wider community of users also may benefit from knowledge of the incident. Often, a report of the incident, once it is closed out, is appropriate for publication to the wider user community.

5.3.5 Public Relations—Press Releases

One of the most important issues to consider is when, to whom, and how much to release to the general public through the press. There are many issues to consider when deciding this particular issue. First and foremost, if a public relations office exists for the site, it is important to use this office as liaison to the press. The public relations office is trained in the type and wording of information released and will help to ensure that the image of the site is protected during and after the incident (if possible). A public relations office has the advantage that you can communicate candidly with them and provide a buffer between the constant press attention and the need of the POC to maintain control over the incident.

If a public relations office is not available, the information released to the press must be considered carefully. If the information is sensitive, it may be advantageous to provide only minimal or overview information to the press. It is quite possible that any information provided to the press will be quickly reviewed by the perpetrator of the incident. As a contrast to this consideration, it was discussed earlier that misleading the press often can backfire and cause more damage than releasing sensitive information.

While it is difficult to determine in advance what level of detail to provide to the press, some guidelines to keep in mind are

- Keep the technical level of detail low. Detailed information about the incident may provide enough information for copy-cat events or even damage the site's ability to prosecute once the event is over.

- Keep speculation out of press statements. Speculation of who is causing the incident or the motives is very likely to be in error and may cause an inflamed view of the incident.

- Work with law enforcement professionals to ensure that evidence is protected. If prosecution is involved, ensure that the evidence collected is not divulged to the press.

- Try not to be forced into a press interview before you are prepared. The popular press is famous for the 2 A.M. interview, where the hope is to catch the interviewee off guard and obtain information otherwise not available.

- Do not allow press attention to detract from the handling of the event. Always remember that the successful closure of an incident is of primary importance.

5.3.6 Who Needs to Get Involved?

There now exists a number of incident response teams (IRTs) such as the CERT and the CIAC (see Section 3.9). Teams exist for many major government agencies and large corporations. If such a team is available for your site, notification of this team should be of primary importance during the early stages of an incident. These teams are responsible for coordinating computer security incidents over a range of sites and larger entities. Even if the incident is believed to be contained to a single site, it is possible that the information available through a response team could help in closing out the incident.

In setting up a site policy for incident handling, it may be desirable to create an incident-handling team (IHT), much like those teams which already exist, that will be responsible for handling computer security incidents for the site (or organization). If such a team is created, it is essential that communication lines be opened between this team and other IHTs. Once an incident is under way, it is difficult to open a trusted dialogue between other IHTs if none has existed before.

5.4 Response

A major topic still untouched here is how to actually respond to an event. The response to an event will fall into the general categories of containment, eradication, recovery, and follow-up.

5.4.1 Containment

The purpose of containment is to limit the extent of an attack. For example, it is important to limit the spread of a worm attack on a network as quickly as possible. An essential part of containment is decision making (i.e., determining whether to shut a system down, to disconnect from a network, to monitor system or network activity, to set traps, to disable functions such as remote file transfer on a Unix system, etc.). Sometimes this decision is trivial: Shut the system down if the system is classified or sensitive or if proprietary information is at risk! In other cases, it is worthwhile to risk having some damage to the system if keeping the system up might enable you to identify an intruder.

The first stage, containment, should involve carrying out predetermined procedures. Your organization or site should, for example, define acceptable risks in dealing with an incident and should prescribe specific actions and strategies accordingly. Finally, notification of cognizant authorities should occur during this stage.

5.4.2 Eradication

Once an incident has been detected, it is important to first think about containing the incident. Once the incident has been contained, it is now time to eradicate the cause. Software may be available to help you in this effort. For example, eradication software is available to eliminate most viruses that infect small systems. If any bogus files have been created, it is time to delete them at this point. In the case of virus infections, it is important to clean and reformat any disks containing infected files. Finally, ensure that all backups are clean. Many systems infected with viruses become reinfected periodically simply because people do not systematically eradicate the virus from backups.

5.4.3 Recovery

Once the cause of an incident has been eradicated, the recovery phase defines the next stage of action. The goal of recovery is to return the system to normal. In the case of a network-based attack, it is important to install patches for any operating system vulnerability which was exploited.

5.4.4 Follow-up

One of the most important stages of responding to incidents is also the most often omitted—the follow-up stage. This stage is important because it helps those involved in handling the incident develop a set of lessons learned (see Section 6.3) to improve future performance in such situations. This stage also provides information that justifies an organization's computer security effort to management and yields information that may be essential in legal proceedings.

The most important element of the follow-up stage is performing a postmortem analysis. Exactly what happened and at what times? How well did the staff involved with the incident perform? What kind of information did the staff need quickly, and how could they have gotten that information as soon as possible? What would the staff do differently next time? A follow-up report is valuable because it provides a reference to be used in case of other similar incidents. Creating a formal chronology of events (including time stamps) is also important for legal reasons. Similarly, it is also important to as quickly obtain a monetary estimate of the amount of damage the incident caused in terms of any loss of software and files, hardware damage, and personnel costs to restore altered files, reconfigure affected systems, and so forth. This estimate may become the basis for subsequent prosecution activity by the FBI, the U.S. Attorney General's Office, etc.

5.4.5 What Will You Do?

- Restore control.
- Relation to policy.
- Which level of service is needed?
- Monitor activity.
- Constrain or shut down system.

5.4.6 Consider Designating a "Single Point of Contact"

When an incident is under way, a major issue is deciding who is in charge of coordinating the activity of the multitude of players. A major mistake that can be made is to have a number of points of contact (POCs) that are not pulling their efforts together. This will only add to the confusion of the event and probably will lead to additional confusion and wasted or ineffective effort.

The single POC may or may not be the person "in charge" of the incident. There are two distinct rolls to fill when deciding who shall be the POC and the person in charge of the incident. The person in charge will make decisions as to the interpretation of policy applied to the event. The responsibility for the handling of the event falls onto this person. In contrast, the POC must coordinate the efforts of all the parties involved with handling the event.

The POC must be a person with the technical expertise to coordinate successfully the efforts of the system managers and users involved in monitoring and reacting to the attack. Often the management structure of a site is such that the administrator of a set of resources is not a technically competent person with regard to handling the details of the operations of the computers but is ultimately responsible for the use of these resources.

Another important function of the POC is to maintain contact with law enforcement and other external agencies (such as the CIA, DoD, U.S. Army, or others) to ensure that multiagency involvement occurs.

Finally, if legal action in the form of prosecution is involved, the POC may be able to speak for the site in court. The alternative is to have multiple witnesses that will be hard to coordinate in a legal sense and will weaken any case against the attackers. A single POC also may be the single person in charge of evidence collected, which will keep the number of people accounting for evidence to a minimum. As a rule of thumb, the more people that touch a potential piece of evidence, the greater the possibility that it will be inadmissible in court. The next section (Legal/Investigative) will provide more details for consideration on this topic.

5.5 Legal/Investigative

5.5.1 Establishing Contacts with Investigative Agencies

It is important to establish contacts with personnel from investigative agencies such as the FBI and Secret Service as soon as possible for several reasons. Local law enforcement and local security offices or campus police organizations also should be informed when appropriate. A primary reason is that once a major attack is in progress, there is little time to call various personnel in these agencies to determine exactly who the correct POC is. Another reason is that it is important to cooperate with these agencies in a manner that will foster a good working relationship, and that will be in accordance with the working procedures of these agencies. Knowing the working procedures in advance and the expectations of your POC is a big step in this direction. For example, it is important to gather evidence that will be admissible in a court of law. If you do not know in advance how to gather admissible evidence, your efforts to collect evidence during an incident are likely to be of no value to the investigative agency with which you deal. A final reason for establishing contacts as soon as possible is that it is impossible to know the particular agency that will assume jurisdiction in any given incident. Making contacts and finding the proper channels early will make responding to an incident go considerably more smoothly.

If your organization or site has a legal counsel, you need to notify this office soon after you learn that an incident is in progress. At a minimum, your legal counsel needs to be involved to protect the legal and financial interests of your site or organization. There are many legal and practical issues, a few of which are:

1. Whether your site or organization is willing to risk negative publicity or exposure to cooperate with legal prosecution efforts.

2. Downstream liability—If you leave a compromised system as is so that it can be monitored and another computer is damaged because the attack originated from your system, your site or organization may be liable for damages incurred.

3. Distribution of information—If your site or organization distributes information about an attack in which another site or organization may be involved or the vulnerability in a product that may affect ability to market that product, your site or organization may again be liable for any damages (including damage of reputation).

4. Liabilities due to monitoring—Your site or organization may be sued if users at your site or elsewhere discover that your site is monitoring account activity without informing users.

Unfortunately, there are no clear precedents yet on the liabilities or responsibilities of organizations involved in a security incident or who might be involved in supporting an investigative effort. Investigators will often encourage organizations to help trace and monitor intruders—indeed, most investigators cannot pursue computer intrusions without extensive support from the organizations involved. However, investigators cannot provide protection from liability claims, and these kinds of efforts may drag out for months and may take lots of effort.

On the other side, an organization's legal council may advise extreme caution and suggest that tracing activities be halted and an intruder shut out of the system. This in itself may not provide protection from liability and may prevent investigators from identifying anyone.

The balance between supporting investigative activity and limiting liability is tricky; you will need to consider the advice of your council and the damage the intruder is causing (if any) in making your decision about what to do during any particular incident.

Your legal counsel also should be involved in any decision to contact investigative agencies when an incident occurs at your site. The decision to coordinate efforts with investigative agencies is most properly that of your site or organization. Involving your legal counsel also will foster the multilevel coordination between your site and the particular investigative agency involved, which in turn results in an efficient division of labor. Another result is that you are likely to obtain guidance that will help you avoid future legal mistakes.

Finally, your legal counsel should evaluate your site's written procedures for responding to incidents. It is essential to obtain a "clean bill of health" from a legal perspective before you actually carry out these procedures.

5.5.2 Formal and Informal Legal Procedures

One of the most important considerations in dealing with investigative agencies is verifying that the person who calls asking for information is a legitimate representative from the agency in question. Unfortunately, many well-intentioned people have unknowingly leaked sensitive information about incidents, allowed unauthorized people into their systems, etc., because a caller has masqueraded as an FBI or Secret Service agent. A similar consideration is using a secure means of communication. Because many network attackers can easily reroute electronic mail, avoid using electronic mail to communicate with other agencies (as well as others dealing with the incident at hand). Nonsecured phone lines (e.g., the phones normally used in the business world) are also frequent targets for tapping by network intruders, so be careful.

There is no established set of rules for responding to an incident when the U.S. federal government becomes involved. Except by court order, no agency can force you to monitor, to disconnect from the network, to avoid telephone contact with the suspected attackers, etc. As discussed in Section 5.5.1, you should consult with your legal counsel, especially before taking an action that your organization has never taken. The particular agency involved may ask you to leave an attacked machine on and to monitor activity on this machine, for example. Your complying with this request will ensure continued cooperation of the agency—usually the best route toward finding the source of the network attacks and, ultimately, terminating those attacks. Additionally, you may need some information or a favor from the agency involved in the incident. You are likely to get what you need only if you have been cooperative. Of particular importance is avoiding unnecessary or unauthorized disclosure of information about the incident, including any information furnished by the agency involved. The trust between your site and the agency hinges on your ability to avoid compromising the case the agency will build; keeping "tight lipped" is imperative.

Sometimes your needs and the needs of an investigative agency will differ. Your site may want to get back to normal business by closing an attack route, but the investigative agency may want you to keep this route open. Similarly, your site may want to close a compromised system down to avoid the possibility of negative publicity, but again, the investigative agency may want you to continue monitoring. When there is such a conflict, there may be a complex set of tradeoffs (e.g., interests of your site's management, amount of resources you can devote to the problem, jurisdictional boundaries, etc.). An important guiding principle is related to what might be called "Internet citizenship"[22,23] and its responsibilities. Your site can shut a system down, and this will relieve you of the stress, resource demands, and danger of negative exposure. The attacker, however, is likely to simply move on to another system, temporarily leaving others blind to the attacker's intention and actions until another path of attack can be detected. Providing that there is no damage to your systems and others, the most responsible course of action is to cooperate with the participating agency by leaving your compromised system on. This will allow monitoring (and ultimately, the possibility of terminating the source of the threat to systems just like yours). On the other hand, if there is damage to computers illegally accessed through your system, the choice is more complicated: Shutting down the intruder may prevent further damage to systems but might make it impossible to track down the intruder. If there has been damage, the decision about whether it is important to leave systems up to catch the intruder should involve all the organizations affected. Further complicating the issue of network responsibility is the consideration that if you do not cooperate with the agency involved, you will be less likely to receive help from that agency in the future.

5.6 Documentation Logs

When you respond to an incident, document all details related to the incident. This will provide valuable information to yourself and others as you try to unravel the course of events. Documenting all details ultimately will save you time. If you do not document every relevant phone call, for example, you are likely to forget a good portion of information you obtain, requiring you to contact the source of information once again. This wastes everyone's time, something you can ill afford. At the same time, recording details will provide evidence for prosecution efforts, providing the case moves in this direction. Documenting an incident also will help you perform a final assessment of damage (something your management as well as law enforcement officers will want to know) and will provide the basis for a follow-up analysis in which you can engage in a valuable "lessons learned" exercise.

During the initial stages of an incident, it is often unfeasible to determine whether prosecution is viable, so you should document as if you are gathering evidence for a court case. At a minimum, you should record

- All system events (audit records)
- All actions you take (time tagged)
- All phone conversations (including the person with whom you talked, the date and time, and the content of the conversation)

The most straightforward way to maintain documentation is by keeping a log book. This allows you to go to a centralized, chronologic source of information when you need it, instead of requiring you to page through individual sheets of paper. Much of this information is potential evidence in a court of law. Thus, when you initially suspect that an incident will result in prosecution or when an investigative agency becomes involved, you need to regularly (e.g., every day) turn in photocopied, signed copies of your logbook (as well as media you use to record system events) to a document custodian who can store these copied pages in a secure place (e.g., a safe). When you submit information for storage, you should in return receive a signed, dated receipt from the document custodian. Failure to observe these procedures can result in invalidation of any evidence you obtain in a court of law.

6. Establishing Postincident Procedures

6.1 Overview

In the wake of an incident, several actions should take place. These actions can be summarized as follows:

1. An inventory should be taken of the systems' assets; i.e., a careful examination should determine how the system was affected by the incident,

2. The lessons learned as a result of the incident should be included in a revised security plan to prevent the incident from recurring,

3. A new risk analysis should be developed in light of the incident.

4. An investigation and prosecution of the individuals who caused the incident should commence if it is deemed desirable.

All four steps should provide feedback to the site security policy committee, leading to prompt reevaluation and amendment of the current policy.

6.2 Removing Vulnerabilities

Removing all vulnerabilities once an incident has occurred is difficult. The key to removing vulnerabilities is knowledge and understanding of the breach. In some cases, it is prudent to remove all access or functionality as soon as possible and then restore normal operation in limited stages. Bear in mind that removing all access while an incident is in progress obviously will notify all users, including the alleged problem users, that the administrators are aware of a problem; this may have a deleterious effect on an investigation. However, allowing an incident to continue also may open the likelihood of greater damage, loss, aggravation, or liability (civil or criminal).

If it is determined that the breach occurred due to a flaw in the system's hardware or software, the vendor (or supplier) and the CERT should be notified as soon as possible. Including relevant telephone numbers (also electronic mail addresses and fax numbers) in the site security policy is strongly recommended. To aid prompt acknowledgment and understanding of the problem, the flaw should be described in as much detail as possible, including details about how to exploit the flaw.

As soon as the breach has occurred, the entire system and all its components should be considered suspect. System software is the most probable target. Preparation is key to recovering from a possibly tainted system. This includes checksumming all tapes from the vendor using a checksum algorithm that (hopefully) is resistant to tampering[10] (see Section 3.9.4.1). Assuming original vendor distribution tapes are available, an analysis of all system files should commence, and any irregularities should be noted and referred to all parties involved in handling the incident. It can be very difficult, in some cases, to decide which backup tapes to recover from; consider that the incident may have continued for months or years before discovery and that the suspect may be an employee of the site or otherwise have intimate knowledge or access to the system. In all cases, the preincident preparation will determine what recovery is possible. At worst case, restoration from the original manufactures' media and a reinstallation of the system will be the most prudent solution.

Review the lessons learned from the incident, and always update the policy and procedures to reflect changes necessitated by the incident.

6.2.1 Assessing Damage

Before cleanup can begin, the actual system damage must be discerned. This can be quite time-consuming but should lead into some of the insight as to the nature of the incident and aid investigation and prosecution. It is best to compare previous backups or original tapes when possible; advance preparation is the key. If the system supports centralized logging (most do), go back over the logs and look for abnormalities. If process accounting and connect time accounting are enabled, look for patterns of system usage. To a lesser extent, disk usage may shed light on the incident. Accounting can provide much helpful information in an analysis of an incident and subsequent prosecution.

6.2.2 Cleanup

Once the damage has been assessed, it is necessary to develop a plan for system cleanup. In general, bringing up services in the order of demand to allow a minimum of user inconvenience is the best practice. Understand that the proper recovery procedures for the system are extremely important and should be specific to the site.

It may be necessary to go back to the original distributed tapes and recustomize the system. To facilitate this worst case scenario, a record of the original systems setup and each customization change should be kept current with each change to the system.

6.2.3   Follow-up

Once you believe that a system has been restored to a "safe" state, it is still possible that holes and even traps could be lurking in the system. In the follow-up stage, the system should be monitored for items that may have been missed during the cleanup stage. It would be prudent to utilize some of the tools mentioned in Section 3.9.8 (e.g., COPS) as a start. Remember, these tools do not replace continual system monitoring and good systems administration procedures.

6.2.4   Keep a Security Log

As discussed in Section 5.6, a security log can be most valuable during this phase of removing vulnerabilities. There are two considerations here: The first is to keep logs of the procedures that have been used to make the system secure again. This should include command procedures (e.g., shell scripts) that can be run on a periodic basis to recheck the security. Second, keep logs of important system events. These can be referenced when trying to determine the extent of the damage of a given incident.

6.3   Capturing Lessons Learned

6.3.1   Understand the Lesson

After an incident, it is prudent to write a report describing the incident, method of discovery, correction procedure, monitoring procedure, and a summary of lessons learned. This will aid in the clear understanding of the problem. Remember, it is difficult to learn from an incident if you don't understand the source.

6.3.2   Resources

Other Security Devices, Methods

Security is a dynamic, not static process. Sites are dependent on the nature of security available at each site and the array of devices and methods that will help promote security. Keeping up with the security area of the computer industry and their methods will ensure taking advantage of the latest technology.

Repository of Books, Lists, Information Sources

Keep an on-site collection of books, lists, information sources, etc. as guides and references for securing the system. Keep this collection up to date. Remember, as systems change, so do security methods and problems.

Form a Subgroup

Form a subgroup of system administration personnel that will be the core security staff. This will allow discussions of security problems and multiple views of the site's security issues. This subgroup also can act to develop the site security policy and make suggested changes as necessary to ensure site security.

6.4 Upgrading Policies and Procedures

6.4.1 Establish Mechanisms for Updating Policies, Procedures, and Tools

If an incident is based on poor policy, unless the policy is changed, then one is doomed to repeat the past. Once a site has recovered from and incident, site policy and procedures should be reviewed to encompass changes to prevent similar incidents. Even without an incident, it would be prudent to review policies and procedures on a regular basis. Reviews are imperative due to today's changing computing environments.

6.4.2 Problem-Reporting Procedures

A problem reporting procedure should be implemented to describe, in detail, the incident and the solutions to the incident. Each incident should be reviewed by the site security subgroup to allow understanding of the incident with possible suggestions to the site policy and procedures.

References

1. Quarterman, J., *The Matrix: Computer Networks and Conferencing Systems Worldwide*, Digital Press, Bedford, Mass., 1990, p. 278.
2. Brand, R., "Coping with the Threat of Computer Security Incidents: A Primer from Prevention through Recovery," June 1990; available on-line from cert.sei.cmu.edu:/pub/info/primer.
3. Fites, M., Kratz, P., and Brebner, A., *Control and Security of Computer Information Systems*, Computer Science Press, 1989.
4. Johnson, D., and Podesta, J,. "Formulating a Company Policy on Access to and Use and Disclosure of Electronic Mail on Company Computer Systems," October 1990; vailable from The Electronic Mail Association (EMA), 1555 Wilson Blvd., Suite 555, Arlington, VA 22209, (703) 522-7111.

5. Curry, D., "Improving the Security of Your Unix System," SRI International Report ITSTD-721-FR-90-21, April 1990.

6. Cheswick, B., "The Design of a Secure Internet Gateway," *Proceedings of the Summer Usenix Conference*, Anaheim, CA, June 1990.

7. Linn, J., "Privacy Enhancement for Internet Electronic Mail: Part I. Message Encipherment and Authentication Procedures," RFC 1113, IAB Privacy Task Force, August 1989.

8. Kent, S., and Linn, J., "Privacy Enhancement for Internet Electronic Mail: Part II. Certificate-Based Key Management," RFC 1114, IAB Privacy Task Force, August 1989.

9. Linn, J., "Privacy Enhancement for Internet Electronic Mail: Part III. Algorithms, Modes, and Identifiers," RFC 1115, IAB Privacy Task Force, August 1989.

10. Merkle, R., "A Fast Software One Way Hash Function," *Journal of Cryptology*, 3(1).

11. Postel, J., "Internet Protocol—DARPA Internet Program Protocol Specification," RFC 791, DARPA, September 1981.

12. Postel, J., "Transmission Control Protocol—DARPA Internet Program Protocol Specification," RFC 793, DARPA, September 1981.

13. Postel, J., "User Datagram Protocol," RFC 768, USC/Information Sciences Institute, August 1980.

14. Mogul, J., "Simple and Flexible Datagram Access Controls for Unix-based Gateways," Digital Western Research Laboratory Research Report 89/4, March 1989.

15. Bellovin, S., and Merritt, M., "Limitations of the Kerberos Authentication System," *Computer Communications Review*, 1990.

16. Pfleeger, C., *Security in Computing*, Prentice-Hall, Englewood Cliffs, N.J., 1989.

17. Parker, D., Swope, S., and Baker, B., *Ethical Conflicts: Information and Computer Science, Technology and Business*, QED Information Sciences, Wellesley, Mass.

18. Forester, T., and Morrison, P., *Computer Ethics: Tales and Ethical Dilemmas in Computing*, MIT Press, Cambridge, Mass., 1990.

19. Postel, J., and Reynolds, J., "Telnet Protocol Specification," RFC 854, USC/Information Sciences Institute, May 1983.

20. Postel, J., and Reynolds, J., "File Transfer Protocol," RFC 959, USC/Information Sciences Institute, October 1985.

21. Postel, J., (Ed.), "IAB Official Protocol Standards," RFC 1200, IAB, April 1991.

22. Internet Activities Board, "Ethics and the Internet," RFC 1087, Internet Activities Board, January 1989.

23. Pethia, R., Crocker, S., and Fraser, B., "Policy Guidelines for the Secure Operation of the Internet," CERT, TIS, CERT, RFC in preparation.
24. Computer Emergency Response Team (CERT/CC), "Unauthorized Password Change Requests," CERT Advisory CA-91:03, April 1991.
25. Computer Emergency Response Team (CERT/CC), "Telnet Breakin Warning," CERT Advisory CA-89:03, August 1989.
26. CCITT, Recommendation X.509, "The Directory: Authentication Framework," Annex C.
27. Farmer, D., and Spafford, E., "The COPS Security Checker System," *Proceedings of the Summer 1990 USENIX Conference*, Anaheim, CA., June 1990, pp. 165—170.

Annotated Bibliography

The intent of this Annotated Bibliography is to offer a representative collection of resources of information that will help the user of this handbook. It is meant to provide a starting point for further research in the security area. Included are references to other sources of information for those who wish to pursue issues in the computer security environment.

Computer Law

[ABA89] American Bar Association, Section of Science and Technology, *Guide to the Prosecution of Telecommunication Fraud by the Use of Computer Crime Statutes*, American Bar Association, 1989.

[BENDER] Bender, D., *Computer Law: Evidence and Procedure*, New York, 1978—present.
Kept up to date with supplements. Years covering 1978 to 1984 focus on computer law, evidence, and procedures. The years 1984 to the present focus on general computer law. Bibliographic references and index included.

[BLOOMBECKER] Bloombecker, B., *Spectacular Computer Crimes*, Dow Jones—Irwin, Homewood, Ill., 1990.

[CCH] Commerce Clearing House, *Guide to Computer Law*, Topical Law Reports, Chicago, Ill., 1989.
Court cases and decisions rendered by federal and state courts throughout the United States on federal and state computer law. Includes case table and topical index.

[CONLY] Conly, C., *Organizing for Computer Crime Investigation and Prosecution*, U.S. Department of Justice, Office of Justice Programs, under Contract Number OJP-86-C-002, National Institute of Justice, Washington, July 1989.

[FENWICK] Fenwick, W., Chair, *Computer Litigation, 1985: Trial Tactics and Techniques*, Litigation Course Handbook Series No. 280, prepared for distribution at the Computer Litigation, 1985: Trial Tactics and Techniques Program, February—March 1985.

[GEMIGNANI] Gemignani, M., "Viruses and Criminal Law," *Communications of the ACM*, 32(6): 669—671, 1989.

[HUBAND] Huband, F., and Shelton, R., (eds.), *Protection of Computer Systems and Software: New Approaches for Combating Theft of Software and Unauthorized Intrusion*, papers presented at a workshop sponsored by the National Science Foundation, 1986.

[MCEWEN] McEwen, J., *Dedicated Computer Crime Units*, prepared for the National Institute of Justice, U.S. Department of Justice, by Institute for Law and Justice, Inc., under Contract Number OJP-85-C-006, Washington, 1989.

[PARKER] Parker, D., *Computer Crime: Criminal Justice Resource Manual*, U.S. Department of Justice, National Institute of Justice, Office of Justice Programs, under Contract Number OJP-86-C-002, Washington, August 1989.

[SHAW] Shaw, E., Jr., "Computer Fraud and Abuse Act of 1986," *Congressional Record*, Washington, 3 June 1986.

[TRIBLE] Trible, P., "The Computer Fraud and Abuse Act of 1986," U.S. Senate Committee on the Judiciary, 1986.

Computer Security

[CAELLI] Caelli, W. (ed.), "Computer Security in the Age of Information," *Proceedings of the Fifth IFIP International Conference on Computer Security*, IFIP/Sec 1988.

[CARROLL] Carroll, J., *Computer Security*, 2d ed., Butterworth Publishers, Stoneham, Mass., 1987.

[COOPER] Cooper, J., *Computer and Communications Security: Strategies for the 1990s*, McGraw-Hill, New York, 1989.

[BRAND] Brand, R., "Coping with the Threat of Computer Security

Incidents: A Primer from Prevention through Recovery," June 1990.

As computer security becomes a more important issue in modern society, it begins to warrant a systematic approach. The vast majority of the computer security problems and the costs associated with them can be prevented with simple, inexpensive measures. The most important and cost-effective of these measures are available in the prevention and planning phases. These methods are presented in this paper, followed by a simplified guide to incident handling and recovery. Available on-line from cert.sei.cmu.edu:/pub/info/primer.

[CHESWICK] Cheswick, B., "The Design of a Secure Internet Gateway," *Proceedings of the Summer Usenix Conference*, Anaheim, Calif., June 1990.

Brief abstract (slight paraphrase from the original abstract): AT&T maintains a large internal Internet that needs to be protected from outside attacks while providing useful services between the two. This paper describes AT&T's Internet gateway. This gateway passes mail and many of the common Internet services between AT&T internal machines and the Internet. This is accomplished without IP connectivity using a pair of machines: a trusted internal machine and an untrusted external gateway. These are connected by a private link. The internal machine provides a few carefully guarded services to the external gateway. This configuration helps protect the internal net even if the external machine is fully compromised.

This is a very useful and interesting design. Most firewall gateway systems rely on a system that if compromised could allow access to the machines behind the firewall. Also, most firewall systems require users who want access to Internet services to have accounts on the firewall machine. AT&T's design allows AT&T internal net users access to the standard services of Telnet and FTP from their own workstations without accounts on the firewall machine. A very useful paper that shows how to maintain some of the benefits of Internet connectivity while still maintaining strong security.

[CURRY] Curry, D, "Improving the Security of Your Unix System," SRI International Report ITSTD-721-FR-90-21, April 1990.

This paper describes measures that you, as a system administrator, can take to make your Unix system(s) more secure. Oriented primarily at SunOS 4.x, most of the information covered applies equally well to any Berkeley UNIX system with or without NFS and/or Yellow Pages (NIS). Some of the information also can be applied to System V, although this is not a primary focus of the paper. A very useful reference, this is also available on the Internet in various locations, including the directory cert.sei.cmu.edu:/pub/info.

[FITES] Fites, M., Kratz, P., and Brebner, A,. *Control and Security of Computer Information Systems,* Computer Science Press, 1989.

This book serves as a good guide to the issues encountered in forming computer security policies and procedures. The book is designed as a textbook for an introductory course in information systems security.

The book is divided into five sections: Risk Management (I), Safeguards: Security and Control Measures, Organizational and Administrative (II), Safeguards: Security and Control Measures, Technical (III), Legal Environment and Professionalism (IV), and CICA Computer Control Guidelines (V).

The book is particularly notable for its straightforward approach to security, emphasizing that common sense is the first consideration in designing a security program. The authors note that there is a tendency to look to more technical solutions to security problems while overlooking organizational controls, which are often cheaper and much more effective; 298 pages, including references and index.

[GARFINKEL] Garfinkel, S., and Spafford, E., *Practical Unix Security,* O'Reilly & Associates, ISBN 0-937175-72-2, May 1991.

Approximately 450 pages, $29.95. Orders: 1-800-338-6887 (U.S. & Canada), 1-707-829-0515 (Europe), e-mail: nuts@ora.com

This is one of the most useful books available on Unix security. The first part of the book covers standard Unix and Unix security basics, with particular emphasis on passwords. The second section covers enforcing security on the system. Of particular interest to the Internet user are the sections on network security, which address many of the common security problems that afflict Internet Unix users. Four chapters deal with handling security incidents, and the book concludes with discussions of encryption, physical security, and useful checklists and lists of resources. The book lives up to its name; it is filled with specific references to possible security holes, files to check, and things to do to improve security. This book is an excellent complement to this handbook.

[GREENIA90] Greenia, M., *Computer Security Information Sourcebook,* Lexikon Services, Sacramento, Calif., 1989.

A manager's guide to computer security. Contains a sourcebook of key reference materials including access control and computer crimes bibliographies.

[HOFFMAN] Hoffman, L., *Rogue Programs: Viruses, Worms, and Trojan*

Horses, Van Nostrand Reinhold, New York, 1990. (384 pages, includes bibliographic references and index.)

[JOHNSON] Johnson, D., and Podesta, J., "Formulating a Company Policy on Access to and Use and Disclosure of Electronic Mail on Company Computer Systems."

A white paper prepared for the EMA, written by two experts in privacy law. Gives background on the issues, and presents some policy options.

Available from The Electronic Mail Association (EMA), 1555 Wilson Blvd., Suite 555, Arlington, Va., 22209. (703) 522-7111.

[KENT] Kent, S., "E-Mail Privacy for the Internet: New Software and Strict Registration Procedures will be Implemented this Year," *Business Communications Review*, 20(1):55, 1990.

[LU] Lu, W., and Sundareshan, M., "Secure Communication in Internet Environments: A Hierachical Key Management Scheme for End-to-End Encryption," *IEEE Transactions on Communications*, 37(10):1014, October 1989.

[LU1] Lu, W., and Sundareshan, M., "A Model for Multilevel Security in Computer Networks," *IEEE Transactions on Software Engineering*, 16(6):647, 1990.

[NSA] National Security Agency, *Information Systems Security Products and Services Catalog*, NSA, Washington, quarterly publication.

NSA's catalogue contains chapters on endorsed cryptographic products list; NSA-endorsed data encryption standard (DES) products list; protected services list, evaluated products list; preferred products list; and endorsed tools list. The catalogue is available from the Superintendent of Documents, U.S. Government Printing Office, Washington, D.C. One may place telephone orders by calling (202) 783-3238.

[OTA] United States Congress, Office of Technology Assessment, "Defending Secrets, Sharing Data: New Locks and Keys for Electronic Information," OTA-CIT-310, October 1987.

This report, prepared for congressional committee considering federal policy on the protection of electronic information, is interesting because of the issues it raises regarding the impact of technology used to protect information. It also serves as a reasonable introduction to the various encryption and information protection mechanisms (185 pages;. available from the U.S. Government Printing Office).

[PALMER] Palmer, I., and Potter, G., *Computer Security Risk Management*,

Van Nostrand Reinhold, New York, 1989.

[PFLEEGER] Pfleeger, C., *Security in Computing*, Prentice-Hall, Englewood Cliffs, N.J., 1989.

A general textbook in computer security, this book provides an excellent and very readable introduction to classic computer security problems and solutions, with a particular emphasis on encryption. The encryption coverage serves as a good introduction to the subject. Other topics covered include building secure programs and systems, security of databases, personal computer security, network and communications security, physical security, risk analysis and security planning, and legal and ethical issues (538 pages including index and bibliography).

[SHIREY] Shirey, R., "Defense Data Network Security Architecture," *Computer Communication Review*, 20(2):66, 1990.

[SPAFFORD] Spafford, E., Heaphy, K., and Ferbrache, D., *Computer Viruses: Dealing with Electronic Vandalism and Programmed Threats*, ADAPSO, Arlington, Va., 1989. (109 pages.)

This is a good general reference on computer viruses and related concerns. In addition to describing viruses in some detail, it also covers more general security issues and legal recourse in case of security problems and includes lists of laws, journals focused on computers security, and other security-related resources. Available from ADAPSO, 1300 N. 17th Street, Suite 300, Arlington Va. 22209; (703) 522-5055.

[STOLL88] Stoll, C., "Stalking the Wily Hacker," *Communications of the ACM*, 31(5):484—497, 1988.

This article describes some of the technical means used to trace the intruder that was later chronicled in *Cuckoo's Egg* (see below).

[STOLL89] Stoll, C., *The Cuckoo's Egg*, ISBN 00385-24946-2, Doubleday, New York, 1989.

Clifford Stoll, an astronomer turned Unix System Administrator, recounts an exciting true story of how he tracked a computer intruder through the maze of American military and research networks. This book is easy to understand and can serve as an interesting introduction to the world of networking. Jon Postel says in a book review, "[this book] . . . is absolutely essential reading for anyone that uses or operates any computer connected to the Internet or any other computer network."

[VALLA] Vallabhaneni, S., *Auditing Computer Security: A Manual with Case Studies*, Wiley, New York, 1989.

Ethics

[CPSR89] Computer Professionals for Social Responsibility, "CPSR Statement on the Computer Virus," *Communications of the ACM*, 32(6):699, 1989.

This memo is a statement on the Internet computer virus by the Computer Professionals for Social Responsibility (CPSR).

[DENNING] Denning, P. J. (ed.), *Computers Under Attack: Intruders, Worms, and Viruses*, ACM Press, New York 1990.

A collection of 40 pieces divided into six sections: the emergence of worldwide computer networks, electronic breakins, worms, viruses, counterculture (articles examining the world of the "hacker"), and finally a section discussing social, legal, and ethical considerations. A thoughtful collection that addresses the phenomenon of attacks on computers. This includes a number of previously published articles and some new ones. The previously published ones are well chosen and include some references that might be otherwise hard to obtain. This book is a key reference to computer security threats that have generated much of the concern over computer security in recent years.

[ERMANN] Ermann, D., Williams, M., and Gutierrez, C. (eds.), *Computers, Ethics, and Society*, Oxford University Press, New York, 1990.

[FORESTER] Forester, T., and Morrison, P., *Computer Ethics: Tales and Ethical Dilemmas in Computing*, MIT Press, Cambridge, Mass., 1990.

From the Preface: "The aim of this book is twofold: (1) to describe some of the problems created by society by computers, and (2) to show how these problems present ethical dilemmas for computer professionals and computer users.

The problems created by computers arise, in turn, from two main sources: from hardware and software malfunctions and from misuse by human beings. We argue that computer systems by their very nature are insecure, unreliable, and unpredictable—and that society has yet to come to terms with the consequences. We also seek to show how society has become newly vulnerable to human misuse of computers in the form of computer crime, software theft, hacking, the creation of viruses, invasions of privacy, and so on."

The eight chapters include Computer Crime, Software Theft, Hacking and Viruses, Unreliable Computers, The Invasion of Privacy, AI and Expert Systems, and Computerizing the Workplace. Includes extensive notes on sources and an index.

[GOULD] Gould, C. (ed.), *The Information Web: Ethical and Social Implications of Computer Networking,*" Westview Press, Boulder, Colo., 1989.

[IAB89] Internet Activities Board, "Ethics and the Internet," RFC 1087, IAB, January 1989; also appears in the *Communications of the ACM,* 32(6):710, 1989.

This memo is a statement of policy by the Internet Activities Board (IAB) concerning the proper use of the resources of the Internet. Available on-line on host ftp.nisc.sri.com, directory rfc, filename rfc1087.txt. Also available on host nis.nsf.net, directory RFC, filename RFC1087.TXT-1.

[MARTIN] Martin, M., and Schinzinger, R., *Ethics in Engineering,* 2d ed., McGraw Hill, New York, 1989.

[MIT89] Massachusetts Institute of Technology, "Teaching Students about Responsible Use of Computers," MIT, 1985—1986; also reprinted in the *Communications of the ACM,* 32(6):704, 1989.

This memo is a statement of policy by the Massachusetts Institute of Technology (MIT) on the responsible use of computers.

[NIST] National Institute of Standards and Technology, *Computer Viruses and Related Threats: A Management Guide,* NIST Special Publication 500-166, August 1989.

[NSF88] National Science Foundation, "NSF Poses Code of Networking Ethics," *Communications of the ACM,* 32(6):688, 1989; also appears in the minutes of the regular meeting of the Division Advisory Panel for Networking and Communications Research and Infrastructure, November 29—30, 1988.

This memo is a statement of policy by the National Science Foundation (NSF) concerning the ethical use of the Internet.

[PARKER90] Parker, D., Swope, S., and Baker, B., *Ethical Conflicts: Information and Computer Science, Technology and Business,* QED Information Sciences, Wellesley, Mass..

Additional Publications on Ethics

The University of New Mexico (UNM). The UNM has a collection of ethics documents. Included are legislation from several states and policies from many institutions. Access is via FTP, IP address ariel.umn.edu. Look in the directory /ethics.

The Internet Worm

[BROCK] Brock, J., "November 1988 Internet Computer Virus and the Vulnerability of National Telecommunications Networks to Computer Viruses," GAO/T-IMTEC-89-10, Washington, July 20, 1989.

Testimonial statement of Jack L. Brock, Director, U. S. Government Information, before the Subcommittee on Telecommunications and Finance, Committee on Energy and Commerce, House of Representatives.

[EICHIN89] Eichin, M., and Rochlis, J., "With Microscope and Tweezers: An Analysis of the Internet Virus of November 1988," Massachusetts Institute of Technology, February 1989.

Provides a detailed dissection of the worm program. The paper discusses the major points of the worm program and then reviews strategies, chronology, lessons and open issues, and acknowledgments; also included are a detailed appendix on the worm program subroutine by subroutine, an appendix on the cast of characters, and a reference section.

[EISENBERG89] Eisenberg, T., Gries, D., Hartmanis, J., et al., "The Computer Worm," Cornell University, February 6, 1989.

A Cornell University report presented to the Provost of the University on February 6, 1989 on the Internet worm.

[GAO] U.S. General Accounting Office, "Computer Security—Virus Highlights Need for Improved Internet Management," United States General Accounting Office, Washington, 1989.

This 36-page report (GAO/IMTEC-89-57) by the U.S. Government Accounting Office describes the Internet worm and its effects. It gives a good overview of the various U.S. agencies involved in the Internet today and their concerns vis-à-vis computer security and networking.

Available on-line on host nnsc.nsf.net, directory pub, filename GAO_RPT, and on nis.nsf.net, directory nsfnet, filename GAO_RPT.TXT.

[REYNOLDS89] "The Helminthiasis of the Internet," RFC 1135, USC/Information Sciences Institute, Marina del Rey, Calif., December 1989.

This report looks back at the helminthiasis (infestation with or disease caused by parasitic worms) of the Internet that was unleashed the evening of November 2, 1988. This document provides a glimpse at the infection, its festering, and cure. The impact of the worm on the Internet community, ethics statements, the role of the news media, crime in the computer world, and future prevention are discussed. A documentation review presents four publications that describe in detail this particular parasitic computer program. Reference and bibliography sections are also included. Available on-line on host ftp.nisc.sri.com directory rfc, filename rfc1135.txt; also available on host nis.nsf.net, directory RFC, filename RFC1135.TXT-1.

[SEELEY89] Seeley, D., "A Tour of the Worm," *Proceedings of 1989 Winter USENIX Conference*, Usenix Association, San Diego, Calif., February 1989.

Details are presented as a "walk through" of this particular worm program. The paper opened with an abstract, introduction, detailed chronology of events on discovery of the worm, an overview, the internals of the worm, personal opinions, and conclusion.

[SPAFFORD88] Spafford, E., "The Internet Worm Program: An Analysis," *Computer Communication Review*, 19(1), 1989. Also issued as Purdue CS Technical Report CSD-TR-823, November 28, 1988.

Describes the infection of the Internet as a worm program that exploited flaws in utility programs in Unix-based systems. The report gives a detailed description of the components of the worm program: data and functions. Spafford focuses his study on two completely independent reverse compilations of the worm and a version disassembled to VAX assembly language.

[SPAFFORD89] Spafford, G., "An Analysis of the Internet Worm," *Proceedings of the European Software Engineering Conference 1989, Warwick England*, Springer-Verlag, Berlin, 1989.

Proceedings published by Springer-Verlag as Lecture Notes in Computer Science No. 387; also issued as Purdue Technical Report #CSD-TR-933.

National Computer Security Center (NCSC)

All NCSC publications, approved for public release, are available from the NCSC Superintendent of Documents. NCSC = National Computer Security Center, 9800 Savage Road, Ft. Meade, Md. 20755-6000; CSC = Computer Security Center, an older name for the NCSC; NTISS = National Telecommunications and Information Systems Security NTISS Committee, National Security Agency, Ft. Meade, Md. 20755-6000; [CSC] Department of Defense, "Password Management Guideline," CSC-STD-002-85, April 12, 1985.

The security provided by a password system depends on the passwords being kept secret at all times. Thus a password is vulnerable to compromise whenever it is used, stored, or even known. In a password-based authentication mechanism implemented on an ADP system, passwords are vulnerable to compromise due to five essential aspects of the password system: (1) a password must be assigned initially to a user when enrolled on the ADP system, (2) a user's password must be changed periodically, (3) the ADP system must maintain a "password database", (4) users must remember their passwords, and (5) users must enter their passwords into the ADP system at authentication time. This guideline prescribes steps to be taken to minimize the vulnerability of passwords in each of these circumstances.

[NCSC1] NCSC, "A Guide to Understanding AUDIT in Trusted Systems," NCSC-TG-001, version 2, June 1, 1988.

Audit trails are used to detect and deter penetration of a computer system and to reveal usage that identifies misuse. At the discretion of the auditor, audit trails may be limited to specific events or may encompass all the activities on a system. Although not required by the criteria, it should be possible for the target of the audit mechanism to be either a subject or an object. This is to say, the audit mechanism should be capable of monitoring every time John accessed the system as well as every time the nuclear reactor file was accessed and likewise every time John accessed the nuclear reactor file.

[NCSC2] NCSC, "A Guide to Understanding DISCRETIONARY ACCESS CONTROL in Trusted Systems," NCSC-TG-003, Version 1, September 30, 1987

Discretionary control is the most common type of access-control mechanism implemented in computer systems today. The basis of this kind of security is that an individual user, or program operating on the user's behalf, is allowed to specify explicitly the types of access other users (or programs executing on their behalf) may have to information under the user's control. Discretionary controls are not a replacement for mandatory controls. In any environment in which information is protected, discretionary security provides for a finer granularity of control within the overall constraints of the mandatory policy.

[NCSC3] NCSC, "A Guide to Understanding CONFIGURATION MANAGEMENT in Trusted Systems," NCSC-TG-006, Version 1, March 28, 1988.

Configuration management consists of four separate tasks: identification, control, status accounting, and auditing. For every change that is made to an automated data processing (ADP) system, the design and requirements of the changed version of the system should be identified. The control task of configuration management is performed by subjecting every change to documentation, hardware, and software/firmware to review and approval by an authorized authority. Configuration status accounting is responsible for recording and reporting on the configuration of the product throughout the change. Finally, though the process of a configuration audit, the completed change can be verified to be functionally correct, and for trusted systems, consistent with the security policy of the system.

[NTISS] NTISS, "Advisory Memorandum on Office Automation Security Guideline," NTISSAM CONPUSEC/1-87, January 16, 1987.

This document provides guidance to users, managers, security officers, and procurement officers of Office Automation Systems. Areas addressed include physical security, personnel security, procedural security, hardware/software security, emanations security (TEMPEST), and communications security for stand-alone OA Systems, OA Systems used as terminals connected to mainframe computer systems, and OA Systems used as hosts in a local-area network (LAN). Differentiation is made between those Office Automation Systems equipped with removable storage media only (e.g., floppy disks, cassette tapes, removable hard disks) and those Office Automation Systems equipped with fixed media (e.g., Winchester disks).

Additional NCSC Publications

[NCSC4] National Computer Security Center, "Glossary of Computer Security Terms," NCSC-TG-004, NCSC, October 21, 1988.

[NCSC5] National Computer Security Center, "Trusted Computer System Evaluation Criteria," DoD 5200.28-STD, CSC-STD-001-83, NCSC, December 1985.

[NCSC7] National Computer Security Center, "Guidance for Applying the Department of Defense Trusted Computer System Evaluation Criteria in Specific Environments," CSC-STD-003-85, NCSC, June 25, 1985.

[NCSC8] National Computer Security Center, "Technical Rationale Behind CSC-STD-003-85: Computer Security Requirements," CSC-STD-004-85, NCSC, June 25, 1985.

[NCSC9] National Computer Security Center, "Magnetic Remanence Security Guideline," CSC-STD-005-85, NCSC, November 15, 1985.

This guideline is tagged as a "For Official Use Only" exemption under Section 6, Public Law 86-36 (50 U.S. Code 402). Distribution is authorized to U.S. government agencies and their contractors to protect unclassified technical, operational, or administrative data relating to operations of the National Security Agency.

[NCSC10] National Computer Security Center, "Guidelines for Formal Verification Systems," Shipping List No. 89-660-P, The Center, Fort George G. Meade, Md., April 1, 1990.

[NCSC11] National Computer Security Center, "Glossary of Computer Security Terms," Shipping List No. 89-254-P, The Center, Fort George G. Meade, Md., October 21, 1988.

[NCSC12] National Computer Security Center, "Trusted Unix Working Group (TRUSIX) Rationale for Selecting Access Control List Features for the Unix System," Shipping List No. 90-076-P, The Center, Fort George G. Meade, Md., 1990.

[NCSC13] National Computer Security Center, "Trusted Network Interpretation," NCSC-TG-005, NCSC, July 31, 1987.

[NCSC14] Tinto, M., "Computer Viruses: Prevention, Detection, and Treatment," National Computer Security Center C1 Technical Report C1-001-89, June 1989.

[NCSC15] National Computer Security Conference, "12th National Computer Security Conference: Baltimore Convention Center, Baltimore, MD, 10—13 October, 1989: Information Systems Security, Solutions for Today—Concepts for Tomorrow," National Institute of Standards and National Computer Security Center, 1989.

Security Checklists

[AUCOIN] Aucoin, R., "Computer Viruses: Checklist for Recovery," *Computers in Libraries*, 9(2):4, 1989.

[WOOD] Wood, C., Banks, W., Guarro, S., et al., *Computer Security: A Comprehensive Controls Checklist*, Wiley, Interscience, New York, 1987.

Additional Publications

Defense Data Network's Network Information Center (DDN NIC). The DDN NIC maintains DDN Security bulletins and DDN Management bulletins on-line on the machine NIC.DDN.MIL. They are available via anonymous FTP. The DDN Security bulletins are in the directory SCC, and the DDN Management bulletins are in the directory DDN-NEWS. For additional information, you may send a message to nic@nic.ddn.mil, or call the DDN NIC at 1-800-235-3155.

[DDN88] Defense Data Network, "BSD 4.2 and 4.3 Software Problem Resolution," DDN MGT Bulletin 43, DDN Network Information Center, November 3, 1988.

A Defense Data Network Management Bulletin announcement on the 4.2bsd and 4.3bsd software fixes to the Internet worm.

[DDN89] DCA DDN Defense Communications System, "DDN Security Bulletin 03," DDN Security Coordination Center, October 17, 1989.

IEEE Proceedings

[IEEE] *Proceedings of the IEEE Symposium on Security and Privacy*, published annually.

IEEE Proceedings are available from Computer Society of the IEEE, P.O. Box 80452, Worldway Postal Center, Los Angeles, Calif. 90080.

Other Publications

Computer Law and Tax Report, Computers and Security Security Management, Magazine Journal of Information Systems Management, Data Processing & Communications Security, SIG Security, Audit & Control Review

Acknowledgments

Thanks to the SSPHWG's illustrious "Outline Squad," who assembled at USC/Information Sciences Institute on June 12, 1990: Ray Bates (ISI), Frank Byrum (DEC), Michael A. Contino (PSU), Dave Dalva (Trusted Information Systems, Inc.), Jim Duncan (Penn State Math Department), Bruce Hamilton (Xerox), Sean Kirkpatrick (Unisys), Tom Longstaff (CIAC/LLNL), Fred Ostapik (SRI/NIC), Keith Pilotti (SAIC), and Bjorn Satdeva (/sys/admin, inc.).

Many thanks to Rich Pethia and the Computer Emergency Response

Team (CERT); much of the work by Paul Holbrook was done while he was working for CERT. Rich also provided a very thorough review of this document. Thanks also to Jon Postel and USC/Information Sciences Institute for contributing facilities and moral support to this effort.

Last, but *not* least, we would like to thank members of the SSPHWG and friends for their additional contributions: Vint Cerf (CNRI), Dave Grisham (UNM), Nancy Lee Kirkpatrick (typist extraordinaire), Chris McDonald (WSMR), H. Craig McKee (Mitre), Gene Spafford (Purdue), and Aileen Yuan (Mitre).

Security Considerations

If security considerations had not been so widely ignored in the Internet, this memo would not have been possible.

Authors' Addresses

J. Paul Holbrook,
CICNet, Inc.,
2901 Hubbard,
Ann Arbor, MI 48105;
Phone: (313) 998-7680
e-mail: holbrook@cic.net.

Joyce K. Reynolds,
University of Southern California
Information Sciences Institute,
4676 Admiralty Way,
Marina del Rey, CA 90292,
Phone: (213) 822-1511,
e-mail: jkrey@isi.edu.

Glossary

ActiveX   A group of technologies introduced by Microsoft to unite the Internet with the PC. ActiveX replaces what was previously marketed as OLE.

API   Application programming interface. A library of software programs that provides access to certain features of an application.

Applet   A small application, usually written in Java.

Applet tag   A way to tell HTML to invoke an applet.

ATM   Asynchronous Transfer Mode. A fixed-length 53-byte packet-based transmission technology that can be used to transmit data, voice, and video traffic. ATM uses cell switching.

Authentication   A way to assure clients that they are connected to an SSL-enabled server. This prevents another computer from impersonating the server or attempting to appear secure when it is not.

Authorization   A way to control who has access to a server or to particular files and directories on it.

Backbone   A centralized high-speed network that connects smaller, independent networks.

Browser   Software used to request and display World Wide Web information. A browser functions as a client program.

Cache   A copy of Web data stored locally so that it doesn't have to be retrieved from a remote server again when requested.

Certificate   A digital file issued by a third party that both communicating parties already trust. It contains the terms of someone's authority to open a particular file or other resource.

certification authority   An authorized individual or organization that issues digital files used for encrypted transactions.

CGI   Common Gateway Interface. A system by which Web servers can interact with other applications such as databases. Programs that are written to use CGI are called *CGI programs* or *CGI scripts*. CGI programs handle forms or perform output parsing not normally done by the server.

Client   A program that requests information and services from a separate server. In Internet technology, a browser is a client.

DNS   Domain Name System. The system used by machines on a network to associate standard IP addresses (such as 198.93.93.10) with host names (such as www.easttech.com). Machines normally get this translated information from a DNS server, or they look it up in tables maintained on their systems.

DNS alias   A host name that points to a different host, specifically a DNS CNAME record. Machines always have one real name, but they can have one or more aliases. For example, an alias such as www.myplace.com might point to a real machine called realthing.myplace.com where the server currently exists.

Document root   A server directory that contains the files, images, and data you want to present to users accessing the server. Web files also can be stored in subdirectories of the document root.

Encryption   The process of transforming information so that it cannot be read by anyone but the intended recipient.

Extranet   An intranet opened to selective access from outside the organization.

File type   The format of a given file. For example, a graphics file does not have the same file type as a text file. File types are usually identified by the file extension (.GIF or .HTML).

Firewall   A network configuration, usually both hardware and software, that forms a barrier between networked computers within an organization and those outside the organization. It is commonly used to protect information such as a network's e-mail and data files within a physical building or organization site.

FTP   File Transfer Protocol. An Internet protocol that allows files to be transferred from one computer to another over a network.

Gateway   A device that is physically connected to multiple networks and/or understands multiple software standards. A gateway acts like a language translator and enables users of otherwise incompatible networks to communicate.

GIF   Graphics Interchange Format. A cross-platform image format originally created by CompuServe and now used widely on the Web. GIF files are usually much smaller in size than other graphic file types such as .BMP or .TIF.

Home page   A document on the server that acts as a catalog or entry point for the server's contents. The location of this document is defined within the server's configuration files.

Host name   A name for a machine in the form

machine.subdomain.domain, which is translated into an IP address. For example, www.easttech.com is the machine *www* in the subdomain easttech and com domain.

HTML Hypertext markup language. A formatting language used for documents on the World Wide Web. HTML files are plain text files with formatting codes that tell browsers such as the Netscape Navigator how to display text, position graphics and form items, and display links to other pages.

HTTP Hypertext Transfer Protocol. A data transfer protocol for transmitting World Wide Web documents between clients and servers on TCP/IP networks.

HTTP-S A secure version of HTTP, implemented using the Secure Sockets Layer (SSL).

Hyperlink An active, embedded reference to a different piece of information. Clicking on the hyperlink with a mouse displays the new information.

Image mapping A process that makes areas of an image active, letting users navigate and obtain information by clicking the different regions of the image.

Internet A worldwide collection of computers that communicate via a set of open software protocols.

Intranet A private TCP/IP network, often found in corporations. Typically protected from the Internet by a firewall.

IP Internet Protocol. *See* TCP/IP.

IP address Internet Protocol address. A set of numbers, separated by dots, that specifies the actual location of a machine on the Internet (e.g., 198.93.93.10).

ISDN Integrated Services Digital Network. A type of telephone service that can carry voice and data transmissions at speeds up to 128 kb/s.

ISP Internet service provider. An organization that provides connections to the Internet.

Java An object-oriented programming language created by Sun Microsystems, Inc. that allows application software to run on a Web client.

JavaScript An object scripting language developed by Sun Microsystems, Inc., and Netscape Communications Corporation that is complementary to Java and can be used to modify the properties and behavior of applets.

LAN   Local-area network. A network that connects computers within a geographically localized environment, such as an office.

MIME   Multipurpose Internet Mail Extensions. This is an emerging standard for multimedia e-mail and messaging.

Object   A software entity that is the basic building block of a program. Normally, an object has one or more attributes (fields) that collectively define the state of the object, behavior defined by a set of methods (procedures) that can modify those attributes, and an identity that distinguishes it from all other objects. Objects can be transient (existing temporarily during the execution of a program) or persistent (existing even after the program is finished).

Platform independence   A characteristic that is assigned to software applications when they can be run on multiple operating systems and hardware platforms.

Portability   The ability of software designed for one computer system to be used on other systems.

Private key   The decryption key used in public key encryption.

Protocol   A set of rules that describes how devices on a network exchange information.

Public key   The encryption key used in public key encryption.

RAM   Random access memory. The physical semiconductor-based memory in a computer.

Redirection   A method with which clients who call a particular URL are sent to a different location, either on the same server or on a different server. This is useful if a resource has moved and you want the clients to use the new location.

Resource   Any document (URL), directory, or program that the server can send to a client that asks for it.

RFC   Request For Comment. A document submitted to the Internet community suggesting new standards and procedures. People can send comments on the technologies before they become accepted standards.

Router   A piece of computer hardware that determines where to send information on a network.

Server root   A directory on the server dedicated to holding the server program, configuration, maintenance, and information files.

SMTP   Simple Mail Transfer Protocol. A software standard for sending and receiving e-mail over TCP/IP networks.

SOCKS   Firewall software that establishes a connection from inside a firewall to the outside when direct connection would otherwise be prevented by the firewall software or hardware (e.g., the router configuration).

SSL   Secure Sockets Layer. A software library establishing a secure connection between two parties (client and server) used to implement S-HTTP, the secure version of HTTP.

T-1   A digital transmission link with a capacity of 1.544 Mb/s.

T-3   A digital transmission link with a capacity of 45 Mb/s.

TCP/IP   Transmission Control Protocol/Internet Protocol. A set of software standards that allows computers with different architectures and operating systems to communicate. All computers on the Internet speak TCP/IP.

TCP/IP   Transmission Control Protocol/Internet Protocol. The main network protocol for the Internet and for intranets and extranets.

Telnet   A protocol under which two machines on the network are connected to each other and support terminal emulation for remote login.

Top-level domain authority   The highest category of host name classification, usually signifying either the type of organization the domain is (e.g., .com is a company, .edu is an educational institution) or the country of its origin (e.g., .us is the United States, .jp is Japan, .au is Australia, .fi is Finland).

Unix   A computer operating system developed by Bell Laboratories in the early 1970s. Most early Internet and Web development was done in Unix.

URL   Uniform Resource Locator. The addressing system used by the server and the client to request documents. It is often called a *location*.

Usenet   A collection of special-interest discussion groups ("news groups") on the Internet.

Virtual private network   A private WAN that uses the Internet for data transport.

WAN   Wide-area network. A network that connects geographically dispersed computers.

Web client   An application program that goes out on the Internet or a private TCP/IP network and retrieves documents and then displays the documents on a user's screen.

Web page   A document on the World Wide Web. Written in HTML.

Web site   A home address for an individual or organization on the World Wide Web. Typically contains dozens or hundreds of documents, product information, press releases, etc. Web sites are built using Web servers, personal computers or workstations, a leased-line connection, a firewall, and various pieces of networking hardware.

Whiteboard   A device that lets you share images, text, and data simultaneously as you speak on the phone with someone else.

Winsock   An industry standard API for Windows that specifies how applications should communicate with TCP/IP protocol software. Adopted by most vendors of network software.

World Wide Web   A collection of linked documents on the Internet and private TCP/IP networks.

Bibliography

Andrews, Whit. 1996. "Mr. Webmaster, Meet Ms. Mainframe." *Web Week,* April 29, 35.

Anthes, Gary. 1996. "Firewall Chaos." *Computerworld,* Feb. 5; available from http://www.computerworld.com.

Anthes, Gary. 1996. "Internet Firewall Market is Ablaze." *Computerworld,* April 1; available from http://www.computerworld.com.

Armstrong, Brent. 1996. "Catching the Intranet Express: Rail Transportation Giant CSX Rides the Java Train to Share Information with Customers." *PC Week,* Sept. 16, 52.

Babcock, Charles. 1996. "Client/Server is Dead; Long Live the Intranet." *Computerworld,* March 11, 126.

———. 1996. "Explainer: Hybrid Firewalls." *Computerworld;* available from http://www.computerworld.com/intranets/9607/intranets/intra_explainer.html.

Baker, Richard H. 1995. *Network Security.* New York: McGraw-Hill.

———. 1996. "Fighting Fire with Firewalls." *Information Week,* Oct. 21, 53—58.

Barry, Dave. 1996. "Lost in Cyberspace." *Newsweek,* Oct. 14, 85—88.

Beckman, Mel. 1996. "ISDN Survival Kit." *InfoWorld,* April 1, 1.

Blackmar, Brian R. 1996. "The Phanton of the Internet." Available from http://www.brba.com/news/apr96/news.htm.

Booker, Ellis. 1996. "For Burlington, Oracle's Web Strategy Looms Key." *Web Week,* Aug. 5; available from http://www.iworld.com.

———. 1996. "Manufacturer Opens a Window onto Its Intranet." *Web Week,* June 30; available from http://www.iworld.com.

Booker, Ellis. 1996. "Manufacturer Opens a Window onto Its Intranet." *Web Week,* June 3, 27.

———. 1996. "Tech Firm Conundrum: Creating an Intranet Amid Babble of Browsers." *Web Week,* Aug. 5; available from http://www.iworld.com.

Bort, Julie. 1996. "Only You Can Prevent Faulty Firewalls." *Open Systems Software,* August, 78—82.

———. 1996. "The Key to Security." *Info World,* Sept. 2, 1.

Bruno, Lee. 1996. "Internet Security: How Much Is Enough?" *Data Communications,* April, 60—72.

557

———. 1996. "Lasting Legacy: Browsing Big Iron on the Web." *Data Communications,* November, 110—120.

Cafasso, Rosemary. "When Security Isn't What It Seems." *Software Magazine,* March, 72—84.

Callaway, Erin. 1996. "Outflanked. Think a Firewall Is Complete Protection from Intruders? It's Not." *PC Week,* June 24, 51.

Campbell, Ian. 1996. *The Intranet: Slashing the Cost of Business.* International Data Corporation; available from http://cgi.netscape.com/cgi-bin/roi_reg.cgi.

Catanzano, Stephen and Kirsten Henderson. 1996. *The Fully Connected Corporation;* available from http://www.shiva.com/remote/40/tb.HTML.

Chapman, D. Brent and Elizabeth D. Zwicky. 1995. *Building Internet Firewalls,* Sebastopol, CA: O'Reilly & Associates.

Crowley, Aileen. 1996. "Extranet Targets Ads. The Advertising Arm of Turner Broadcasting Taps an Intranet to Communicate with Clients." *PC Week*, Sept. 2, 44.

Currid, Cheryl. 1996. "Somebody Out There Is Watching You. Be Careful What You and Your Users Say and Do on the Net. It Could Come Back to Haunt You." *Windows Magazine,* September, 57.

Dern, Daniel P. 1996. "Building Web Sites that Can Take a Hit." *Network World,* Nov. 4, 61.

Dodge, John. 1996. "Intranets: 'Client/Server Done Right.'" *PC Week,* June 17, 12.

Duffy, Tom. 1996. "Intranet Radically Reduces Costs. MTC Telemanagement's Global Intranet Saves Big Bucks." *PC Week,* May 27, N3.

———. 1996. "Intranet Radically Reduces Costs." *PC Week,* May 30; available from http://www.pcweek.com/@netweek/0527/27mtc.html.

Elgamal, Taher, Jeff Treuharf, and Frank Chen. 1996. *Securing Communications on the Intranet and Over the Internet.* Netscape Communications Corp. Available from http://home.netscope.com/newsref/ref/128bit.html.

Frank, Alan. 1996. "HTML and CGI," Part II. *LAN Magazine,* September; available from http://www.lanmag.com/9609/tut.htm.

Gannon, Joseph. 1996. "Creating HTML Forms for the World Wide Web." *Intercom,* October, 10—13.

Garfinkel, Simson, and Gene Spafford. 1991. *Practical Unix Security.* Sebastopol, CA: O'Reilly & Associates.

Garfinkel, Simson. 1995. *Pretty Good Privacy.* Sebastopol, CA: O'Reilly & Associates.

Genentech, Inc. 1996. "About Access Excellence." Available from http://www.gene.com/.

Gibbs, Mark. 1996. "The Common Gateway Interface: Unlocking Back-End Applications." *Network World Intranet Magazine,* September, 10.

———. 1996. "Building a Better Mousetrap: O'Reilly's WebSite Professional." *Network World Intranet,* October; available from http://www.nwfusion.com, document no. 2113.

Grygo, Eugene. 1996. "Intranet Reality Check." *Client/Server Computing,* May, 22—32.

Held, Gilbert. 1996. "Revving Up Your Web Server. On Today's Information Superhighway, a Sluggish Web Server Just Doesn't Cut It. Here Are Some Ways to Turbocharge Your System for Optimal Performance." *LAN Magazine,* November, 45—50.

Holbrook, J. P., and J. K. Reynolds. 1991. "The Site Security Handbook" (RFC 1244); available from ftp://archie.au/rfc/rfc1244.au.gz or at http://ds.internic.net/ds/dspg2intdoc.html.

Hudgins-Bonafield, Christine. 1996." Will Spies Hold Your Keys?" *Network Computing,* March 15, 78.

Karve, Anita. 1996. "In the Line of Fire." *LAN Magazine,* October, 62.

Levitt, Lee. 1996. "Intranets: Internet Technologies Deployed Behind the Firewall for Corporate Productivity." Process Software; available from http://www.process.com/news/intrawp.htp.

Levy, Steven. 1996. "Trying to Find the Key." *Newsweek,* Oct. 14, 91.

Lipschutz, Robert P. 1996." Web Wiozardy 101." *Mobile Computing and Communications,* November, 89.

Maglitta, Joseph. 1996. "Net Gains, Net Pains. ROI: Payoffs Can Be Big. But There Is No Free Lunch." *Computerworld,* insert June 24; available from http://www.computerworld.com/intranets/9606/intra_analysis.HTML.

Maglitta, Joseph. 1996. "Projects: AT&T's New Intranet Brings Automated Business Procedures to the Desktops of 10,000 Customer Service Reps." *Computerworld;* available from http://www.computerworld.com/intranets/9607/intranets/intra_projects.html.

McWilliams, Brian S. 19XX "Double Duty: Trans Ocean Piggybacks an Intranet on Its Web Home Page." *Computerworld;* available from http//www.computerworld.com/intranets/9606/intranets/intra_projects.html.

Memon, Farhan. 1996. "Patients Log onto Medical Tutorials." *Inter@ctive Week*, Sept. 30, 55.

Methvin, David W. 1996. "Instant Intranet. Data on Demand Within Your Enterprise Can Be Simple with an Intranet." *Windows Magazine*, September, 224—228.

———. 1996. Safety on the Net. *Windows Magazine*, August, 164—180.

Microsoft Corporation. 1996. "Microsoft Server Installation and Administration Guide". Available from http://www.microsoft.com/ntserver/iis/.

Mier, Edwin E. 1996. "Web Server Market Springs to Life." *Network World*, March 25, 61—64.

Moad, Jeff. "Running on Empty: CGI Has Lost Its Pep for Many Driving Mission-Critical Web Applications." *PC Week*, Nov. 25, 43.

Morrisey, Peter. 1996. "Striking Just the Right Firewall Match." *Network Computing*, Sept. 15, 158—166.

Moschella, David. 1996. "Why Intranets Are a Missed Opportunity." *Computerworld*, Aug. 12, 37.

Mullich, Joe. 1996. "On the Cutting Edge of Cutthroat: Vanguard Uses Intranet Customer Service to Vie in the Dog-Eat-Dog World of Financial Services." *PC Week*, Oct. 21, 54.

Murphy, Kathleen. 1996. "HP's Internal Web Aids Worldwide Sales Force." *Web Week*, March 1; available from http://www.iworld.com.

Nash, Kim S. 1996 "Extranet: Best of Both 'Nets." *Computerworld*, Aug. 12, 1.

Netscape Communcations Corporation. 1996. "Netscape Enhances Communcations at Eli Lilly & Co." Available from http://home.netscape.com/comprod/at_work/customer_profiles/lilly.html.

———. 1996. "Netscape Enhances Employee Efficiency and Productivity at Genentech." Available from http://www.home.netscape.com.

———. 1996. "John Deere Harvests the Benefits of Information Integration with an Intranet." Available from http://home.netscape.com/comprod/at_work/customer_profiles/john_deere.html.

———. 1996. "McDonnell Douglas Streams Document Distribution with Netscape." Available from http://home.netscape.com/.

———. 1996. "The Web Forges New Links Between Mobil and Its Customers, Partners, and Employees." Available from http://home.netscape.com/comprod/at_work/customer_profiles/mobil.html.

————. 1996. "Intranets Redefine Corporate Information Systems." Available from http://home.netscape.com/comprod/at_work/white_paper/indepth.html.

————. 1996. "AT&T Uses Netscape and the Web to Build a New Infrastructure for Information Access and Communication." Available from http://www.home.netscape.com.

Newman, David. 1996. "Web Servers: Digging into Corporate Data." *Data Communications,* Nov. 21, 57.

Nolle, Thomas. 1996. "Intranet Management: It Won't Work Until We Take a Different View." *Network World,* Sept. 16, 86.

Oakes, Chuck (Interview). 1996. "User Close-up: Diamond Shamrock, Inc." *Computerworld;* available from http://www.computerworld/com/intranets/9606/intranets/intra_usersspeak.html.

Olivetti, Ricerca. 1996. "An Intranet Solution to Foster Innovation and Streamline Processes." Available from http://www.olivetti.com/info/oliric.htm.

Pace, Mark, Brooks Talley, and Michelle Murdock. 1996. "Internet Firewalls: It's Between You and Them." *Infoworld,* July 29, 70—72.

Panone, Joe. 1996. "Feds Loosen Security Noose." *LAN Times,* Oct. 28, 41.

Paul, Lauren Gibbons. 1996. "Eureka! Levi Finds Gold Mine of Data." *PC Week,* May 13, 53.

Paul, Lauren Gibbons. 1996. "Intranet in the Middle: Marshall Drives Home Its Service Model Using Its Multifaceted Network to Foster Communications among Customers, Suppliers, and Partners." *PC Week,* Sept. 23, 54; available from http://www.pcweek.com/builder/0923/23marsh.html.

Pincince, Thomas J., David Goodtree, and Carolyn Barth. 1996. "Network Strategy Service." *The Forrester Report,* March 1; available from http://www.forrester.com/winreg/forreg.dll/EXIST?jmp=mar96nsr.htm.

Power, Richard. 1996. "Follow the Money: Management Wants Electronic Commerce, But Is Your Network Secure Enough? Your Information Systems May Be More Vulnerable than You Think." *LAN Magazine,* October, 54—60; available from http://www.lanmag.com/9610elec.htm.

Quinn, Jane Bryant. "HTTP://WWW.JBQOK.COM. The Internet Is Safer for Business than You Think. Your Password Is the Weakest Link." *Newsweek,* Oct. 14, 71.

Rice, Valerie. 1996. "Building the Case for your Intranet." *PC Week*, April 29, 53.

———. 1996. "When Is an Intranet Not an Intranet?" *PC Week*, Sept. 30, 52.

Roberts, Bill. 1996. "Lots of Data Types, One Front End: At 3M Spinoff, Web Unites Notes, Oracle, and MVS Systems." *Web Week*, Aug. 19; available from http://www.iworld.com.

Rodger, Will. 1996. "Keeping Medical Records Cybersafe." *Inter@ctive Week*, June 24, 47.

Rodger, Will. 1996. "New Privacy Bill Pushes Technological Protection." *Inter@ctive Week*, June 24, 15.

———. 1996. "Will Export Law Loophole Set Crypto Free?" *Inter@ctive Week*, June 24, 16.

Rodriguez, Karen. 1996. "Company Networks Cut Paper Trail." *Inter@ctive Week*, June 17, 31.

Salamone, Salvatore. 1996. "How to Put Mainframes on the Web." *Byte*, June, 53.

Schultz, Beth. 1996. "Companies Lured by Intranets, But at What Cost? Figuring out the Dollars and Cents of an Intranet Is Not as Simple as 1,2,3." *IntraNet Magazine*, September; available from http://www.nwfusion.com.

Schultz, Beth. 1996. "Hawking the Intranet." *IntraNet Magazine*, July, 45.

Schultz, Beth. 1996. "Safe and Sound?" *Network World IntraNet*, October; available at http://www.nwfusion.com.

Scott, Clint, and Lloyd Hopkins. 1996. "Integrating the World Wide Web and Oracle Order Entry." *Oracle Magazine*, May/June, 77—82.

Shimmin, Bradley F. 1996. "Comparison: Enterprise-Wide Webs." *LAN Times*, May 27, 57.

Siyan, Karanjit, and Chris Hare. 1995. *Internet Firewalls and Network Security*. Indianapolis, New Riders Publishing.

Speicher, Gene (Interview). 1996. "Project Summary: AT&T Corp." *Computerworld*; available from http://www.computerworld.com/intranets/9607/intranets/intra_usersspeak.html.

Strom, David. 1996. "Creating Private Intranets: Challenges and Prospects for IS," Attachmate Corp.; available from http://www.attachmate.com/intranet/intranetp.html.

Sullivan, Kristina B. 1996. "Security and Speed Vary Among Firewall Flavors." *PC Week*, Oct. 7, 99.

Sun Microsystems. 1996. "How to Develop a Network Security Policy." Available from http://www.sun.com/solstice/networking-products/networksec.html.

Tilton, Eric. 1996. "Composing Good HTML." Available from http://www.cs.cmu.edu/~tilt/cgh/.

Tolly, Kevin, John Curtis, and Elke Passarge. 1996. "Firewalls: Defending the Front Line." *LAN Times*, June 17, 49—59.

University of Illinois. 1996. "A Beginner's Guide to HTML." Available from http://www.ncsa.unic.edu/general/internet/www/htmlprimer-all.html.

Vaca, John. 1996. *Internet Security Secrets*. Foster City, CA: IDG Books.

Valigra, Lori. 1996. "Why Web Servers Need 64 Bits." *Client/Server Computing*, November, 43—37.

Vegvari, Ted. 1996. "It's Time For `Name That Server.'" *Computerworld*, Oct. 28, 85.

Vonder Haar, Steven. 1996. "Firewalls Address the Threat Within." *Inter@ctive Week*, Jan. 29, 23.

———. 1996. "John Deere Gets the Picture." *Inter@ctive Week*, May 6, 41.

———. 1996. "Telegroup Automates International Sales Force." *Inter@ctive Week*, Dec. 4, 48.

Wagner, Mitch. 1996. "Bank One Checks Out Web." *Computerworld*, Aug. 26, 69.

Watt, Peggy. 1996. "Come, Collaborate on the Intranet." *Network World*, Sept. 16; available from http:/www.nwfusion.com.

Wilde, Candee. 1996. "The Vanguard Group: Company Uses the Web to Make Investment Planning Easier—and More Lucrative." *Computerworld Client/Server Journal*, August, 14—15.

Wiseth, Kelli. 1996. "Safety Net: Balancing Security and Communication in a Distributed World." *Oracle Magazine*, July/August, 43—58.

Wong, William. 1996. "Create a Tough Firewall." *Network VAR*, October, 35—39.

INDEX

D

About the Author

As editorial director of Courseware Development Group in Houston, Texas, Richard H. Baker designs and develops computer skills training products for Fortune 1000 clients. He is the author of 15 computer books; his McGraw-Hill titles include *Wiring the Workgroup, Networking and the Enterprise: How to Build Client/Server Systems That Work, Network Security,* and *Downsizing: How to Get Big Gains from Smaller Computer Systems.*